A SPECIAL ISSUE OF
LANGUAGE AND COGNITIVE PROCESSES

PROCESSING EAST ASIAN LANGUAGES

edited by

Hsuan-Chih Chen
Department of Psychology, The Chinese University of Hong Kong, Shatin, Hong Kong

Xiaolin Zhou
Department of Experimental Psychology, University of Cambridge, Cambridge, UK

Psychology Press
Taylor & Francis Group
New York London

First published 1999 by Psychology Press Ltd.
711 Third Avenue, New York, NY 10017
27 Church Road, Hove, East Sussex, BN3 2FA

First issued in paperback 2014

Psychology Press is an imprint of the Taylor & Francis Group, an informa business

ISBN 13: 978-1-138-87721-4 (pbk)
ISBN 13: 978-0-86377-660-1 (hbk)

Typeset by Mendip Communications, Frome, Somerset

Contents

---

* This book is also a special issue of the journal *Language and Cognitive Processes* which forms Issues 5 & 6 of Volume 14 (1999). The page numbers used here are taken from the journal and so begin on p. 425.

LANGUAGE AND COGNITIVE PROCESSES, 1999, *14* (5/6), 425–428

Processing East Asian Languages: An Introduction

Hsuan-Chih Chen
The Chinese University of Hong Kong

Xiaolin Zhou
Cambridge University and Peking University

INTRODUCTION

There has been substantial progress over the past decades in understanding the processes underpinning various language activities. However, most research in this field has been carried out using materials in English or other European languages, and only a small amount has been addressed to non-European languages. This bias presents a serious obstacle to the development of a general theory of language processing for at least two reasons (for relevant discussions see Chen, 1992, 1996).

First, because there are striking differences between European and non-European languages, it is by no means self-evident that the same processes are used in the different languages. For instance, contemporary theories of language processing unexceptionally consider words as the basis of complex comprehension processes (Marslen-Wilson & Tyler, 1980; Rayner & Pollatsek, 1989). This is not surprising, because, after all, words are transparent units for speakers of European languages. However, it is not obvious whether the same arguments and conclusions relating to word processing that have been reached through psycholinguistic studies with European languages can be generalised to other languages, such as

Requests for reprints should be addressed to H.-C. Chen, Department of Psychology, The Chinese University of Hong Kong, Shatin, N.T., Hong Kong. Email: hcchen@psy-cuhk.eduhk

We thank the many reviewers for providing helpful comments on the manuscripts submitted to this special issue, and Jackie Tsang for extensive assistance during all phases of this project. We also acknowledge support from the Research Grants Council of Hong Kong to H.-C. Chen and from the Economic and Social Research Council (UK) to X. Zhou.

Chinese, in which words are not transparent units (Chen, 1999; Hoosain, 1992).

Second, a psycholinguistic theory developed from a limited set of languages may not account for the roles in processing played by the orthographic and linguistic properties not existing in that specific set of languages. Take lexical tone as an example. In order to understand how tone is used in word recognition and language processing (Cutler & Chen, 1997; Ye & Connine, this issue; Zhou & Marslen-Wilson, 1997), one has no choice but to study non-European languages, such as Chinese and many African languages, because tone is not used in major European languages to distinguish lexical items.

Fortunately, there has recently been acceleration in both the recognition and correction of this bias for solely using European languages to study language processing. In fact, there has been in recent years an upsurge of interest in the processing of major East Asian languages such as Chinese, Japanese, and Korean. These languages, due to their salient differences in structure from European languages, provide challenging opportunities to explore both language-specific processes involved in comprehension and communication, and the universality of theories developed from the study of European languages.

CONTENTS OF THIS SPECIAL ISSUE

The 11 papers in this special issue on processing East Asian languages deal with a range of topics in psycholinguistics, and all of them report new, empirical research. These papers can be grouped into two parts. Part one includes seven papers on lexical and sub-lexical processing.

The first three papers focus on the possible role of phonology in processing a visually presented lexical item. This issue has been the focus of a great deal of research in the literature, but no consensus has been reached to date. In the first of these, Shen and Forster, by using a masked priming paradigm with naming and lexical decision tasks, demonstrate that phonological priming effects in Chinese character recognition are task-dependent. Wong and Chen (the second paper) investigate the time course of orthographic and phonological activation in reading Chinese text by analysing different types of eye movement data. Cho and Chen (the third paper) examine the activation of graphemic and phonological information in the semantic processing of Korean Hanja (a logographic script originally borrowed from the Chinese) and Hangul (a phonetic script). They also explore whether proficiency in Hanja affects the use of phonology in comprehending Hanja characters. The results from all three studies converge to show that phonology is not likely to play a significant role in processing logographic characters for skilled adult readers.

As mentioned above, words are not transparent units in Chinese where they can be made up of one or more characters. Chinese characters, however, are distinct orthographic units of the language and are typically morphemes. Different characters are made up of strokes and radical components. The following two articles are concerned with the sub-morphemic and supra-morphemic levels of processing in Chinese. Wu, Zhou, and Shu (the fourth paper) look at the development of sublexical processing in naming Chinese characters. They suggest that character components are processed and used in character recognition from the very beginning of learning to read. In the following paper (the fifth), Zhou, Marslen-Wilson, Taft, and Shu examine the activation and use of different types of lexical information in processing two-character compound words in Chinese.

An interesting property of written Japanese is that it simultaneously uses several different scripts, including logographic Chinese (Kanji), two forms of a phonetic script called Kana (Hiragana and Katakana), Roman letters, and Arabic numerals. The next paper in the special issue addresses the processing of mixed-script materials in Japanese. Shafiullah and Monsell (the sixth paper) demonstrate that there is a cost in switching from logographic Kanji to syllabic Kana in naming and semantic categorisation and discuss the possible source of the cost.

Whereas the first six papers are concerned with the processing of visually presented materials, Ye and Connine (the seventh paper) turn their attention to an important issue in processing spoken Chinese, namely the use of tonal information. They argue that the processing of tone draws on both perceptual and lexical processes in spoken word recognition.

Part two comprises four papers on parsing and discourse comprehension. The first two papers are concerned with parsing in Japanese, a head-final language. Kamide and Mitchell (the eighth paper) demonstrate that the attachment decision of a verb-argument can be made before the head verb of the relevant phrase is encountered and argue that head-driven parsing is not universal. Miyamoto, Gibson, Pearlmutter, Aikawa, and Miyagawa (the ninth paper) investigate the attachment preferences of head-final relative clauses and find a non-monotonic preference to attach according to locality. They interpret their results within a framework in which both locality and another factor (predicate proximity or anaphor resolution) constrain the attachment of relative clauses in Japanese. Whereas a considerable amount of parsing work has been done in Japanese, Kim (the tenth paper) extends the work to Korean, which is also a head-final language where the positions of clause boundaries cannot be predicted easily. He demonstrates that case marking information is used to reduce syntactic ambiguity in processing Korean sentences. In the final paper of this special issue, Yang, Gordon, Hendrick, and Wu explore how different types of pronouns in Chinese are processed and argue that anaphora resolution in Chinese can be understood using a model previously developed in English.

This special issue attempts to provide a representative sample of the most recent research on the processing of major East Asian languages and to communicate the current thinking in the field. The papers in this issue reveal both the potential of this relatively new research area and also many intriguing questions that studying Chinese, Japanese, and Korean has raised, thus pointing out a number of possible directions for future research. It will, we hope, provide stimulating and enjoyable reading to anyone interested in the psychology of language in general and cognitive processing in the three target languages in particular.

REFERENCES

Chen, H.-C. (1992). Reading comprehension in Chinese: Implications from character reading times. In H.-C. Chen & O.J.L. Tzeng (Eds), *Language processing in Chinese* (pp.175–205). Amsterdam: North-Holland.

Chen, H.-C. (1996). Chinese reading and comprehension: A cognitive psychology perspective. In M.H. Bond (Ed.), *The handbook of Chinese psychology* (pp.43–62). Hong Kong: Oxford University Press.

Chen, H.-C. (1999). How do readers of Chinese process words during reading for comprehension? In J. Wang, A.W. Inhoff, & H.-C. Chen (Eds), *Reading Chinese script: A cognitive analysis* (pp.257–278). Mahwah, NJ: Lawrence Erlbaum Associates Inc.

Cutler, A., & Chen, H.-C. (1997). Lexical tone in Cantonese spoken-word processing. *Perception & Psychophysics*, *59*, 165–179.

Hoosain, R. (1992). Psychological reality of the word in Chinese. In H.-C. Chen & O.J.L. Tzeng (Eds), *Langauge processing in Chinese* (pp.111–130). Amsterdam: Elsevier.

Marslen-Wilson, W.D., & Tyler, L.K. (1980). The temporal structure of spoken language understanding. *Cognition*, *8*, 1–71.

Rayner, K., & Pollatsek, A. (1989). *The psychology of reading*. Englewood Cliffs, NJ: Prentice-Hall.

Zhou, X., & Marslen-Wilson, W.D. (1997). The abstractness of phonological representation in the Chinese mental lexicon. In H.-C. Chen (Ed.), *Cognitive processing of Chinese and related Asian languages* (pp.3–26). Hong Kong: The Chinese University Press.

LANGUAGE AND COGNITIVE PROCESSES, 1999, *14* (5/6), 429–459

Masked Phonological Priming in Reading Chinese Words Depends on the Task

Di Shen and Kenneth I. Forster
Department of Psychology, University of Arizona, Tucson, Arizona, USA

In two masked priming experiments with Chinese characters, orthographic priming effects were observed in lexical decision and naming tasks despite the fact that the primes were phonologically unrelated to the target characters. In contrast, phonological priming was found only in naming, a task that explicitly required a vocal response. No additional priming effects were obtained for masked primes that were simultaneously visually similar and phonologically identical to the targets. The data suggest that the recovery of lexical information for Chinese characters does not depend on the prior activation of phonological information.

INTRODUCTION

An important issue in the study of visual word recognition concerns the possible role of phonological information in the process of identifying words. Central to the inquiry is the question of whether phonological information of a word is activated in the process of retrieving its lexical properties from the mental lexicon, and if so, what contribution it makes to this process. To recognise a visually presented word, its orthographic features, e.g., sequences of letters in an alphabetic language, or stroke configurations in a logographic language, must first be transformed into a

This research was supported in part by National Multipurpose Research and Training Grant #1P60 DC01409 from the National Institute on Deafness and other Communication Disorders to the National Center for Neurogenic Communications Disorders at the University of Arizona, and by a grant from the McDonnell-Pew Foundation Cognitive Neurosciences Program.

Correspondence concerning this article should be addressed to K.I. Forster, Department of Psychology, University of Arizona, Tucson, AZ 85721. Electronic mail may be sent to kforster@u.arizona.edu format that is compatible with the way lexical information (e.g., its meaning, pronunciation, syntactic status and so forth) is represented in the memory system. Whether this process of transformation is mediated by phonological codes has been the focus of debate and empirical investigations ever since the turn of the century. This issue is fundamental for psychologists interested in modelling reading processes, neuroscientists attempting to understand acquired reading disorders and their neurological causes, the educators concerned with the acquisition of reading comprehension skills.

The possibility that the pronunciation of a word influences its identification in reading has been repeatedly affirmed and denied throughout the history of reading research (for reviews see Berent & Perfetti, 1995; Carr & Pollatsek, 1985; Frost, 1998; Humphreys & Evett, 1985; McCusker, Hillinger, & Bias, 1981; Patterson & Coltheart, 1987; Van Orden, Pennington, & Stone, 1990). Despite extensive research on this topic, empirical studies to date have not come up with anything that even resembles a conclusive resolution. The status quo in the field is that evidence consistent with either the phonological mediation hypothesis or the direct visual access position is readily available (McCusker et al., 1981; Seidenberg, 1992). The controversial findings in the literature may be due partially to the choice of stimulus materials, the types of subjects, the kinds of experimental paradigms, or a combination of any of these and other possible factors. Another important reason why there has been no straightforward answer to the question is no doubt related to the confound between the spelling and pronunciation in alphabetic languages, which has been the predominant focus of published research. In English for example, with the exception of a very few examples such as *ate* vs. *eight*, words which sound identical (i.e., homophones) typically have substantial spelling overlap and, consequently, visual and phonological information are confounded in many studies. Attempts to control for this confound by the inclusion of orthographic controls have been frustrated by the lack of any accepted criterion of orthographic similarity (e.g., see Taft, 1982).

Considering the intractable ambiguities in the literature, a better approach may be to investigate word recognition in languages with nonalphabetic orthographies, where the way in which a word is pronounced is typically unrelated to the way in which it is written, for example, Chinese or Japanese Kanji. As a nonalphabetic language, Chinese naturally separates the appearance of a written character from its phonology. This is especially relevant in priming studies, since the effects of phonological similarity between prime and target can be studied independent of orthographic similarity, and just as important, the effects of orthographic similarity can be studied without any confound with phonological similarity.

Phonological Mediation Hypothesis

This hypothesis comes in several forms. The strongest form assumes that visual word recognition is a process that transforms spelling to sound and then maps sound to meaning. Specifically, recognition of the orthographic features of a word recovers its corresponding phonological representation which, in turn, is used as *the* internal code to access its corresponding meaning in a phonology-based lexicon, and there is essentially no direct link between orthographic representations and semantic representations. A weaker version of the hypothesis assumes that there is a direct link between orthographic codes and semantic codes, but this link is so weak that access to meaning is faster if this orthographic route operates in conjunction with a phonologically mediated route (e.g., Perfetti, Zhang & Berent, 1992; Seidenberg, 1992; Van Orden et al., 1990). A still weaker version is that the phonological code generated from the visual stimulus is an alternative procedure for accessing the lexical entry, but serves mainly as a back-up procedure in case the visually based process fails (Coltheart, 1978).

Exactly how the printed form is converted into phonology is still a topic under debate. In an alphabetic language, phonological coding can be achieved by either of two possible mechanisms, or "routes". First, the pronunciation could be computed from print by applying a set of rules that summarises correspondences between spelling and pronunciation, or through a set of weighted connections in a neural network. Computationally, this process involves a set of transformations that convert minimal orthographic units to minimal phonological units. This is the so-called assembled, or non-lexical route, and it proceeds independently of any lexical information. The second mechanism, usually described as the direct or lexical route, is based on the use of word-specific association mechanisms. Readers identify a word as a visual pattern or a token of a particular lexical type that allows access to the appropriate representation in lexical memory, which in turn enables the retrieval of the stored phonological code corresponding to the word (Coltheart, 1978; Forster & Chambers, 1973). This retrieval process can be implemented either as a table look-up procedure, or in terms of a network. The distinction between the non-lexical and lexical routes can be made explicit (e.g., Coltheart, Curtis, Atkins, & Haller, 1993; Forster & Davis, 1991), or implicit (e.g., Seidenberg & McClelland, 1989).

The non-lexical assembly route is perfectly reliable if the relationship between orthography and phonology is fully isomorphic, i.e., each graphic symbol corresponds to one phoneme and vice versa. However, this is not the case for an alphabetic writing system like English where letter-phoneme correspondences are highly variable. This inconsistency has been exploited by many investigators, who have shown that performance with so-called exception words (where the assembled pronunciation does not correspond to the lexical pronunciation) suffers from some type of interference (e.g., Andrews, 1982; Glushko, 1979, 1981). However, this research has failed to demonstrate that phonological recoding is essential to access, since it is perfectly possible that the phonological codes are activated relatively late, and serve mainly to interfere with an already successfully completed access guided purely by orthographic information.

The issue of whether phonological recoding is obligatory in visual word recognition involves two extreme proposals: (1) phonological recoding is the one and only route for gaining access to lexical memory (i.e., the strong form of the hypothesis); and (2) phonological recoding always occurs but it is not necessarily used as an access code for word meaning (i.e. the weak form). Adopting the strong position, Van Orden et al. (1990) proposed that all bottom-up access in word recognition from orthography to meaning is solely based on phonological coding of the orthographic string, and that there is no procedure enabling direct access from orthography to meaning. Such a proposal would predict that the phonological properties of a visually presented word or letter string must affect the way it accessed. These phonological effects should be manifest in any kind of experimental conditions or paradigms that are assumed to involve lexical access. Moreover, no difference should be found between readers, old or young, skilled or unskilled. This position has the virtue of being relatively easy to verify. In contrast, the weak form is more difficult to verify because the hypothesis itself offers less precise and explicit predictions (cf. Ziegler & Jacobs, 1995). Consider for an example the universal phonological principle proposed by Perfetti and associates (Perfetti et al., 1992; Perfetti & Zhang, 1995; Tan & Perfetti, 1997). This hypothesis suggests that visual word recognition activates multiple levels of phonology in all writing systems. Orthographic characteristics of a writing system determine the details of how various phonological levels are activated. The theory essentially emphasises automatic activation of word phonology as an essential constituent of identification, but is not explicit on the role that phonological information plays in the process of lexical access.

Phonological Recoding in Chinese

The mere existence of grapheme-phoneme correspondence in alphabetic languages makes the phonological mediation mechanism at least a plausible account for processing printed words. But this model is claimed to represent a universal framework that underlies word processing in *all* languages, including logographic languages like Chinese (e.g., Perfetti & Zhang, 1995; Tan & Perfetti, 1997; Van Orden et al., 1990). Katz and Frost

(1992) point out that although Chinese appears to be a particularly poor candidate for the strong version of the phonological mediation hypothesis, there is still evidence that phonological processes play a role there as well.[1]

How could the phonological properties of a Chinese word be determined prior to lexical access? According to the structural formation of characters, modern Chinese characters fall into four principal categories, namely, pictograms, simple ideograms, compound ideograms, and logographic-phonetic compounds. The fourth category is the most frequent (nearly 90% of modern Chinese characters by type, and about 40.87% by token, (Zhu, 1988). These compounds consist of two or more radicals, usually one semantic radical providing some clue to the meaning, and one phonetic radical providing some clue to the pronunciation of the resultant character. For example, 伴 (companion) is comprised of a semantic radical 人 (human) and a phonetic radical 半 (half). This compound character is pronounced /ban/, identical with its phonetic radical.

These compounds have prompted some researchers to argue that the phonological information represented in the phonetic radical may allow for the possibility of prelexical or presemantic phonological recoding in much the same fashion as in alphabetic languages (e.g., Cheng, 1992; Hung & Tzeng, 1981; Seidenberg, 1985; Tan, Hoosain, & Peng, 1995; Tzeng & Hung, 1988). In these models, the phonetic radical is first mapped onto a phonological code, which then serves as the basis for subsequent access of meaning.

It might be useful to review some of the critical features of these logographic-phonetic characters before evaluating the plausibility of phonological mediation in reading this type of characters. First of all, the distinction between a semantic radical and a phonetic radical is only functional, rather than visual or graphic. A radical (e.g., 木 /mu/) that serves as a phonetic radical in one character, e.g., 沐 (bath /mu/), could be a semantic radical in another, e.g., 桌 (desk /zhuo/). That is, there is nothing in a radical that indicates whether it is phonetic or semantic. A radical has to be recognised before its status can be determined. Second, a character may consist of two radicals that are both pronounceable and used as phonetic radicals in other characters, e.g., 埋 (土, 里). But the pronunciation of the compound could be related to either, or neither of the constituent radicals. Third, the position of a phonetic radical in a character is probabilistic rather than deterministic. Although a large percentage of phonetic radicals occur to the right of a character, there are many types of exceptions. Relative to the semantic radical, the phonetic radical could be

[1] This could be taken as a firm indication that the evidence is not relevant to the question of phonological mediation. If Chinese shows the same kinds of phonological effects as English, then these effects must be due to something other than phonological mediation.

in any possible position in a character, e.g., to the left or to the right, above or below, inside or outside (Sun, 1980). Sometimes a phonetic radical (a semantic radical as well) can even be separated into two halves with another radical positioned in the middle, e.g., 辩 (argue). Fourth, the phonetic radical in a character, generally speaking, is not a reliable clue to pronouncing a compound character. The majority of logographic-phonetic compounds differ to varying degrees from constituent phonetic radicals. Of 5990 logographic-phonetic compounds collected in Ni's (1975) Modern Chinese Logographic-phonetic Compounds, only 26.3% (1578) characters share identical pronunciation with their respective phonetic radicals (Fan, Gao, & Ao, 1984). But many of these compound characters are typically uncommon in use and, therefore, these "phonologically transparent" characters (sometimes also known as phonograms) only account for 18.5% by token (Zhu, 1988). More importantly, there is nothing in the graphic shape of a compound that indicates whether the phonetic radical is valid or not. Finally, compound characters also contain semantic radicals which serve a cueing function for the meaning of a compound character. Within the framework of the phonological mediation theory, the cueing function of semantic radicals would be left totally unaccounted for.

In general, a phonetic radical provides but a rough clue to the pronunciation of a compound character. Six possibilities ranging from complete to partially identical to completely different pronunciations are: (1) the radical and the compound character may have identical pronunciation; (2) identical pronunciation but with different tones; (3) identical initial but different rimes; (4) identical rime but different initials; (5) completely different; and (6) identical in one but different in other contexts when the compound is a polyphonic character (e.g., 堡 /bao/, /bu/, /pu/). More important, nothing in the graphic form of a character indicates which solution is correct nor which component is the phonological radical. From a total of 1522 phonetic radicals in modern Chinese, only 18 provide consistent pronunciations for more than three compound characters, totalling 98 characters (Gao, 1983). Other phonetic radicals either are not productive or provide inconsistent clues for pronunciation. Such an unreliable and unsystematic correspondence between orthography and phonology in the Chinese writing system would most probably encourage Chinese readers to use the whole character as a basic unit for lexical search and retrieval, whether it is for character meaning or character pronunciation.

Prelexical or presemantic phonology

It is claimed that in Chinese, phonological information is activated prior to semantic information (Perfetti & Zhang, 1995; Tan et al., 1995), giving rise to the term "prelexical phonology". What is prelexical phonology? There appears to be no generally agreed-upon definition for the concept. But most researchers would probably agree that a prelexical phonological representation for a letter sequence, word or nonword, is a pronunciation compiled on the basis of the letter sequence without regard to its lexical properties. A specific example would be when one attempts to pronounce a letter sequence that has never been seen or heard before. The pronunciation is generated by putting together a sequence of phonemes each of which corresponds to an individual letter or letter cluster. This is typically described as a rule-based assembly process where the rules are implicit in a native speaker's internalised knowledge about his language. Obviously, essential to this concept of prelexical phonology is that the generated pronunciation is decomposable into phonemes which have direct correspondence to the orthographic constituents. Under this definition, prelexical phonology is possible in an alphabetic language because a word can be broken down into letters or letter clusters that correspond directly to phonemes in the pronunciation of that word.

Under the same definition, prelexical phonology is immediately ruled out as a plausible mechanism for reading Chinese characters. The graphemic features in Chinese writing system are not isomorphic to phonemic features. The smallest orthographic unit in a character is a stroke but the individual strokes do not themselves represent any aspects of character phonology. In other words, a character cannot be decomposed phonemically like an alphabetic word. Reliable or systematic relationships between graphemes and phonemes do not exist in the scripts (otherwise why should an artificial phonetic system such as Pinyin be created?). Thus there is no way to assemble the phonological code for a character before its lexical representation has been accessed.

However, it is possible that a phonological code could still be generated from the phonetic radical considered as a whole, rather than from its constituent elements. For example, in English, the character "$" can be considered as analogous to a phonetic radical in Chinese. There is nothing about the constituents of this character that determine its pronunciation. But this is also true of the character "B". Before prelexical phonology can be computed, the pronunciation of this letter must be determined, and no rule-based system can do this. Some kind of arbitrary mapping or table lookup operation is required. The same is required for "$". So determining the pronunciation of "$" prelexically is really no different from determining the pronunciation of "BAT" prelexically, and therefore there is nothing strange about the idea of determining the pronunciation of phonetic radicals prelexically.

From one point of view, it might seem to be inappropriate to describe this process as prelexical, because the phonological information is retrieved from what amounts to a dictionary representation. Further, the procedure is somewhat indirect, since the phonetic radical must still be combined with the semantic radical (for which there is no phonetic information) to determine the meaning. Given this problem, one might as well propose that the phonological information is retrieved for the character as a whole (ignoring the constituent radicals), in which case, a lexicon is definitely involved, since whole words are being associated with their pronunciations. But this is evidently not a conventional lexicon, because it contains no information about meaning. To obtain the meaning, a totally new look-up procedure is required, even though the word has already been recognised.

Setting this problems to one side, it might be suggested that the term "prelexical" is probably confusing, and that the term "presemantic" gives a clearer idea of the actual proposal. Retrieving the phonology does involve a limited form of lexical access, but it is still presemantic in the sense that access to meaning is only achieved at a later stage of processing. But could this phonological information serve as an effective access code for retrieving semantic properties? Clearly this hypothesis has to presume that the phonological representation and semantic representation of a lexical item are accessed independently (e.g., stored completely separately), and that the connections linking orthography to semantics are much weaker than the connections linking orthography to phonology, and also are weaker than those linking phonology to semantics (or simply that there is no direct connection between orthography and semantics).

Evidence for Presemantic Phonological Involvement in Chinese

Much of the work on phonological processes in reading demonstrates merely that the phonological properties of the target word must have been established before some overt response is made to the target word. For example, it has been found that the homophone interference effects in semantic categorisation observed by Van Orden (1987) also occur in Chinese (e.g., Leek, Weekes & Chen, 1994; Wydell, Patterson & Humphreys, 1993). Such an effect could be the result of phonological code activation occurring after the lexical entry has been located. It could be that all lexical codes are automatically activated once a word has been accessed. Another possibility is that the phonological code becomes active before access takes place, but actually plays no direct role in activating the relevant lexical entry. For example, the assembled phonology may be determined very rapidly, but is not used until the addressed phonology is retrieved from the lexical entry and compared with it.[2]

Of more relevance is evidence that phonological codes are activated earlier than semantic codes in backward masking experiments (Perfetti & Zhang 1995; Perfetti et al., 1992; Tan & Perfetti, 1997). These experiments might demonstrate that the phonological code is activated both rapidly and automatically, but they do not necessarily establish that semantic codes are dependent on the prior activation of the phonological code. Furthermore, recent evidence (Chen, 1998; Chen, Flores d'Arcais, & Cheung, 1995) suggests that semantic activation in reading Chinese characters can occur without prior phonological activation.

Perhaps the strongest case in support of the presemantic hypothesis is provided by phonological priming studies, where it is shown that recognition of a target word is facilitated by the prior presentation of a homophonic stimulus. In this case, the causal agent (the phonological nature of the priming stimulus) is clearly available before the target word has been accessed, and hence there is less doubt about when the phonological cue is potentially operative.

The earliest phonological priming study with Chinese characters was carried out by Hsieh (1982). Lexical decision responses to the target characters were faster when preceded by homophonic characters relative to controls, regardless of their visual similarity to the targets. More recently, Cheng (1992) also showed that lexical decisions to a target character were faster when preceded by a homophonic character. This homophone priming effect was found to be independent of the stimulus-onset asynchrony (SOA), which ranged from 50 to 750 msec, with the target always being presented for 1000 msec. Again, this effect was independent of visual similarity between the prime and the target characters.

Similar effects have been reported in English (e.g. Meyer, Schvaneveldt & Ruddy, 1974). However, these effects have proved difficult to replicate (Martin & Jensen, 1988), and in any event, it is debatable whether the observed facilitation in lexical decision is a direct consequence of faster lexical access *per se*. For example, such effects could be explained in a post-access checking account (Forster, 1992), originally proposed to explain semantic and sentential priming effects in word recognition. Upon lexical access, the retrieved lexical information of the target word is

[2] We acknowledge that in some network models (e.g., Seidenberg & McClelland, 1989; Van Orden et al., 1990), many of these distinctions may be meaningless, since all lexical codes are being computed simultaneously. However, this does not mean that these distinctions are invalid. It means only that these models are incapable of expressing these distinctions.

checked to establish some meaningful relationship between the just-accessed word and the prior context. If some kind of congruence is detected, the decision process is facilitated, otherwise it is delayed. In other words, conscious awareness of the relationship between the prime and the target may change the way in which the subject responds to the target stimulus, rather than the way the target is perceptually processed.

In an attempt to minimise such effects, Forster and Davis (1984) introduced the masked priming paradigm to assess repetition effects in the lexical system. A typical trial consists of three stimuli presented in quick succession: a forward pattern mask (500 msec), a priming stimulus in lower-case letters (50–60 msec), and a target item in upper-case letters (500 msec). The subject's task is to classify the target as a word or not as rapidly as possible. Because the prime is exposed briefly, and is masked both forwards and backwards, the prime is virtually invisible for the majority of subjects. It is assumed that this lack of awareness of the prime means that the nature of the prime is not made available to the decision process, and hence cannot produce congruency effects.

Masked Phonological Priming

The evidence for phonological effects with masked priming is not absolutely clear. Ferrand and Grainger (1992, 1993, 1994) used the masked priming paradigm with the lexical decision task in an attempt to assess the time course for orthographic and phonological activation in the recognition of French words. They concluded that as the prime exposure duration increased from 14 ms to 64 msec there was a relatively steady increase in the size of phonological priming effects, whereas the effects of orthographic priming increased from 14 msec to 29 msec and then decreased with longer prime exposures.[3] More specifically, only orthographic facilitation (relative to phonological controls) was observed with 29 and 32 ms prime durations, but with longer durations (43–64 msec) significant phonological priming was obtained.

Ferrand and Grainger interpreted these results to support a hypothesis that both orthographic and phonological information play a fundamental role in the process of visual word recognition and that lexical representations can be accessed on the basis of both types of code. They proposed a framework, based on McClelland and Rumelhart's (1981) interactive activation (IA) model, consisting of a tripartite structure of sublexical

[3] In fact, the orthographic priming effect remained constant while the phonological effect increased as the SOA increased. Given the increase in phonological priming and the fact that the overall priming effect remained unchanged, Ferrand and Grainger reasoned the orthographic component must be decreasing.

orthographic units linked to their corresponding phonological units, both of which are directly connected to word units. That proposal is essentially a reinstated version of Seidenberg's (1985) time course model in localist terms, with an additional assumption of within-level inhibition. The connections between word units are uniquely inhibitory while connections between different types of units (orthographic, phonological, word) are primarily facilitatory. Like Seidenberg's time course model, what is crucial in this model appears to be the assumed indirectness of the phonological activation, which lags behind the build-up of activation at the orthographic level. In the case of masked priming, Ferrand and Grainger (1994) proposed that, at very short prime exposure (e.g., 29 to 32 msec), only orthographically similar primes would facilitate subsequent target recognition whereas, at longer prime exposures (e.g., 43 to 64 msec), only homophonic primes would benefit target recognition, regardless of their orthographic similarity to the target. Further, orthographically similar but nonhomophonic primes would only inhibit target recognition because of within-level inhibition between activated word nodes.[4] This account of masked priming effects obviously runs counter to other studies using exactly the same experimental procedures but yielding robust orthographic priming effects at durations of 60 msec (e.g., Forster, Davis, Schoknecht, & Carter, 1987; Forster & Taft, 1994; Sereno, 1991). To account for the discrepancy, Ferrand and Grainger (1994) offered an explanation in terms of prime-target orthographic overlap, which was greater in the cited studies (as many as 6 out of 7 letters in common) than in their own (3 out of 4 letters in common).

Additional support for the existence of phonological priming effects has been provided by Lukatela and colleagues (Lukatela, Lukatela & Turvey, 1993; Lukatela & Turvey, 1991; Lukatela & Turvey, 1993), who have reported a series of experiments examining the role of homophones and pseudohomophones as associative primes in a speeded naming task. A typical trial consists of a prime stimulus presented in upper case for 40 msec, an interstimulus interval (ISI) of 60 msec, and a lower-case target exposed for 400 msec. On critical trials, the prime is either a pseudohomophone or a homophone of a word which is semantically related to the target (e.g., *TAYBLE-chair; TOWED-frog*). The results show that an associated pseudohomophone (e.g., *TAYBLE*) as a prime could facilitate the naming of a subsequent target (e.g., *chair*) to a degree comparable with an associated word (e.g., *TABLE*), whereas a spelling control for the pseudohomophone (e.g., *TARBLE*), failed to prime

[4] The inhibitory effect was not reflected in the orthographic priming effect which, in fact, remained constant over SOAs ranging from 43 to 64 msec.

(Lukatela & Turvey, 1991). Lukatela and colleagues argued that these results could not be explained by any model of word recognition that did not provide a central role for assembled or computed phonology, or by any dual-route theory in which phonological recoding was useful only for new words or low-frequency regular words.

These results are surprising, especially given that associative priming effects (e.g., *table-CHAIR*) with masked primes are notoriously weak (Perea & Gotor, 1997). One might have expected that a phonologically mediated associated priming effect would have been even weaker, but this is not what was found. One possible explanation is that the primes in these experiments were not heavily masked, since no forward mask was used, and the effective duration of the prime was probably closer to 100 msec, which is considerably longer than in most masked priming experiments.

Another relevant consideration is the fact that all the experiments reporting mediated associative priming effects used a naming task only. It is perhaps not surprising that phonological processes are actively engaged when the task requires articulatory output, particularly when the subjects were overtly informed before the experiment that silently reading the primes might help them in reading aloud the target stimuli (Lukatela & Turvey, 1993, p.175). If these associative priming effects were indeed produced by activating the lexical representations of the target, then such effects should be observable in any task that is sensitive to lexical access, for example, the lexical decision task. As a matter of fact, Lukatela, Lukatela, and Turvey (1993) explicitly argued for the advantages of both lexical decision and naming tasks over the semantic categorisation task (p.462). Moreover, there appears to be nothing in their experiments that inherently prevented them using a lexical decision task. With results coming from the naming task alone, one could argue that these phonologically mediated priming effects might only occur because the task requirements effectively forced subjects into a recoding strategy.[5]

A totally different picture emerges from the work of Davis, Castles, and Iakovidis (1998). These investigators used a masked priming paradigm with a forward mask, and found no evidence for phonological priming in English, either for adults or children. The task in this case was lexical decision, not naming. Special consideration was given to the possibility that phonological priming effects might be obtained only when the orthographic overlap between prime and target is high, but this variable had no noticeable effect on the amount of priming.

[5] A recent paper obtaining masked homophone priming effects with a lexical decision task appears to be an exception (Lukatela, Frost, & Turvey, 1998), although the authors claim that this effect occurs only under very limited conditions.

The masked priming paradigm has also been used to explore phonological processes in nonalphabetic languages. Forster and Yoshimura (1994) investigated phonological priming effects in a lexical decision task using primes and targets written in either Japanese Kanji (logographic) or Hiragana (syllabic) scripts. No phonological priming was obtained when both the prime and target were Kanji characters, where the orthography is totally unrelated to the phonology. In contrast, strong priming effects were found when the prime and target were both written in Hiragana where orthography and phonology are correlated. In addition, Hiragana–Kanji pairs also yielded weak but significant priming effects. These results so far appear to be consistent with the orthographic depth hypothesis (Katz & Frost, 1992), and the weak version of the phonological mediation hypothesis, i.e., visual word recognition is phonologically mediated in orthographies where prelexical phonology is possible, but probably not in logographic orthographies. Such a hypothesis would then predict that logographic Kanji primes homophonic to the target should never show phonological priming effects. But exactly the opposite patterns was found in the study. Briefly presented Kanji primes also primed Hiragana target words. This was a puzzling result, since Kanji–Kanji pairs showed no priming. Forster and Yoshimura proposed that this phonological priming was a consequence of the task requirement: the Hiragana target words used in this experiment would normally be written with Kanji characters, and hence a "sounding out" process was required in order to decide whether they were words (i.e., they were essentially equivalent to pseudohomophones such as *rayn* in an English experiment). Hence it is not entirely surprising that this sounding out process might have been facilitated by the phonological code activated post-lexically by the Kanji prime.

This hypothesis that phonological priming effects are task-dependent is further supported by results from unpublished masked priming experiments in Chinese (Xing & Forster, 1996). In two experiments using naming and lexical decision tasks, high and low frequency two-character target words were paired with identity (repetition) primes, pseudohomophone primes and unrelated primes. A pseudohomophone prime consisted of two characters, homophonic to the two characters in the target word, but meaningless when used together as a word. An unrelated prime was a two-character word neither orthographically nor phonologically similar to the target, serving as a baseline condition. Identity primes produced strong masked priming effects in both naming and lexical decision tasks, independent of word frequency, whereas pseudohomophone primes yielded a significant priming effect only in the naming task. The absence of homophonic priming effects in lexical decision was interpreted to suggest that the involvement of articulation in the task is a critical requirement for the occurrence of such effects. In the naming task where phonological processing is required in the naming response, the phonological code of a pseudohomophone prime could be retrieved and collected by the articulatory production system to prepare a phonetic plan for articulation, resulting in facilitation in pronouncing a target homophonic to the prime. But in the lexical decision task where only a motor response (pressing YES or NO buttons) is required, the articulation system is less likely to be engaged during the identification process, consequently no phonological priming effects are obtained. In contrast, the identity priming effects that were consistently found across both tasks must have occurred as a result of a change in the state of the lexical entry, not as a result of a change in the pathway leading to the entry (Forster & Davis, 1984).

The research to be reported here is essentially a follow-up of this work. The effect of masked homophonic primes in Chinese are examined in both a naming task and a lexical decision task. In addition, the effect of orthographically similar primes are examined.

EXPERIMENT 1: NAMING

Chinese orthography permits the presentation of a homophonic prime that is orthographically quite unrelated to the target. By the same token it permits the presentation of an orthographically similar prime that is phonologically quite unrelated to the target, and also, a prime that is both orthographically and phonologically similar to the target. Such a combination of prime conditions enables us to put several contrasting hypotheses against each other in one experiment. First, the visual or direct access theory would predict comparable amounts of priming for orthographically similar primes, regardless of phonology, but no priming from orthographically different primes. Conversely, the extreme version of the phonology-based access hypothesis would predict that the amount of priming from phonological primes should be independent of orthography, and there should be no effects from the orthographically similar prime. Third, Van Orden et al.'s (1990) proposal (phonological mediation if and only if the prime and the target are visually similar) would predict additional priming effects from the primes that are both homophonic and orthographically similar to the target.

In order to test the hypothesis that phonological priming effects are task-dependent, the same set of materials were tested in a naming task and a lexical decision task. The following describes the naming experiment.

	Orthographically Similar Prime	Phonologically Identical Prime	Orth. Similar & Phonologically Identical Prime	Target Character
Simple Characters	牛 [niu] cow	五 [wu] five	N/A	午 [wu] noon
Compound Characters	埋 [mai] bury	礼 [li] polite	俚 [li] slang	理 [li] reason

FIG. 1. Illustration of items used in both Experiments 1 and 2. Pronunciations are given in brackets.

Method

Participants. Twenty-four volunteer native speakers of Mandarin from China participated in the experiment. Most of them were graduate students enrolled in various departments at the University of Arizona, and the rest were their spouses, with ages ranging from 21 to 45. They all had normal or corrected-to-normal vision.

Materials and Design. The target stimuli consisted of 30 simple characters and 32 compound characters. Simple and compound character targets were run in separate sessions because they were paired with different numbers of prime types. Each simple character target was associated with three types of primes: orthographically related, phonologically related and control. An orthographic prime was a visually similar character (defined in terms of shared strokes), but phonologically unrelated to its prospective target character. The prime differed in no more than two strokes from the target, the mean number of different strokes being 1.20. A phonological prime was a character that was homophonic (both in pronunciation and tone) with the target, but visually unrelated to it. Finally, a control prime was completely unrelated to the target in any respect. None of the primes were semantically related to their corresponding targets. In addition, 10 compound characters were embedded as fillers. Three sets of materials were constructed such that each target occurred in each condition across the sets, but appeared only once within any one set. The complete set of materials is listed in the Appendix.

Each compound character target was tested under four prime conditions: orthographic, phonological, orthographic plus phonological, and control. An orthographic plus phonological prime was visually similar as well as homophonic to its target character. Specifically, such a prime was a compound character which shared the phonetic radical with the corresponding target. Both the prime and the target were phonologically transparent in the sense that the pronunciation of the phonetic radical was the same as the pronunciation of the whole word. The pronunciation of the prime and the target were identical (including tone). The semantic radical of the prime was different from that of the target character, but every effort was made to ensure that the visual difference between the two semantic radicals was minimised as well. In addition, 8 simple characters were embedded as fillers. Four counterbalanced sets of materials were constructed such that each target was tested in each priming condition.

Procedure. Each trial consisted of the following sequence of three stimuli: first a forward pattern mask was presented for 500 msec; this was immediately followed by presentation of the prime for 50 msec, which was immediately replaced by the target presented for 500 msec. The pattern mask was about 30 × 30 mm in size, the target character was 25 × 25 mm, and the prime character was slightly smaller than the target. To reduce their physical similarity, the target and the prime characters were always presented in different fonts (targets in Songti font and primes in Kaiti font). The character stimuli were generated by a Chinese word processing program and stored as individual image files. Each stimulus was presented in the centre of the display and was superimposed on the preceding item. The instructions specified that the task was to pronounce the target character loudly into a microphone. The participants were encouraged to do so as quickly and as accurately as possible. Stimulus presentation and recording of RTs was controlled by the DMASTR system (Forster & Forster, 1990). Naming times were measured from the target onset to the triggering of a voice key. The sessions were monitored by an assistant who checked the accuracy of each response. After a response was made, a feedback message appeared on the screen specifying the accuracy of the response as well as the RT. Instructions as well as 13 practice items were presented before the test stimuli.

Results

Trials on which an incorrect response was made, or the voice key was not triggered were discarded. The mean naming latencies and error rates averaged over individuals for each of the masked priming conditions for simple target characters and compound target characters are shown in Table 1.

TABLE 1
Mean Naming Times (in msec) and Error Rates (in Percentages) to Simple and Compound Target Characters Preceded by Orthographic, Phonological, Orthographic Plus Phonological, and Control Masked Primes in Experiment 1

Priming Conditions	*RT*	*Error*	*Priming*
Simple Characters			
Orthographic	624	2.5	+40
Phonological	634	4.1	+30
Control	664	4.6	
Compound Characters			
Orthographic	699	3.1	+32
Phonological	714	3.1	+17
Orth + Phon	696	2.1	+35
Control	731	6.3	

Simple character targets. An omnibus test of the naming latencies indicated a significant main effect of prime type, both for the subject analysis, $F_1(2,23) = 5.76$, $P < .001$, and for the item analysis, $F_2(2,87) = 4.39$, $P < .05$. Further pairwise analyses showed that the mean naming times in the orthographic priming condition were significantly faster than in the unrelated control condition, $F_1(2,23) = 9.56$, $P < .001$; $F_2(1,58) = 8.78$, $P < .001$. The mean latencies in the phonological condition were also faster than the control condition. This difference was significant by subjects, $F_1(2,23) = 4.70$, $P < .05$, and marginally significant by items, $F_1(1,58) = 3.56$, $P = .06$. However the difference between the orthographic and phonological priming conditions was not significant (both Fs < 1). None of the differences in the error data were significant.

Compound character targets. The results for the compound character targets revealed a similar pattern, although some of the priming effects were not strong enough to reach significance (due to the smaller number of items in each condition). The naming latencies in the orthographic priming condition were faster than in the control condition, which was significant by subjects, $F_1(2,23) = 5.22$, $P < .05$, but only marginally so for items, $F_2(1,62) = 3.42$, $P = 0.69$. The phonological primes also facilitated naming of the targets, but this 17 msec effect was not at all reliable, $F_1(1,23) = 1.19$, $P > .05$; $F_2(1,62) = 1.82$, $P > .05$. A larger effect (35 msec) was obtained for the orthographic plus phonological condition, but again this was not reliable, $F_1(1,23) = 4.22$, $P = .052$; $F_2(1,62) = 1.09$, $P > .05$. None of the differences in error rates were significant, except for the reduction in errors for the orthographic plus phonological condition (3.17%), $F_1(1{,}23) = 4.60$, $P < .05$; $F_2(1{,}62) = 3.66$, $P = .06$.

Combined analysis. To increase the power of statistical analysis, the naming data from these two experiments were collapsed across the simple and compound character targets. The overall analysis of variance showed a significant main effect of prime type, ($F_1(2{,}94) = 7.26$, $P < .005$); ($F_2(2{,}183) = 4.43$, $P < .05$). Targets were named faster under the orthographic prime condition than the control condition, $F_1(1{,}47) = 14.57$, $P < .001$, $F_2(1{,}122) = 8.26$, $P < .005$. The phonological condition also produced significant priming effects compared to the controls, $F_1(1{,}47) = 5.15$, $P < .05$; $F_2(1{,}122) = 3.82$, $P < .05$. However, the difference between the two masked priming conditions was not significant by either analysis. None of the error data revealed any significant differences.

Discussion

The results from the naming task indicate that the naming of Chinese characters, simple or compound, was facilitated by masked primes characters that were related either orthographically or phonologically, or both, to the target characters. Since no subjects reported seeing another character (i.e., the prime) presented before the target, the possibility must be minimal that naming was facilitated because the subjects noticed the congruence between the target and the prime.

The facilitation in the orthographic condition provides a clearer case for the existence of "pure" orthographic priming effects, given that the prime was phonologically unrelated to the target character. The proponents of phonological recoding (e.g. Lukatela et al., 1993; Lukatela & Turvey, 1993; Van Orden et al., 1990) have argued that although there is now plenty of evidence for the role played by phonological codes in visual word recognition, there is no clear-cut positive evidence for the role played by orthographic codes (other than subserving phonological code activation). Until now, the evidence in favour of direct orthographic mediation has generally taken the form of an absence of phonological effects (Van Orden et al., 1992). But the orthographic priming effects observed here provide clear positive evidence for the role played by orthographic codes.

At the same time, these results also show that naming of Chinese characters was facilitated by masked homophone primes. The independent contribution made by the homophone primes to target naming lends support to the hypothesis of a phonology-assisted access. In addition, this result indicates that a masked homophone prime does not have to be orthographically related to the target in order for priming to occur.

The existence of masked homophone priming effects also suggests that phonologically mediated access is possible in reading logographic characters, with or without phonetic radicals. But considering that prelexical assembled phonology is implausible in Chinese, we have to assume the basic unit of phonological encoding of a Chinese character is the whole character (or the whole radical when it is a valid phonetic radical). The orthographic features of a character are mapped onto its phonological representation, and its phonological codes are then used to access lexical semantics (supposing that we could solve the problem of one-to-many relationship in case of a homophone character). For instance, a visually different homophone prime could not activate the target entry or node by its orthographic codes but it could if its phonological codes could be recovered very early in the process and then used to activate the target. This view is therefore consistent with the hypothesis of presemantic phonology proposed specifically to account for reading Chinese (e.g., Tan et al., 1995) in that character phonology is recovered as character specific information, but preceding access to character meaning. Of course, the presemantic phonology account is fundamentally congruent with the hypothesis of prelexical phonological mediation in stressing the role of phonological codes as the primary access code for visual word recognition.

The failure of the orthographic plus phonological related condition to produce stronger priming in the compound characters does not support a co-operative model, in which both codes independently activate lexical representations. This result is exactly what the strong phonological mediation view would predict, since orthographic similarity to the target is irrelevant. However, this view then needs to explain the orthographic effects obtained with the simple characters. This would not in fact be difficult to do if these primes had been non-characters, and had been formed from the target character by changing one or two strokes. In this case, the mapping function would still be able to recover the phonological properties of the target (or something very similar) from the prime, since the prime is just a slightly distorted version of the target, and any best-match function should be able to cope with this distortion. However, in fact the primes were well-formed characters in their own right, and hence the best-match function would recover a phonological pattern completely unrelated to the target, and therefore no priming should occur.

Closely related is the issue of how a briefly presented masked prime facilitates the subsequent processing of the target stimulus. Forster and Davis (1984) proposed that masked priming (e.g., by identity of form primes) might occur as a result of a change in the state of the lexical entry itself, not as a result of a change in the path leading to the entry. However, it appears that the naming task can yield misleading results with a masked priming procedure, since the subject evidently attempts to pronounce the prime as well as the target, which leads to response competition (Forster & Davis, 1991). This produces an *onset effect*, in which prime-target pairs that share just the onset produce faster naming times (e.g., *belly-BREAK*). An obvious extension of this response competition argument to the case of phonological priming is that if the prime is a homophone of the target, then not only would response competition be reduced to a minimum, but there could be a large savings effect as well, since what amounts to the pronunciation of the target may already have been determined by the time the target is presented. This represents a case of articulatory priming (Forster, 1998) and may have little to do with lexical access, since phonological priming effects in the naming task are found with nonword targets as well as word targets.

Whether such effects also occur in a logographic language is not known. Pronunciation in an alphabetic language via a sub-lexical route can proceed in an incremental left-to-right fashion, so that only part of the pronunciation of the prime might be determined by the time the target is presented. This would still be sufficient to produce response competition effects and articulatory priming. However, in a logographic script, an incremental procedure is not possible, and the pronunciation of the whole character must be determined, which may not be possible in the time available. Hence it is possible that there are no articulatory priming effects in a Chinese naming experiment. The easiest way to determine whether this is the case is to repeat the experiment using a lexical decision task, where onset effects do not occur. This was done in the next experiment.

EXPERIMENT 2: LEXICAL DECISION

This experiment used exactly the same set of stimuli and masked priming conditions as in the previous experiment, but the task was lexical decision. An equal number of noncharacters was added to serve as distractors. The subjects were instructed to read the target presented on the screen and decide whether the stimulus was a Chinese character that they knew.

The hypothesis was that if orthographic priming or phonological priming effects observed in the preceding naming experiments were lexical effects, then a similar pattern of masked priming effects should be revealed in the lexical decision task.

Method

Participants. Twenty-four native speakers of Mandarin Chinese from the same population as in Experiment 1 were tested on the simple characters, and an additional 8 were tested on the compound character targets, making 32 in all.

Materials and design. Exactly the same set of test materials, the pattern mask, target and prime characters, from the preceding experiment were used. In addition, 30 simple noncharacters and 32 compound noncharacters were embedded in the stimulus set as distractor targets. Simple noncharacters were created by editing strokes in an existing simple character, none of which appeared as a character stimulus in the experiment while compound noncharacters were constructed by combining two or more radicals which are used in existing compound characters.

All the noncharacters in these two experiments were created by using Font Maker, a computer program designed to create or edit Chinese characters. For a simple noncharacter, an existing Chinese character was first retrieved, in the same font and size as the character targets (Kaiti, Size 48), onto the editing platform of Font Maker. One, or at most, two strokes (with a mean of 1.25) were either added to or deleted from that character and extreme care was taken in the process so that the noncharacter thus created still looked like a real Chinese character. Compound noncharacters were created by retrieving two or more radicals in Kaiti font onto the editing platform. The sizes of these radicals were adjusted proportionally such that the compound noncharacter was of exactly the same size as a target character. A new code was attached to each of the noncharacters which was then stored in the character dictionary. The individual noncharacters, as well as characters, were later retrieved and stored as bit-mapped images which could then be read and displayed by the DMASTR program.

Procedure. The method of presenting the mask, prime and target was identical with Experiment 1. The subjects were asked to make a lexical decision by pressing either a YES or a No button to indicate whether the display corresponded to a known character or not. They were encouraged to do so as quickly and as accurately as possible. For the same reason as stated earlier, the simple and compound character targets were tested in separate sessions.

Results

Trials on which an incorrect response occurred were discarded. The mean lexical decision times and error rates for each masked priming condition are given in Table 2.

Simple character targets. An overall analysis of the lexical decision times revealed that the main effect of masked priming types was significant by subjects, $F_1(2,23) = 10.51$, $P < .001$, and marginally significant for the items, $F_2(2,87) = 2.69$, $P = .07$. Further subanalyses showed that the simple

TABLE 2
Mean Lexical Decision Times (in msec) and Error Rates (in Percentages) to Simple and Compound Target Characters Preceded by Orthographic, Phonological, Orthographic Plus Phonological, and Control Masked Primes in Experiment 2

Priming Conditions	*RT*	*Error*	*Priming*
Simple Characters			
Orthographic	541	5.0	+35
Phonological	578	5.4	−2
Control	576	3.3	
Compound Characters			
Orthographic	521	6.3	+20
Phonological	537	9.4	+4
Orth + Phon	517	6.6	+24
Control	541	6.3	

character targets primed by orthographically similar masked primes were recognised significantly faster than the unrelated control condition, $F_1(1,23) = 11.64$, $P < .001$; $F_2(1,58) = 4.20$, $P < .05$. The orthographic priming condition was also significantly faster than the phonological priming condition, $F_1(1,23) = 21.92$, $P < .001$; $F_2(1,58) = 4.34$, $P < .05$. In contrast, the 2 msec difference between the phonological priming and control conditions was not (both Fs < 1). There were no significant effects in the error analysis.

Compound character targets. A similar pattern of results was obtained for the compound characters. Both the orthographic and the orthographic plus phonological priming conditions produced faster responses compared to the control condition, whereas the priming effect from the phonological alone condition was close to zero. Moreover, there appears to be very little difference in priming between the orthographic and the orthographic plus phonological conditions.

Both the orthographic condition ($F_1(1,31) = 5.52$, $P < .05$, $F_2(1,62) = 3.32$, $P = .073$) and the orthographic plus phonological condition $F_1(1,31) = 11.81$, $P < .01$, $F_2(1,62) = 4.43$, $P < .05$) produced reliable priming effects compared to the baseline control. In contrast, no priming effects were obtained for the phonological conditions (both Fs < 1). Most important of all, there was virtually no difference in priming effects between the orthographic and the orthographic plus phonological conditions (both Fs < 1), demonstrating that a homophone prime that was orthographically similar to the target did not produce additional priming effects above and beyond the priming effects produced by an orthographically similar prime.

Combined analysis. Combined analyses were also conducted on the lexical decision latencies collapsed across the two types of target characters. Pairwise comparisons showed the orthographic condition produced significant facilitation compared to the control condition ($F_1(1,47) = 13.57$, $P < .001$, $F_2(1,122) = 4.42$, $P < .05$), as well as compared to the phonological priming condition, $F_1(1,47) = 8.22$, $P < .001$; $F_2(1,122) = 3.88$, $P = .05$). In contrast, the difference between the phonological and the control condition was not significant (both *F*s < 1). None of the error data revealed significant differences.

Discussion

The most critical result of this experiment is the disappearance of phonological priming effects in the lexical decision task,. even for compound characters with valid phonetic radicals. This strongly suggests that the phonological effects observed in the first experiment depended on the task being naming, and that the mechanism of priming there had more to do with articulatory processes than lexical access *per se*.

On the other hand, what was clearly revealed in both naming and lexical experiments is that orthographically similar primes produced strong and robust priming effects in both tasks despite the fact they were phonologically unrelated to the target characters. The fact that such primes were only visually similar to the target characters demonstrates that the masked priming effects can be orthographic in nature, and the fact that these primes were phonologically unrelated to the targets rules out the possibility that orthographic codes were only subserving phonological code activation (Van Orden et al., 1990). Thus, these orthographic priming provide convincing evidence for direct orthographic access to lexical representations in memory (cf. Lukatela et al., 1993; Van Orden et al., 1990).

Finally, the lexical decision experiments revealed no additional priming effects due to the combination of visual plus phonological similarity, essentially replicating the pattern of the naming data in Experiment 1, and the results of Davis et al. (1998) in English. As argued earlier, this is inconsistent with a co-operative model, in which both orthographic and phonological codes play a role in retrieving lexical properties.

GENERAL DISCUSSION

The results of these experiments demonstrate for the first time convincing evidence of facilitatory orthographic priming effects that are dissociated from any possible phonological effects. They also suggest that evidence for phonological priming effects derived from naming studies should be interpreted with caution, since these effects may not generalise to other tasks, such as lexical decision.

Given that it has become commonplace to question the results obtained with lexical decision, some thought should be given to the possibility that the way in which lexical decisions are reached may have obscured the phonological effects so clearly evident in the naming task. One thing that this task is often criticised for is its sensitivity to postlexical decision processes. A difficult decision on a stimulus will result in longer reaction time and a prolonged decision process could perhaps obscure phonological priming effects. Two arguments can be made against this hypothesis. First, if a prolonged decision process in lexical decision obscured phonological effects, the same would apply to orthographic priming effects. But we have observed robust effects of orthographic priming across both tasks. Second, if the decision process in lexical decision were difficult and prolonged, we would expect to find much longer response times in lexical decision compared to naming. However, naming times for logographic characters are typically longer (by as much as 100 msec) than lexical decision times.

Ferrand and Grainger (1994) attempted to explain the absence of phonological effects in most masked priming studies in terms of inhibitory processes generated by partial orthographic overlap, which cancel the facilitatory effects produced by the homophonic prime. But this argument cannot apply in the current situation, since the homophonic primes were orthographically unrelated to the targets, and the overlap in terms of strokes between the prime and target was close to 0%. Thus, there is no reason to suppose that these primes generated any more within-level inhibition than the control primes. Ferrand and Grainger's hypothesis should predict stronger phonological priming effects when the homophone primes are orthographically unrelated to the targets. Obviously that was not the case.

Another possibility that needs to be considered is that lexical decisions may be triggered by the overall level of activation in a lexical network, rather than the discovery of a lexical representation that matches the input. Coltheart, Davelaar, Jonasson, and Besner (1977) first suggested such a mechanism, and it has subsequently been adopted by Monsell, Doyle and Haggard (1989), and Jacobs and Grainger (1992). The upshot of this strategy is that a positive decision might be reached long before the input has in fact been recognised. If it were argued that phonological effects were only involved at a relatively late stage of access (when semantic properties are being determined), then it could be argued that lexical decisions were generated too early for phonological processes to have any influence.

Such an argument creates a number of difficulties. Most of the emphasis in studies reporting phonological effects has been on demonstrating that phonology plays a role very early in access, not late. Also, the effects are supposed to be presemantic, which again suggests an early influence. Another problem is that if phonology is relevant only when semantic properties are being retrieved, then the results from naming studies become irrelevant, and this is the main source of evidence in favour of phonological priming. However, the most critical problem is that the phonological mediation hypothesis would require that lexical activation could only occur as a *result* of phonological activation, and hence it would be impossible for activation-based lexical decisions to be generated before phonological processes came into play.

The simplest explanation of why lexical decision should be insensitive to phonological priming, but sensitive to orthographic priming, appears to be that phonological effects depend on the involvement of phonological articulatory processes in the task. Naming involves such processes, lexical decision does not. This position is also consistent with the results of other studies. For example, Ferrand, Grainger, and Segui (1994) obtained strong masked priming effects in naming studies when the prime matched only the onset or initial syllable of the target, but no such effects were found in the lexical decision task using exactly the same set of stimuli and method or presentation. Similarly, Taft and van Graan (1998) showed that a phonological property such as regularity had no effect in a category decision task, although it did reliably affect performance in a naming task.

However, there are situations in which phonological effects occur, but the task requirements do not emphasise phonological processing. The clearest case is the homophone interference effect obtained in semantic categorisation (Van Orden, 1987; Van Orden et al., 1992). However, the interpretation of this effect is open to question. When a subject miscategorises homophones like *creak* as A SMALL STREAM, or takes longer to make a correct rejection, this effect could be interpreted as a joint effect of phonological and orthographic similarity (e.g., Besner, Dennis, & Davelaar, 1985), or it could be attributed to the fact that the category name A SMALL STREAM is so narrowly defined that a subject could easily preassemble a list of items that might include the correct exemplar which happens to be a homophone of the target (Jared & Seidenberg, 1991). In addition, homophone interference could occur when the phonological code retrieved for the homophone foil is stored in working memory and then used to initiate a reaccess for the correct exemplar (for discussion see Taft, 1991).

Another issue concerns the point at which phonological information exerts an influence. For example, Coltheart, Laxon, Richard, and Elton (1988) reported that homophone interference was observed with irregular words. Since the homophonic pronunciation of their exception words could not be determined by prelexical rules, the phonological codes must have been retrieved from the corresponding lexical entries, having been accessed on the basis of purely visual information. Moreover, the homophone interference effects associated with irregular words were just as strong as for regular words. Thus it is possible to argue that homophone interference effects in semantic categorisation (and lexical decision) occur post-lexically. Just as the irrelevant semantic properties of a word cause interference in the Stroop task (Stroop, 1935), the irrelevant phonological properties of a word may also cause interference in categorisation tasks. This interference arises because all lexical codes associated with a word may be automatically activated whenever any one type of code is activated. That is, it may not be possible to selectively activate the semantic code, without activating the corresponding phonological code. In turn, this phonological code may act to generate its own semantic codes, which will be quite misleading in the case of a homophone.

In a recent discussion, Van Orden, Holden, Podgornik, and Aitchison (1999) accept that homophone effects in categorisation depend on a number of task parameters, such as the narrowness of the category, or the relative frequency of the homophone, but deny that this invalidates the claim that phonology is involved in reading. Instead, they argue that these contextual factors affect the dynamics of the reading process, so that on occasion, relatively minor alterations in the parameter settings completely nullify any effects of phonology. As support for this view, they report evidence that homophone effects can be generated for high frequency words in a categorisation task when the category is presented 200 msec *after* the target word (e.g., *BREAK* : : *part of a car*), although the very same items produced no effect when the category was presented just before the target word. This finding clearly supports a dynamical systems interpretation, but at the same time, it must be pointed out that this is just what might be expected if the interfering phonological code is generated well after the target word has been recognised.

We would concede that the evidence presented here deals with a very restricted set of task parameters, namely, a lexical decision task in a logographic language, involving homophones that are orthographically quite unrelated, and a priming situation in which the prime is presented very briefly, and of which the subject is unaware. This combination of conditions could hardly be more tilted against phonological mediation. Yet, if priming had been observed in such conditions, this would have represented the strongest possible case for phonological mediation, and hence it is important to know whether such an effect can be observed. Our conclusion is that this effect is only observed when the task emphasises rapid mapping from an orthographic code to a phonological code.

In conclusion, we agree that phonological representations are recovered as part of the word identification process, even in a logographic language.

We agree that a reader is sensitive to the phonological properties of written words at *some* stage of the reading process, but this stage is probably so late that phonology plays little or no role in the identification of the word, but probably does play a role in postaccess comprehension.

REFERENCES

Andrews, S. (1982). Phonological recoding: Is the regularity effect consistent? *Memory & Cognition, 10*, 565–575.

Berent, I., & Perfetti, C. (1995). A rose is a REEZ: The two cycles model of phonology assembly in reading English. *Psychological Review, 102*, 146–184.

Besner, D., Dennis, I., & Davelaar, E. (1985). Reading without phonology? *Quarterly Journal of Experimental Psychology: Human Experimental Psychology, 37*, 477–491.

Carr, T.H., & Pollatsek, A. (1985). Recognition of printed words: A look at current models. In D. Besner, T.G. Waller, & G.E. MacKinnon (Eds), *Reading research, Vol. 5* (pp.1–82). New York: Academic Press.

Chen, H.-C., Flores d'Arcais, & Cheung, S.-L. (1995). Orthographic and phonological activation in recognizing Chinese characters. *Psychological Research, 58*, 144–153.

Chen, H.-C. (1998). Semantics without phonology: Evidence from replications of Perfetti and Tan (JEP:LMC, 1998). Paper presented at the 39th Annual Meeting of the Psychonomic Society, Dallas.

Cheng, C.-M. (1992). Lexical access in Chinese: Evidence from automatic activation of phonological information. In H.-C. Chen & O.J.L. Tzeng (Eds) *Language processing in Chinese* (pp.67–91). Elsevier Science Publishers B.V.

Coltheart, M (1978). Lexical access in simple reading tasks. In G. Underwood (ed.), *Strategies of information processing* (pp.151–216). London: Academic Press.

Coltheart, M., Curtis, B., Atkins, P., & Haller, M. (1993). Models of reading aloud: dual-route and Parallel-distributed-processing approaches. *Psychological Review, 4*, 589–608.

Coltheart, M., Davelaar, E., Jonasson, J.T., & Besner, D. (1977). Access to the internal lexicon. In S. Dornic (Ed.), *Attention and performance, XI* (pp.535–555). Hillside, NJ: Lawrence Erlbaum Associates Inc.

Coltheart, V., Laxon, V., Richard, M., & Elton, C. (1988). Phonological recoding in reading for meaning by adults and children. *Journal of Experimental Psychology: Learning, Memory, and Cognition, 14*, 387–397.

Davis, C., Castles, A., & Iakovidis, E. (1998). Masked homophone and pseudohomophone priming in children and adults. *Language and Cognitive Processes, 13*, 625–651.

Fan, K.Y., Gao, J.Y., & Ao, X.P. (1984). Pronunciation principles of Chinese characters and alphabetic writing scripts. *Chinese Character Reform, 4*, 23–27.

Ferrand, L., & Grainger, J. (1992). Phonology and orthography in visual word recognition: Evidence from masked nonword priming. *Quarterly Journal of Experimental Psychology, 45A*, 353–372.

Ferrand, L., & Grainger, J. (1993). The time-course of orthographic and phonological code activation in the early phases of visual word recognition. *Bulletin of the Psychonomic Society, 31*, 119–122.

Ferrand, L., & Grainger, J. (1994). Effects of orthography are independent of phonology in masked form priming. *Quarterly Journal of Experimental Psychology, 47A*, 365–382.

Ferrand, L., Grainger, J., & Segui, J. (1994). A study of masked priming in picture and word naming. *Memory & Cognition, 22*, 431–441.

Forster, K.I. (1992). Lexical processing. In D.N. Osherson & A. Lasnik (Eds), *An invitation to cognitive science: Language* (Vol. 1, pp.95–131). Cambridge, Mass: MIT Press.

Forster, K.I. (1998). The pros and cons of masked priming. *Journal of Psycholinguistic Research*, *27*, 203–233.

Forster, K.I., & Chambers, S.M. (1973). Lexical access and naming time. *Journal of Verbal Learning and Verbal Behavior*, *12*, 627–635.

Forster, K.I., & Davis, C. (1984). Repetition priming and frequency attenuation in lexical access. *Journal of Experimental Psychology: Learning, Memory, and Cognition*, *10*, 680–698.

Forster, K.I., & Davis, C. (1991). The density constraint on form-priming in the naming task: Interference effects from a masked prime. *Journal of Memory and Language*, *30*, 1–25.

Forster, K.I., Davis, C. Schoknecht, C., & Carter, R. (1987). Masked priming with graphemically related forms: Repetition or partial activation? *Quarterly Journal of Experimental Psychology*, *39A*, 211–251.

Forster, K.I., & Forster, J.C. (1990). *User's guide to the DMASTR display system.* Department of Psychology, University of Arizona.

Forster, K.I., & Taft, M. (1994). Bodies, antibodies, and neighbourhood density effects in masked form-priming. *Journal of Experimental Psychology: Learning, Memory, and Cognition*, *20*, 844–863.

Forster, K.I., & Yoshimura, K. (1994). Phonological processes in visual word recognition: Masked priming experiments in Japanese and Chinese. Paper presented at the *Asian–Australian Workshop on Cognitive Processing of Asian Languages*, Sydney, Australia.

Frost, R. (1998). Toward a strong phonological theory of visual word recognition: True issues and false trails. *Psychological Bulletin*, *123*, 71–99.

Gao, J.Y. (1983). Functions of phonetic radicals and other uses. *YuWen XuiXi* (*Language Studies*), *9*, 53–55.

Glushko, R.J. (1979). The organization and activation of orthographic knowledge in reading aloud. *Journal of Experimental Psychology: Human Perception and Performance*, *5*, 674–691.

Glushko, R.J. (1981). Principles of pronouncing print: The psychology of phonography. In A.M. Lesgold & C.A. Perfetti (Eds.), *Interactive processes in reading*, pp.61–84. Hillsdale, NJ: Lawrence Erlbaum Associates Inc.

Hsieh, N.M. (1982). *Reading of Chinese characters and words and phonological recoding.* Unpublished M.S. thesis: National Taiwan University.

Humphreys, G.W., & Evett, L.J. (1985). Are there independent lexical and nonlexical routes in word processing? An evaluation of the dual route theory of reading. *Behavioral and Brain Sciences*, *8*, 689–740.

Hung, D.L., & Tzeng, O.J.L. (1981). Orthographic variations and visual information processing. *Psychological Bulletin*, *90*, 377–414.

Jacobs, A.M., & Grainger, J. (1992). Testing a semistochastic variant of the Interactive Activation Model in different word recognition experiments. *Journal of Experimental Psychology: Human Perception and Performance*, *18*, 1174–1188.

Jacobs, A.M., & Grainger, J. (1994). Models of visual word recognition – sampling the state of the art. *Journal of Experimental Psychology: Human Perception and Performance*, *20*, 1311–1334.

Jared, D., & Seidenberg, M.S. (1991). Does word recognition proceed from spelling to sound to meaning? *Journal of Experimental Psychology: General*, *120*, 358–394.

Jiatong University (1988). *Dictionary of Chinese character information.* Shanghai: Science Press.

Katz, L., & Frost, R. (1992). The reading process is different for different orthographies. The orthographic depth hypothesis. In R. Frost & L. Katz (Eds), *Orthography, phonology, morphology, and meaning*, pp.67–84. Amsterdam: Elsevier Science.

Leck, K.J., Weekes, B.S., & Chen, M.J. (1994). Visual and phonological pathways to the lexicon: Evidence from Chinese readers. Paper presented at the *Asian-Australian Workshop on Cognitive Processing of Asian Languages*, Sydney, Australia.

Lukatela, G., Frost, S.J., & Turvey, M.T. (1998). Phonological priming by masked nonword primes in the lexical decision task. *Journal of Memory & Language, 39*, 666–683

Lukatela, G., Lukatela, K., & Turvey, M.T. (1993). Further evidence for phonological constraints on visual lexical access: Towed primes frog. *Perception and Psychophysics, 53*, 461–466.

Lukatela, G., & Turvey, M.T. (1991). Phonological access of the lexicon: Evidence from associative priming with pseudohomophones. *Journal of Experimental Psychology: Human Perception and Performance, 17*, 951–966.

Lukatela, G., & Turvey, M.T. (1993). Similar attentional, frequency, and associative effects for pseudohomophones and words. *Journal of Experimental Psychology: Human Perception and Performance, 19*, 166–178.

Martin, R.C., & Jensen, C.R. (1988). Phonological priming in the lexical decision task: A failure to replicate. *Memory and Cognition, 16*, 505–521.

McClelland, J.L., & Rumelhart, D.E. (1981). An interactive activation model of context effects in letter perception: Part 1. An account of basic findings. *Psychological Review, 88*, 375–407.

McCusker, L.X., Hillinger, M.L., & Bias, R.G. (1981). Phonological recoding and reading. *Psychological Bulletin, 89*, 217–245.

Meyer, D.E., Schvaneveldt, R.W., & Ruddy, M.G. (1974). Functions of graphemic and phonemic codes in visual word recognition. *Memory and Cognition, 2*, 309–321.

Monsell, S., Doyle, M.C., & Haggard, P.N. (1989). Effects of frequency on word recognition tasks: Where are they? *Journal of Experimental Psychology: General, 118*, 43–71.

Monsell, S., Patterson, K.E., Graham, A., Hughes, C.H.C.H., & Milroy, R. (1992). Lexical and sublexical translation of spelling to sound: Strategic anticipation of lexical status. *Journal of Experimental Psychology: Learning, Memory, and Cognition, 18*, 452–467.

Ni, H.S. (1975). *Modern Chinese logographic-phonetic compounds.* Beijing: Yuwen Press.

Patterson, K.E., & Coltheart, V. (1987). Phonological processes in reading: A tutorial review. In M. Coltheart (Ed.), *Attention and performance XII: The psychology of reading*, pp.421–447. Hove, UK: Lawrence Erlbaum Associates Ltd.

Perea, M., & Gotor, A. (1997). Associative and semantic priming effects occur at very short stimulus-onset asynchronies in lexical decision and naming. *Cognition, 62*, 223–240.

Perfetti, C.A., & Tan, L.H. (1998). The time course of graphic, phonological, and semantic activation in Chinese character identification. *Journal of Experimental Psychology: Learning, Memory, and Cognition, 24*, 101–118.

Perfetti, C.A., & Zhang, S. (1991). Phonological processes in reading Chinese words. *Journal of Experimental psychology: Learning, Memory, and Cognition, 17*, 633–643.

Perfetti, C.A., & Zhang, S. (1995). Very early phonological activation in Chinese reading. *Journal of Experimental Psychology: Learning, Memory, and Cognition, 21*, 24–33.

Perfetti, C.A., Zhang, S., & Berent, I. (1992). Reading in English and Chinese: Evidence for a "universal" phonological principle. In R. Frost, & L. Katz (Eds), *Orthography, phonology, morphology, and meaning* (pp.227–248). Amsterdam: North-Holland.

Seidenberg, M.S. (1985). The time course of phonological code activation in two writing systems. *Cognition, 19*, 1–30.

Seidenberg, M.S. (1992). Beyond orthographic depth in reading: Equitable division of labor. In R. Frost & L. Katz (Eds), *Orthography, phonology, morphology, and meaning* (pp.85–118). Elsevier Science Publishers B.V.

Seidenberg, M.S., & McClelland, J.L. (1989). A distributed, developmental model of word recognition and naming. *Psychological Review, 96*, 523–568.

Sereno, J.A. (1991) Graphemic, associative, and syntactic priming effects at a brief stimulus onset asyncrony in lexical decision and naming. *Journal of Experimental Psychology: Learning, Memory, and Cognition, 17*, 459–477.

Stroop, J.R. (1935). Studies of interference in serial verbal reactions. *Journal of Experimental Psychology, 18*, 624–643.

Sun, J.X. (1980). *Essential knowledge about Chinese characters.* Shijiazhuang, China: Hebei People's Press.

Taft, M. (1982). An alternative to grapheme-phoneme conversion rules? *Memory and Cognition, 10*, 465–474.

Taft, M. (1991). *Reading and the mental lexicon.* Hove, UK: Lawrence Erlbaum Associates Ltd.

Taft, M., & van Graan, F. (1998). Lack of phonological mediation in a semantic categorization task. *Journal of Memory and Language, 38*, 203–224.

Tan, L.H., Hoosain, R., & Peng, D.-L. (1995). Role of early presemantic phonological code in Chinese character identification. *Journal of Experimental Psychology: Learning, Memory, and Cognition, 21*, 43–54.

Tan, L.H., & Perfetti, C.A. (1997). Visual Chinese character recognition: Does phonological information mediate access to meaning? *Journal of Memory and Language, 37*, 47–51.

Tzeng, O.J.L., & Hung, D.L. (1988). Cerebral organization: Clues from scriptal effects on lateralization. In I. Liu, H.-C. Chen & M.J. Chen (Eds), *Cognitive aspects of the Chinese language, Vol. 1.* Hong Kong: Asian Research Service.

Van Orden, G.C. (1987). A ROWS is a ROSE: Spelling, sound and reading. *Memory and Cognition, 15*, 181–198.

Van Orden, G.C., Holden, J.G., Podgornik, M.N., & Aitchison, C.S. (1999). What swimming says about reading: Coordination, context, and homophone errors. *Ecological Psychology, 11*, 45–79.

Van Orden, G.C., Pennington, B.F., & Stone, G.O. (1990). Word identification in reading and the promise of a subsymbolic psycholinguistics. *Psychological Review, 97*, 488–522.

Van Orden, G.C., Stone, G.O., Garlington, K., Markson, L., Pinnt, G., Simonfy, C., & Brichetto, T. (1992). "Assembled" phonology and recoding: A case study in how theoretical perspective shapes empirical investigation. In R. Frost & L. Katz (Eds), *Orthography, phonology, morphology, and meaning* (pp.249–292). Amsterdam: Elsevier Science.

Wydell, T.N., Patterson, K.E., & Humphreys, G.W. (1993). Phonologically mediated access to meaning for Kanji: Is a rows still a rose in Japanese Kanji? *Journal of Experimental Psychology: Learning, Memory and Cognition, 19*, 491–514.

Xing, K.L., & Forster, K.I. (1996). Masked phonological priming in reading Chinese characters. Unpublished paper, University of Arizona.

Zhu, X. (1988). Dynamic account of the functions of phonetic radicals in modern Chinese character. In X. Yuan (Ed.), *Written language and culture.* BeijingGuanming Daily Publish House.

Ziegler, J.C., & Jacobs, A.M. (1995). Phonological information provides early sources of constraint in the processing of letter strings. *Journal of Memory and Language, 34*, 567–593.

APPENDIX

Targets and Primes used in Experiments 1 and 2.

Target	Primes	
	Visual	Phon.
今	令	斤
天	夫	添
刁	习	碉
刃	刀	任
申	中	身
由	田	尤
木	本	目
吏	史	立
午	牛	五
末	未	莫
韭	非	九
业	亚	页
士	土	示
兔	免	吐
巨	臣	具
瓜	爪	刮
人	入	仁
尸	户	失
矛	予	毛
万	方	腕
九	丸	酒
去	丢	趣
叉	又	插
旦	且	淡
良	民	凉
目	日	牧
尤	龙	油
母	毋	亩
牙	乐	崖
乌	鸟	污

Target	Primes		
	Visual	Phon.	Vis. + Phon.
理	埋	李	俚
肝	肚	柑	杆
材	村	裁	财
忘	忌	旺	妄
饭	饮	犯	贩
柱	栏	助	住
铭	铬	明	酩
伴	佯	扮	拌
仲	伸	众	种
侍	待	室	恃
估	枯	孤	姑
址	扯	纸	趾
柚	抽	犹	蚰
沾	沽	瞻	粘
译	泽	益	怿
铀	钿	游	油
泳	冰	勇	咏
冼	洗	显	铣
绶	缓	售	授
驶	驮	屎	使
迷	述	弥	谜
牲	性	声	胜
楫	缉	集	辑
忧	扰	悠	优
钉	针	定	订
栋	栎	洞	冻
绅	坤	深	伸
酪	酪	涝	烙
扬	仍	阳	扬
绞	纹	脚	狡
坪	圩	凭	评
扦	托	铅	仟

LANGUAGE AND COGNITIVE PROCESSES, 1999, *14* (5/6), 461–480

Orthographic and Phonological Processing in Reading Chinese Text: Evidence From Eye Fixations

Kin Fai Ellick Wong and Hsuan-Chih Chen
The Chinese University of Hong Kong, Hong Kong

The use of orthographic and phonologic information in reading Chinese text was investigated using an eye-monitoring technique. The basic manipulation was to change a critical character in a short passage so that various combinations of orthographic and phonological information were altered. Patterns of disruption caused by different manipulations were compared in order to reveal the use of orthographic and phonological information from individual characters during reading for comprehension. Results showed that orthographic manipulations produced reliable and early disruption in first fixation duration at the target word position. In contrast, phonological effects were only found in the measure of a relatively late stage of processing (i.e., total reading time) at the target position, but not in early measures of processing. These results supported the position that it is orthography rather than phonology, which plays an early and dominant role in reading Chinese.

INTRODUCTION

One of the most debated issues in the field of language processing has been the role of phonology in reading. A number of different positions have been proposed in the literature to account for how a printed word is processed for comprehension (Baron, 1973; Carr & Pollatsek, 1985; Coltheart, 1978; Coltheart, Curtis, Atkins, & Haller, 1993; Daneman &

Requests for reprints should be sent to Hsuan-Chih Chen, Department of Psychology, Chinese University of Hong Kong, Shatin, N.T., Hong Kong. Email: hcchen@psy.cuhk.edu.hk

This research was supported by Earmarked Research Grants from the Research Grants Council of Hong Kong to H.-C. Chen. We are grateful to Eyal Reingold for helpful discussions, to Matthew Chung for technical assistance, to Jackie Tsang and Xiu Yu Wu for aid in sorting and analysing the data, and to Xiaolin Zhou, Albrecht Inhoff, and Sandy Pollatsek for their comments and suggestions on an earlier draft.

Reingold, 1993; Lesch & Pollatsek, 1993; Lukatela & Turvey, 1991; Rubenstein, Lewis & Rubenstein, 1971; Van Orden, 1987). For instance, the phonological mediation hypothesis postulates that the orthographic input of a printed word first activates its phonology and then the semantics of the word are accessed by the phonology. In contrast, the direct access hypothesis argues that the semantics of a printed word are directly accessed by its orthographic input, bypassing its phonology. An alternative position (e.g., the dual-route hypothesis) assumes that both direct access and phonological mediation can contribute to the task of semantic access under certain conditions. The debate mainly focuses on whether phonological mediation or direct access is the predominant route in reading for skilled readers.

Although a great deal of research has been devoted to investigating the role of phonology in reading, however, past research on this issue using English as stimuli has failed to yield a consistent pattern of findings. For example, by using an eye-monitoring technique, Daneman, Reingold, and Davidson (1995; Daneman & Reingold, 1993) demonstrated that reading a homophonic word in a passage (i.e., a word such as "hare" which was homophonic to a contextually appropriate word "hair", but was itself contextually inappropriate), as manifested by the gaze duration of the word, was as disruptive as reading a non-homophonic control word such as "hire" which was unrelated to any contextually appropriate word. In contrast, Rayner, Pollatsek, and Binder (1998) reported that reading homophonic words was less disruptive than reading non-homophonic control words, especially for homophones which were orthographically similar to the contextually appropriate words (see also Pollatsek, Lesch, Morris, & Rayner, 1992).

Similar controversial results have also been observed in studying word recognition in isolation. For instance, in a semantic categorisation task, Van Orden (1987) reported that homophonic foils (i.e., targets which were homophonic to the correct exemplars) were more likely to be mis-classified as correct exemplars relative to unrelated controls. These findings were interpreted as indicating that semantic access of a word are phonologically mediated. Yet, recently, Taft and Van Graan (1998) found that regular and irregular words (e.g., PLANK and PINT, respectively) showed a difference in a naming task, but not in the semantic categorisation task. Given that the regularity effects found in naming are generally considered as reflecting phonological mediation, the results of Taft and Van Graan led them to conclude that semantic access may not necessarily be phonologically mediated (see also Jared and Seidenberg, 1991).

Why are the findings in English with respect to the role of phonology in reading so inconsistent? One possible reason is that in languages with alphabetic scripts (including English), each written symbol represents the elementary unit in speech, namely the phoneme. Orthography and phonology in most alphabetic scripts are consequently confounded to a considerable extent. Thus, it may be difficult to examine the unique contributions of orthography and phonology in reading English (for relevant discussions, see Shen & Forster, this issue).

However, a similar confounding between orthography and phonology is absent in those languages using a logographic script (e.g., Chinese). To illustrate, for the Chinese character 搏 (pronounced as /bok3/ in Cantonese), we can easily find an orthographically similar and phonologically identical (O+P++) character 博 (/bok3/), an orthographically similar but phonologically different (O+P−) character 傅 (/foo6/), an orthographically dissimilar but phonologically identical (O−P++) character 駁 (/bok3/), and an orthographically dissimilar and phonological dissimilar (O−P−) character 間 (/gaan1/). The present study was therefore designed to examine the unique contributions of orthography and phonology in reading Chinese (see Chen, 1992, 1996, for discussions on properties of written Chinese and their potential psychological implications).

The present study adopted a violation paradigm similar to the one used by Daneman et al. (1995) and Rayner et al. (1998). Specifically, subjects in our study were required to read short passages displayed on a computer monitor. In some of the passages, one character was chosen to be the critical character and was replaced by a contextually inappropriate target character in one of the O+P++, O+P−, O−P++, and O−P− conditions. In other words, the orthographic and phonological information carried by the critical character was systematically violated by substituting it with a target character. By observing and comparing the patterns of disruptions caused by different types of target characters on eye movement data, the role of orthography and phonology in reading Chinese can then be assessed.

Three types of eye movement data (i.e., first fixation duration, gaze duration and total reading time) were collected in the present study to reveal the time course of lexical processing during reading for comprehension (for relevant findings and discussions on the issue, see Daneman et al., 1995; Rayner et al., 1998). The first fixation duration on a word is simply the time that the eyes initially fixate on the word independent of the number of fixations on the word. It has been shown that first fixation duration is sensitive to a relatively early stage of processing in reading (Balota, Pollatsek, & Rayner, 1985; Inhoff, 1984; 1985; Inhoff & Rayner, 1986; Just & Carpenter, 1980; Lima, 1987; Lima & Inhoff, 1985). The gaze duration on a word is the total amount of time that the eyes fixate on the word before moving on to another word. Therefore, gaze duration includes the first fixation duration plus any subsequent time spent in consecutive fixations on the same word and should reflect later processing relative to first fixation duration (Inhoff, 1984). Finally, the total reading time on a word includes the gaze duration plus any subsequent time spent in regressive fixations to the word and can presumably reveal a relatively late stage of processing (Daneman et al., 1995). Apart from these dependent variables, we also analysed skipping rate (i.e., the likelihood of a word being completely skipped in reading), because it has been shown to be sensitive to various lexical properties in reading Chinese (Chen, Lau, & Wong, 1998).

Since first fixation duration is presumably the earliest measure of processing in reading, this dependent measure can be observed to reflect the role of phonology in early processing (Rayner et al., 1998). Specifically, if reading of a character involves activation of its phonological representation as an access code to the mental representation of the character (i.e., phonology plays a crucial role in an early stage of processing), then it is expected to find phonological effects (i.e., reading a homophonic character is less disruptive than reading a non-homophonic character) with first fixation duration. In contrast, if phonology's significant role is not in the early stage but rather the later stages of reading, it is expected that reading homophones is as disruptive as reading non-homophones in the first fixation duration, and perhaps in the gaze duration as well. However, in the total reading time reading homophones may show advantages over non-homophones, as the total reading time has been shown to be sensitive to the relatively late stages of lexical processing (Daneman et al., 1995).

The contribution of orthography in reading may also be examined by a similar logic. That is, if the meanings of a character are accessed directly from its visual input during the reading of a passage rather than from phonological mediation, then it is expected that orthographic similarity effects (i.e., the advantages of reading orthographically similar characters over reading orthographically dissimilar characters) will be observed in the first fixation duration, but not phonological effects. Similar predictions can also be generated for other dependent measures.

METHOD

Participants

Thirty-two undergraduates participated in the present experiment for research credit in an introductory psychology course at the Chinese University of Hong Kong. They were all native Cantonese speakers with normal or corrected-to-normal vision.

Materials

The stimuli included 40 experimental passages and 40 error-free filler passages. The mean number of characters per experimental passage was 50, ranging from 40 to 60. Each experimental passage included a critical character, which was always the first character of a two-character word (e.g., the character "栽" from the word "栽培"). These two-character words were in the centre of a sentence and were neither at the line boundaries nor at the clause boundaries. Each experimental passage had four versions, O+P++, O+P−, O−P++, and O−P−, which were created by replacing the critical character with an orthographically similar homophone character[1] (e.g., "哉"), an orthographically similar but phonologically dissimilar character (e.g., "截"), an orthographically dissimilar homophone character (e.g., "災"), and an orthographically dissimilar and phonologically dissimilar character (e.g., "紗"), respectively. The mean frequency of the target characters according to the character frequency counts developed by the Hong Kong Education Department (1986) for O+P++, O+P−, O−P++, and O−P− conditions were 104, 103, 164, and 121 occurrences per million, respectively, with no significant frequency effect found between conditions. The complexity of the target characters in the four conditions was also matched (i.e., the mean number of strokes for O+P++, O+P−, O−P++, and O−P− were 11.9, 12.3, 11.7, and 11.8, respectively). The target characters are listed in Appendix A.

The four versions of the passages were used to create four experimental lists, each of which contained 10 passages from each of the four experimental conditions. Passages that contained one type of the target characters on one list contained another type of the target characters on another list, with passage type counterbalanced across lists.

In constructing the stimuli, care was taken to ensure that the original critical characters were not easily predictable from prior context and that the target characters in the four conditions did not fit in the context. This was done intentionally to maximise the likelihood that readers would not skip the characters. To confirm whether the stimuli were constructed as planned, another group of 26 undergraduates were recruited to judge how predictable the critical and target characters were from prior context and how well they fitted in the context. The mean predictability of the critical character in the passage was 2.5% as determined by norms collected from the judges (i.e., they were presented the passages up to the occurrence of the critical character and guessed what the next word would be), whereas

[1] Homophony and the phonological manipulations adopted in the study were defined in Cantonese (i.e., the native language of the subjects in the present study).

none of the target characters in the four conditions was predicted (i.e., the mean predictability was 0% for all four conditions). Also, the original critical characters were judged to be appropriate according to the context 100% of the time, while the corresponding data for the target characters in the O+P++, O+P–, O–P++, and O–P– conditions were 5%, 3%, 3%, and 3%, respectively (the passages were presented with the critical or target characters underlined and the subjects were asked to judge whether the underlined character fitted in the context).

Apparatus

An EIZO T562 17-inch SVGA monitor with 0.25 mm dot pitch was used to display text. All stimuli were shown in black on a grey background. Eye movements were recorded with an EyeLink video-based eyetracking system that calculated the x- and y-coordinates of the reader's point of regard every 4 ms.

All characters were presented in traditional 24-point Kai-Ti font. From the subject's viewing distance of about 0.7 m, each character subtended approximately 1.2 degrees of visual angle both in width and in height. The centre to centre inter-character distance subtended approximately 1.4 degrees of visual angle. Each text was displayed in the centre of the monitor as a 14 characters × 11 rows matrix. Reading was done from left to right within each row and from top to bottom row by row.

Procedure

Each of the 32 subjects participated in a 75-min experiment. The experiment included a calibration phase and an experimental phase. In the calibration phase, each subject performed a formal 9-point calibration procedure to make sure that the tracker was accurate to 0.5 degrees of visual angle to either side of the reader's fixation centre. The experimental phase began after the calibration.

At the beginning of the experimental phase, subjects were asked to read short passages displayed on the computer screen for comprehension at their normal pace and to answer three multiple-choice comprehension questions after reading each passage. They were told that some of the passages might contain a misplaced character, but that they did not need to worry about it and not to re-read the passages.

The subjects were asked to fixate on the dot appeared at the top left corner of the monitor indicating the position of the first character of the passage and then to press the start button on a response pad to initiate a trial. Once the start button was pressed, the entire passage was displayed on the screen. After reading a passage, the subjects pressed the end button on the response pad to clear the screen. Three multiple-choice questions were then presented on the screen and the subjects answered each of them by pressing the appropriate keys on the response pad. The fixation dot of the next passage would display on the screen automatically after the last question was answered. Each subject saw in total 80 short passages (i.e., 40 experimental passages and 40 filler ones) presented in a random order and was allowed to have a short break after reading every 20 passages.

Design and Data Analysis

There were two within-subjects factors: orthographic similarity (orthographically similar *vs.* orthographically dissimilar) and phonological similarity (phonologically identical *vs.* phonologically dissimilar).

Four types of eye movement measures (i.e., first fixation duration, gaze duration, total reading time, and skipping rate) were analysed with respect to the target character (i.e., position N). In addition, because the target character appeared always at the first character of a two-character word, the data were also analysed with respect to the target word (i.e., Nw; the region used for computing the various measures included both character positions N and N + 1). Specifically, the data for Nw included trials on which either the target character or the N + 1 character (or the area in between the two) being fixated on the first pass. Finally, we found in our previous research (Chen, 1999) that the violation effects resulting from replacing an original character with anomalous ones in a text often appeared not immediately at the place where the manipulation was introduced but at one or two characters after the target position. Thus, we also analysed the data with respect to the two characters after the target ones (character positions N + 1 and N + 2). To maximise the likelihood of detecting the potential effects of various manipulations, in the computations for the date for N + 1 and N + 2, only trials on which the target character was fixated on the first pass were included. Thus, for instance, the date for the position N + 1 included trials on which both the target character and the N + 1 character being fixated.

RESULTS

Two 2 (orthographic similarity) × 2 (phonological similarity) analyses of variance (one by subjects and one by items) on each of the dependent measures for the target character position N, the target word position Nw, the character position N + 1, and the character position N + 2 were carried out.

Character Position N

The mean dependent measures at position N are shown in Table 1.

First fixation duration and gaze duration. No effects were significant in the analyses (all *F*s < 1).

Total reading time. The main effect of orthographic similarity was significant [$F_1(1,31) = 16.44$, $P < .001$; $F_2(1,39) = 4.78$, $P < .05$], indicating that the mean total reading time was shorter for the orthographically similar conditions (396 ms) than the orthographically dissimilar conditions (469 ms). The main effect of phonological similarity was also significant [$F_1(1,31) = 15.16$, $P < .001$; $F_2(1,39) = 10.5$, $P < .005$], indicating that the mean total reading time was shorter for the phonologically identical condition (383 ms) than the phonologically dissimilar condition (482 ms). The orthographic similarity × phonological similarity interaction was not significant (*F*s < 1).

TABLE 1
Mean First Fixation Duration, Gaze Duration, Total Reading Time, and Skipping Rate as a Function of Phonological and Orthographic Similarity at the Target Character Position N

		Control–Experimental
First fixation duration (ms)		
O+P++	254	+2
O+P–	255	+1
O–P++	257	–1
O–P–	256	
Gaze duration (ms)		
O+P++	282	+16
O+P–	311	–13
O–P++	302	–3
O–P–	298	
Total reading time (ms)		
O+P++	346	+173
O+P–	446	+73
O–P++	420	+99
O–P–	519	
Skipping rate (%)		
O+P++	47	–12
O+P–	45	–10
O–P++	38	–3
O–P–	35	

Skipping rates. The main effect of orthographic similarity was significant [$F_1(1,31) = 15.82$, $P < .001$; $F_2(1,39) = 13.02$, $P < .001$], indicating that the average skipping rate was higher for the orthographically similar conditions than the orthographically dissimilar conditions (46.5% and 36.5%, respectively). No other effects were significant (all $Fs < 1.5$).

Word Position Nw

The mean dependent measures at position Nw are shown in Table 2.

First fixation duration. The main effect of orthographic similarity was significant [$F_1(1,31) = 6.1$, $P < .05$; $F_2(1,39) = 13.35$, $P < .001$], indicating that the mean first fixation duration was shorter for the orthographically similar conditions (252 ms) than the orthographically dissimilar conditions (271 ms). No other effects were significant (all $Fs < 1$).

TABLE 2
Mean First Fixation Duration, Gaze Duration, Total Reading Time, and Skipping Rate as a Function of Phonological and Orthographic Similarity at the Target Word Position Nw

		Control–Experimental
First fixation duration (ms)		
O+P++	254	+18
O+P–	250	+22
O–P++	269	+3
O–P–	272	
Gaze duration (ms)		
O+P++	338	+93
O+P–	369	+62
O–P++	422	+9
O–P–	431	
Total reading time (ms)		
O+P++	523	+406
O+P–	642	+287
O–P++	661	+268
O–P–	929	
Skipping rate (%)		
O+P++	7	–4
O+P–	5	–2
O–P++	4	–1
O–P–	3	

Gaze duration. The main effect of orthographic similarity was significant [$F_1(1,31) = 34.79$, $P < .0001$; $F_2(1,39) = 16.49$, $P < .001$] (i.e., 353 and 426 ms for the orthographically similar and dissimilar conditions, respectively). The main effect of phonological similarity was not significant by subjects [$F_1(1,31) = 1.54$, $P > .1$], but was significant by items [$F_2(1,39) = 7.92$, $P < .01$], indicating that the mean gaze duration tended to be shorter for the phonologically identical conditions (380 ms) than the phonologically dissimilar conditions (400 ms). The orthographic similarity × phonological similarity interaction was not significant (Fs < 1).

Total reading time. The main effect of orthographic similarity was significant [$F_1(1,31) = 71.33$, $P < .0001$; $F_2(1,39) = 34.05$, $P < .0001$] (i.e., 583 and 795 ms for the orthographically similar and dissimilar conditions, respectively). The main effect of phonological similarity was significant [$F_1(1,31) = 34.05$, $P < .0001$; $F_2(1,39) = 26.14$, $P < .0001$] (i.e., 592 and 786 ms for the phonologically similar and dissimilar conditions, respectively). Furthermore, the orthographic similarity × phonological similarity interaction was also significant [$F_1(1,31) = 5.04$, $P > .05$; $F_2(1,39) = 5.29$, $P < .05$], indicating that either orthographic or phonological similarity alone could produce a reliable effect on total reading time at the position Nw, but together they produced the strongest effect.

Skipping rate. The main effect of orthographic similarity was significant [$F_1(1,31) = 6.2$, $P < .05$; $F_2(1,39) = 4.33$, $P < .05$], indicating that the mean skipping rate was higher for the orthographically similar conditions (5.9%) than the orthographically dissimilar conditions (3.4%). No other effects were significant (all Fs < 1.5).

Character Position $N + 1$

The mean dependent measures at position N + 1 are shown in Table 3. Two subjects' data were not included in the subject-based analyses for first fixation duration, gaze duration, and total reading time, because they skipped all items at position N + 1 in some of the conditions. Two items (out of the 40 items) were excluded from the item-based analyses for a similar reason.

First fixation duration. The main effect of orthographic similarity was significant by subjects [$F_1(1,29) = 4.33$, $P < .05$] but not by item ($F_2 < 1$), indicating that the mean first fixation duration tended to be shorter for the orthographically similar conditions (251 ms) than the orthographi-

TABLE 3
Mean First Fixation Duration, Gaze Duration, Total Reading Time, and Skipping Rate as a Function of Phonological and Orthographic Similarity at the Character Position $N + 1$

		Control–Experimental
First fixation duration (ms)		
O+P++	248	+31
O+P−	255	+24
O−P++	267	+12
O−P−	279	
Gaze duration (ms)		
O+P++	283	+56
O+P−	305	+34
O−P++	318	+21
O−P−	339	
Total reading time (ms)		
O+P++	389	+218
O+P−	433	+174
O−P++	463	+144
O−P−	607	
Skipping rate (%)		
O+P++	38	−20
O+P−	26	−8
O−P++	25	−7
O−P−	18	

cally dissimilar condition (273 ms). No other effects were significant (all Fs < 2).

Gaze duration. The main effect of orthographic similarity was significant by subjects [$F_1(1,29) = 5.05$, $P < .05$] but not by items [$F_2(1,37) = 1.75$, $P > .1$] (i.e., 294 and 328 ms for the orthographically similar and dissimilar conditions, respectively). The main effect of phonological similarity was not significant by subjects [$F_1(1,29) = 1.76$, $P > .1$], but was marginally significant by items [$F_2(1,37) = 3.13$, $P = .08$]. The orthographic similarity × phonological similarity interaction was not significant (Fs < 1).

Total reading time. The main effect of orthographic similarity was significant [$F_1(1,29) = 29$, $P < .0001$; $F_2(1,37) = 9.26$, $P < .005$] (i.e., 411 and 535 ms for the orthographically similar and dissimilar conditions, respectively). The main effect of phonological similarity was also significant [$F_1(1,29) = 15.06$, $P < .001$; $F_2(1,37) = 6.05$, $P < .05$] (i.e.,

426 and 520 ms for the phonologically identical and dissimilar conditions, respectively). The orthographic similarity × phonological similarity interaction was not significant [$F_1(1,29) = 2.76$, $P > .1$; $F_2(1,37) = 2.17$, $P > .1$].

Skipping rate. The main effect of orthographic similarity was significant by subjects [$F_1(1,31) = 10.82$, $P < .005$], and was marginally significant by items [$F_2(1,39) = 3.42$, $P = .07$] (i.e., 32% and 21% for the orthographically similar and dissimilar conditions, respectively). The main effect of phonological similarity was significant [$F_1(1,31) = 8.18$, $P < .01$; $F_2(1,39) = 5.19$, $P < .03$] (i.e., 31% and 22% for the phonologically identical and dissimilar conditions, respectively). The orthographic similarity × phonological similarity interaction was not significant (*F*s < 1).

Character Position *N* + 2

The mean dependent measures at position N + 2 are shown in Table 4. There were four items at position N + 2 excluded in the item-based analyses for first fixation duration, gaze duration, and total reading time, because they were skipped by all subjects in some conditions.

First fixation duration. The main effect of orthographic similarity was significant [$F_1(1,31) = 7.35$, $P < .05$; $F_2(1,35) = 8.14$, $P < .01$] (i.e., 218 and 244 ms for the orthographically similar and dissimilar conditions, respectively). The main effect of phonological similarity was significant by subjects [$F_1(1,31) = 4.31$, $P < .05$], but was not significant by subjects ($F_2 < 1$). The orthographic similarity × phonological similarity interaction was not significant (*F*s < 1.05).

Gaze duration. The main effect of orthographic similarity was significant [$F_1(1,31) = 11.64$, $P < .005$; $F_2(1,35) = 19.17$, $P < .001$] (i.e., 226 and 268 ms for the orthographically similar and dissimilar conditions, respectively). The main effect of phonological similarity was also significant (i.e., 234 and 260 ms for the phonologically identical and dissimilar conditions, respectively), [$F_1(1,31) = 7.42$, $P < .05$; $F_2(1,35) = 4.8$, $P < .05$]. The orthographic similarity × phonological similarity interaction was not significant [$F_1 < 1$; $F_2(1,35) = 1.72$, $P > .1$]

Total reading time. The main effect of orthographic similarity was significant (i.e., 298 and 394 ms for the orthographically similar and dissimilar conditions, respectively) [$F_1(1,31) = 18.93$, $P < .001$; $F_2(1,35) = 20.23$, $P < .0001$]. The main effect of phonological similarity was

TABLE 4
Mean First Fixation Duration, Gaze Duration, Total Reading Time, and Skipping Rate as a Function of Orthographic and Phonological Similarity at the Character Position $N + 2$

		Control–Experimental
First fixation duration (ms)		
O+P++	211	+32
O+P–	226	+27
O–P++	234	+19
O–P–	253	
Gaze duration (ms)		
O+P++	216	+69
O+P–	235	+50
O–P++	252	+27
O–P–	285	
Total reading time (ms)		
O+P++	290	+156
O+P–	306	+140
O–P++	342	+104
O–P–	446	
Skipping rate (%)		
O+P++	38	–17
O+P–	38	–17
O–P++	33	–12
O–P–	21	

significant by subjects [$F_1(1,31) = 9.52$, $P < .005$], and was only marginally significant by items [$F_2(1,35) = 2.94$, $P = .09$] (i.e., 316 and 376 ms for the phonologically identical and dissimilar conditions, respectively). The orthographic similarity × phonological similarity interaction was not significant by subjects [$F_1(1,31) = 2.41$, $P > .1$]; but was significant by items [$F_2(1,35) = 6.43$, $MSE = 24316$, $P < .05$], suggesting that a clear effect of phonological similarity was shown in the orthographically dissimilar conditions (104 ms) but not in the orthographically similar conditions (16 ms).

Skipping rate. The main effect of orthographic similarity was significant [$F_1(1,31) = 16.21$, $P < .0005$; $F_2(1,39) = 7.68$, $P = .01$] (i.e., 38% and 27% for the orthographically similar and dissimilar conditions, respectively). The main effect of phonological similarity was marginally significant by subjects [$F_1(1,31) = 3.38$, $P = .08$], but was not significant by items [$F_2(1,39) = 2.59$, $P > .1$]. The orthographic similarity × phonological similarity interaction was significant [$F_1(1,31) = 5.9$, $P < .05$; $F_2(1,39) = 4.13$, $P = .05$], indicating that the effect of phonological similarity was observed in the orthographically dissimilar condition (12%) but not in the orthographically similar condition (0%).

DISCUSSION

The present study was designed in an attempt to reveal the use of orthographic and phonological information in reading Chinese text. The results can be summarised easily. Although we did not find any reliable effects in first fixation duration at the target character position (N), orthographic manipulations produced robust interference at the target word position (Nw), whereas phonological manipulations showed a relatively weak trend of delayed disruption at the N + 1 and N + 2 positions. A similar pattern of results emerged from both skipping rates (i.e., reliable orthographic effects appeared immediately at the target character position and continued through to the N + 2 position, while weaker but nevertheless significant phonological effects were found at the N + 1 and N + 2 positions) and gaze duration (i.e., early and strong orthographic effects but weak and late phonological effects). However, a slightly different picture was shown in total reading time; both orthographic and phonological effects were significant starting at the target character position and continuing through the N + 2 position.

As indicated in the introduction, both phonological mediation and direct access have been proposed to account for the roles of orthographic and phonological activation in reading. Can either of these two hypotheses provide a reasonable explanation for the present results? Let us look at phonological mediation first. The phonological mediation hypothesis postulates that the phonologically mediated route plays a major role in semantic access. The strongest version of the hypothesis actually assumes that since orthographic representations are not directly connected with semantic representations, semantic access is done exclusively via phonological mediation (Frost, 1998; Van Orden, Pennington, & Stone, 1990). This version of the hypothesis would predict that whereas strong phonological effects should occur early, orthographic effects might not appear in the earliest measures of processing such as first fixation duration. A weak version of the phonological mediation hypothesis assumes that the link between the orthographic representation and the semantic representation exists, but is relatively weak (e.g., Seidenberg, 1992). Hence, semantic access is generally faster for the phonological mediation route than the direct route. This version of the phonological mediation hypothesis would predict strong and early phonological effects and weak orthographic effects.

However, the present results provide practically no evidence for either the strong or the weak version of the phonological mediation hypothesis.

The phonological effects were not only slower but also weaker than the orthographic effects for almost all the dependent measures except for total reading time, the measure of a relatively late stage of processing. In addition, even in total reading time, both phonological and orthographic effects appeared at the same location and with similar strength. These results, thus, are difficult to reconcile with the notion that semantic access is exclusively or predominantly via the phonological mediation route.

In contrast to phonological mediation, the direct access hypothesis generally postulates that reading comprehension does not require the mediation of phonology and is accomplished mainly by a direct, visual access path. This hypothesis would predict that there should be early and strong orthographic effects in first fixation duration, but either weak phonological effects or no such effects at all at the target character or word position.

Interestingly, as indicated earlier, we did not find any reliable effects in early measures of processing, such as first fixation duration and gaze duration, at the target character position where the orthographic and phonological manipulations were introduced. Nevertheless, when we expanded the region used for computing the various fixation time measures from the target character position (N) to the target word position (Nw), a clear pattern of results emerged: Robust orthographic effects appeared in both first fixation duration and gaze duration, while a somewhat less reliable trend of phonological effects was revealed only in gaze duration, and not in first fixation duration. These results seem to suggest that orthographic processing plays a prominent role in the early stage of reading Chinese, but phonological processing does not (for a similar suggestion, see, e.g., Chen, 1998; Chen, Flores d'Arcais, & Cheung, 1995). The present findings, thus, appear to be compatible with the direct access hypothesis.

Furthermore, our finding that reliable effects were only found in first fixation duration at the target word position but not at the target character position seems to suggest that our subjects might have utilised information obtained from more than a single character to carry out various processes involved in reading (for discussions on comprehension processes involved in reading Chinese, see Chen, 1992, 1996, 1999). In other words, it seems plausible that the various types of lexical information from an individual character are not used independently, but are activated and used together with those from the coming character which is likely to be used to form a word (for relevant discussions on the representations and processing of Chinese characters and words, see Taft, Liu, and Zhu, 1999). This interesting possibility warrants future research.

It is important to note that although our results are more in line with the direct access rather than the phonological mediation hypothesis, there is indeed evidence to show that phonological processing does exist in the comprehension of Chinese. As indicated earlier, we found reliable phonological effects across different positions in the measure of a relatively late stage of processing (i.e., total reading time; for relevant discussions and results using different versions of a self-paced moving-window paradigm, see, e.g., Wu, Shu, Zhou, & Shi, 1998; Wong & Chen, 1999). In addition, we found a slowly emerging trend of phonological effects in those measures reflecting early processing (i.e., first fixation duration and gaze duration). These results, thus, seem to suggest that while phonological processing does have a role to play in reading Chinese, it simply is too slow and weak to affect the early stages of processing (for a similar suggestion, see Shen & Forster, this issue).

Note that, similar to our results found in reading Chinese text, robust orthographic effects together with null or weak phonological effects have been documented in studies using either isolated Chinese characters or two-character Chinese words as stimuli in a variety of tasks, including semantic categorisation (e.g., Chen et al., 1995), backward masking (Perfetti & Zhang, 1991), phonologically mediated priming (Zhou, Shu, Bi, & Shi, 1999; Zhou & Marslen-Wilson, 1999), masked priming with lexical decision (Shen & Forster, this issue; Zhou et al., 1999), and even primed-naming (Chen, 1998). Evidence for the notion that phonology plays a critical role in an early stage of Chinese character identification has also been reported (Perfetti & Tan, 1998; Tan & Perfetti, 1997). However, it has been shown that some of the most striking phonological effects documented in the literature (Perfetti & Tan, 1998; Tan & Perfetti, 1997) could not be replicated, though the same stimuli and procedures were used (Chen 1998; Wu, 1998; Zhou & Marslen-Wilson, 1999; for relevant discussions, see, Wu & Chen, 1999). These reports attest to the central importance of replication in the study of reading and related processes in Chinese, particularly because the research in this interesting area is still relatively new.

In conclusion, the independent relationship between the visual and phonological forms in Chinese provides an excellent opportunity to examine the relative contributions of orthography and phonology during the reading of Chinese text. In the present study, we found compelling evidence in various types of eye movement data that it is orthographic rather than phonological activation, which plays an early and dominant role in the early stage of reading for comprehension, indicating that the meaning of a Chinese word is possibly accessed by orthography directly. On the other hand, phonology seems to play a more active role in the later stages of processing in reading, possibly because it can contribute to working memory and/or to the recovery from lexical impairment (see Daneman et al., 1995).

REFERENCES

Balota, D.A., Pollatsek, A., & Rayner, K. (1985). The interaction of contextual and parafoveal visual information during eye fixations in reading. *Cognitive Psychology*, *17*, 364–390.

Baron, J. (1973). Phonemic stage not necessary for reading: Lexical access and/or production? *Quarterly Journal of Experimental Psychology*, *25*, 241–246.

Carr, T.H., & Pollatsek, A. (1985). Recognizing printed words: A look at current models. In D. Besner, T.G. Waller, & G.E. MacKinnon (Eds), *Reading research: Advances in theory and practice*, Vol. 5, pp.1–82. Orlando, FL: Academic Press.

Chen, H.-C. (1992). Reading comprehension in Chinese: Implications from character reading times. In H.-C. Chen & O.J.L. Tzeng (Eds), *Language processing in Chinese*, pp.175–205. Amsterdam: North-Holland.

Chen, H.-C. (1996). Chinese reading and comprehension: A cognitive psychology perspective. In M.H. Bond (Ed.) *The handbook of Chinese psychology*, pp.43–62. Hong Kong: Oxford University Press.

Chen, H.-C. (1999). How do readers of Chinese process words during reading for comprehension? In J. Wang, A.W. Inhoff, & H.-C. Chen (Eds), *Reading Chinese script: A cognitive analysis*, pp.257–278. Mahwah, NJ: Lawrence Erlbaum Associates Inc.

Chen, H.-C. (1998). *Semantics without phonology: Evidence from replications of Perfetti and Tan (1998).* Paper presented at the 39th Annual Meeting of the Psychonomic Society, Dallas, Texas, USA.

Chen, H.-C., Flores d'Arcais, G.B., & Cheung, S.L. (1995). Orthographic and phonological activation in recognizing Chinese characters. *Psychological Research*, *58*, 144–153.

Chen, H.-C., Lau, W.Y.L., & Wong, K.F.E. (1998). *Reading Chinese: Implications from character reading times and eye movements.* Paper presented at the First International Workshop of Writing Language Processing, Sydney.

Coltheart, M. (1978). Lexical access in simple reading tasks. In G. Underwood (Ed.), *Strategies of information processing*, pp.151–216. New York: Academic Press.

Coltheart, M., Curtis, B., Atkins, P., & Haller, M. (1993). Models of reading aloud: Dual-route and parallel-distributed-processing approaches. *Psychological Review*, *100*, 589–608.

Daneman, M., & Reingold, E.M. (1993). What eye fixations tell us about phonological recoding during reading. *Canadian Journal of Experimental Psychology*, *47*, 153–178.

Daneman, M., Reingold, E.M., & Davidson, M. (1995). Time course of phonological activation during reading: Evidence from eye fixations. *Journal of Experimental Psychology*, *21*, 884–898.

Frost, R. (1998). Toward a strong phonological theory of visual word recognition: true issues and false trials. *Psychological Bulletin*, *123*, 71–99.

Hong Kong Education Department (1986). *Frequency count of Chinese words used in Hong Kong secondary school reading materials.* Hong Kong: Hong Kong Government Press.

Inhoff, A.W. (1985). The effect of factivity on lexical retrieval and postlexical processing during eye fixations in reading. *Journal of Psycholinguistic Research*, *14*, 45–56.

Inhoff, A.W. (1984). Two stages of word processing during eye fixations in the reading of prose. *Journal of Verbal Learning and Verbal Behavior*, *23*, 612–624.

Inhoff, A.W., & Rayner, K. (1986). Parafoveal word processing during eye fixations in reading: Effects of word frequency. *Perception and Psychophysics*, *40*, 431–439.

Jared, D., & Seidenberg, M.S. (1991). Does word identification proceed from spelling to sound to meaning? *Journal of Experimental Psychology: General*, *120*, 358–394.

Just, M.A., & Carpenter, P.A. (1980). A theory of reading: From eye fixation to comprehension. *Psychological Review*, *87*, 329–354.

Lesch, M.F., & Pollatsek, A. (1993). Automatic access of semantic information by phonological codes in visual word recognition. *Journal of Experimental Psychology: Learning, Memory, and Cognition*, *19*, 285–294.

Lukatela, G., & Turvey, M.T. (1991). Phonological access of the lexicon: Evidence from associative priming with pseudohomophones. *Journal of Experimental Psychology: Human Perception and Performance*, *17*, 951–966.

Lima, S.D. (1987). Morphological analysis in sentence reading. *Journal of Memory and Language*, *26*, 84–99.

Lima, S.D., & Inhoff, A.W. (1985). Lexical access during eye fixations in reading: Effects of word-initial letter sequence. *Journal of Experimental Psychology: Human Perception and Performance*, *11*, 272–285.

Perfetti, C.A., & Tan, L.H. (1998). The time course of graphic, phonological, and semantic activation in Chinese character identification. *Journal of Experimental Psychology: Learning, Memory, and Cognition*, *24*, 101–118.

Perfetti, C.A., & Zhang, S. (1991). Phonemic processes in reading Chinese words. *Journal of Experimental Psychology: Learning, Memory, and Cognition*, 17, 633–643.

Pollatsek, A., Lesch, M.F., Morris, R.K., & Rayner, K. (1992). Phonological codes are used in integrating information across saccades in word identification and reading. *Journal of Experimental Psychology: Human Perception and Performance*, *18*, 148–162.

Rayner, K., Pollatsek, A., & Binder, K.S. (1998). Phonological codes and eye movements in reading. *Journal of Experimental Psychology: Learning, Memory, and Cognition*, *24*, 476–497.

Rubenstein, H., Lewis, S.S., & Rubenstein, M.A. (1971). Evidence for phonemic recording in visual word recognition. *Journal of Verbal Learning and Verbal Behavior*, *10*, 645–657.

Seidenberg, M.S. (1992). Beyond orthographic depth in reading: Equitable division of labor. In R. Frost & L. Katz (Eds), *Orthography, phonology, morphology, and meaning*, pp.85–118. Amsterdam: Elsevier.

Shen, D., & Forster, K.I. (this issue). Masked phonological priming in reading Chinese words depends on the task. *Language and Cognitive Processes*, *14*, 429–459.

Taft, M., & Van Graan, F. (1998). Lack of phonological mediation in a semantic categorization task. *Journal of Memory and Language*, *38*, 203–224.

Taft, M., Liu, Y., & Zhu, X. (1999). Morphemic processing in reading Chinese. In J. Wang, A.W. Inhoff, & H.-C. Chen (Eds), *Reading Chinese script: A cognitive analysis*, pp.91–113. Mahwah, NJ: Lawrence Erlbaum Associates Inc.

Tan, L.H., & Perfetti, C.A. (1997). Visual Chinese character recognition: Does phonological information mediate access to meaning? *Journal of Memory and Language*, *37*, 41–57.

Van Orden, G.C. (1987). A ROWS is a ROSE: Spelling, sound and reading. *Memory and Cognition*, *15*, 181–198.

Van Orden, G.C., Pennington, B.F., & Stone, G.O. (1990). Word identification in reading and the promise of subsymbolic psycholinguistics. *Psychological Review*, *97*, 488–522.

Wong, K.F.E., & Chen, H.-C. (1999). The role of orthographic and phonological processing in reading Chinese. *Acta Psychologica Sinica*, in press.

Wu, H. (1998). *The role of phonological information in processing single- and two-character words in Chinese.* Unpublished M.S. Thesis. National Chung-Cheng University, Taiwan.

Wu, J.-T., & Chen, H. (1999). Evaluating semantic and homophonic priming in Chinese character recognition and naming. *Chinese Journal of Psychology*, in press.

Wu, N., Shu, H., Zhou, X., & Shi, D. (1998). The role of phonology and orthography in Chinese reading comprehension: A moving window study. *Acta Psychologica Sinica*, *30*, 154–160.

Zhou, X., & Marslen-Wilson, W. (1999). Orthography, phonology, and semantic activation in reading Chinese. *Journal of Memory and Language*, in press.

Zhou, X., Shu, H., Y. Bi, & Shi, D. (1999). Is there phonologically mediated access to lexical semantics in reading Chinese? In J. Wang, A.W. Inhoff, & H.-C. Chen (Eds), *Reading Chinese script: A cognitive analysis*, pp.135–171. Mahwah, NJ: Lawrence Erlbaum Associates Inc.

APPENDIX

Base Word	O+P++	O+P−	O−P++	O−P−
栽培	哉	截	災	紗
抗議	伉	坑	擴	紋
蟬聯	禪	彈	簷	礦
唯一	維	誰	遺	恨
儒家	孺	懦	虞	頡
積木	漬	債	織	亂
趾頭	址	扯	咫	旱
江山	肛	虹	岡	抹
肢體	枝	技	姿	呀
怡和	貽	抬	夷	烙
狐臭	弧	抓	湖	忠
媒介	煤	謀	玫	搬
錄音	綠	緣	陸	腦
理由	浬	埋	李	存
逍遙	消	稍	燒	責
場地	腸	錫	翔	裸
辯論	辨	辦	便	器
乒乓	兵	岳	冰	伸
桃園	逃	挑	塗	怒
精神	睛	猜	晶	梁
撤退	澈	撒	設	誤
鎖匙	瑣	銷	所	線
綿羊	棉	錦	眠	氰
搏鬥	博	傅	駁	敝
惆悵	綢	調	酬	隔
抉擇	決	快	厥	弟
流水	琉	梳	榴	訴
喚叫	煥	噢	緩	瞞
構造	購	講	寇	齊
姓氏	性	牲	聖	致
晴朗	情	倩	澄	境
揣摩	喘	瑞	忖	彪
池水	弛	牠	祠	狗
深澳	琛	探	森	堅
熾熱	幟	識	賜	摸
賭場	睹	諸	島	暴
楊柳	揚	湯	洋	署
愉快	瑜	偷	娛	副
輝煌	揮	渾	徽	鎖
譯本	繹	擇	液	憤

LANGUAGE AND COGNITIVE PROCESSES, 1999, *14* (5/6), 481–502

Orthographic and Phonological Activation in the Semantic Processing of Korean Hanja and Hangul

Jeung-Ryeul Cho
Kyungnam University, Masan, South Korea

Hsuan-Chih Chen
The Chinese University of Hong Kong, Shatin, N.T., Hong Kong

The Korean orthography includes alphabetic *Hangul* and logographic *Hanja* scripts. Two experiments investigated whether (a) the role of phonological and orthographic activation differs during semantic processing of Hangul and Hanja and (b) proficiency in Hanja would affect the way that phonology is used in the comprehension of Hanja characters. In Experiment 1, in which Hanja was tested, less-skilled Hanja readers produced more false positive categorisation errors on homophone foils, as well as on visually similar foils, than on their corresponding controls. Skilled Hanja readers however, produced reliable visual similarity effects, but not homophonic effects. These results indicate that phonology plays a prominent role in the semantic processing of logographic Hanja for the less-skilled readers, but not for the skilled readers. In Experiment 2, in which Hangul was tested, both skilled and less-skilled Hanja readers displayed strong homophonic effects for pseudohomophones, suggesting that phonology plays a crucial role in the semantic processing of Hangul. Overall, the results indicate that both language proficiency and script difference can affect the pattern of semantic processing of written language.

Requests for reprints should be addressed to Hsuan-Chih Chen, Department of Psychology, The Chinese University of Hong Kong, Shatin, N.T., Hong Kong. Email: hcchen@psy.cuhk.edu.hk

This research was supported by a Research Grant from the Korea Research Foundation to J.R. Cho and by Earmarked Research Grants from the Research Grants Council of Hong Kong to H.-C. Chen. The first version of the manuscript was done while J.R. Cho was a Visiting Scholar at the Department of Psychology, the Chinese University of Hong Kong. We are grateful to Kyung-Soon Yoo, Hae-Gon Rhoo, and Jackie Tsang for their assistance in data collection, computer programming, and data analyses, to Jung-Oh Kim for advice and encouragement in early stages of this research, and to Xiaolin Zhou, Greg Simpson, and Sandy Pollatsek for their comments and suggestions on an earlier draft.

INTRODUCTION

Orthographies in the world vary substantially in how they represent meaning in written forms. For instance, most European languages adopt an alphabetic system in which the solution developed is to use the written language to represent the spoken one. In alphabetic systems, symbols are typically made to correspond to elementary units in speech, that is, phonemes. There are, however, other orthographies that have been developed following a logographic principle (that is, one in which symbols directly encode meaning). Chinese characters, for example, generally represent basic units of meaning, that is, morphemes. Given that various orthographies are constructed on distinct principles, it is interesting and important to know whether the same processes are activated in accessing the meanings of a printed word written in the different orthographies.

In the literature, several different hypotheses have been proposed to account for how a printed word is processed for meaning. For example, the dual-route hypothesis proposed by Coltheart (1980) assumes that there are basically two possible ways of semantic access: (1) a phonologically mediated path, which goes from orthography to phonology, and then from phonology to meaning, and (2) a direct path, where access to meaning proceeds directly from orthography. Whether the phonologically mediated path or the direct path plays a dominant role in processing a printed word can be determined by factors such as the specific properties of an orthography (Frost, Katz, & Bentin, 1987) and reading proficiency (Backman, Bruck, Hebert, & Seidenberg, 1984; Doctor & Coltheart, 1980; Rusted, 1989). An alternative hypothesis, usually known as the phonological mediation hypothesis, postulates that the semantic processing of a printed word depends solely upon phonological mediation (Lesch & Pollatsek, 1993; Lukatela & Turvey, 1991; Rubenstein, Lewis, & Rubenstein, 1971; Van Orden, 1987; see Frost, 1998, for a recent review on relevant issues). In contrast to the two mentioned positions, the direct access hypothesis argues that reading comprehension does not require the mediation of phonology and is accomplished mainly by a direct, visual access path (Baron, 1973; Daneman & Reingold, 1993).

To explore whether phonological mediation is necessary for access to meaning in processing printed words in English, Van Orden and his colleagues (e.g., Van Orden, 1987; Van Orden, Johnston, & Hale, 1988) carried out a series of experiments using a semantic categorisation task. In these experiments, subjects were given a category name and had to decide whether a subsequently presented target was a member of the category. The main manipulation in their studies was to present to the subjects a target word (e.g., *rows*) which was a homophone of a real exemplar (e.g. *rose*) of the category (in this case, *flower*). The results showed a highly reliable homophony effect: subjects made more errors and spent longer times on homophone foils than on spelling controls (e.g., *robs* when the category is *flower*). A significant homophony effect was still found even when the orthographic similarity was low between homophone foils and corresponding category exemplars (Van Orden, 1987; Experiment 1). A similar pattern was also observed when immediate backward pattern masking was introduced to control for possible confoundings from orthographic information (Van Orden, 1987; Experiment 2). These results suggest that phonology plays a crucial role in the access to meaning of written English.

Note that phonology and orthography of printed words in languages using an alphabetic script are closely related, whereas a similar confounding is absent in those using a logographic script. A number of researchers have adopted the semantic categorisation task used in the Van Order (1987) study to examine the role of phonology in semantic processing of logographic Chinese (Chen, Flores d'Arcais, & Cheung, 1995; Leck, Weekes, & Chen, 1995). For instance, Chen et al. (1995) demonstrated clear effects of orthographic similarity (i.e., subjects made more errors and produced longer response times on orthographically similar foils than on the corresponding controls) but not homophonic effects (i.e., subjects produced the same proportion of false positive categorisation errors and showed the same decision latencies on homophonic foils and non-homophonic controls). Similar findings (i.e., visually similar foils produced more false positive errors, but homophonic foils did not) have also been reported by Leck et al. The absence of purely phonological effects and the presence of visual similarity effects for Chinese characters indicate that phonology is not crucial during the comprehension of Chinese characters.

Working along similar lines, Wydell, Patterson, and Humphreys (1993) tested the use of phonological information in Kanji word recognition, also using a semantic categorisation task. Japanese Kanji words are formed by logographic characters originally borrowed from the Chinese. Using two-character Kanji words as stimuli, Wydell et al. found homophony effects with visually similar, homophonic foils but not with visually dissimilar, homophonic foils (for similar results, see Sakuma, Sasanuma, Tatsumi, & Masaki, 1998). In addition, a stronger effect was found with the visually similar homophones than with the visually dissimilar non-homophones. These results were interpreted as indicating that both orthography and phonology contribute to meaning activation in processing multi-character Kanji words.

Note that there is an important difference between the Chinese and Japanese studies reviewed above. Specifically, the Chinese studies used single character words, whereas the Japanese studies used two-character words. In fact, for instance, the orthographic similarity was introduced in the Japanese studies by using identical characters (i.e., morphemes) in both the orthographically similar distracters and the corresponding exemplars, while it was done in the Chinese studies by using identical character components. Consequently, using multi-character words as stimuli can activate additional morphological processing (e.g., interaction between individual morphemes), which would not appear in the semantic processing of single character words (for relevant discussions about the orthographic and phonological manipulations in the Japanese studies reviewed above, see, e.g., Zhou & Marslen-Wilson, in press). This is probably why the Chinese and the Japanese studies noted above do not totally agree on the role of phonology in the process of semantic activation during visual word recognition. In fact, it has been shown that phonology plays a more prominent role in processing multi-character Chinese words than in processing single character words (Wu, Chou, & Liu, 1994).

In the present study, in contrast to earlier investigations on the role of phonology in the semantic processing of a printed item in different scripts, we have chosen to test this issue in one single language, namely Korean. Written Korean uses both an alphabetic script, Hangul, and a logographic script, Hanja (see Taylor, 1997, for a detailed description of the Korean orthography). Hence, it provides an excellent opportunity to test whether universal or script-specific strategies are utilised in scripts with different orthographic depths. A brief description of some features of Korean orthography follows.

For many centuries, Koreans used logographic characters borrowed from the Chinese, and these characters are known as Hanja. In the 15th century, the alphabetic Hangul was invented. Hangul has 24 letters, each representing a phoneme of the Korean language. Although it is an alphabet, the alphabetic characters are written like a syllabary in which two or more letters are clustered into a syllabic block. Hangul is fundamentally a phonetic script, so that a syllable block can be pronounced by analysing it into its constituent phonemes.

In spite of the invention of Hangul, Hanja characters are still used by the Koreans. Hanja characters typically have the same shape as the original Chinese characters and have similar meanings. In terms of phonology, Hanja characters approximate the sounds of the corresponding Chinese characters, but without the tones. The use of Hanja in Korea has decreased in the past several decades, with about 1800 Hanja currently used for educational purposes. Children begin to learn Chinese Hanja only in middle school.

Note that Korean grammatical morphemes can only be written in Hangul, so it is possible to write exclusively in Hangul but not in Hanja, and in general, Hangul is far more frequently used than Hanja. Hanja may be used for the purpose of emphasis, much like using italics or bold type in English; it is also used to resolve homography in Korean because each meaning of a Hangul homograph will map onto a different Hanja character.

Alphabetic Hangul words, which encode phonological information directly and unambiguously, are assumed to access their meanings by a phonologically mediated route. Thus, phonological information presumably plays a major role in the processing of printed Hangul words. However, in the case of logographic Hanja, which directly represents meaning but not phonology, it is expected that the meanings of Hanja are activated directly from orthography rather than through phonological mediation.

Though quite scarce, there are indeed studies on Korean word recognition (Park, 1990; Simpson & Kang, 1994). However, the focus of most, if not all, lexical studies in Korean is not directly on the issue of semantic access but on phonological activation. For instance, Simpson and Kang (1994) compared naming latencies for high- and low-frequency Hangul words embedded in a list of additional Hangul words, Hanja words, or Hangul non-words. The results showed that only in the context of Hanja words were high-frequency Hangul words named faster than low-frequency Hangul words. In the context of Hangul non-words and Hangul words, Hangul frequency did not affect naming time. The data suggested that Korean readers favoured the use of an assembly (non-lexical) route to a word's pronunciation when filler words (a context) were printed in Hangul words or Hangul pseudowords. But when most of the words are printed in the logographic Hanja, Korean readers showed the evidence of using a direct (lexical) route to the phonology of a word. According to Simpson and Kang, these results are consistent with the notion that alphabetic Hangul favours the phonologically mediated route; but logographic Hanja favours a direct route to word recognition.

Working on a similar topic, Park (1990) reported evidence for phonological processing in the reading of Hanja using a primed lexical decision task with a 500-ms stimulus-onset asynchrony. In the study, all targets were in Hangul, while primes were in Hanja. The phonological relation of a prime and a target was not directly varied in the study. Rather, it was done via a third word. Specifically, the relation between a Hanja prime in the homophonic condition and the corresponding Hangul target was established through another Hanja word, which was homophonic to the prime, but semantically related to the target. Park found that homophonic Hanja primes (either words or non-words) facilitated lexical decision of Hangul targets relative to the non-homophonic controls, indicating that phonological information was activated during the processing of Hanja words.

There are a number of points in the reviewed Korean studies that deserve our attention. First of all, different tasks (i.e., naming *vs.* primed lexical decision) were adopted in those studies, which makes the comparison across experiments difficult. Second, Korean readers vary considerably in their Hanja proficiency. This important factor, however, was not examined in the previous Korean studies.

In the present study, we have chosen Korean Hanja and Hangul to test whether the role of phonology differs in the semantic processing of a printed item in different orthographies. Following previous studies on this issue, we adopted the semantic categorisation task in this study. Furthermore, to explore whether Hanja proficiency would affect the way that phonology is used in the comprehension of logographic Hanja, we recruited both skilled and less-skilled Hanja readers in our study. The first experiment assesses the semantic processing of Hanja; the second experiment examines the comprehension of Hangul.

EXPERIMENT 1: LOGOGRAPHIC HANJA

This experiment was designed to examine orthographic and phonological activation in semantic processing of Hanja for skilled and less-skilled Hanja readers. The task was a semantic categorisation task, in which subjects were given in each trial a category name in Hangul, followed by a Hanja character that in the experimental trials was either a homophone foil, a non-homophone control, a visually similar foil, or a visually dissimilar control. Figure 1 illustrates the materials used.

If phonology plays a crucial role during semantic activation, then we should expect a possible interference effect from the homophones (i.e., a tendency to produce more false alarms and/or longer correct rejection latencies in the homophone condition relative to the control condition). On the other hand, if phonology is not crucial in semantic access, then we should not expect any difference in latencies or in the error rates between the homophones and their corresponding controls. Similar predictions can also be made for the visually similar condition.

The present experiment focuses on comparing performance of skilled Hanja readers and less-skilled readers in semantic categorisation because it is possible for the two groups with different proficiencies in Hanja to differ in their use of phonological and orthographic information in accessing the meaning of Hanja. Since less-skilled readers are presumably not as efficient as skilled readers in visual encoding of the printed Hanja, it is more likely for relatively well-established phonological activation to influence word recognition. Indeed, there is evidence that less-skilled readers tend to rely more upon and utilise more phonological information in the initial recognition of written words (Backman et al., 1984; Doctor &

	Category	Target word	Correct Exemplar
Homophone Distracter			
Example	옷감	面	綿
Pronunciation		/myun/	/myun/
Translation	cloth	subcounty	cotton
Homophone Control			
Example	성직자	面	
Pronunciation		/myun/	
Translation	priest	subcounty	
Visually Similar Distracter			
Example	옷감	結	綿
Pronunciation		/kyul/	/myun/
Translation	cloth	end	cotton
Visually Similar Control			
Example	과일	結	
Pronunciation		/kyul/	
Translation	fruit	end	

FIG. 1. Examples of materials used in Experiment 1.

Coltheart, 1980). This is probably because novice readers are explicitly taught to carry out conversions from printed words to phonological representations. If this is the case, less-skilled readers would be expected to reveal a reliable homophonic effect. Moreover, if the access to meaning for Hanja depends entirely on phonological mediation, both skilled and less-skilled groups should not differ in the magnitude of homophony effects.

Method

Subjects. Forty undergraduates of Kyungnam University in Korea participated in this experiment. Among them, half were less-skilled Hanja readers and the other half were skilled Hanja readers. These subjects were selected on the basis of their performance in a semantic categorisation test similar to the one used in the experiment but with a different set of materials (i.e., none of the items used in the pretest appeared in the formal experiment). This pretest included 20 common Hanja characters and 20 common Hangul words as targets, and in each of Hanja and Hangul target groups, 10 were category exemplars and 10 were non-exemplars. The Hanja and Hangul targets were randomly presented in the pretest. The purpose of including Hangul words as targets was to use the same pretest in Experiment 2, which tested Hangul. In addition to the semantic test, all participants in the pretest were asked to rate their proficiency in reading Hanja using a 7-point scale, with 1 indicating extremely low proficiency and 7 indicating extremely high proficiency.

Forty participants in the pretest whose error rates for Hanja were less than 50% were selected as subjects for the formal experiment. These participants were further divided into two groups of 20 each using a median-split method based on their Hanja performance in the pretest. The average reaction times in the pretest for the skilled and less-skilled Hanja readers were 1059 ms (15.2% error) and 1860 ms (28.7% error), respectively, in the case of Hanja; and 925 ms (8.0% error) and 1152 ms (4.7% error), respectively, in the case of Hangul. The self-reported proficiencies in reading Hanja for the skilled and less-skilled subjects were 5.4 and 4.8 respectively.

Apparatus. Stimulus presentation and response recording were controlled by 386 IBM compatible computers. All stimuli were presented on a SAMBO colour monitor. From the subjects' viewing distance of about 50 cm, a Hanja character subtended about 0.8 degrees of visual angle both in width and in height. A Hangul syllabic item subtended about 0.57 degrees of visual angle in width and about 0.8 degrees in height.

Stimuli. All target stimuli were single-character Hanja words, all of which are taught in secondary school. These included 20 homophonic distracters, 20 homophone controls, 20 visually similar distracters, and 20 visual controls. To ensure subjects' comprehension of category names and to prevent the possible overlap in semantic radical between a category name and a target when presenting both in Hanja, all the category names were presented in Hangul.

A homophonic distracter was a homophone of a real exemplar of the corresponding category; it differed from the real exemplar both in visual shape and in meaning. Each homophonic distracter appeared twice across subjects; once as a homophonic distracter and once as a homophone control. An English analogue of this manipulation is as follows: One subject can see "flower" as a category name and "rows" as a target item, while another subjects sees "rows" as a target following "a kind of food" as a category name. The reason for this manipulation is to rule out possible item-specific effects, in which results might have been partially contaminated by peculiarities of the stimulus itself (e.g., Wydell et al., 1993). The visually similar distracters differed from the corresponding category exemplars in meaning and pronunciation, but they had similar graphic construction (most of them shared at least one major component radical). The visual controls were constructed in the same method as the homophone controls (i.e., the visual controls and visually similar distracters were actually the same items, but were presented following different category names).

To ascertain the homophonic distracters, the visual distracters, and the corresponding category exemplars were roughly equivalent in terms of their familiarity to the subjects. These items (20 exemplars, 20 homophones, and 20 visually similar distracters) together with 30 fillers were given to a new group of 45 subjects, who were from the same subject pool but did not participate in the main experiment, to rate for familiarity using a 5-point scale. In the scale, 1 indicated that the item was totally unfamiliar and 5 indicated that it was highly familiar. The average familiarity ratings for the exemplars, homophones, and visual distracters, were 4.1, 3.9, and 3.8, respectively; an analysis of variance (ANOVA) across items showed no significant difference between the three types of items [$F(2,38) = 1.24$].

For each subject, there were 100 pairs of category names and targets, 40 of which were for yes-trials and the rest for no-trials. The 60 no-trials were formed by 20 no-fillers and 40 critical trials. In addition, 20 practice words with 10 category exemplars and 10 non-exemplars were used. The critical experimental targets consisted of 10 visually dissimilar, homophonic distracters, 10 homophone controls, 10 visually similar distracters, and 10 visual controls. The order of presentation for the practice trials and for the filler experimental trials was determined randomly and was fixed for all subjects. The critical trials, which included distracters and controls, were randomly filled for each subject in fixed presentation slots. Each trial was separated by one, two, or three filler trials.

To avoid overactivating one category, the 40 critical targets were chosen on the basis of exemplars from 19 different semantic categories. Most exemplars were selected from the category norms of Lee (1991), and the rest of the exemplars were chosen by the experimenters.

Design and procedure. The design included two within-subjects factors: Types of similarity (homophone *vs.* visual similarity) and relation (distracter *vs.* control). A between-subjects factor was reading proficiency in Hanja (skilled *vs.* less-skilled readers).

Each subject received 20 practice trials and 100 experimental trials. Each trial began with the presentation of a category name and, directly under it, a cross as a fixation point. Both were exposed for the duration of 1500 ms. The fixation point was then replaced by a Hanja target item, which remained on the screen for 500 ms. The target was replaced by a pattern mask of '*****' which was the same size as occupied by the Hanja character. The subjects were instructed to read the category name silently and then to look at the fixation point. Upon the presentation of the target word, the subject had to judge whether the target was a member of the category just presented by pressing as rapidly and accurately as possible a "yes" or a "no" response key on the computer keyboard. No feedback concerning speed or accuracy was given. Each trial was initiated by the subject's pressing of the keyboard's space bar.

Results

The results consisted of the errors (false alarms) and of the response latencies for the correct "no" responses.

False positive error rates to critical trials. The overall error rates to critical trials are given in Table 1. The percentages of errors were subjected to two ANOVAs (one by subjects and one by items). There was a significant effect of proficiency [$F_1(1,38) = 13.25$, $P < .001$] by subjects and [$F_2(1,76) = 24.35$, $P < .001$] by items. Less-skilled readers made more errors (25%) than skilled readers (14.5%). There were significant effects of relation [$F_1(1,38) = 98.73$, $P < .001$; $F_2(1,76) = 19.78$, $P < .001$]; and a two-way interaction of proficiency and relation [$F_1(1,38) = 10.62$, $P < .005$; $F_2(1,76) = 5.67$, $P < .05$]. A three-way interaction of proficiency, similarity, and relation was also significant [$F_1(1,38) = 5.67$, $P < .05$, $F_2(1,76) = 4.13$, $P < .05$]. An interaction of similarity and relation was significant by subjects [$F_1(1,38) = 5.04$, $P < .05$], but not by items [$F_2(1,76) = 1.38$, $P = .24$].

TABLE 1
Mean Percentages of False Positive Categorisation Responses and Average Reaction Times (ms) of Correct Categorisation Responses (Experiment 1)

	Error percentages		*Reaction times*	
	Less-skilled readers	*Skilled readers*	*Less-skilled readers*	*Skilled readers*
Homophone distracter	35.0 (3.5)	13.0 (2.3)	1332 (68)	1014 (60)
Control	14.5 (2.9)	11.0 (2.3)	1362 (61)	989 (39)
Visual distracter	35.5 (3.5)	26.5 (3.7)	1309 (79)	1063 (65)
Control	15.0 (3.3)	7.5 (1.4)	1291 (57)	994 (48)

Post hoc comparisons for the three-way interaction were conducted using the protected *t*-test procedure. Less-skilled Hanja readers produced more errors on homophone distracters than on controls [$t_1(38) = 6.48, P < .001$; $t_2(76) = 4.70, P < .001$], and also made more errors on visually similar distracters than on controls [$t_1(38) = 6.48, P < .001$; $t_2(76) = 4.58, P < .001$]. However, skilled readers were not different between homophone distracters and their controls (*t*s < 1), but they made more errors on visually similar distracters than controls [$t_1(38) = 6.01, P < .001$; $t_2(76) = 4.25, P < .001$].

Latencies for the correct "No" responses. The mean latencies for the correct responses in the critical trials are also shown in Table 1. The ANOVA showed a significant effect of proficiency [$F_1(1,38) = 18.37, P < .001$; $F_2(1,76) = 83.23, P < .001$]. The average reaction time of skilled readers (1015 ms) was much faster than that of less-skilled readers (1323 ms). No other effects were significant.

Discussion

The results showed that less-skilled Hanja readers made about twice as many errors (25%) and took longer times (1323 ms) in making semantic categorisation responses than skilled readers (14.5% and 1015 ms). In addition, the skilled and less-skilled readers differed in their homophony effects. The less-skilled readers made more errors on homophone distracters than on their corresponding controls (i.e., a 20.5% difference). However, the skilled readers were not reliably different in their error performance between homophone distracters and controls (i.e., a 2% difference).

Note that although for the skilled readers the difference between the homophone distracters and controls was extremely small and was far from being significant, the direction of this difference is in line with that for the less-skilled readers. Thus, one might ask whether we can trust this "null" result. We believe the result for the skilled Hanja readers is valid for the following reason. The presence of a homophony effect for the less-skilled Hanja readers indicates that the semantic categorisation task and the homophony manipulation adopted in the present experiment are clearly sensitive enough to reveal effects resulting from phonological activation in visual word recognition. Given this, one cannot argue that the absence of a reliable effect of homophony for the skilled Hanja readers is due to the power of the experiment being low. Thus, it seems reasonable to conclude that homophony effects were found only in the less-skilled Hanja readers and not in the skilled readers. The homophony effects found in the present experiment indicate that phonology plays a crucial role in the semantic processing of Hanja characters for the less-skilled readers but not for the skilled readers.

Although skilled and less-skilled Hanja readers differed in homophony effects, the present experiment demonstrated that the two groups of readers were compatible in visual similarity effects. Specifically, subjects in both groups made more errors on visually similar foils than on the corresponding controls. Moreover, a similar trend was also found in reaction times for both groups, though the differences between the visually similar distracters and controls were not statistically reliable. The visual similarity effects found in the present experiment suggest that both groups rely heavily on graphic information in the semantic processing of a Hanja item. Note, however, that no theory, including the phonological mediation hypothesis, would deny that the fact that visual-spatial analysis plays a crucial role in visual word recognition. For instance, if we assume that a strong version of the phonological mediation position (e.g., Van Orden, 1987) is correct. This means that the primary analysis goes directly from visual form to phonology to semantics, and then another visual and/or orthographic analysis is made of the stimulus to sort out cases where there is something suggesting that the original analysis may be in error. Following this logic, it would not be too surprising to find a considerable amount of errors for the visually similar distracters, because these characters are likely to be misidentified as the other characters. Thus, the visual similarity effect found in the present experiment should be explained with caution. This effect by itself cannot be used as evidence for the direct visual route to semantic access. Rather, it needs to be explained together with the homophony effects found in the current experiment. Since the visual similarity effect was demonstrated in the absence of a noticeable homophony effect for the skilled Hanja readers, these results seem to suggest that orthographic processing plays a prominent role in the semantic processing of logographic Hanja for skilled readers, but phonological processing does not (for a similar conclusion see Chen et al., 1995). On the other hand, the results of less-skilled readers in this experiment were similar to those of Van Orden's (1987) English study, showing both effects of orthographic similarity and homophony on semantic judgements. Thus our findings suggest that both orthographic and phonological processing contribute to the activation of Hanja for less-skilled readers.

The results that homophony effects were found in less-skilled readers but not in skilled readers appear to be in line with the notion that less-skilled readers rely more heavily on phonological activation to access the meaning of words (Doctor & Coltheart, 1980). Consistent with the present results, Song, Zhang, and Shu (1995) have found that less-skilled Chinese readers experience more difficulty finding semantically anomalous homophone characters than irrelevant control characters in a proof-reading task. Improvement in reading skills apparently moves the phonologically mediated access to the direct access to the meaning of words, probably because the phonologically mediated route is not as reliable and efficient as the direct route especially in a logographic system such as Hanja.

In short, the present results suggest that both phonological and graphic information contribute to the activation of the meaning of Hanja for less-skilled readers. However, for skilled readers, only graphic information contributes to the semantic processing of Hanja.

EXPERIMENT 2: HANGUL

The present experiment investigated phonological and visual contributions to the semantic processing of alphabetic Hangul words. As noted earlier, Hangul is a very shallow orthography which has a regular phoneme-grapheme correspondence. This study used pseudohomophones in a semantic categorisation paradigm. A pseudohomophone is a non-word that has the same pronunciation as a real word. Pseudohomophones were tested by Van Orden et al. (1988) in semantic categorisation tasks, using English. Van Orden and colleagues found significant homophony effects by using non-word homophone foils as targets. False positive errors to pseudohomophone foils (e.g., *sute* for the category "an article of clothing") substantially exceed false positive errors to non-word spelling controls (e.g., *blane* for the same category). They argued that since non-words are not represented in the lexicon, the categorisation errors occur because a phonological code is computed non-lexically. Furthermore, the false positive error rate to pseudohomophones was virtually identical to that of homophones (21.3% and 21.8%, respectively), which suggested phonological access to meaning for both homophones and pseudohomophones. On the basis of these results, Van Orden and his colleagues argued that word recognition depends entirely upon phonological mediation.

In the present experiment pseudohomophones were created in Hangul with the same method that Kang and Simpson (1996) used in their experiments. In order to make pseudohomophones this experiment takes advantage of the syllable-blocking characteristic of Hangul and the phonological process of liaison. In liaison, some Korean consonants vary in their pronunciation according to whether they are followed by another consonant or a vowel. Because of the syllable printing, this phonological process of liaison has a unique effect in Hangul: If a final consonant of a syllable is followed by a vowel, the following syllable takes the pronunciation of the syllable-final consonant. A non-word was created by moving a syllable-final consonant to the beginning of the next syllable such that the non-word has the same pronunciation in rapid speech as a real word. An English analogue of this manipulation is to spell "ice pick" as "I spick". Figure 2 illustrates the materials used.

If the phonological code of a pseudohomophone distracter becomes automatically available, then this should result in a tendency to produce more false alarms and/or longer correct (No) response latencies than the control conditions. If phonological information is not activated in this task, then any difference in latencies and in the error rates is not expected between the pseudohomophones and the control conditions.

In this experiment, performance of skilled and less-skilled Hanja readers was compared. In Experiment 1, the proficiency in Hanja reading affected the use of phonology in accessing the meaning of written Hanja: less-skilled Hanja readers showed reliable homophony effects whereas skilled readers did not. This suggests that less-skilled readers rely more heavily on phonological processes, but skilled readers do not. The present experiment examined whether the same pattern of homophony effects by skilled and

	Category	Target Nonword	Correct Exemplar
Pseudohomophone Distracter			
Example	직업	구닌	군인
Pronunciation		/ku-nin/	/kun-in/
Translation	job		soldier
Pseudohomophone Control			
Example	금속	구닌	
Pronunciation		/ku-nin/	
Translation	metal		
Visually Similar Nonword Distracter			
Example	직업	굴닌	군인
Pronunciation		/kul-nin/	/kun-in/
Translation	job		soldier
Visually Similar Nonword Control			
Example	무기	굴닌	
Pronunciation		/kul-nin/	
Translation	weapon		

FIG. 2. Examples of materials used in Experiment 2.

less-skilled Hanja readers in Experiment 1 would be found in the semantic processing of Hangul.

Method

Subjects and apparatus. Forty undergraduates of Kyungnam University of Korea participated in this experiment. Among them half were less-skilled Hanja readers and the other half were skilled Hanja readers. None of the subjects had participated in Experiment 1.

The same pretest and the same criteria as used in Experiment 1 were given to the subjects in order to select skilled and less-skilled Hanja readers. But a self-report was not given in this experiment because it did not provide any interesting new information in Experiment 1. These participants were further divided into two groups of 20 each using a median-split method based on their performance on Hanja in the pretest. The average reaction times in the pretest for the skilled and less-skilled Hanja readers were 1083 ms (11.5% errors) and 1700 ms (23.0% errors), respectively, in the case of Hanja; and 862 ms (6.7% errors) and 1064 ms (4.7% errors), respectively, in the case of Hangul. These pretest results were generally compatible with those found in Experiment 1, indicating that the skilled and less-skilled Hanja subjects clearly differed in their proficiency in semantic processing of Hanji and that the less-skilled Hanja readers were somewhat slower (but tended to be more accurate) than the skilled readers in processing of Hangul.

The same experimental setups were used in this experiment as in Experiment 1. From the subjects' viewing distance of about 50 cm, a Hangul character subtended about 0.57 degrees of visual angle in width and about 0.8 degrees in height. All target items and category names were written in Hangul, which ranged from one to four syllables in length.

Stimuli. All stimuli, including both targets (i.e., disyllabic Hangul words) and category names, were shown in Hangul. There were 128 pairs of category names and target words, 64 of which were yes-trials and the other 64 were no-trials. The 64 no-trials were formed by 32 fillers and 32 critical trials. The critical trials were formed by using 16 pseudohomophone distracters and 16 visually similar non-word distracters. The same distracters were also used as the corresponding controls following different category names, as in Experiment 1. Figure 2 illustrates the experimental materials.

A pseudohomophone distracter was a non-word homophone of a real exemplar of the corresponding category. It was created by moving a syllable-final consonant to the beginning of the next syllable. Visually similar non-word distracters were created by moving the fist syllable-final consonant to the next syllable, as with the pseudohomophone distracters, and then introducing a new syllable-final consonant. Thus, the pseudohomophone distracters and the visually similar non-word distracters were matched in terms of their visual similarity to the corresponding exemplars, but they differed in whether they sounded like the exemplars. To verify the validity of our phonological manipulation, we asked 50 subjects who had not been involved in any aspect of the present experiment (or in Experiment 1) to rate the phonological similarity between either the pseudohomophones and the corresponding exemplars or the visually similar non-words and the exemplars using a 5-point scale. In the scale, 1 indicated that the two items in each pair were totally different in their pronunciation and 5 indicated that they were identical in pronunciation. The average ratings for the exemplar-homophone pairs and exemplar-visually similar distracters were 4.6 and 1.8, respectively; a t-test across pairs showed a significant difference between the two types of stimuli [$t(15) = 22.85$, $P < .001$]. Therefore, any effect that occurs with pseudohomophone distracters can be attributed to phonological factors beyond those based on visual similarity.

Two different stimulus files were created. Each subject saw only one stimulus file. Across subjects, there were 16 pseudohomophone distracters, 16 pseudohomophone controls, 16 visually similar non-word distracters, and 16 visual controls. Half the pseudohomophones appeared as pseudohomophone distracters for one subject group and as controls for the other subject group, as in Experiment 1. The same manipulation also applied to the visual controls and the visually similar distracters.

Design and procedure. The design included two within-subjects factors: Type of similarity (pseudohomophones *vs.* visually similar non-words) and type of relation (distracter *vs.* control). A between-subjects factor was reading proficiency of Hanja (skilled *vs.* less-skilled readers). Each subject received 20 practice trials and 128 experimental trials.

The experimental procedures were the same as those used in Experiment 1.

Results

The results consisted of the errors (false alarms) and of the latencies for the correct "no" responses.

False positive error rates to critical trials. The overall error rates are given in Table 2. The percentages of errors were subjected to an analysis of variance (ANOVA). There was a significant effect of relation [$F_1(1,38) = 26.74$, $P < .000$; $F_2(1,60) = 15.63$, $P < .001$]. An interaction between

TABLE 2
Mean Percentages of False Positive Categorisation Responses and Average Reaction Times (ms) of Correct Categorisation Responses (Experiment 2)

	Error percentages		*Reaction times*	
	Less-skilled readers	*Skilled readers*	*Less-skilled readers*	*Skilled readers*
Pseudohomophone distracter	15.6 (4.7)	14.4 (3.4)	1232 (82)	971 (94)
Control	1.9 (1.0)	0.6 (0.6)	1098 (66)	920 (77)
Visual distracter	8.1 (2.4)	8.8 (2.6)	1151 (66)	984 (72)
Control	3.8 (1.6)	3.1 (1.5)	1180 (75)	931 (80)

similarity and relation type was significant by subjects [$F_1(1,38) = 8.63$, $P < .01$], and marginally so by items [$F_2(1,60) = 3.40$, $P < .07$].

Post hoc comparisons for the interaction of similarity and relation by subjects were conducted using the protected *t*-test procedure. Pseudohomophone distracters (15.0%) had more errors than controls (1.2%) [$t(38) = 6.15$, $P < .001$], whereas relatively small differences were found between visually similar distracters (8.4%) and controls (3.4%) [$t(38) = 2.24$, $P < .05$]. Moreover, the phonological similarity effect was significantly larger than the visual similarity effect [$t(38) = 4.18$, $P < .01$].

Latencies for the correct "No" responses. The mean latencies for the correct responses of the critical trials are also shown in Table 2. The ANOVAs revealed a significant effect of proficiency [$F_1(1,38) = 4.09$, $P < .05$; $F_2(1,60) = 73.65$, $P < .001$]. Skilled Hanja readers were generally faster in making a correct rejection (951 ms) than the less-skilled Hanja readers (1165 ms). The main effect of relation [$F_1(1,38) = 11.10$, $P < .005$], and an interaction between similarity and relation [$F_1(1,38) = 5.47$, $P < .05$], were significant by subjects, but not by items. A three-way interaction of proficiency, similarity and relation was significant by subjects [$F_1(1,38) = 5.71$, $P < .05$], but marginally so by items [$F_2(1,60) = 3.89$, $P = .053$]. The three-way interaction by subjects showed that less-skilled readers spent longer times on pseudohomophone distracters (1232 ms) than on controls (1098 ms) [$t(38) = 3.88$, $P < .005$], but there were no other reliable differences between distracters and their corresponding controls.

Discussion

Experiment 2 examined the effects of orthographic similarity and homophony on semantic decisions involving Hangul words. This experiment included visually similar pseudohomophones and visually similar non-homophones and their corresponding controls. The analysis of errors showed that skilled and less-skilled Hanja readers were almost the same in the effects of homophony and visual similarity, although they differed in their response speed. Both groups of the subjects made more false-positive errors on pseudohomophone foils than their controls (i.e., the differences in errors for the skilled and less-skilled readers were 13.8% and 13.7%, respectively). In addition, both groups also made more errors on visually similar non-word distracters than controls (i.e., the differences in errors for the skilled and less-skilled readers were 5.7% and 4.3%). These results thus seem to suggest that both phonology and orthography contribute to the activation of the meaning of Hangul words.

It is also interesting to note that homophony effects by pseudohomophones (about 13.7% in errors on average) were much stronger than visual similarity effects (about 5% on average), suggesting that phonology seems like the primary source of the activation of the meaning of alphabetic Hangul. The strong homophony effects found in this experiment are in line with the findings of previous English studies (Van Orden, 1987; Van Orden et al., 1988) which support the hypothesis that phonological activation plays a prominent role in the semantic processing of an alphabetic word.

GENERAL DISCUSSION

The present study investigated the role of orthographic and phonological activation in the comprehension of Hanja and Hangul. The results can be summarised as follows. In Experiment 1 where Hanja characters were used, there was a reliable homophony effect for the less-skilled Hanja readers, but not for the skilled readers. Also, there was a significant effect of visual similarity for both groups of readers. In Experiment 2 with Hangul stimuli, however, there were reliable effects of both homophony and visual similarity for both skilled and less-skilled Hanja readers. These results indicate that, at least for skilled readers, phonology does not play a crucial role in semantic access for logographic characters (for similar arguments and relevant findings, see Chen et al., 1995; Shen & Forster, 1999; Zhou, Shu, Bi, & Shi, 1999), though it does seem to play a more prominent role in accessing meaning for words written in phonetic based writing systems such as those in Hangul. In other words, the present findings for skilled Korean readers demonstrate for the first time clear evidence that phonology plays different roles in semantic processing of logographic Hanja and alphabetic Hangul. These results are in line with the notion that the role of phonology in semantic access during visual word recognition can be script dependent (Chen et al., 1995; Katz & Frost, 1992).

However, in addition to orthographic variation, can there be other explanations for different effects in Experiments 1 and 2 for skilled Hanja readers? Note that, for instance, the pseudohomophones in Experiment 2 were visually similar to the corresponding exemplars, whereas the homophones in Experiment 1 were not. Given this, one might ask whether this difference in phonological manipulation could have affected the present findings. This does not seem likely, however, because it has been shown in studies with Chinese stimuli where visual similarity and homophony were manipulated in a factorial design (Shen & Forster, this issue), the effects from using visually similar homophones were comparable in size relative to those from using visually similar but phonologically different stimuli, indicating that using homophonic stimuli did not create additional effect over and above those produced from visual similarity. The findings of Shen and Forster in Chinese stand in interesting contrast to what we found in Experiment 2 with Hangul stimuli (i.e., the phonological effect was significantly larger than the visual similarity effect), indicating the difference in phonological manipulation across Experiments 1 and 2 cannot be used to account for the different results in the two experiments.

Furthermore, one might ask whether factors such as the power of experiment or the range of reading skill covered could affect the present results for skilled Hanja readers in Experiment 1 (e.g., what would happen if extremely proficient Hanja readers were tested or if more stimuli were used?). We do not think this is likely for the following reasons. First, the presence of reliable effects of visual similarity and homophony in both Experiments 1 and 2 clearly indicate the semantic task adopted in the present study is sensitive enough to reveal effects coming from non-semantic sources of information processing, including both orthographic and phonological activation. Second, the overall pattern of results for the skilled Hanja readers demonstrated in the present study and that from other studies using the same task but with extremely skilled Chinese readers (Chen et al., 1995) are highly comparable. Consequently, one cannot attribute the absence of a reliable effect of homophony for skilled readers in Experiment 1 to factors such as the sensitivity of the experiment or the range of reading skill involved. On the basis of the arguments mentioned above, orthographic variation seems like the only factor that can be used to account for the different findings of skilled Hanja readers in the two experiments.

Another issue of concern in the present study was whether the level of proficiency in Hanja would affect the cognitive processes involved in the comprehension of Hanja. The answer is affirmative according to the results of Experiment 1 for skilled and less-skilled readers (i.e., the absence of a reliable homophony effect for the skilled readers and the presence of homophony effect for the less-skilled readers). In fact, our results clearly indicate that the level of proficiency of a reader can affect the pattern of word comprehension in reading. These results are in line with those of prior research (Backman et al., 1984; Doctor & Coltheart, 1980; Kang & Simpson, 1996; Seidenberg, 1985), indicating that the level of reading proficiency is indeed an important factor in studies of visual word recognition.

However, because Hanja is a logographic script and its construction properties apparently do not require or encourage the activation of phonology in comprehending a Hanja character (e.g., Chen, 1996; Chen & Juola, 1982), it is striking to find that less-skilled Hanja readers show clear evidence of phonological activation during the process of visual word identification. A possible explanation is that comprehension of the printed Hanja is a skill that is not yet fully developed for less-skilled Hanja readers, and, consequently, it is more likely for well-established phonological activation to influence word identification. This explanation can account for the present results of the less-skilled Hanja readers and the results of less-skilled Chinese readers from Song et al. (1995). This line of reasoning is consistent with the notion that phonology plays a crucial role for beginning and/or less-skilled readers when recognising written words (Bosman & de Groot, 1996; Doctor & Coltheart, 1980; but see Davis, Castles, & Iakovidis, 1998), although we need to bear in mind that in reading a logographic script such as Chinese or Hanja, phonology cannot be obtained in the same way as in alphabetic reading where the process of assembling a pronunciation is possible. Furthermore, since the less-skilled Hanja readers in the present study were also fluent Hangul readers, our results can possibly be explained by another explanation that the less-skilled Hanja reader engages in a translation process, mentally converting the Hanja character into Hangul, where it is vulnerable to phonological effects, as shown in Experiment 2. Unfortunately, we cannot verify these two explanations based on the present results. Therefore, it seems that the way in which phonology is used by less-skilled readers in comprehending Hanja remains an open question which warrants future research.

In short, the present results demonstrate that both orthographic variation and the level of proficiency in reading are main determinants for the patterns of meaning access in visual word recognition. These results are inconsistent with the view that either phonological mediation or direct access plays a crucial role in visual word recognition across different orthographics. Rather, they are more in line with the dual-route models (Coltheart, 1980; Doctor & Coltheart, 1980) and the orthographic variation hypothesis (Biederman & Tsao, 1979; Chen & Juola, 1982; Hoosain, 1991; Hung & Tzeng, 1981), which assume that the pattern of lexical processing and memory can be affected by factors such as reading proficiency and properties of the orthography. Furthermore, the present findings attest the importance of carrying out reading research across different orthographies, because it can reveal both universal and orthography-specific patterns of comprehension processes, which in turn can help to build a truly comprehensive theory of how people read and comprehend written information.

REFERENCES

Backman, J., Bruck, M., Hebert, M., & Seidenberg, M. (1984). Acquisition and use of spelling-sound correspondences in reading. *Journal of Experimental Child Psychology, 38*, 114–133.

Baron, J. (1973). Phonemic stage not necessary for reading: Lexical access and/or production? *Quarterly Journal of Experimental Psychology, 25*, 241–246.

Biederman, I., & Tsao, Y.C. (1979). On processing of Chinese ideographs and English words: Some implications from Stroop test results. *Cognitive Psychology, 11*, 125–132.

Bosman, A.M., & de Groot, A.M.B. (1996). Phonological mediation is fundamental to reading: Evidence from beginning readers. *Quarterly Journal of Experimental Psychology, 49A*, 715–744.

Chen, H.-C. (1996). Chinese reading and comprehension: A cognitive psychology perspective. In M.H. Bond (Ed.), *Handbook of Chinese psychology*, pp.43–62. Hong Kong: Oxford University Press.

Chen, H.-C., Flores d'Arcais, G.B., & Cheung, S.L. (1995). Orthographic and phonological activation in recognizing Chinese characters. *Psychological Research/Psychologische Forschung, 58*, 144–153.

Chen. H.-C., & Juola, J.F. (1982). Dimensions of lexical coding in Chinese and English. *Memory and Cognition, 10*, 216–224.

Cheng, C.M. (1992). Lexical access in Chinese: Evidence from automatic activation of phonological information. In H.-C. Chen & O.J.L. Tzeng (Eds), *Language Processing in Chinese*, pp. 67–91. Amsterdam: North-Holland.

Coltheart, M. (1980). Reading phonological recoding and deep dyslexia. In M. Coltheart, K. Patterson, & J.C. Marshal (Eds), *Deep dyslexia*, pp.197–226. London: Routledge & Kegan Paul.

Daneman, M., & Reingold, E.M. (1993). What eye fixations tell us about phonological recoding during reading. *Canadian Journal of Experimental Psychology, 47*, 153–178.

Davis, C., Castles, A., & Iakovidis, E. (1998). Masked homophone and pseudohomophone priming in children and adults. *Language and Cognitive Processes, 13*, 625–651.

Doctor, E.A., & Coltheart, M. (1980). Children's use of phonological encoding when reading for meaning. *Memory and Cognition, 8*, 195–209.

Frost, R. (1998). Toward a strong phonological theory of visual word recognition: True issues and false trials. *Psychological Bulletin, 123*, 71–99.

Frost, R., Katz, L., & Bentin, S. (1987). Strategies for visual word recognition and orthographic depth: A multilingual comparison. *Journal of Experimental Psychology: Human Perception and Performance, 13*, 104–115.

Hoosain, R. (1991). *Psycholinguistic implications for linguistic relativity: A case study of Chinese.* Hillsdale, NJ: Lawrence Erlbaum Associates Inc.

Hung, D.L., & Tzeng, O.J.L. (1981). Orthographic variations and visual information processing. *Psychological Bulletin, 90*, 377–414.

Kang, H., & Simpson, G.B. (1996). Development of semantic and phonological priming in a shallow orthography. *Developmental Psychology, 32*, 860–866.

Katz, L., & Frost, R. (1992). The reading process is different for different orthographies: The orthographic depth hypothesis. In R. Frost & L. Katz (Eds), *Orthography, phonology, morphology, and meaning*, pp.67–84. North-Holland: Elsevier Science Publishers B.V.

Leck, K.J., Weekes, B.S. & Chen, M-J. (1995). Visual and phonological pathways to the lexicon: Evidence from Chinese readers, *Memory and Cognition*, *23*, 468–476.

Lee, Kwan-Yong. (1991). Korean category norms: Survey on exemplar frequency norm, typicality, and features. *Korean Journal of Experimental and Cognitive Psychology*, *3*, 131–160 (in Korean).

Lesch, M.F., & Pollatsek, A. (1993). Automatic access of semantic information by phonological codes in visual word recognition. *Journal of Experimental Psychology: Learning, Memory, and Cognition*, *19*, 285–294.

Lukatela, G., & Turvey, M.T. (1991). Phonological access of the lexicon: Evidence from associative priming with pseudohomophones. *Journal of Experimental Psychology: Human Perception and Performance*, *17*, 951–966.

Park, T.J. (1990). Phonological encoding when reading Chinese-character-words in Korean. *Korean Journal of Experimental and Cognitive Psychology*, *2*, 90–102 (in Korean).

Rubenstein, H., Lewis, S.S., & Rubenstein, M.A. (1971). Evidence for phonemic recording in visual word recognition. *Journal of Verbal Learning and Verbal Behavior*, *10*, 645–657.

Rusted, J. (1989). Developmental differences in the influence of orthographic and phonological information in visual word recognition. *British Journal of Developmental Psychology*, *7*, 73–81.

Sakuma, N., Sasanuma, S., Tatsumi, I.F., & Masaki, S. (1998). Orthography and phonology in reading Japanese Kanji words: Evidence from the semantic decision task with homophones. *Memory and Cognition*, *26*, 75–87.

Seidenberg, M.S. (1985). The time course of phonological code activation in two writing systems. *Cognition*, *19*, 1–30.

Shen, D., & Forster, K.I. (1999). Masked phonological priming in reading Chinese words depends on the task. *Language and Cognitive Processes*, *14*, 000–000.

Simpson, G.B., & Kang, H. (1994). The flexible use of phonological information in word recognition in Korean. *Journal of Memory and Language*, *33*, 319–331.

Song, H., Zhang, H., & Shu, H. (1995). The developmental shift of the role of graphic code and phonetic code in Chinese reading. *Acta Psychologica Sinica*, *27*, 139–144.

Taylor, I. (1997). Psycholinguistic reasons for keeping Chinese characters in Korean and Japanese. In H.-C. Chen (Ed.), *Cognitive Processing of Chinese and Related Asian Languages*, pp.299–319. Hong Kong: Chinese University Press.

Van Orden, G.C. (1987). A ROWS is a ROSE: Spelling, sound and reading. *Memory and Cognition*, *15*, 181–198.

Van Orden, G.C., Johnston, J.C., & Hale, B.L. (1988). Word identification in reading proceeds from spelling to sound to meaning. *Journal of Experimental Psychology: Learning, Memory, and Cognition*, *14*, 371–385.

Wu, J.T., Chou, T.L., & Liu, I.M. (1994). The locus of the character/word frequency effect. In H.W. Chang, J.T. Huang, C.W. Hue & O.J.L. Tzeng (Eds), *Advances in the study of Chinese Language Processing*, Vol. 1, pp.31–58. Taipei: Department of Psychology, National Taiwan University.

Wydell, N., Patterson, K.E., & Humphreys, G.W. (1993). Phonologically mediated access to meaning for Kanji: Is a Rows still a Rose in Japanese Kanji? *Journal of Experimental Psychology: Learning, Memory, and Cognition*, *19*, 491–514.

Zhou, X., & Marslen-Wilson, W. (1999). Orthography, phonology, and semantic activation in reading Chinese. *Journal of Memory and Language*, in press.

Zhou, X., Shu, H., Bi, Y., & Shi, D. (1999). Is there phonologically mediated access to lexical semantics in reading Chinese? In J. Wang, A.W. Inhoff, & H.-C. Chen (Eds), *Reading Chinese script: A cognitive analysis*, pp.135–171. Mahwah, NJ: Lawrence Erlbaum Associates Inc.

LANGUAGE AND COGNITIVE PROCESSES, 1999, *14* (5/6), 503–524

Sublexical Processing in Reading Chinese: A Development Study

Ningning Wu
Beijing Normal University

Xiaolin Zhou
Peking University and University of Cambridge, Cambridge, UK

Hua Shu
Beijing Normal University

Three primed naming experiments were conducted to investigate the development of sublexical processing in reading Chinese. Target characters were either homophonic to (Experiments 1 and 2) or semantically related to (Experiment 3) phonetic radicals embedded in irregular complex characters, but not to the complex character themselves. For both the third and sixth grade school children, targets were named faster when they were preceded by such complex characters than by unrelated primes, although the semantic effect of complex characters was not significant for the third grade children. It is argued that, from early on in learning to read Chinese, phonetic radicals embedded in complex characters are decomposed from visual input and used to activate their own phonological and semantic properties, in parallel to the processing of whole characters.

INTRODUCTION

Most complex Chinese characters are composed of a semantic radical and a phonetic radical (Li, 1993; Yin & Rohsenhow, 1994). While semantic radicals have the function of indicating the semantic category of

Requests for reprints should be addressed to Xiaolin Zhou, Department of Experimental Psychology, University of Cambridge, Cambridge CB2 3EB, UK. Email: xz104@cam.ac.uk

This research was suppoted in part by grants from China National Science Foundation to Hua Shu and to Xiaolin Zhou and in part by a grant from UK Economic and Social Research Council to William Marslen-Wilson and Xiaolin Zhou. We thank Ike Chen, Laurie Feldman, and Catherine McBride-Chang for their helpful comments on an earlier version of this paper.

morphemes corresponding to whole characters, phonetic radicals have the function of pointing to the pronunciations of whole characters. However, due to the evolution of the writing system, many such characters are no longer pronounced in the same way as their phonetic radicals. Previous studies (Hue, 1992; Peng, Yang, & Chen, 1994; Seidenberg, 1985) have found that the "regularity" of phonetic radicals in encoding phonological information for whole characters influences phonological processing of these characters, at least when they are of low frequency. Regular complex characters, which are pronounced in the same way as their phonetic radicals, are named faster than frequency-matched simple characters, which have no phonetic radicals, or irregular complex characters, which have different pronunciations from their phonetic radicals. These findings are often interpreted as suggesting that phonetic radicals embedded in complex characters are decomposed from visual input and mapped onto their own phonological representations as well as representations of other characters containing these radicals. The co-operative and competitive interaction between phonological processing of whole characters and their phonetic radicals leads to the "regularity" and "consistency" effect in naming complex characters (Seidenberg, 1985; Zhou & Marslen-Wilson, 1999a). Thus, sublexical processing of phonetic radicals in reading Chinese is thought as analogous to sublexical processing of letter strings in reading alphabetic words, whose function is to provide sources of phonological activation (and semantic activation) for whole words (Coltheart, Curtis, Atkins, & Haller, 1993; Plaut, McClelland, Seidenberg, & Patterson, 1996; Seidenberg & McClelland, 1989). Some researchers (Cheng, 1992; Flores d'Arcais, Saito, & Kawakami, 1995), however, went so far to suggest that, because the phonetic radical-sound correspondences are over-learned in Chinese, they could be used in the same way as the grapheme-phoneme correspondences in alphabetic languages, presumably to compute "pre-lexical" phonology for whole characters.

The main purpose of this study was to investigate how school children, in learning to read complex Chinese characters, use phonological information provided by phonetic radicals and whether sublexical processing of phonetic radicals embedded in complex characters is restricted to phonology, involving only activation of phonological information associated with the phonetic radicals. Before presenting our experiments, we give a brief introduction to the structural properties of Chinese characters and previous research on sublexical processing of phonetic radicals.

THE STRUCTURE OF CHINESE CHARACTERS AND SUBLEXICAL PROCESSING OF PHONETIC RADICALS

The Chinese writing system is often described as logographic or morphosyllabic, where the basic orthographic units, the characters, correspond directly to morphemic meanings and syllables. With some exceptions, each character in isolation represents one morpheme and has one pronunciation, although different characters may have the same pronunciations. Modern Chinese characters can be broadly differentiated into two categories (Li, 1993); simple and complex,[1] both of which are composed of strokes and arranged in squares of similar size. Simple characters (e.g., 土 tu[3], *soil*, *earth*) make up about 5% of the total characters in Modern Chinese. They are holistic visual patterns that cannot be divided meaningfully into sublexical units. Complex characters constitute about 95% of all modern Chinese characters (Li, 1993; Yin & Rohsenow, 1994) and 87% of characters learned by Chinese school children (Shu, Wu, Zheng, & Zhou, 1998). Most of these characters are composed of a semantic radical on the left and a phonetic radical on the right (e.g., 城 cheng[2], *city*, in which the phonetic radical is 成 cheng[2], *become*),[2] although some arrange their radicals in other ways (see Yin & Rohsenow, 1994).

As far as the phonological relations between complex characters and their phonetic radicals are concerned, there are about one third of the complex characters ("regular" characters, e.g., 清 qing[1], *clear*, whose phonetic radical is 青 qing[1], *blue*) that have exactly the same pronunciations as their phonetic radicals (Fan, Gao, & Ao, 1984; Li & Kang, 1993). About one third of complex characters ("irregular" characters, 猜 cai[1], *guess*) bear no phonological relations with their phonetic radicals at all. The final one third share some aspect of their phonology, such as segmented rhyming parts (e.g., 精 jing[1], *essence*), or the initial consonants (e.g., 倩 qian[4], *pretty*) with their phonetic radicals. Most phonetic radicals can be involved in both regular and irregular characters. Unlike letter clusters or graphemes in alphabetic words,

---

[1] Characters were differentiated into six categories (pictographic, indicative, associative, picto-phonetic, notative, and burrowed) in a classic work (Shuwen Jiezi, 121 A.D., see Yin & Rohsenow, 1994), which is still referred to today. While the first four categories were based on the way the characters were created, the last two refer to the expansion of the use of existing characters. It seems that there is little psychological relevance of many of these categories (e.g., pictograms or ideograms).

[2] Throughout this paper, the pronunciations of Chinese characters are given in *pinyin*, the alphabetic system used in mainland China. Numbers in brackets or parentheses represent the lexical tones of syllables.

phonetic radicals provide clues to the pronunciations of whole characters, rather than to a part of them. Moreover, most phonetic radicals (92%) can stand alone as meaningful characters, even though their meanings mostly have nothing to do with the meanings of whole characters.

From early on school children are exposed to different types of characters and different phonological relations between complex characters and their phonetic radicals. According to our analyses of characters learned by Chinese school children (Shu et al., 1998), the proportion of regular complex characters (disregarding the tonal differences between whole characters and their phonetic radicals) increases from 31% of all complex characters learned in the second grade to 41% in the sixth grade, while irregular characters (having segmental differences between complex characters and their phonetic radicals) increases from 40% in the second grade to about 46% in the sixth grade. Simple characters take about 45% and 29% respectively of all characters learned in the first and second grades. Among them, over 75% become phonetic radicals of complex characters learned in the later grades. Simple characters learned in school usually have higher frequency than complex characters that use them as phonetic radicals. The average frequency of phonetic radicals as independent characters is 730 per million in adult reading materials while the average frequency of complex characters containing these radicals is 15 per million. By the end of the third grade, children have learned about 2000 characters. By the end of the sixth grade, children have learned about 3260 characters, which are not far away from the 4570 characters covering most adult reading materials (Institute of Language Teaching and Research, 1986).

There have been a number of studies on sublexical or subcharacter processing of phonetic radicals in skilled reading of Chinese (Fang, Horng, & Tzeng, 1986; Flores d'Arcais et al., 1995; Hue, 1992; Peng et al., 1994; Seidenberg, 1985; Taft & Zhu, 1997; Zhou, 1994). With few exceptions (Zhou and Marslen-Wilson, 1999a, 1999b), studies of phonetic radicals concentrate on phonological activation of phonetic radicals and its influence on phonological processing of whole characters. Seidenberg (1985) found that regular complex characters, or characters having the same pronunciations as their phonetic radicals, were named faster than frequency-matched simple characters, although this effect was restricted mostly to low frequency characters. Fang et al. (1986) investigated regularity and consistency effects in naming characters, where consistency was defined according to whether *all* complex characters containing a particular phonetic radical are pronounced in the same way as the radical. They observed a significant consistency effect but not regularity effect. Regular-consistent characters (e.g., 材 cai[2], *materials*) were named faster than regular-inconsistent characters (e.g., 油 you[2], *oil*; which contained the phonetic radical 由 you[2], *cause*), although the latter were not named faster than irregular-inconsistent characters (e.g., 抽 chou[1], *lash*). Subsequent studies using similar designs, however, found both regularity and consistency effects for low frequency complex characters (Hue, 1992; Peng et al., 1994).[3]

The effect of sublexical phonological processing and its interaction with the frequency of complex characters were examined more directly in a study using a primed naming task. Zhou and Marslen-Wilson (1999a) used paired characters in which primes were high or low frequency irregular complex characters (e.g., 猜 cai[1], *guess*) and targets were characters (e.g., 轻 qing[1], *light*) that were homophonic to the phonetic radicals (e.g., 青 qing[1], *blue*) embedded in the complex characters but not to the characters themselves. They found that targets preceded by low frequency complex characters were named faster than when they were preceded by unrelated characters. Targets preceded by high frequency complex characters, however, did not show significant facilitation in naming. This pattern of priming effects, together with the regularity and consistency effects in single-character naming, suggests that in processing complex characters, phonetic radicals are decomposed from visual input and used to access their own phonological representations. However, the ability to decompose phonetic radicals and gain access to their phonology is modulated by the frequency of complex characters containing these radicals. Reading high frequency complex characters may involve little decomposition, as the highly efficient processing of whole characters leaves little time for the sublexical processing of their phonetic radicals. Alternatively, the phonological activation of phonetic radicals embedded in complex characters is transient and already suppressed by the phonological activation of whole characters by the time probing targets are presented.

Phonological processing of phonetic radicals and its influences on the processing of whole characters have also been investigated for school children. Shu and Zeng (1996) asked the second, fourth, and sixth grade children to write down, in terms of *pinyin*, the pronunciations of familiar and unfamiliar characters. They found that children's performance was influenced by the regularity of complex characters in relation to their phonetic radicals, with better scores on regular characters than on irregular characters. Children were able to use phonological cues provided by phonetic radicals to guess the pronunciation of unfamiliar characters, and this ability improved as they grew older. Yang and Peng (1997) asked

[3] A potential problem with these studies is that stimuli for different categories were not purposely matched on their initial phonemes in pronunciation. This may explain some of the conflicts between these studies.

participants to name complex characters and recorded their naming latencies. They found that both the third and sixth grade school children showed the consistency effect (as defined in Fang et al., 1986) but only the third grade, not the sixth grade children showed regularity effect. The latter result was probably due to the selection of stimuli. Shu and Wu (1996) used the same design and task as Yang and Peng (1997) and found that both the fourth and sixth grade children showed regularity and consistency effects while the third grade children showed neither of them. In another study, Shu, Zhou, and Wu (in press) asked children to judge whether two characters having the same phonetic radical were homophones. In each pair, the first character was a familiar one while the second character was an unfamiliar one. In guessing the pronunciation of the second character and making judgement, children had to be aware of the orthographic structure of the familiar and unfamiliar characters and use the phonological information provided by the phonetic radical. It was found that children's judgement was influenced by the consistency of phonetic radicals in providing phonological cues to whole characters. Pairs containing consistent radicals were less likely to be judged as non-homophones than pairs containing inconsistent radicals. This effect was pronounced as children were getting older.

All these studies suggest that in reading complex Chinese characters, skilled readers and school children rely on their knowledge about the structure of characters to decompose the visual input of whole characters, and use phonological cues provided by phonetic radicals to help retrieve phonological information of whole characters. Sublexical processing of embedded phonetic radicals, like sublexical processing of letter strings in reading alphabetic words, could be therefore primarily a phonological event, computing phonological output for the whole words (Coltheart et al., 1993; Plaut et al., 1996; Seidenberg & McClelland, 1989).

A study by Zhou and Marslen-Wilson (1999b), however, found that sublexical processing of phonetic radicals activates not only the phonological information corresponding to the radicals, but also the semantic information associated with the radicals. The appearance of complex character 猜 (cai[1], *guess*) activates the semantic representation corresponding to its radical 青 (qing[1], *blue*), leading to facilitation in naming the target character 紫 (zi[3], *purple*), which is semantically related to the phonetic radical, but not to the complex character itself. Moreover, the presence of semantic associates to phonetic radicals also activates the semantic and phonological representations of the radicals, creating phonological competition with the irregular complex characters and delaying the vocalisation of these characters. These findings suggest that sublexical processing of phonetic radicals in reading complex characters is not exactly the same as sublexical processing in reading monomorphemic alphabetic words or semantically opaque compound words, in which the processing of letter strings does not engage semantic activation for the sublexical orthographic units themselves, even when these units happen to be words on their own (e.g., *boy* in *boycott* or *mail* in *blackmail*; see Sandra, 1990; Zhou & Marslen-Wilson, 1999b; Zwitserlood, 1994).

The present study was firstly to examine how children use phonological cues of phonetic radicals embedded in complex characters. Do they treat the phonetic radical-sound correspondences in the same way as the grapheme-phoneme correspondences in alphabetic scripts and compute "prelexical" phonology for whole characters (e.g., Cheng, 1992; Flores d'Arcais et al., 1995)? Or do they decompose the visual input and use phonetic radicals to activate phonological representations of their own as well as characters containing these radicals (Seidenberg, 1985; Zhou & Marslen-Wilson, 1999a)? Secondly, this study was to investigate whether school children's sublexical processing of phonetic radicals is just a phonological event, involving only computing phonology from the decomposed visual input, or is also a semantic event, involving activating semantic information corresponding to these phonetic radicals.

This study used essentially the same designs and technique as Zhou and Marslen-Wilson (1999a,b) to address the above issues. Experiments 1 and 2 examined whether phonetic radicals in complex characters were decomposed by the third and sixth grade children and used to activate phonological representations of these radicals. Experiment 3 examined whether semantic properties corresponding to phonetic radicals were also activated in reading complex characters. In both Experiments 1 and 3, both the third and sixth grade children were tested in order to track the development of sublexical processing.

EXPERIMENT 1

This experiment had two purposes. The first one was to investigate, in children's reading of complex characters, whether phonetic radicals were decomposed from visual input and used to activate their own phonological representations, even though this phonological activation could only interfere with the processing of complex characters themselves. The second purpose was to examine the development of sublexical phonological processing across different ages (or educational levels).

To index the phonological activation of phonetic radicals embedded in complex characters, irregular complex characters (e.g., 海 hai[3], *sea*) were used as primes and characters (e.g., 美 mei[3], *beautiful*) that were homophonic to phonetic radicals (每 mei[3], *every*) embedded in the primes but not to the primes themselves were used as targets (see Table 1). If phonetic radicals are decomposed and used to access their own

TABLE 1
Experiment 1: Design and Sample Stimuli

	Homophone	*Complex*	*Control*	*Target*
Character	每	海	低	美
Pinyin	mei(3)	hai(3)	di(1)	mei(3)
Gloss	*every*	*sea*	*low*	*beautiful*
Frequency	873	270	270	548
Stroke	6.1	9.3	8.8	8.4

Homophone primes are characters embedded in irregular complex primes as phonetic radicals. "Frequency" refers to average frequency of primes or targets (per million). "Stroke" refers to average number of strokes of primes or targets (per character).

phonological representations, the activation of these representations in the lexicon should facilitate the processing of targets, which share phonological properties with the radicals. The reason for using irregular rather than regular complex characters as primes was to make sure that any priming effects were from sublexical or subcharacter processing of phonetic radicals, rather than from lexical level processing of whole characters. It would be impossible to determine the source of facilitation in naming if targets were homophonic to both the whole characters and their phonetic radicals. The same design and stimuli were applied to both the third and sixth grade children.

In this and other experiments, we tested school children of the third and sixth grades. By the third grade, children should have learned large numbers of simple and complex characters (Shu et al., 1998) and have sufficient knowledge about the structure of complex characters and the function of their phonetic and semantic radicals (e.g., Shu et al., in press). Moreover, they can follow instructions to carry out the on-line experimental naming task (Zhou, Wu, & Shu, 1998). The sixth grade children clearly show advantages over lower grade children in their lexical processing. Indeed the pattern of their phonological and semantic processing is very similar to that of skilled adult readers (Zhou et al., 1998), with equally efficient phonological and semantic activation.

Method

Design and Materials. The experimental design and sample stimuli are presented in Table 1. Thirty irregular complex characters with left–right structure were selected from the "Database of Chinese Characters Learned in School", which indexed, according to grades, the first appearance of characters in textbooks used by school children in Beijing. All the selected complex characters were supposed to have been taught to the third grade children. All the phonetic radicals embedded in complex primes were real characters on their own and they were also presented alone as homophone primes. Targets were chosen to be homophonic to the radicals but not to the complex primes. Targets had no orthographic or semantic relations with either complex primes or homophone (or radical) primes.

Another thirty irregular complex characters with left-right structure were also chosen as control primes. There were no orthographic, phonological, or semantic relations between control primes and targets at either lexical or sublexical level. Because our main interest was in phonological priming of phonetic radicals contained in complex primes, control primes were matched in fequency, visual complexity (in terms of the number of strokes), and orthographic structure (left-right composition of phonetic and semantic radicals) with the complex primes, rather than with homophone primes. Since there were no frequency counts for characters used by school children in different grades, the frequency information in Table 1 came from a corpus study of 1.8 million Chinese characters (Institute of Language Teaching and Research, 1986). The familiarity of characters for children was closely correlated to the usage of characters in print (Shu et al., 1998).

Besides the critical stimuli, the experiment also included 50 pairs of filler characters to discourage participants from using potential response strategies. Primes and targets in filler pairs were neither semantically nor orthographically nor phonologically related. Characters used as fillers were of various orthographic structures and with various frequencies. They, and their corresponding phonological forms (i.e., syllables), were not used in the critical stimuli. There were also 20 pairs of practice items, with similar composition as the formal stimuli.

A Latin square design was used to assign the critical primes and their targets into three counter-balanced test versions. In each version, the same targets appeared only once and one third of the targets were preceded by one of the three types of primes. The same filler prime-target pairs were used in the three test versions. A pseudo-random ordering was used to arrange the stimuli in each version, so that, across the test versions, the primes and targets from the same quintets of critical stimuli appeared at the same position in the testing sequence. The SOA between primes and targets was set at 100 ms. At this SOA, school children are capable of producing significant phonological, orthographically, or semantically based priming effects in naming (Wu, 1998; Zhou et al., 1998).

Procedure. The preparation of stimuli was as follows. All primes and targets (in 48 × 48 *songti* font) were generated by a computer program and stored as individual image files on a hard disk. A character was about

2.4 × 1.6 cm in size. The presentation of stimuli to participants and recording of reaction times were controlled by the dual-screen version software DMASTR, made available to us by Ken Forster. In each trial, an eye fixation signal ("+") was first presented at the centre of a computer screen for 300 ms, followed by a 300 ms blank interval. A prime was then presented for 100 ms and overwritten immediately by the corresponding target, which was presented for 400 ms. There was a 3-second interval between the disappearance of the last target and the appearance of the next eye fixation point. Participants were tested individually. They were seated about 60 cm from the screen and were asked to read into a microphone as quickly and as accurately as possible the second character of each trial. The microphone was interfaced with the computer to record voice onset latencies. Participants' performance was monitored by an experimenter and naming errors were recorded by hand in pre-printed scoring sheets.

Each participant saw first a list of 20 prime-target practice items. There was a break after practice. The first three pairs after the break were fillers. The complete test session for each participant lasted less than 15 minutes.

Participants. A total of 82 participants were tested, 39 from the third grade and 43 from the sixth grade. All participants were native speakers of Mandarine Chinese and were school children at the Affiliated School of Beijing Normal University.

Results

Nine participants at the third grade were excluded from analyses because of their high (over 20%) response errors. Three targets were also deleted for the third grade children because over half of participants in one or more test versions made mistakes in response. Mean naming latencies, based on correct responses, were then computed for each participant and each item, and the overall mean reaction times for each condition are presented in the upper part of Table 2.

Overall analyses were first conducted, with the grade as a between-subject factor and prime type as a within-subject factor. The main effect of grade was significant [$F_1(1,71) = 68.29$, $P < .001$; $F_2(1,26) = 182.29$, $P < .001$], indicating that the third grade children were slower than the sixth grade children in naming targets. The main effect of prime type was also significant [$F_1(2,142) = 11.89$, $P < .001$; $F_2(2,52) = 6.77$, $P < .01$]. Post hoc Newman-Keuls tests showed that the mean reaction times for homophone (radical) primes and complex primes were significantly faster than the time for control primes ($P < .01$ and $P < .05$ respectively), indicating that the phonological processing of targets was facilitated both by radical primes

TABLE 2
Experiments 1 and 2: Mean Naming Latencies (ms) and Error Percentages

Experiment	*Grade*	*Homophone*	*Complex*	*Control*
Exp. 1	Third	709 (14.6)	715 (10.0)	756 (10.3)
	Sixth	607 (5.8)	629 (4.5)	628 (5.5)
Exp. 2	Sixth	656 (4.5)	665 (4.5)	690 (3.5)

presented alone as homophone primes and by radicals embedded in irregular complex primes. However, the interaction between grade and prime type was also significant [$F_1(2,142) = 9.19$, $P < .01$; $F_2(2,52) = 3.76$, $P < .05$], suggesting that the priming patterns were not exactly the same for the two grades. The analyses of error rates produced a significant main effect of grade [$F_1(1,71) = 9.25$, $P < .05$; $F_2(1,26) = 10.43$, $P < .05$], with more errors made by the third grade children than by the sixth grade children. The main effect of prime type was not significant [$F_1(2,142) = 1.72$, $P > .1$; $F_2(2,52) = 2.89$, $P > .1$].

Separate analyses were conducted for reaction times for the third and sixth grade children. For the third grade, the main effect of prime type was significant [$F_1(2,58) = 8.36$, $P < .001$; $F_2(2,52) = 7.07$, $P < .01$]. Newman-Keuls tests showed that, against control primes, priming effects for both radical homophone primes and complex primes were significant ($P < .01$), although there was no significant difference between these two ($P > .1$). For the sixth grade, the main effect of prime type approached significance [$F_1(2,84) = 6.83$, $P < .01$; $F_2(2,58) = 2.02$, $.05 < P < .1$]. Newman-Keuls tests showed that the effect for radical homophone primes was significant against control primes ($P < .01$). However, there was no significant difference between complex primes and control primes ($P > .1$).

Discussion

The significant homophone priming effects in the primed naming task, although may have been overestimated due to higher frequency and simpler visual configuration of homophone primes than control primes, were consistent with a number of studies, both with skilled readers (Perfetti & Zhang, 1991; Zhou & Marslen-Wilson, 1999a, in press) and with school children (Wu, 1998; Zhou et al., 1998). These effects indicated that, even for the third grade school children, the pre-activation of phonological information can produce strong facilitatory effects in naming. What is most interesting in this experiment, however, is the finding that irregular complex primes were capable of facilitating the processing of targets that were homophonic not to the primes but to the phonetic radicals embedded in these primes. This sublexical phonological priming effect appeared only for the third grade children, not for the sixth grade children.

The significant priming effect for complex primes demonstrated that in reading complex primes, school children, like skilled readers, decompose the visual input of the whole characters and use their phonetic radicals to activate phonological representations corresponding to the radicals (possibly as well as representations corresponding to other characters containing these radicals), in parallel to the processing of whole characters. Why then did the sixth grade children not show such sublexical phonological activation of phonetic radicals?

As we reviewed earlier, Zhou and Marslen-Wilson (1999a) found that low frequency complex primes, but not high frequency complex primes, facilitated the processing of targets homophonic to the embedded phonetic radicals, consistent with the interaction between regularity and frequency in single-character naming (Hue, 1992; Peng et al., 1994; Seidenberg, 1985). The absence of a significant priming effect for high frequency characters was attributed to the fewer opportunities in decomposing phonetic radicals from high frequency complex characters and/or the strong competition between phonological activation of whole characters and sublexical phonetic radicals. Was it possible that the lack of a significant priming effect for the sixth grade here was because these complex characters had already become high frequency characters for these children? After all, the stimuli were chosen according to their appearance in the third grade textbooks. These complex characters were likely to be used repeatedly after their initial acquisition.

The purpose of the next experiment was therefore to investigate whether sublexical phonological activation of phonetic radicals could be observed for the sixth grade children when complex characters were of relatively low frequency to them.

EXPERIMENT 2

Method

Design and stimuli. The experimental design and critical stimuli were essentially the same as Experiment 1 (see Table 1), except that a few complex primes used in Experiment 1 were replaced with low frequency characters having the same phonetic radicals. All the phonetic radicals (embedded in complex primes and also presented in isolation as homophone primes) and all the targets were the same as those used in Experiment 1. A few control primes were also replaced to match with the new complex primes in frequency and visual complexity. The average frequency of complex primes and the average frequency control primes were both 129 per million. The average numbers of strokes were 10.0 and 9.9 per character respectively for the two types of primes. According to the "Database of Chinese Characters Learned in School", all the new primes had been taught to the sixth grade children.

Procedure. The preparation of stimuli and the test of participants were conducted in the same way as Experiment 1.

Participants. Thirty children of the sixth grade at Beijing Ji Jia Miao school were tested, 10 in each test version. All of them were native speakers of Mandarin Chinese.

Results

Mean naming latencies were computed on the bases of correct responses and they, together with error rates, are reported in the lower part of Table 2. One-way ANOVAs conducted for reaction times revealed a significant main effect of prime type [$F_1(2,58) = 9.31$, $P < .001$; $F_2(2,58) = 6.13$, $P < .01$]. Newman-Keuls tests showed that the mean reaction time for homophone (radical) primes was significantly faster than the time for control primes ($P < .01$). More importantly, the mean reaction time for complex primes was also faster than the time for control primes ($P < .1$ by participants and $P < .05$ by item). The difference between homophone and complex primes was not significant ($P > .1$). The analyses of error rates did not find significant results ($F_1 < 1$, $F_2 < 1$).

Discussion

The finding of a significant priming effect for irregular complex primes for the sixth grade children was consistent with the significant effect for the third grade children in Experiment 1. This effect demonstrated again that in reading complex characters children decompose the phonetic radicals from the whole characters and use them to access their own phonological representations, in parallel to the processing of whole characters. The presence of a significant effect for complex primes, contrasting with the absence of such an effect for the sixth grade children in Experiment 1, also demonstrated that sublexical phonological processing of phonetic radicals is strongly modulated by the frequency of complex characters. Complex primes in this experiment had lower mean frequency than the primes in Experiment 1. Moreover, the sixth grade children tested for this experiment were probably less skilful in reading than the sixth grade children tested for Experiment 1, as demonstrated by the difference (about 50 ms) in average mean reaction times between the two groups.[4] This could mean that the same complex characters were of even lower frequency for the children tested in this experiment than for the children tested in Experiment 1. Phonetic radicals in low frequency complex characters may have more opportunities to decompose and to activate their own phonological representations.

EXPERIMENT 3

The previous two experiments demonstrated that there is a decompositional process in reading complex Chinese characters and that phonological properties associated with the phonetic radicals embedded in complex characters are activated even though this phonological activation can only interfere with phonological activation of whole characters. The ability to decompose characters and conduct sublexical phonological processing develops no later than the third grade; until then school children have acquired about 2000 characters (Shu et al., 1998). The purpose of this experiment was to demonstrate that sublexical processing of phonetic radicals is not only a phonological event, involving computation from orthographic to phonology, but also a semantic event, involving activation of semantic properties associated with the radicals, even though this sublexical semantic activation can only interfere with the processing of whole characters.

In this experiment, irregular complex characters (e.g., 帕 pa[4], *handkerchief*) were used as primes, and characters (e.g., 黑 hei[1], *black*) that were semantically related to the phonetic radicals embedded in these primes (e.g., 白 bai[3], *white*) but not to the primes themselves were used as targets. If reading complex characters involves decomposing phonetic radicals and using them to access their own semantic representations, this sublexical semantic activation should be able to facilitate the processing of targets. Since decomposition and sublexical processing is likely to be

[4] Children tested in Experiment 1 were from a "key" school in Beijing while children tested in this experiment were from an ordinary school. It was possible that these children had different family backgrounds and there were general differences in educational standard between these schools.

modulated by frequency of complex characters, separate sets of complex primes were used here for the third and sixth grade children.

Method

Design and materials. The design and sample stimuli are presented in Table 3. A total of 60 irregular complex characters (e.g., 帕 pa[4], *handkerchief*) were used as complex primes, 30 each for the third and sixth grade children. These two groups of complex primes, sharing most common characters, had the same set of phonetic radicals (e.g., 白 bai[3], *white*). These radicals were presented on their own as semantic primes. The same sets of targets (e.g., 黑 hei[1], *black*) were used for the two groups of complex primes. Targets were semantically related to the phonetic radicals, but not to the complex primes themselves. All complex primes were of left-right structure with phonetic radicals on the right. Control primes were selected to match with the complex primes on frequency, visual complexity, and orthographic structure. The semantic relatedness between phonetic radicals (i.e., semantic primes) and targets was checked in a pretest, in which 40 children, 20 each from the third and sixth grades, was asked to judge the semantic relatedness on a 7-point scale, ranging from 1 (unrelated) to 7 (highly related). The average points were 5.4 and 5.8 respectively for the third and sixth grade children, indicating that, given time, both the third and sixth grade children can effectively activate semantic properties of radical-target pairs and make conscious judgements.

TABLE 3
Experiment 3: Design and Sample Stimuli

Grade		*Semantic*	*Complex*	*Control*	*Target*
Third	Character	白	拍	泪	黑
	Pinyin	bai(2)	pai(1)	lei(4)	Hei(1)
	Gloss	*white*	*clap*	*tear*	*Black*
	Frequency	807	239	235	1403
	Stroke	5.8	9.3	10.2	9.6
Sixth	Character	白	帕	桶	黑
	Pinyin	bai(2)	pa(4)	tong(3)	Hei(1)
	Gloss	*white*	*handkerchief*	*bucket*	*Black*
	Frequency	807	177	172	1403
	Stroke	5.8	9.6	10.4	9.6

Semantic primes are characters embedded in irregular complex primes as phonetic radicals. "Frequency" refers to average frequency of primes or targets (per million). "Stroke" refers to average number of strokes of primes or targets (per character).

For the two groups of stimuli, a Latin square design was used to assign the critical primes and their corresponding targets into three counterbalanced test versions. Each version in each group had 30 critical targets, 10 of them preceded by one of the three types of primes. Another 50 pairs of characters that were neither semantically, phonologically, nor orthographically related were used as fillers and added to each test version. Characters and syllables used in the critical stimuli were not used again in fillers. A pseudo-random ordering was used to arrange the stimuli so that, across the three test versions in each group, the same targets appeared at the same positions. Twenty pairs of practice items were also used. The SOA between primes and targets was against set at 100 ms.

Procedure. The preparation of stimuli and test of participants were carried out in the same way as Experiments 1 and 2.

Participants. A total of 74 children at Beijing Ji Jia Miao school were tested, 39 from the third grade and 35 from the sixth grade. All of them were native speakers of Mandarin Chinese.

Results

Mean naming latencies and response error percentages are reported in Table 4. ANOVAs were conducted on reaction times, with prime type as a within-subject factor and grade as a between-subject factor. The main effect of grade was highly significant [$F_1(1,67) = 37.56$, $P < .001$, $F_2(1,27) = 260.09$, $P < .001$], indicating that the overall naming latency for the sixth grade children was much faster than the latency for the third grade children. More importantly, the main effect of prime type was significant [$F_1(2,134) = 8.55$, $P < .001$, $F_2(2,54) = 8.46$, $P < .001$]. Newman-Keuls tests showed that the overall naming latency for semantic primes was significantly faster than the latency for control primes ($P < .01$). The overall naming latency for complex primes was also significantly faster than the latency for controls ($P < .05$). The difference between semantic

TABLE 4
Experiment 3: Mean Naming Latencies (ms) and Error Percentages

Grade	*Semantic*	*Complex*	*Control*
Third	714 (7.3)	727 (5.5)	729 (6.6)
Sixth	612 (4.6)	624 (4.6)	645 (4.6)

primes and complex primes was significant ($P < .05$). Moreover, the interaction between prime type and grade was not significant by participants ($F_1 < 1$), but it was marginally significant by items [$F_2(2,54) = 2.60$, $.05 < P < .1$]. Planned tests involving only complex and control primes found a stronger interaction between prime type and grade: [$F_1(1,67) = 2.25$, $P = .1$, $F_2(1,27) = 4.31$, $P < .05$), indicating that although the third grade children exhibited the same trend, as the sixth grade children in semantic and sublexical semantic priming, the priming effect for complex primes was greatly reduced or non-existent for the third grade. Indeed the 2 ms difference between complex primes and control primes for the third grade was not significant. The analyses of error rates did not find a significant main effect of either prime type [$F_1 < 1$, $F_2 < 2$], or grade [$F_1(1,67) = 3.89$, $P = .1$, $F_2(1,27) = 1.19$, $P > .1$].

Discussion

The strong semantic priming effect for the sixth grade children and the non-significant semantic effect for the third grade children were consistent with our other studies (Wu, 1998; Zhou et al., 1998), which had better matched semantic and control primes and which observed essentially the same pattern of semantic priming for children of these two grades. Given the finding that the mean naming latencies for the third grade children were significantly longer than those for the sixth grade, it is reasonable to assume that the third grade children needed more time to process the primes and activate their semantic properties.

The most interesting finding in this experiment was that there was an overall priming effect for complex primes, although this effect came mainly from the sixth grade children. This effect, based on semantic relations between targets and phonetic radicals embedded in complex primes, suggested that in reading complex primes, school children decomposed the phonetic radicals from the visual input of complex primes and used them to activate semantic properties corresponding to the phonetic radicals. This semantic activation spread to the semantic representations corresponding to the target characters, leading to facilitation in naming.

It is clear from Table 4 that the effect for complex primes was greatly reduced, if it did exist, for the third grade children. The absence of significant sublexical semantic activation for the third grade children follows the general weakness of lexical level semantic priming for the third grade children (Wu, 1998; Zhou et al., 1998). It is possible that it requires more processing time for these children to decompose the radicals and activate their semantic properties. The priming effects for semantic and complex primes could be larger when a SOA longer than 100 ms is used.

GENERAL DISCUSSION

In this study, we investigated whether school children, in reading complex characters, engage sublexical processing of phonetic radicals in a way similar to skilled readers and how their sublexical processing is developed over age and schooling. Three experiments, using a primed naming task, found significant priming effects for targets that were either phonologically or semantically related to phonetic radicals embedded in irregular complex primes. In Experiment 1, targets were homophonic to phonetic radicals which were either embedded in complex primes or presented on their own as homophone primes. The same set of stimuli were applied to the third and sixth grade children. Significant priming effects were found for homophone radical primes for children of both grades. However, while the priming effect for complex primes was significant for the third grade children, it was not for the sixth grade children. In Experiment 2, the same design was used on the (possibly less skilled) sixth grade children but with complex primes of lower frequency. Priming effects were significant for both homophone radical primes and complex primes. Experiment 3 used characters that were semantically related to phonetic radicals as targets and complex characters. Significant overall priming effects were found for both semantic (radical) primes and complex primes, although the effect of complex primes was not significant for the third grade children. The patterns of priming effects across the three experiments were, in general, consistent with what were found with skilled adult readers (Zhou & Marslen-Wilson, 1999a,b).

Nevertheless, it seems that there is dissociation between sublexical phonological and sublexical semantic processing of phonetic radicals for the third grade children. This dissociation is indeed parallel to the dissociation between lexical level phonological and semantic processing. There were strong homophone and sublexical phonological priming effects (Experiment 1), in contrast with the weak semantic and sublexical semantic priming effects (Experiment 3). This contrast may be taken as evidence that, for younger children, phonological activation in reading Chinese characters is more efficient than semantic activation, although it is also possible that the larger phonological effects were partly due to the naming task, which is biased towards the use of phonological rather than semantic information.

However, even in such a task, semantic effects were equally strong as phonological effects for the sixth grade children (see Tables 2 and 4). Here we saw equally efficient phonological and semantic activation in reading Chinese (see also Zhou et al., 1998, which compared directly homophone and semantic priming effects for both the third and sixth grade children), similar to what was observed for adult readers (Zhou & Marslen-Wilson, in press). Moreover, sublexical phonological activation of phonetic radicals for these children (Experiments 1 and 2) was modulated by the frequency of complex characters in the same way as for adults (Zhou & Marslen-Wilson, 1999a). The pattern of sublexical semantic activation (Experiment 3) was also similar to the pattern for adults (Zhou & Marslen-Wilson, 1999b). The sixth grade children may have already developed essentially the same structure of the mental lexicon and the same mechanisms of lexical processing as skilled adult readers. This is consistent with the fact that the sixth grade children may have acquired about 3200 characters (Shu et al., 1998), which cover about 99.765% of adult reading materials (Institute of Language Teaching and Research, 1986).

What are the theoretical implications of the priming effects across the three experiments? Clearly, these effects suggest that in reading complex characters, the embedded phonetic radicals are decomposed and mapped onto their own phonological and semantic representations, in parallel to the mapping for whole characters. This sublexical processing is likely to be automatic or mandatory, in the sense that it takes place whether or not it helps lexical processing of whole characters. Indeed, semantic activation of phonetic radicals almost always interferes with semantic activation of whole characters since semantic properties corresponding to phonetic radicals have little in common with those of whole characters containing these radicals.[5] Zhou, Lu, and Shu (in press) found that, for semantic radicals that can stand alone as independent characters, sublexical processing of these radicals activates not only semantic information associated with the radicals (Feldman & Siok, 1999; Zhou & Marslen-Wilson, 1999a), but also phonological information corresponding to the radicals. The presentation of a complex character 躲 (duo[3], *avoid*), for example, facilitates the naming of the target 深 (shen[1], *deep*), which is homophonic to the semantic radical 身 (shen[1], *body*). This sublexical phonological processing of pronounceable semantic radicals embedded in (low) frequency complex characters is another piece of evidence supporting the notion of automatic decomposition in lexical access and parallel processing of whole characters and their constituent radicals.

Thus, sublexical processing of phonetic radicals is both a phonological event, involving computing phonology from decomposed phonetic radicals, and a semantic event, involving activating semantic representations corresponding to the phonetic radicals themselves. There are no fundamental differences between sublexical processing of phonetic (and

[5] When irregular complex characters were used as targets rather than as primes, Zhou and Marslen-Wilson (1999a,b) found that the processing of complex characters is delayed by the presence of semantic associates of their phonetic radicals. This finding suggests that sublexical semantic activation of the embedded phonetic radicals is not under strategic control.

semantic) radicals and lexical processing of simple and complex characters. The proposition treating sublexical processing of phonetic radicals in reading complex characters in the same way as using grapheme-phoneme correspondence in reading alphabetic words is clearly untenable. Lexical processing in reading complex characters is, after all, more analogous to lexical processing of semantically transparent compound words, where semantic properties of both whole words and their constituent morphemes are activated in parallel in reading (Sandra, 1990; Zhou & Marslen-Wilson, 1999b; Zwitserlood, 1994). Moreover, sublexical phonological and semantic processing of phonetic radicals embedded in complex characters has a clear pattern of development over age and schooling.

We believe that sublexical phonological and semantic activation of phonetic radicals in reading complex Chinese characters is partly due to the structure of these characters, the function of the embedded phonetic and semantic radicals, and learning processes in acquiring these characters (Zhou & Marslen-Wilson, 1999b). Structurally, phonetic radicals are integrated orthographic units, whose constituents (e.g., strokes) have no systematic correspondences to phonology or semantics. There are usually clear visual separations between phonetic and semantic radicals, at least for complex characters with left-right structure. This provides clear cues for visual decomposition of phonetic and semantic radicals in lexical access. Functionally, both phonetic and semantic radicals can have their own semantic properties. Most phonetic radicals and some semantic radicals also have their own phonological properties. Phonetic radicals are not only meaningful characters by themselves, being acquired very early in learning and having much higher frequency than complex characters containing them (Shu et al., 1998), but also repeatedly used in different characters. Complex characters are therefore more similar to compound words rather than to monomorphemic words, having functionally salient components. Furthermore, the relations between phonetic and semantic radicals and the complex characters are either explicitly or implicitly taught to children when they learn characters. For example, one way to teach children to learn characters, used by some parents and in some schools in mainland China, is to group together characters with the same phonetic (or semantic) radicals and ask children to pay special attention to the structure and composition of these characters. Also, since a common way for Chinese dictionaries to arrange characters is to group characters according to their orthographic structure and common components (usually semantic radicals) and to use these components as indexes, school children and adult readers have to decompose characters and use their critical component a searching cues when they use dictionaries.

All these properties make phonetic radicals very salient orthographic and functional units in complex characters. Decomposing such units from visual input and activating their corresponding phonological and semantic properties in the lexicon thus becomes not only natural but also mandatory. The parallel processing of whole characters and sublexical radicals appears not only in skilled reading, but also in the early stage of learning.

REFERENCES

Cheng, C.M. (1992). Lexical access in Chinese: Evidence from automatic activation of phonological information. In H.-C. Chen & O.J.L. Tzeng (Eds), *Language processing in Chinese*, pp.67–91. Amsterdam: North-Holland.

Coltheart, M., Curtis, B., Atkins, P., & Haller, M. (1993). Models of reading aloud: Dual-route and parallel-distribution-processing approaches. *Psychological Review*, *100*, 589–608.

Fan, K.Y., Gao, J.Y., & Ao, X.P. (1984). Pronunciation principles of the Chinese character and alphabetic writing scripts. *Chinese Character Reform*, *3*, 23–27.

Fang, S.-P., Horng, R.-Y., & Tzeng, O. (1986). Consistency effects in the Chinese character and pseudo-character naming tasks. In H.S.R. Kao & R. Hoosain (Eds), *Linguistics, psychology, and the Chinese language*, pp.11–21. Hong Kong, China: Center of Asian Studies, University of Hong Kong.

Feldman, L.B., & Siok, W.T. (1999). Semantic radicals in phonetic compounds: Implications for visual character recognition in Chinese. In J. Wang, A. Inhoff, & H.-C. Chen (Eds), *Reading Chinese scripts: A cognitive analysis*, pp.19–35. Mahwah, NJ: Lawrence Erlbaum Associates Inc.

Flores d'Arcais, G.B., Saito, H., & Kawakami, M. (1995). Phonological and semantic activation in reading Kanji characters. *Journal of Experimental Psychology: Learning, Memory, and Cognition*, *21*, 34–42.

Hue, C.-W. (1992). Recognition processes in character naming, H.-C. Chen & O.J.L. Tzeng (Eds), *Language processing in Chinese*, pp.93–107. Amsterdam: North-Holland.

Institute of Language Teaching and Research (1986). *A frequency dictionary of Modern Chinese*. Beijing: Beijing Language Institute Press.

Li, D. (1993). *A study of Chinese characters*. Beijing: Peking University Press.

Li, Y., & Kang, J. (1993). A statistic analysis of phonetic radicals in Modern Chinese picto-phonetic characters. In *Information analyses of Modern Chinese characters*, pp.29–36. Shanghai: Shanghai Education Press.

Peng, D., Yang, H., & Cheng, Y. (1994). Consistency and phonetic-independency effects in naming tasks of Chinese phonograms. In Q. Jing, H. Zhang, & D. Peng (Eds), *Information processing of the Chinese language*, pp.26–41. Beijing: Beijing Normal University Press.

Perfetti, C.A., & Zhang, S. (1991). Phonological processes in reading Chinese words. *Journal of Experimental Psychology: Learning, Memory, and Cognition*, *17*, 633–643.

Plaut, D.C., McClelland, J.L., Seidenberg, M.S., & Patterson, K.E. (1996). Understanding normal and impaired word reading: Computational principles in quasi-regular domains. *Psychological Review*, *103*, 56–115.

Sandra, D. (1990). On the representation and processing of compound words: Automatic access to constituent morphemes does not occur. *Quarterly Journal of Experimental Psychology*, *42A*, 529–567.

Seidenberg, M.S. (1985). The time course of phonological code activation in two writing systems. *Cognition*, *19*, 1–30.

Seidenberg, M.S., & McClelland, J.L. (1989). A distributed, developmental model of visual word recognition and naming. *Psychological Review*, *96*, 523–568.

Shu, H., & Wu, N. (1996). *The regularity and consistency effects in children's reading of Chinese characters.* Unpublished manuscript, Department of Psychology, Beijing Normal University, Beijing, China.

Shu, H., Wu, N., Zheng, X., & Zhou, X. (1998). Children's learning of Chinese characters: A corpus analysis. *Applied Linguistics, 2*, 63–68.

Shu, H., & Zheng, H. (1996). Children's awareness of phonological cues in Chinese characters. *Acta Psychologica Sinica, 3*, 227–233.

Shu, H., Zhou, X., & Wu, N. (in press). Utilizing phonological cues in Chinese characters: A developmental study. *Acta Psychologica Sinica.*

Taft, M., & Zhu, X. (1997). Submorphemic processing in reading Chinese. *Journal of Experimental Psychology: Learning, memory, and Cognition, 23*, 761–775.

Wu, N. (1998). *The nature and development of sublexical processing in Chinese character recognition.* Unpublished Master dissertation, Beijing Normal University, Beijing, China.

Yang, H., & Peng, D.L. (1997). The learning and naming of Chinese characters of elementary school children. In H.-C. Chen (Ed.), *Cognitive processing of Chinese and related Asian languages*, pp.323–346. Hong Kong: The Chinese University Press.

Yin, B., & Rohsenow, J.S. (1994). *Modern Chinese characters.* Beijing: Sinolingua.

Zhou, X. (1994). *Sub-lexical processing in reading Chinese.* Paper presented at the Inaugural Asian-Australian Workshop on Cognitive Processing of Asian Languages, Sydney, Australia.

Zhou, X., Lu, X., & Shu, H. (in press). The nature of sublexical processing in reading Chinese: Phonological activation of semantic radicals. *Acta Psychologica Sinica.*

Zhou, X., & Marslen-Wilson, W. (1999a). Sublexical processing in reading Chinese. In J. Wang, A. Inhoff, & H.-C. Chen (Eds), *Reading Chinese script: A cognitive analysis*, pp.37–63. Mahwah, NJ: Lawrence Erlbaum Associates Inc.

Zhou, X., & Marslen-Wilson, W. (1999b). The nature of sublexical processing in reading Chinese characters. *Journal of Experimental Psychology: Learning, Memory, and Cognition, 25*, 1–19.

Zhou, X. & Marslen-Wilson, W. (in press). The relative time course of semantic and phonological activation in reading Chinese. *Journal of Experimental Psychology: Learning, Memory, and Cognition.*

Zhou, X., Wu, N., & Shu, H. (1998). The relative time course of semantic and phonological activation in reading Chinese: Evidence from child development. *Psychological Sciences, 21*, 498–501.

Zwitserlood, P. (1994). The role of semantic transparency in the processing and representation of Dutch compounds. *Langauge and Cognitive Processes, 9*, 341–368.

LANGUAGE AND COGNITIVE PROCESSES, 1999, *14* (5/6), 525–565

Morphology, Orthography, and Phonology in Reading Chinese Compound Words

Xiaolin Zhou
Cambridge University and Peking University

William Marslen-Wilson
MRC Cognition and Brain Sciences Unit

Marcus Taft
University of New South Wales

Hua Shu
Beijing Normal University

The interaction between morphological, orthographic, and phonological information in reading Chinese compound words was investigated in five sets of experiments, using both masked priming and visual-visual priming lexical decision tasks. Words sharing common morphemes were consistently found to facilitate each other, although the priming effects were modulated by spatial overlap of orthographic forms in masked priming. Priming effects were also found for words having homographic-homophonic characters, but the effect tended to be inhibitory when the SOA between primes and targets was long and when the competing morphemes corresponding to the characters were at the initial constituent position of primes and targets.

The research reported here was supported in part by a grant from UK Economic and Social Research Council to William Marslen-Wilson and Xiaolin Zhou and in part by a grant from China National Natural Science Foundation to Xiaolin Zhou. Most of the data has been presented at the 7th International Conference on the Cognitive Processing of Chinese and other Asian Languages (Hong Kong, December 1995). The trip to the conference was partially funded by the Tregaskis Bequest of London University. We thank Yanchao Bi and other students at the Cognitive Laboratories of Beijing Normal University for helping us test subjects in Beijing. We also thank H.-C. Chen, Joe Devlin, and Kevin Miller for their comments on an earlier version of this paper.

Requests for reprints should be addressed to Xiaolin Zhou, Department of Experimental Psychology, Cambridge University, Cambridge CB2 3EB, UK. Email: xz104@cam.ac.uk

Priming effects between words having homographic but non-homophonic characters were more inhibitory, compared with effects between words having homographic-homophonic characters. Words having orthographically different homophonic morphemes did not prime each other throughout the experiments. The results were discussed in terms of how lexical representations incorporate morphological structure and how morphological, orthographic, and phonological information interacts in constraining semantic activation of constituent morphemes and compound words.

INTRODUCTION

Most Chinese words are compound words, composed of two or more constituent morphemes. According to the Institute of Language Teaching and Research (1986), compound words are over 70% of all words used in Chinese. A crucial issue in the study of lexical processing of Chinese is therefore how compound words are represented in the mental lexicon and how their lexical knowledge is accessed in visual or spoken word recognition. In recent years, there have been several studies of the role of morphological structure in lexical representation and processing of Chinese compound words (Taft & Zhu, 1995; Zhang & Peng, 1992; Zhou & Marslen-Wilson, 1994, 1995), and many studies of phonological and orthographic activation in reading Chinese single-character words (Chen, Cheung, & Flores d'Arcais, 1995; Leck, Weekes, & Chen, 1995; Perfetti & Zhang, 1991, 1995; Zhou, 1997; Zhou & Marslen-Wilson, 1999b in press a, b). Few studies, however, have tried to combine the two lines of approaches and to investigate how morphological, orthographic, phonological, and semantic information interacts in lexical processing of compound words. The main purpose of this research was therefore to fill in this gap. Specifically, we examined how lexical processing in reading Chinese compound words is constrained by morphological processing of their constituent morphemes and to what extent orthographic and phonological properties of constituent morphemes interact with morphemic processing and semantic activation of whole words.

In investigating lexical representation and morphological processing, it is essential to distinguish different types of morphological process, in particular between inflectional, derivational, and compounding procedures. Although the linguistic boundaries between these different types of word-formation process are sometimes blurred (Bybee, 1985), there are nonetheless potentially significant differences in the mental representation and processing of each type of complex word. The term "morphological processing" is being used here specifically in relation to the processing (and representation) of compound words and, perhaps more importantly, to the form and semantic processing of their constituent morphemes.

Further studies are needed to examine whether the arguments and the generic representation model proposed below for compound words can be applied to other types of polymorphemic words.

MORPHOLOGICAL AND PHONOLOGICAL PROCESSING IN CHINESE

In Mandarin Chinese, a morpheme usually corresponds to a syllable in spoken form and to a character in written form. Because the number of syllables used in the language is limited to about 1300 whereas the number of commonly used morphemes is over 5000, homophonic morphemes are the rule rather than the exception in the language.[1] However, such ambiguity rarely exists for written morphemes. With a few exceptions, each morpheme is written as a specific character, corresponding to a specific syllable. The homophonic morphemes, unlike their counterparts in English, may have no orthographic similarities at all. Occasionally, different morphemes may correspond to the same character, with the same or different pronunciations.

Morphemes used as constituents in compounds are usually words by themselves, although there are also bound morphemes in the language. There are also a few disyllabic monomorphemic words that are either descendants of Classic Chinese or loan words from other languages. The loan words follow the same phonotactic rules (e.g., having lexical tones) as other Chinese words and usually have fixed written forms. The phonological forms of compound words are usually the simple concatenations of the syllables corresponding to their constituent morphemes, although under certain circumstances the tone of one constituent can be altered due to the influence of the neighbouring tone. The orthographic forms of compound words or disyllabic, two-character monomorphemic words are always the concatenations of the orthographic forms (i.e., characters) of their constituents. In both orthographic and phonological forms, there are clear clues to the boundaries between constituents of Chinese two-character words.

The few previous studies on morphological processing in Chinese addressed the issue of how compound words are represented in the lexicon. Zhang and Peng (1992) found that both word and character (morpheme) frequencies affect lexical decision times to visually presented compounds. In auditory word recognition, Zhou and Marslen-Wilson

[1] Syllables with the same segmental elements but different tones are treated as different syllables. Tones are used to differentiate between lexical items. If tones are not counted, there are only about 400 syllables in Mandarin Chinese. The four tones are represented by numbers in parentheses in this paper.

(1994) observed similar word and morpheme frequency effects, together with a syllable frequency (i.e., cumulative frequency of homophonic morphemes) effect. These findings, however, led the authors to suggest different models of lexical representation. While Zhang and Peng (1992) maintained a decomposed lexical structure in which compound words are represented in terms of their constituent morphemes, Zhou and Marslen-Wilson (1994, 1995) proposed a multi-level representational model which distinguished a syllabic (phonological) layer, a morphemic layer, and a whole word layer. The morphological structure of compound words is represented or marked at all the levels, with constituent morphemes linking to whole word representations through excitatory connections, and homophonic morphemes linking to each other through inhibitory connections. A similar kind of structure was also suggested by Taft and Zhu (1995, 1997) to account for lexical processing in reading compound words.

In an auditory-auditory priming study, Zhou and Marslen-Wilson (1995) systematically manipulated morphological and phonological relations between primes and targets and the constituent positions of related morphemes in primes and targets. While consistent facilitatory priming effects were found for words sharing common morphemes, the priming effects between words having homophonic morphemes could be either inhibitory, facilitatory, or null, depending on the constituent positions of critical morphemes in primes and targets (see also Chen & Cutler, 1997). These positional priming effects between words having homophomic morphemes are difficult to explain in a lexical representation model with a single layer of morphemic representation. The multi-level morphological representation model, on the other hand, fits the data well. The complicated pattern of priming effects between words having homophonic morphemes was interpreted as the result of interactions between homophonic morphemes and between morpheme- and word-level representations in the time course of lexical activation.

However, the multi-level lexical representation model was not explicit about (a) what the nature of morphemic and whole word representations is and (b) whether it is necessary to arrange morpheme and word representations in a hierarchy. Zhou and Marslen-Wilson (1997) suggested that morpheme and whole-word representations in the multi-level representation model are semantic in nature. They are semantic representations corresponding to constituent morphemes and whole words. It follows that semantic representations for morphemes and whole words can be arranged at the same level, with phonological representations (i.e., syllables) connecting to both of them. It also follows that semantic representations of words and morphemes can be seen as composed of semantic features, with representations for words and representations for their constituent morphemes sharing some of their features, depending on semantic compositionality (transparency) of compound words (Zwitserlood, 1994).

The modified model can easily incorporate orthographic representations (Zhou & Marslen-Wilson, 1999c). It can be envisaged that there are orthographic representations for constituent morphemes that connect directly to their phonological and semantic representations, as well as to semantic representations of compound words containing these morphemes. Figure 1 illustrates prototypical orthographic (O), phonological (P), and semantic (S) representations and connections between them for a compound word (O1O2, such as *bathroom* or *butterfly*). Both compound words and their constituents are represented at orthographic, phonological, and semantic levels. However, the representations for compound words are not independent from the representations for the constituent morphemes. At orthographic, phonological and semantic levels, the representations for compound words have much overlap with the representations for morphemes. In most cases, the orthographic and phonological representations of compound words are simply concatenations of the forms of their constituent morphemes. There are no separate representations at these levels for whole words. Similarly at the semantic

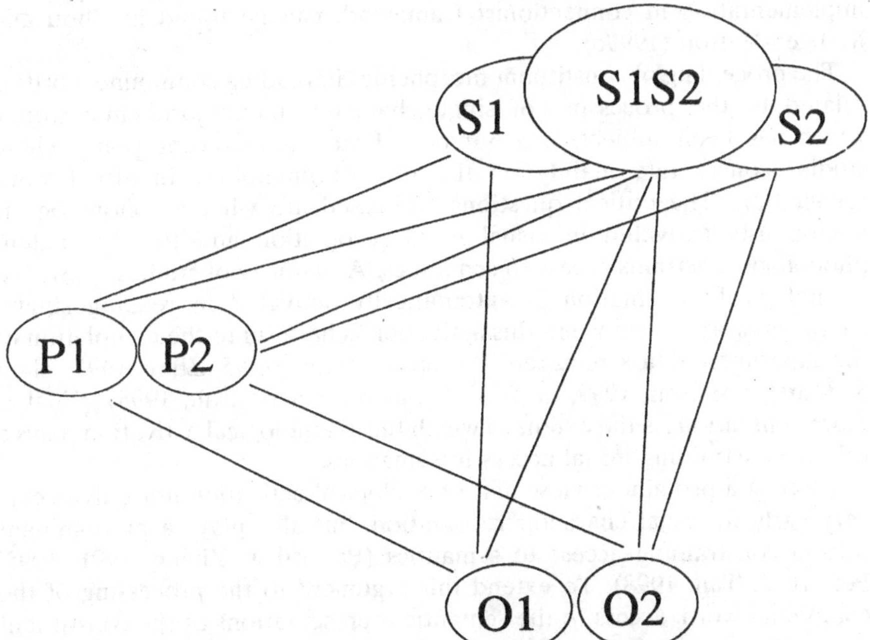

FIG. 1. A prototypical model of lexical representation of compound words.

level, compound words may share many semantic features with constituent morphemes. The degree of overlap reflects the semantic transparency of compound words. Representations at different levels are excitatorily connected, so that activation spreads bidirectionally between them.

Clearly, the schematic model illustrated in Fig. 1 assumes triangular relations between orthography, phonology, and semantics (Seidenberg & McClelland, 1989), where activation can spread either directly between two types of representations or indirectly via a third type of representation. In visual word recognition, access to semantics could be through direct links between orthographic and semantic representations and through activation of phonological representations. Moreover, this model assumes that the morphological structure of Chinese compound words is explicitly used to guide the mapping of visual input onto lexical representations. In projecting onto the lexicon, the visual input of a compound word is decomposed into smaller units, which activate orthographic (i.e., character) and phonological (i.e., syllable) representations of constituent morphemes, and semantic representations of both morphemes and the whole word. Morphological effects in lexical processing of compound words come from the interaction between form and meaning of constituent morphemes and the interaction between constituent morphemes and whole words. A more detailed discussion of this model and its possible implementation in connectionist framework can be found in Zhou and Marslen-Wilson (1999c).

The processing of constituent morphemes in reading compound words is related to the processing of single-character, monomorphemic words, which has been subject to a number of studies in recent years. These studies concentrate mainly on the role of phonology in visual word recognition. The critical questions addressed are whether phonology is mandatorily activated in visual word recognition and to what extent phonology constrains access to semantics. A majority of studies show that phonological information is automatically activated in reading single-character words, even when this activation is harmful to the completion of the experimental task required (Perfetti & Zhang, 1995; Zhou, 1997; Zhou & Marslen-Wilson, 1999, in press a; but see Chen et al., 1995). What is more contentious is the extent to which this phonological activation plays a role in constraining initial access to semantics.

There is a prominent view that phonological activation not only occurs very early in visual character recognition, but also plays a predominant role in constraining access to semantics (Perfetti & Zhang, 1991, 1995; Perfetti & Tan, 1998). To extend this argument to the processing of the compound word, access to the semantic representations of the constituent morphemes and of the whole word could be assumed to be mainly mediated by the phonological activation of constituent syllables (and information about the co-occurrence of these syllables, see Zhou & Marslen-Wilson, 1999a). Direct access from orthography to semantics could play at most a minor role. One problem with this strong phonological view, however, is that most of the supporting experimental evidence, which is mainly based on the comparison of the relative time course of phonological and semantic activation in reading characters, proves to be difficult to replicate (see, for example, Chen & Shu, 1997; Zhou & Marslen-Wilson, in press a, b).

Zhou and Marslen-Wilson (in press a, b) promoted an interactive view according to which access to semantics in reading Chinese is constrained by both orthography and phonology operating in interaction with each other. Both direct computation from orthography to semantics and mediation through phonological activation and the interaction between the two routes play roles in the multiple constraint-satisfaction process of accessing semantics in skilled reading. Based on evidence from studies using different experimental paradigms tapping directly into semantic activation, including semantic categorisation (Chen et al., 1995; Leck et al., 1995; Sakuma, Sasanuma, Tatsumi, & Masaki, 1998; Wydell, Patterson, & Humphreys, 1993), semantic judgment (Xu, Pollatsek, & Potter, 1999; Zhou, Pollatsek, & Marslen-Wilson, 1999), and phonologically mediated semantic priming (Zhou, 1997; Zhou & Marslen-Wilson, in press b), Zhou and his colleagues further argued that it is orthography, rather than phonology, that plays a relatively more important role in determining semantic activation in reading Chinese.

In this study, we investigated whether this interactive view applies to visual recognition of two-character, two-syllable compound words. We used masked and visual-visual priming lexical decision tasks and manipulated systematically the morphological, orthographic, and phonological relations between primes and targets. The stimulus onset asynchrony (SOA) between primes and targets was also manipulated to track the time course of orthographic and phonological activation and their constraints on semantic activation. Masked and visual-visual priming and the SOA between primes and targets were manipulated as a between-subject factor, with each sub-experiment for each SOA condition.

The lexical decision task was used to focus participants more on semantic processing than processing of orthographic or phonological forms of compound words. The notion of wordhood can be ambiguous for some Chinese compound words. Subjects in this study were explicitly instructed that real words were those used in the language and had relatively fixed meanings while non-words were those not used in the language and had no fixed or commonly accepted meanings. Because nonwords were composed of meaningful characters, both words and nonwords could activate orthographic and phonological forms and indeed morphemic meanings of their constituent morphemes. Although theoretically the activation of co-occurrence information between constituent orthographic forms or syllables could be used to discriminate real words from nonword, such information by itself does not seem to be used efficiently in lexical decision (see Zhou & Marslen-Wilson, 1999a). Consequently lexical decision to compound words is biased towards the use of semantic information of whole words.

EXPERIMENT 1

Experiment 1 and the following Experiments 2 and 3 were essentially the visual version of the auditory-auditory priming experiments reported in Zhou and Marslen-Wilson (1995). In the present experiments, primes and targets either shared a common morpheme, or had homophonic-homographic morphemes, or had orthographically different homophonic morphemes. The crucial questions for these experiments were, firstly, whether morphological relations between primes and targets influence the processing of target compound words; secondly, whether morphological effects on lexical processing can be separated from the influences of orthographic and phonological forms of constituent morphemes, and thirdly, how orthographic and phonological processing of constituent morphemes interacts with morphological processing and with access to semantics of compound words.

Table 1 presents the design and sample stimuli of Experiment 1. A target word (e.g., 华贵 hua[2] gui[4], *luxurious*) was preceded by four types of primes. The first was a morphological prime (e.g., 华丽 hua[2] li[4], *magnificent*) which shared the initial constituent morpheme with the target. The shared morpheme exhibited the same orthographic and phonological form in the two compounds. The second type was a character prime (e.g., 华侨 hua[2] qiao[2], *overseas Chinese*) whose initial morpheme had the same orthographic and phonological forms with the initial morpheme of the target. However, the same character represented two different morphemes, i.e., having different morphemic meanings, in the prime and target (e.g., 华 means "magnificent" in 华贵 hua[2] gui[4], *luxurious*, and "Chinese" in 华侨 hua[2] qiao[2], *overseas Chinese*). The

TABLE 1
Design and Sample Stimuli for Experiment 1

MORPH	*CHAR*	*HOM*	*CON*	*TARGET*
华丽 hua(2) li(4) *magnificent*	华侨 hua(2) qiao(2) *overseas Chinese*	滑翔 hua(2) xiang(2) *glide*	完整 wan(2) zheng(3) *intact*	华贵 hua(2) gui(4) *luxurious*

initial morpheme of the third type of prime (e.g., 滑翔 hua[2] xiang[2], *glide*) was homophonic to the initial morpheme of the target. These homophonic morphemes, however, had different orthographic forms and different morphemic meanings. Finally, the same target was also preceded by a morphologically, semantically, orthographically and phonologically unrelated compound word (e.g., 完整 wan[2] zheng[3], *intact*).

There were at least two reasons for predicting a facilitatory priming effect between words sharing initial morphemes. Firstly, repeated access to morphemes shared between primes and targets, i.e., their orthographic and phonological forms and morphemic meaning, should facilitate the form and semantic activation of the targets. Secondly, primes and targets as wholes were semantically related as well, in the same way as words sharing no common morphemes (e.g., 医生 yi[1] sheng[1], *doctor*; and 护士 hu[4] shi[4], *nurse*). For words having homographic and homophonic morphemes (e.g., 华侨 hua(2) qiao(2), *overseas Chinese* and 华贵 hua(2) gui(4), *luxurious*), one would normally predict an inhibitory effect between them in visual-visual priming. The visual input of the critical character in a prime should activate two different morphemic meanings, one corresponding to the morpheme in the prime and one corresponding to the morpheme in the target. There should be competition between the activation of these morphemic meanings, with the one used in the prime taking the upper hand. When the target is presented, the critical morphemic meaning used in the prime is initially activated further. It takes time for the morphemic meaning used in the target to overcome this competition and to activate semantics of the whole word (Laudanna, Bedecker, & Caramazza, 1989, 1992; Zhou & Marslen-Wilson, 1995). On the other hand, it was not clear what kind of effects we would expect for masked priming. Words sharing orthographic properties tend to facilitate each other in this paradigm (e.g., Shen & Forster, this issue), but competition between morphemic meanings would reduce this facilitatory effect.

The prediction for the priming effect between words having orthographically different homophonic morphemes (e.g., 滑翔 hua[2] xiang[2], *glide*; and 华贵 hua[2] gui[4], *luxurious*) depends crucially on whether phonological mediation is the predominant route for accessing semantics. If phonology plays a predominant role in lexical processing of Chinese, we should expect to find a facilitatory effect in processing the compound target. At least at a short SOA, the processing of the initial morpheme of the prime should activate the semantic representation of the initial homophonic morpheme of the target. Because constituent morphemes share many semantic properties with the whole compounds, this morphemic semantic activation should lead to a facilitatory effect in lexical decision to the target. On the other hand, if phonological activation by itself has limited effects on semantic activation (Zhou, 1997; Zhou &

Marslen-Wilson, in press a, b), pre-activating a constituent syllable of the target may have no significant influence on lexical processing of the target.

Method

Design and Materials

Forty compound words were selected as targets, completed with the four types of primes illustrated in Table 1. The four priming conditions were labelled respectively as MORPH (for morphological priming), CHAR (for character priming), HOM (for homophonic or phonological priming), and CON (for control priming). Reaction times to targets in the CON condition provided baselines for measuring priming effects in other conditions. MORPH primes were not only morphologically but also semantically related to the target words, as indicated in a semantic relatedness judgement pretest. The average semantic relatedness between these words was 6.4 on a 9-point scale, where 1 represented "completely unrelated" and 9 "highly related". CHAR, HOM and CON primes were not semantically related to the targets. The average frequencies were 22, 23, 19, 20 per million respectively for the four types of primes. The average frequency of targets was 47 per million.

In addition to the critical word design, a nonword design was also created. Not only did the lexical decision task require nonword foils, but also the nonword stimuli could be organised to act as the counterpart of the word design and to provide additional information concerning the extensiveness of morphemic or form priming and strategic contribution to priming effects. The nonword design here mirrored the word design. In the BASE condition, a nonword target (i.e., 掩该 yan[3] gai[1]) was preceded by its base word (e.g., 掩盖 yan[3] gai[4], *conceal*) from which the nonword was derived. The creation of nonword targets were carried out by replacing the second constituents of BASE primes with characters sharing segmental templates or rhyming parts with the base characters. In the MORPH condition, the same nonword target was preceded by a compound word sharing the initial morpheme with the BASE prime (e.g., 掩护 yan[3] hu[4], *cover*). In the HOM condition, the initial morpheme of the prime (e.g., 演变 yan[3] bian[4], *evolve*) was homophonic to, but orthographically different from the initial morpheme of the BASE prime and nonword target. Finally, the nonword target was also preceded by an unrelated word (e.g., 填补 tian[2] bu[3], *fill*). Note, nonword targets here and other nonword fillers were all composed of meaningful morphemes.

There were 40 nonword targets, each having the four types of primes. Fifty-four word-word pairs and 54 word-nonword pairs were also used as fillers in the experiment. The primes and targets in these pairs were neither semantically nor orthographically nor phonologically related. None of the syllables or characters in the filler primes and targets had been used in the critical primes and targets. Twenty prime-target practice pairs, which had the same compositions as formal test items, were also selected.

A Latin square design was used to assign critical primes and their targets to four counter-balanced test versions. In each version, there were ten primes from each of the four priming conditions for the critical word targets, and ten primes for each of the four priming conditions for the critical nonword targets. The same 108 filler prime-target pairs were used in the four test versions. A single pseudo-random order was used to arrange prime-target pairs, so that the same targets appeared at the same positions across the four test versions. The only difference between versions was that the primes for a particular critical word or nonword target were different. Not more than four consecutively presented targets were words or nonwords.

Procedure

All the stimuli were generated using a computer word processing program and captured as pictures on the screen by a snapshot program. Each word or nonword was excised and stored as an image file on a computer hard disk. Because primes and targets sometimes shared the same characters, they were created respectively in *kaiti* and *songti* fonts to avoid the abnormality of the shared characters being fixed on the computer screen in visual presentation. A target was about 3.4 × 5.4 cm in size and the prime was slightly smaller.

The presentation of stimuli to subjects and the recording of reaction times and response errors were controlled by the experimental software DMASTR, developed by Ken and Jonathan Forster. In visual-visual priming, an eye fixation signal ("+") was first presented at the centre of the screen for 300 ms, followed by a 300 ms blank interval. A prime was then presented either for 57 ms or for 200 ms, depending on the SOA, followed immediately by the corresponding target, which was presented for 400 ms. Both primes and targets were presented at the centre of the screen, with targets overwriting primes. In masked priming, a pattern mask, composed of lines and with a similar size to a compound word, were presented at the centre of screen for 300 ms, followed immediately by a prime, which was presented for 57 ms. The target was then presented for 400 ms. In this situation, subjects could not report the prime and most of them were not even aware of the presence of the prime. There was a 3-s interval between the disappearance of the last target and the appearance of the next eye fixation signal or the pattern mask.

Subjects were seated in a quiet room in groups of three or less, about 60 cm away from the screen. They were told to decide as quickly and as accurately as possible, by pressing "yes" and "no" buttons on the response boxes in front of them, whether each target was a real word or not. The dominant hand was used for the "yes" keys. Each subject saw first a list of 20 prime-target practice items. There was a break after practice and a break in the middle of the main test session. The first three pairs after each break were always fillers. The complete test session for each subject was less than 20 minutes.

Subjects

A total of 137 native speakers of Mandarin Chinese were tested, 52 in masked priming, 45 in visual-visual priming with SOA of 57 ms, and 40 in visual-visual priming with SOA of 200 ms. Each test version had roughly equal number of subjects. Subjects in masked priming and in visual-visual priming with SOA of 200 ms were either students or visiting scholars at universities in London while subjects in visual-visual priming with SOA of 57 ms were undergraduate students at Beijing Normal University. They all were paid for their participation.

Results

Three words in masked priming, four words in visual-visual priming with SOA of 57 ms, and two words in visual-visual priming with SOA of 200 ms were deleted from analyses because over 50% of responses to these items in one or more test versions were incorrect. Mean reaction times, based on correct responses and without trimming, and percentages of response error were then computed for each subject and each item. Table 2 reports mean reaction times and error percentages to critical word targets in both masked and visual-visual priming.[2] Priming effects for word targets, as assessed against control baselines, are also plotted in Fig. 2. Analyses of variance were performed on reaction times and error rates in overall analyses with sub-experiment as a between-subject factor and prime type as a within-subject factor having four levels (MORPH, CHAR, HOM, and CON). Only items included in all sub-experiments were entered into item tests. Separate analyses were also conducted for different priming conditions.

There was a significant main effect of sub-experiment in the analyses of reaction time [$F_1(2,134) = 3.82$, $P < .05$, $F_2(2,70) = 26.74$, $P < .001$], indicating that subjects in different sub-experiments were not equally fast. More importantly, the main effect of prime type was highly significant

[2] No significant differences between priming conditions in the nonword design were found in this and the following experiments. To save space, we do not report the nonword data in this paper.

TABLE 2
Mean Reaction Times (ms) and Error Percentages in Experiment 1

	MORPH	*CHAR*	*HOM*	*CON*
Masked	563	583	611	609
	(5.1)	(9.1)	(10.1)	(8.1)
SOA 57 ms	575	595	628	618
	(5.8)	(7.6)	(9.3)	(6.2)
SOA 200 ms	606	648	637	644
	(3.7)	(7.1)	(6.8)	(7.1)

[$F_1(3{,}402) = 42.038$, $P < .001$, $F_2(3{,}105) = 16.63$, $P < .001$]. Post hoc Newman–Keuls tests showed that the mean reaction times for MORPH primes (580 ms) and CHAR primes (608 ms) were all significantly shorter ($P < .01$ or $.05$) than the times for HOM primes (625 ms) and CON primes (623 ms). Moreover, while the 28 ms difference between MORPH primes and CHAR primes was significant ($P < .01$), the 2 ms difference between HOM and CON primes was not ($P > .1$), indicating that words having orthographically different homophonic morphemes did not prime each other. The interaction between prime type and sub-experiment was

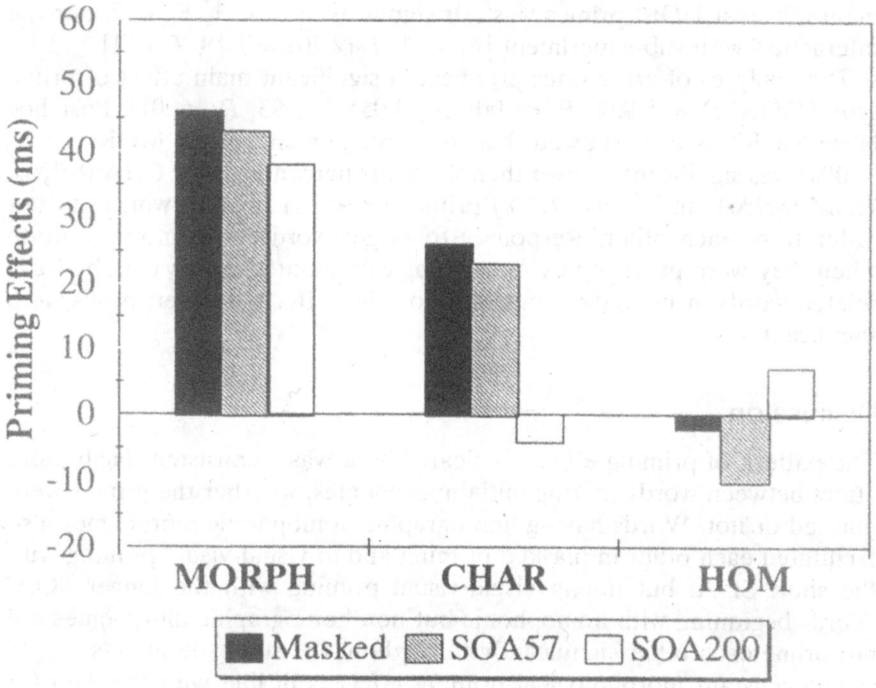

FIG. 2. Priming effects (ms) in Experiment 1.

significant by subjects [$F_1(6,402) = 2.99$, $P < .01$], and marginally significant by items [$F_1(6,210) = 2.08$,$.05 < P < .1$], suggesting that the patterns of priming effects were not uniform across sub-experiments. Figure 2 suggests that this interaction was mainly due to the change of priming direction of CHAR primes.

Detailed analyses of priming effects, as assessed against control priming conditions, were conducted respectively for MORPH, CHAR, and HOM primes. The main effect of morphological priming was highly significant [$F_1(1,134) = 80.73$, $P < .001$, $F_2(1,35) = 37.40$, $P < .001$]. This effect did not vary significantly across sub-experiments, as its interaction with sub-experiment was not significant [$F_1 < 1$, $F_2 < 1$]. The priming effect of CHAR primes was significant [$F_1(1,134) = 8.38$, $P < .01$, $F_2(1,35) = 4.29$, $P < .05$], and interacted with sub-experiment [$F_1(2,134) = 4.26$, $P < .05$, $F_2(2,70) = 2.52$, $.05 < P < .1$], indicating that CHAR primes did not produce the same pattern of priming effects across sub-experiments. In planned tests, the 26 ms facilitatory effect in masked priming was significant [$t_1(51) = 3.24$, $P < .01$, $t_2(35) = 3.46$, $P < .01$], as was the 23 ms effect in visual-visual priming with SOA of 57 ms [$t_1(44) = 2.97$, $P < .01$, $t_2(35) = 2.02$, $.05 < P < .01$. But the 4 ms inhibitory effect in visual-visual priming with SOA of 200 ms was not significant, [$t_1 < 1$, $t_2 < 1$]. The main effect of HOM primes was not significant [$F_1 < 1$, $F_2 < 2$, nor the interaction with sub-experiment [$F_1 < 1$, $F_2(2,70) = 1.18$, $P < 1$].

The analyses of error rates produced a significant main effect of prime type [$F_1(3,402) = 5.922$, $P < .001$, $F_2(3,05) = 3.93$, $P < .01$]. Post hoc Newman–Keuls tests showed that the error percentage for MOR primes (5.0%) was significantly lower than the error percentages for CHA (8.2%), HOM (8.9%), and CON (7.3%) primes ($P < .01$ or .05), which did not differ from each other. Responses to target words were more accurate when they were preceded by morphologically related words than by form related words or unrelated controls. No other effects or interactions were significant.

Discussion

The pattern of priming effects is clear. There was a consistent facilitatory effect between words sharing initial morphemes, whether the primes were masked or not. Words having homographic-homophonic morphemes also facilitated each other in masked priming and in visual-visual priming with the short SOA, but not in visual-visual priming with the longer SOA. Words beginning with homophonic but non-homographic morphemes did not prime each other significantly throughout the sub-experiments.

The constant morphological priming effect is in line with the data for auditory priming for Chinese compound words (Zhou & Marslen-Wilson,

1995). This effect can be interpreted as indicating that compound words are represented in the lexicon as individual morphemes and repeated access to the same morphemes induces the priming effect for target words. The model illustrated in Fig. 1, however, provides us with a more explicit way to account for the priming effect—in terms of activation of semantic (and form) properties of compound words and their constituent morphemes. In this semantic account, the activation of constituent orthographic representations of primes leads to the activation of semantic representations of both the whole words and the initial morphemes. The visual input of the initial characters of targets maps onto the same constituent orthographic and phonological representations, activating further the constituent semantic representations. Because semantic representations of target words share many properties with their constituent morphemes, the processing of target words is thus facilitated. Primes and targets could also share some semantic properties that were not shared with the critical constituent morphemes and these shared properties contributed to the priming effect of MORPH primes as well.[3] We will try to tear apart the morphological priming effect from the "pure" semantic effect in later experiments.

The variation in priming effects between words having homographic-homophonic morphemes can also be accommodated by the semantic account of morphological priming. The activation of orthographic and phonological representations of the initial morpheme of a CHAR prime spreads to all the morphemic semantic representations corresponding to this character. When the CHAR prime is masked or presented for a short time, there is little competition between semantic activation of the homographic-homophonic morphemes. Consequently the semantic representation of the target word, which shares many properties with its initial morpheme, is pre-activated. This semantic activation leads to the facilitatory effect in lexical decision. When the CHAR prime is presented for a relatively long time, however, strong competition seems to develop between the alternative semantic representations of the homographic-homophonic morphemes. Consequently the semantic representation of the initial morpheme of the target, and hence the semantic representation of the target, are not activated or even inhibited.

The absence of significant priming effects between words having orthographically different homophonic morphemes is inconsistent with the strong phonological mediation view of semantic activation. It is likely that the constituent phonological representations of the initial morphemes

[3] Occasionally the second constituent morphemes of MORPH primes and targets were semantically related. But we do not expect this casual semantic relation to have a significant contribution to the priming effects.

of HOM primes and targets were activated when the primes were presented.[4] However, this phonological activation by itself had little effect on the activation of morphemic semantic representations of the initial morphemes. The projection of visual input of the initial morphemes of targets onto the already activated morphemic phonological representations does not contribute much to the semantic activation of these initial morphemes and of the whole targets.

EXPERIMENT 2

Experiment 2 was essentially a replication of Experiment 1, but with the critical morphemes now at the second constituent position of both primes and targets. The purpose of this experiment was to collect converging evidence concerning morphological, orthographic and phonological processing of compound words. The empirical question was whether the pattern of priming effects in Experiment 1 was retained when the activation of critical morphemes in primes and target was more constrained by the processing of the initial morphemes of compound words.

In auditory-auditory priming, such a change of constituent position of critical morphemes in primes and targets resulted in different patterns of priming effects for words having homophonic morphemes (Chen & Cutler, 1997; Zhou & Marslen-Wilson, 1995). Facilitatory priming effects were found for words having homophonic morphemes at the second constituent position while inhibitory effects were found for words having such morphemes at the first constituent position. The positive effect was interpreted as due to the change of interactive relations between morphemic and whole word representations over time course of activation. The directional mapping of speech input onto the lexicon over time means that the processing of the initial morphemes in primes and targets provides a context to constrain the semantic activation of homophonic morphemes occurring in the second position. In the present visual priming experiments, however, the processing of constituent morphemes of compounds is much less directional, leaving little room for intra-word constraints

[4] When we run a naming version of Experiment 1, we found graded priming effects for MORPH, CHAR, and HOM primes. This naming experiment included all the critical stimuli and 94 pairs of unrelated word-word fillers. Forty subjects were tested, with the SOA of 100 ms between primes and targets. The mean naming latencies for the three types of primes and control primes were 555, 573, 595, and 610 ms respectively. All the differences between priming conditions were statistically significant. Thus, the phonological properties of constituent morphemes of compound words are activated, at least when the experimental task demands their activation.

between the first and second constituents. We therefore expect to observe a similar pattern of priming effects as in Experiment 1.

Method

Design and Materials

The experimental design was very similar to the one illustrated in Table 1, except that the critical morphemes were at the second constituent position. A target word (e.g., 简易 jian[3] yi[4], *simple*, *unsophisticated*, in which 易 means "easy") was preceded either by a word sharing the second constituent morpheme (e.g., 轻易 qing[1] yi[4], *easily*, *rashly*), by a word having a homographic-homophonic second constituent (e.g., 贸易 mao[4] yi[4], *trade*, in which 易 means "exchange"), by a word having an orthographically different homophonic second constituent (e.g. 压抑 ya[1] yi[4], *inhibit*, *constrained*), or by an unrelated word (e.g., 诬陷 wu[1] xian[4], *frame a case against*). There were 40 quartets of primes, which were matched on word frequency, with means of 14, 19, 16, and 18 per million respectively. The mean frequency of target words was 40 per million. The average semantic relatedness between MORPH primes and targets was 6.1 in the 9-point scale.

There was also a nonword design, similar to the one in Experiment 1. The second constituents of 40 nonword targets and their critical primes were related in a similar way as in the word design. A nonword target (e.g., 魂暗 hun[2] an[4]) was created by replacing the first constituent of a base word (e.g., 昏暗 hun[1] an[4], *dim*, *dusky*) with another character sharing the segmental template or rhyming part. The same nonword target was not only preceded by the base word, but also by a MORPH prime, a HOM prime, and a control prime, all selected in the same way as Experiment 1. There were 40 such nonword targets. Because critical primes had no significant influences on lexical decision to the nonword targets, the design and data are not reported in this paper.

Besides the critical stimuli, there were also 50 word-word and 50 word-nonword pairs in the experiment. These pairs were used as fillers and were not related. Another 20 word-word and word-nonword pairs were selected as practice items, with a similar composition as the formal stimuli. No syllables or characters were used twice unless it was intended in the critical designs. The creation of test versions, preparation of stimuli, and subject testing were conducted in the same way as Experiment 1.

Subjects

One hundred and forty-six undergraduate students at Beijing Normal University were tested, 50 in masked priming, 52 in visual-visual priming with SOA of 57 ms, and 44 in visual-visual priming with SOA of 200 ms. They were native speakers of Mandarin Chinese and were paid for their participation. Each test version of each sub-experiment had roughly equal numbers of subjects.

Results

In each sub-experiment, one target was deleted from the analyses because over half of subjects in one or more test versions made incorrect responses. One subject in masked priming was also excluded due to his high response error rate (over 30%). The mean reaction times and error percentages are reported in Table 3. Figure 3 also reports the priming effects for MORPH, CHAR and HOM primes, as assessed against their control primes.

Overall analyses were conducted, with prime type as a within-subject factor and sub-experiment as a between-subject factor. The main effect of prime type was highly significant [$F_1(3,426) = 62.81$, $P < .001$, $F_2(3,114) = 15.77$, $P < .001$]. Post hoc Newman–Keuls tests showed that the mean reaction time to target words was significantly shorter for MORPH primes (548 ms) than for CHAR primes (575 ms), HOM primes (589 ms), and control primes (594 ms) ($P < .01$). The mean reaction time for CHAR primes was also significantly shorter than the time for HOM primes ($P < .05$). In contrast, the difference between HOM primes and control primes was not significant ($P > .1$). The interaction between prime type and sub-experiment was significance by subjects [$F_1(6,426) = 2.71$, $P < .05$], although not by items, $F_2 < 1$.

Separate analyses were conducted respectively for MORPH, CHAR, and HOM priming effects, as assessed against control primes. For MORPH primes, the priming effect was highly significant [$F_1(142) = 156.77$, $P < .001$, $F_2(1,38) = 43.31$, $P < .001$]. Moreover, the interaction between priming effect and sub-experiment was not significant [$F_1(2,142) = 1.80$, $P > .1$, $F_2 < 1$], indicating that the morphological priming effect was essentially the same across three sub-experiments. The same pattern

TABLE 3
Mean Reaction Times (ms) and Error Percentages in Experiment 2

	MORPH	*CHAR*	*HOM*	*CON*
Masked	536 (3.4)	557 (5.1)	582 (5.0)	588 (6.7)
SOA 57 ms	554 (3.4)	586 (6.0)	604 (6.0)	603 (6.5)
SOA 200 ms	553 (0.7)	581 (4.7)	582 (4.2)	593 (5.1)

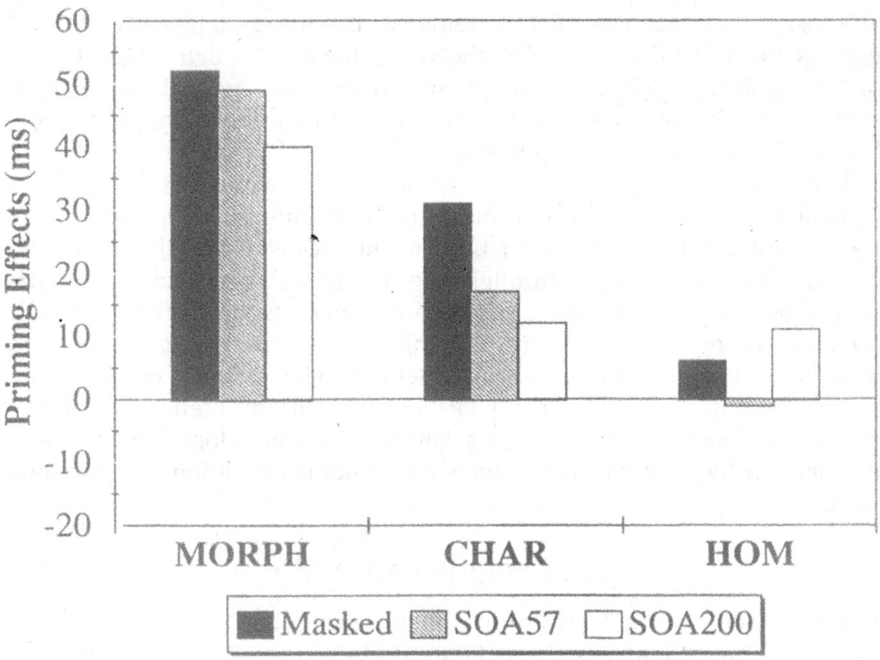

FIG. 3. Priming effects (ms) in Experiment 2.

was observed for CHAR primes. Here the priming effect was significant [$F_1(1,142) = 27.07$, $P < .001$, $F_2(1,38) = 4.30$, $P < .05$], but the interaction between priming effect and sub-experiment was not [$F_1(2,142) = 2.05$, $P >$ .1, $F_2(2,76) = 1.21$, $P < .1$]. No significant priming effect was found for HOM primes [$F_1(1,142) = 2.82$, $.05 < P < .1$, $F_2 < 1$], nor any interaction with sub-experiment ($F_1 < 1$, $F_2 < 2$).

In the analyses of error rates, the main effect of prime type was significant [$F_1(3,426) = 7.463$, $P < .001$, $F_2(3,114) = 4.99$, $P < .01$]. Post hoc tests showed this effect was mainly due to the significant differences between MOR condition (2.5%) and other conditions (5.3% for CHAR, 5.1% for HOM, and 6.2% for CON). The differences between the latter three conditions were not significant ($P > .1$). The main effect of prime type did not interact with sub-experiment ($F_1 < 1$, $F_2 < 1$).

Discussion

Clearly, the pattern of priming effects was very similar to the one in Experiment 1. In both masked priming and visual-visual priming, words sharing common morphemes facilitated each other. Words having homographic-homophonic morphemes also facilitated each other, although this effect was slightly reduced as subjects had more time to process the CHAR primes. On the other hand, although words having orthographically different homophonic morphemes tended to facilitate each other in masked priming and in visual-visual priming with the longer SOA, this effect was not significant.

The strong priming effect between words having common morphemes is consistent with the assumption that in reading Chinese compound words, the semantic representations of both whole words and their constituent morphemes are activated through constituent orthographic representations. The priming effect for CHAR primes suggests that both morphemic semantic representations corresponding to the critical characters were activated when the primes were presented. The absence of significant priming effects for words having orthographically different homophonic morphemes is consistent with the argument that phonology of constituent morphemes by itself has little effects on semantic activation of compound words.

EXPERIMENT 3

In Experiments 1 and 2, critical morphemes in primes and targets were at the same constituent positions. One consequence of this was that the critical morphemes had the same spatial positions in the presentation of primes and targets.[5] In Experiment 3, we put the critical morphemes in primes and targets at different spatial positions. Specifically, all the critical morphemes in primes were the second constituents and all the critical morphemes in targets were the first constituents of compounds. The critical question was whether the same pattern of priming effects as Experiments 1 and 2 would be observed here. If the significant priming effects for MORPH and CHAR primes in Experiments 1 and 2 were mainly due to semantic activation of the critical morphemes and of the whole-words, the change of spatial position of critical morphemes should not have drastic influence on the pattern of priming effects.

Method

Design and materials

The design was similar to Experiments 1 and 2 (see Table 1). A target word (e.g. 容忍 rong[2] ren[3], *tolerate*, in which 容 means "tolerate") was

[5] Another consequence was that the shared morphemes were likely to function in the same way as constituent morphemes (e.g., as the linguistic head of the compounds), even though we did not control the internal morphological relations between the initial and second constituent morphemes.

preceded by four types of primes: a MORPH prime (e.g., 宽容 kuan[1] and rong[2], *lenient*) which shared a common morpheme with the target; a CHAR prime (e.g., 笑容 xiao[4] rong[2], *smiling expression*, in which 容 means "appearance") which had a homographic-homophonic character with the target; a HOM prime (e.g., 繁荣 fan[2] rong[2]) whose second constituent was homophonic to, but orthographically different from the initial morpheme of the target; and an unrelated control prime. MORPH primes and targets were also semantically related, with an average point of 6.2 in the 9-point scale. The four types of primes were matched on frequence, with means of 14, 16, 14, and 16 per million respectively. The average frequency of targets was 30 per million.

As Experiments 1 and 2, there was also a nonword design, mirroring the word design. Nonword targets were preceded by BASE, MORPH, CHAR and CONT primes. Additional 55 word-word pairs and 55 word-nonword pairs were selected for use as fillers. Primes and targets here were neither orthographically, nor phonologically, nor semantically related. The creation of four test versions, preparation of stimuli, and test of subjects were conducted in the same way as Experiments 1 and 2.

Subjects

A total of 136 undergraduate students at Beijing Normal University were tested, 41 for masked priming, 55 for visual-visual priming with SOA of 57 ms, and 40 for visual-visual priming with SOA of 200 ms. They were native speakers of Mandarin Chinese and were not tested for Experiments 1 and 2.

Results

Three targets in masked priming, three in visual-visual priming with SOA of 57 ms, and two in visual-visual priming with SOA of 200 ms were deleted from the analyses because of excess error rates (over 50%) in one or more test versions. Mean reaction times and response error rates are reported in Table 4. Priming effects for MORPH, CHAR, and HOM primes, as assessed against control primes, are also plotted in Fig. 4.

In the overall analyses of reaction times, the main effect of prime type was highly significant [$F_1(3,399) = 42.387$, $P < .001$, $F_2(3,108) = 27.54$, $P < .001$]. Post hoc Newman-Keuls tests found that the mean reaction time for MORPH primes (569 ms) was significantly shorter than the times for CHAR, HOM, and CON primes ($P < .01$). Responses for CHAR primes (594 ms) was also significantly faster than responses for HOM primes (616 ms) and CON primes (612 ms), which did not differ from each other. The interaction between prime type and sub-experiment was significant by

TABLE 4
Mean Reaction Times (ms) and Error Percentages in Experiment 3

	MORPH	*CHAR*	*HOM*	*CON*
Masked	593 (2.2)	600 (5.8)	615 (9.5)	621 (8.0)
SOA 57 ms	564 (5.0)	596 (8.4)	623 (11.2)	614 (10.5)
SOA 200 ms	552 (2.1)	587 (7.9)	612 (7.6)	603 (5.8)

subjects [$F_1(6,399) = 2.283$, $P < .05$], and by items [$F_2(6,216) = 2.32$, $P < .05$].

Separate analyses were conducted for priming effects for MORPH, CHAR, and HOM primes across sub-experiments. For MORPH primes, the main prime effect was highly significant [$F_1(1,133) = 91.54$, $P > .001$, $F_2(1,36) = 50.71$, $P < .001$]. The interaction between priming effect and sub-experiment was marginally significant [$F_1(2,133) = 2.43$, $.05 < P < .1$, $F_2(2,72) = 2.54$, $.05 < P < .1$], indicating that the MORPH priming effect

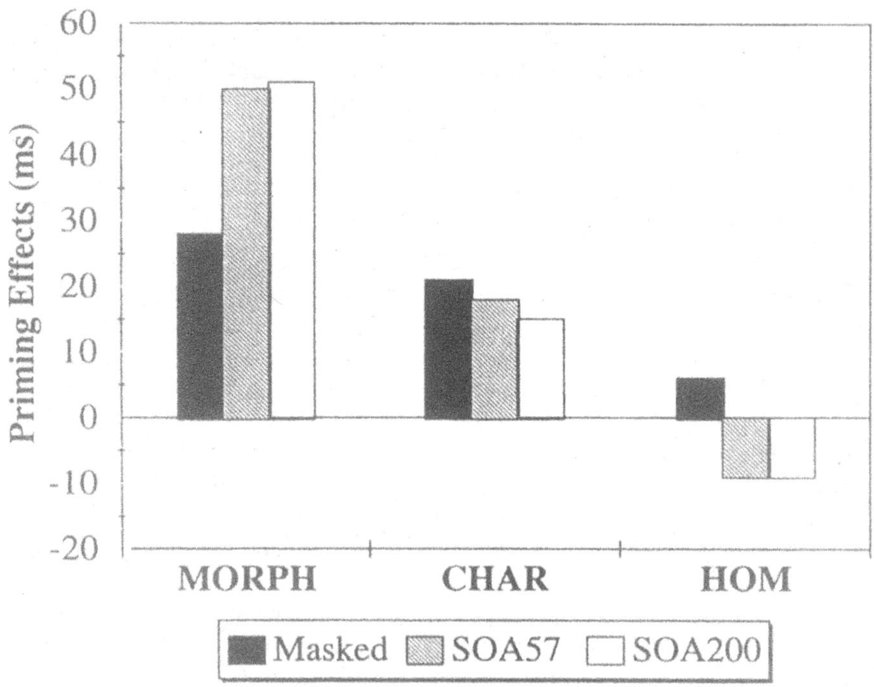

FIG. 4. Priming effects (ms) in Experiment 3.

was smaller in masked priming than in visual-visual priming (see Fig. 4). For CHAR primes, the priming effect was significant [$F_1(1,133) = 15.23$, $P < .001$, $F_2(1,36) = 9.07$, $P < .001$], but not the interaction between priming effect and sub-experiment ($F_1 < 1$, $F_2 < 1$). No significant priming effect was found for HOM primes ($F_1 < 1$, $F_2 < 1$). The interaction between this effect and sub-experiment was not significant either, [$F_1(2,133) = 1.04$, $P > .1$, $F_2(2, 72) = 1.30$, $P > .1$].

The analyses of error rates found a significant main effect of prime type [$F_1(3,399) = 13.90$, $P < .001$, $F_2(3,108) = 3.08$, $P < .05$]. Post hoc tests showed that this effect was mainly due to the differences between MORPH primes and the other three types of primes ($P < .01$ or $.05$). There were no significant differences between the later three types of primes ($P > .1$). The interaction between prime type and sub-experiment was significant by items [$F_2(6,216) = 2.99$, $P < .01$], but not by subjects ($F_1 < 1$).

Discussion

The pattern of priming effects was similar to the ones in Experiments 1 and 2, although the MORPH priming effect was reduced in masked priming. This reduction indicates that the priming effects between words sharing morphemes were not simply due to repeated access to morphemic semantic representations through character forms and the consequent semantic activation of whole words. This semantic activation is also influenced significantly by the orthographic relationship between critical morphemes in masked priming. Although the importance of orthographic form is masked priming has long been recognised (Forster & Davis, 1991; Forster, Davis, Schoknecht, & Carter, 1987), this experiment suggests that the spatial overlap of orthographic forms also plays an important role in determining morphological priming. Significant priming effects for CHAR primes throughout the three sub-experiments indicated that, even though the processing of the initial morphemes of the primes serves as a strong contextual constraint on the semantic activation of the second constituent, this does not seem to suppress the alternative semantic activation of the critical morphemes in the targets (Zhou & Marslen-Wilson, 1995). The non-significant priming effects for HOM primes demonstrated again the weakness of "pure" phonology in constraining semantic activation.

EXPERIMENT 4

The pattern of priming effects between words having homographic-homophonic characters in Experiments 1, 2, and 3 suggested parallel access to semantic representations of homophonic morphemes through common orthographic forms. The semantic representations of alternative morphemes may compete with each other in the time course of activation. It follows that if a character corresponding to a morpheme in the prime does not have a corresponding competitive morpheme in the target, there should be no competition between alternative morphemic semantic representations. Consequently processing of the target should not be hampered by morphemic competition, even though it contains the critical character used by the prime. The priming effect for the CHAR prime should therefore be larger than what was found in the previous experiments.

One way to have characters representing no competing morphemes in targets is to use two-character monomorphemic words (e.g., 沙发 sha[1] fa[1], *sofa*). In such words, characters are used mainly for the purpose of representing the sound of the word, even though syllables in these words use only specific characters (from sets of homophones). On the other hand, most of the characters used in monomorphemic words are also used as morphemes in isolation and in compound words (e.g. 沙 sha[1], means "sand" and 发 fa[1] means "hair" or "develop" in isolation). These monomorphemic words can therefore be taken as semantically opaque compound words. If similar patterns of priming effects are obtained for such monomorphemic words as for compound words in previous experiments, it could be argued that semantically transparent and opaque compound words are represented in essentially the same way in the lexicon.

Another purpose of Experiment 4 was to investigate further the role of phonology in processing compound words. Although "pure" phonological overlap between homophonic morphemes having no orthographic similarity does not have significant effects on lexical decision to compound targets, phonological information may have nevertheless played a role in producing the priming effects between words having homographic-homophonic morphemes. In other words, the priming effects for CHAR primes in Experiments 1, 2, and 3 were not solely based on orthographic overlap between primes and targets. Phonological information carried by the homographic characters may interact with orthographic information and this interaction constrains semantic activation of homographic morphemes and compound words (for further argument and evidence, see Zhou & Marslen-Wilson, 1999a, in press b).

Experiment 4 used compound words that had homographic, but not homophonic morphemes (e.g., 重复 chong[2] fu[4], *repeat*; 重量 zhong[4] liang[4], *weight*, where 重 can be chong[2], *repeat*, or zhong[4], *heavy*). If the pattern of priming effects between such words is different from the one between words having homographic-homophonic morphemes in Experiment 1 (e.g., 华侨 hua[2] qiao[2], *overseas Chinese* and 华贵 hua[2] gui[4], *luxurious*, where 华 hua[2] is either *Chinese* or *magnificent*), we may conclude that phonological information of constituent morphemes interacts with orthographic information in constraining semantic activation of morphemes and compound words.

Method

Design and materials

There were two sets of critical target words. In Experiment 4A, all the targets were two-character monomorphemic words, such as 沙发 (sha[1] fa[1], *sofa*). Each target was preceded by a compound word (CHAR prime, 沙滩 sha[1] tan[1], *sandy beach*) which had the same initial character as the target. The same target was also preceded by a word (HOM prime, 杀害 sha[1] hai[4], *kill*) whose initial morpheme was homophonic to but orthographically different from the initial character of the target. This target was also preceded by an unrelated control prime (请求 qing[3] qiu[2], *request*). This design was very similar to the one in Experiment 1, except that the target words here were monomorphemic words. Because of restrictions in finding appropriate stimuli, there were only 18 monomorphemic targets. The average frequences of the three types of primes and of the targets were 13, 15, 13, and 13 per million respectively.

In Experiment 4B, both primes and targets were compound words, where the initial morphemes of the CHAR primes (e.g., 重复 chong[2] fu[4], *repeat*) shared the orthographic form with the initial morphemes of targets (e.g., 重量 zhong[4] liang[4], *weight*). However, the homographic morphemes had different pronunciations in primes and targets. Because Experiment 4B was run in conjunction with Experiment 4A, two types of control primes were used to create balanced test versions. For one type, the initial constituents of control primes (e.g., 崇高 chong[2] gao[1], *lofty, high*) were homophonic to the initial constituents of the CHAR primes. The second type of control primes (e.g., 绝望 jue[2] wang[4], *give up all hope*) was not related to either the targets or the CHAR primes. No significant difference in lexical decision to targets was expected for the two types of control primes. Again, there were 18 quintets of stimuli, with average frequences of 47, 51, 40, and 43 per million respectively for the three types of primes and the targets.

Besides the critical stimuli, there were also 16 word-nonword pairs that shared the initial characters. These pairs were used to prevent subjects from using response strategies based on orthographic or phonological overlap between primes and targets. Another 26 word-word pairs and 49 word-nonword pairs that were not semantically, orthographically, or phonologically related were selected as fillers. There were also 20 pairs of word-word and word-nonwords practice items that had the similar composition as critical stimuli.

Experiments 4A and 4B were run concurrently as a single experiment. The procedures of creating test versions, preparing stimuli, and testing subjects were the same as Experiment 1. Because the patterns of priming effects in masked priming and in visual-visual priming with SOA of 57 ms were essentially the same in Experiments 1, 2, and 3, we did not test subjects for visual-visual priming with the SOA of 57 ms in this and the following Experiment 5.

Subjects

Sixty-three subjects in London were tested, 30 in visual priming and 33 in masked priming. Many of them had participated in Experiment 1. However, there was an interval of at least three months between the two experiments. Another 71 subjects were tested in Beijing in a replication of this experiment, with 36 in masked priming and 35 in visual-visual priming. These subjects were undergraduate students at Beijing Normal University and were not tested in the previous experiments.

Results

Because essentially the same patterns of priming effects were found for subjects in London and in Beijing, the analyses reported here were based only on the London data.[6] Mean reaction times and error percentages are reported in Table 5. Separate analyses were conducted for monomorphemic targets and phonologically altered (non-homophonic homographic) targets.

TABLE 5
Mean Reaction Times (ms) and Error Percentages in Experiment 4

	Experiment 4A			*Experiment 4B*		
	CHAR	*HOM*	*CON*	*CHAR*	*CON1*	*CON2*
Masked	648 (4.0)	684 (7.6)	694 (4.5)	680 (6.6)	693 (6.1)	689 (3.5)
SOA 200 ms	652 (3.8)	671 (2.2)	664 (3.9)	683 (4.9)	661 (7.2)	655 (5.6)

[6] For Beijing subjects, the mean reaction times in responding to monomorphemic targets (Experiment 4A) were 625, 675, and 680 ms respectively for CHAR, HOM, and CON primes in masked priming, and were 662, 679, and 687 ms in visual-visual priming. The mean reaction times in responding to targets of Experiment 4B were 669, 673, and 671 ms respectively for CHAR, CON1, and CON2 primes in masked priming, and were 696, 665, and 652 ms in visual-visual priming.

Experiment 4A

The overall analyses were conducted with prime type as a within-subject factor and sub-experiment as a between-subject factor. The main effect of prime type was significant by subjects but not by items [$F_1(2,122) = 3.51$, $P < .05$, [$F_2(2,34) = 1.07$, $P > .1$], and similarly for the interaction between prime type and sub-experiment [$F_1(2,122) = 3.74$, $P < .05$, [$F_2(2,34) = 2.30$, $P > .1$]. The item tests were not as powerful as subject tests, as there were only 18 targets in total.

Separate analyses were conducted for masked priming and the visual-visual priming with SOA of 200 ms. In masked priming, the main effect of prime type was significant by subjects, [$F_1(2,64) = 7.28$, $P < .005$], and marginally significant by items [$F_2(2,34) = 3.09$, $.05 < P < .1$]. Post hoc Newman-Keuls tests showed that responses to targets were significantly faster for CHAR primes than for HOM or CON primes ($P < .01$ by subjects and $.05 < P < .1$ by items). However, the difference between HOM and CON condition was not significant ($P > .1$). The analyses of error rates did not produce significant results. In visual-visual priming, the main effect of prime type was not significant in either reaction times or error rates ($F_1 < 1$, $F_2 < .1$).

Experiment 4B

In the overall analyses of reaction times, the main effect of prime type was not significant ($F_1 < 1$, $F_2 < .1$). The interaction between prime type and SOA was significant by subjects [$F_1(2,122) = 3.86$, $P < .05$], although not by items ($F_2 < 1$). This indicated that the pattern of priming effects in masked priming was not the same as the pattern in visual-visual priming. Separate analyses found no significant main effect of prime type in masked priming ($F_1 < 1$, $F_2 < 1$). But this main effect was significant in visual-visual priming [$F_1(2,58) = 5.36$, $P < .01$, $F_2(2,34) = 2.61$, $.05 < P < .1$]. Post hoc tests showed that responses to targets for CHAR prime were slower than responses for the two types of control primes ($P < .05$ by subjects and $.05 < P < .1$ by items). No differences were found between the two types of control primes. The analyses of error rates did not reveal any effects significant.

Discussion

The pattern of priming effects in Experiment 4A was generally similar to that in Experiment 1, even though different types of two-character words were used as targets. The null effect between words having orthographically different homophonic morphemes replicated Experiments 1, 2, and 3. In both masked and visual-visual priming, however, the priming effects between words sharing homophonic characters, were larger than the effects for compound targets in Experiment 1: the effects for monomorphemic targets increased by 15 ms in masked priming and by 20 ms in visual-visual priming (see Fig. 5). We discuss the implications of these findings later.

The pattern of priming effects for compound words having initial homographic but non-homophonic morphemes (Experiment 4B) was clearly different from the pattern for compound words having initial homographic-homophonic morphemes (Experiment 1). In masked priming, no significant effect was found here while a significant facilitatory effect was found in Experiment 1. In visual-visual priming, an inhibitory effect was found here whereas no significant effect was found in Experiment 1 (see Fig. 6). These differences suggest that phonological information carried by homographic characters has a significant influence on the processing of these characters and compound words containing these characters. This phonological effect, contrasting with the null effect between words having orthographically different homophonic morphemes, indicate that phonological activation, when it interacts with activation of appropriate orthographic information, could have significant

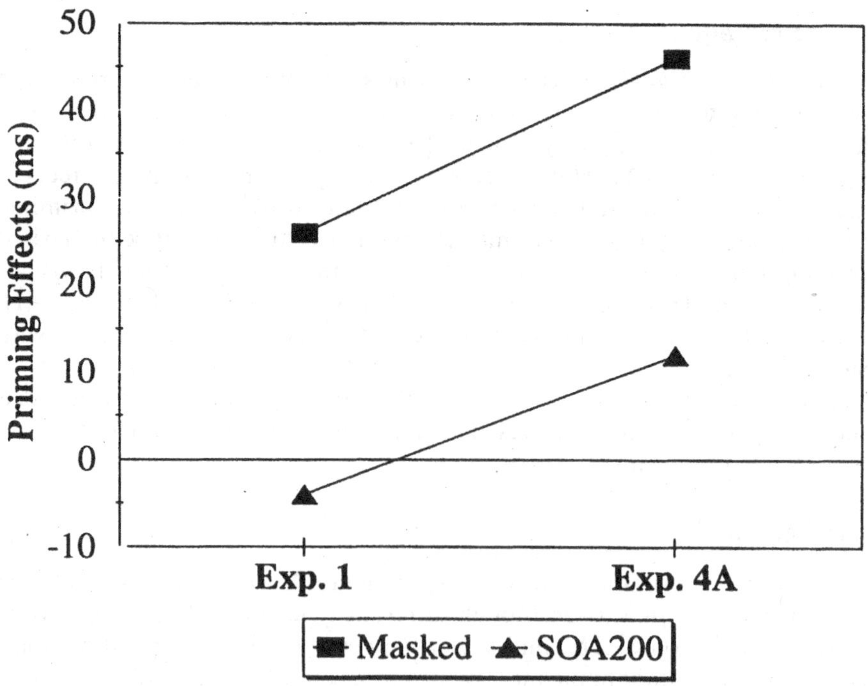

FIG. 5. Priming effects (ms) for CHAR primes in Experiments 1 and 4A.

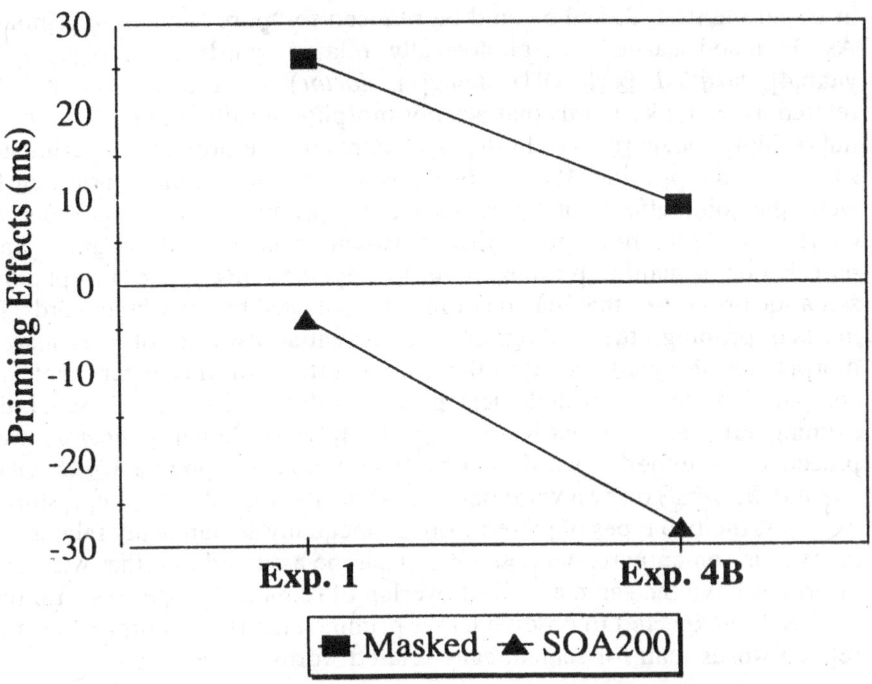

FIG. 6. Priming effects (ms) for CHAR primes in Experiments 1 and 4B.

influences on semantic activation of constituent morphemes and compound words.[7] In the General Discussion we discuss how the model sketched in Fig. 1 handles these findings.

EXPERIMENT 5

The purpose of this experiment was to examine whether the apparent morphological priming effects between words having common morphemes

[7] Because the mean reaction times in Experiment 4B were about 50 ms longer than the times in Experiment 1, one might argue that the more inhibitory effects for targets having non-homophonic homographic characters than for targets having homophonic-homographic characters were not due to the interaction between orthographic and phonological information carried by the homographic characters, but due to the slower reaction times themselves. More phonological information was allowed to come into play when responses were slowed down. It should be noted, however, that the null priming effects between words having orthographically different homophonic morphemes did not change according to the speed of responses (see Tables 1 and 5). Moreover, representing priming effects in terms of the proportion of mean reaction times in control conditions does not change the general pattern of the comparison between experiments.

in Experiments 1, 2, and 3 could be reduced to "pure" semantic priming. As discussed earlier, morphologically related words (e.g., 医院 yi[1] yuan[4], *hospital*; 医生 yi[1] sheng[1], *doctor*) are mostly semantically related as well, like words that are not morphologically related (e.g., 护士 hu[4] shi[4], *nurse*; 医生 yi(1) sheng[1], *doctor*). The previous experiments suggested that priming effects between words sharing common morphemes were the joint effects of "pure" semantic priming, due to the general overlap of semantic properties between primes and targets, and morphemic semantic priming, due to repeated access to morphemic semantic properties that may be or may be not used by the whole words. In masked priming, the orthographic and spatial overlap of the shared morphemes also contributed to the priming effects. In this experiment, we compared directly morphological priming effects with "pure" semantic priming effects. A target word (e.g., 医生 yi[1] sheng[1], *doctor*) was preceded by either a word sharing a common morpheme (医院 yi[1] yuan[4], *hospital*) or by a word only semantically related (护士 hu[4] shi[4], *nurse*). If the two types of paired words are equally semantically related, as indexed in semantic relatedness tests, it can be assumed that the two types of primes have the same extent of overlap of semantic properites with the targets. We expected to observe larger priming effects for morphologically related words than for semantically related words.

Method

Design and materials

Each target word was paired with three types of primes. In MORPH condition, a prime and its target had the same initial morpheme, which was written and pronounced in the same way in the prime and target. The same target was also preceded by a semantically related compound word in the SEM condition. The SEM prime and target shared no morphemes and no phonological and orthographic similarities. Meanings of the constituent morphemes in the prime and target were not related either. In the control priming (CON) condition, the target was also paired with a morphologically, semantically, orthographically, and phonologically unrelated word.

Forty-five target words and their MORPH and SEM primes were selected from a pool of potential stimuli, which underwent a semantic relatedness pretest. Thirty subjects were asked to judge the semantic relatedness between primes and targets on a 9-point scale, with 1 representing "completely unrelated" and 9 "very related". The primes and targets were split into two versions so that half MORPH primes and half SEM primes were in one version. Subjects were also split into two groups so that they never saw the same targets twice. For the selected set of stimuli, the average point of semantic relatedness to targets was 7.9 for

MORPH primes and 7.8 for SEM primes. The average word frequencies were 18 and 28 per million respectively for the two types of primes. The mean frequency of control primes was 23 per million.

To prevent subjects from using response strategies based on orthographic overlap between MORPH primes and targets, the experiment included 10 word-nonword pairs that shared their initial characters. These nonword targets were derived from real words that shared the initial morphemes with the primes. There were also 45 word-word pairs and 80 word-nonword pairs that were not morphologically, semantically, orthographically, or phonologically related. These pairs acted as fillers to reduce the proportion of critically related items in a test version. The creation of test versions, preparation of stimuli and tests of subjects were carried out in the same ways as previous experiments. As in Experiment 4, only masked priming and visual-visual priming with SOA of 200 ms were conducted.

Subjects

Sixty-two undergraduate students at Beijing Normal University were paid to participate in the experiment. Thirty-two of them were tested for visual-visual priming and 30 for masked priming. They were native speakers of Mandarin Chinese and were not tested for the previous experiments or for the semantic relatedness pretests.

Results

One subject and two items in masked priming were deleted from analyses because of high error rates. Mean reaction times, based on correct, untrimmed response times, and response error rates are reported in Table 6.

TABLE 6
Mean Reaction Times and Error Percentages of Experiment 5

	MORPH	*SEM*	*CON*
Masked	530 (1.9)	566 (3.2)	583 (5.0)
SOA 200 ms	536 (1.6)	548 (2.2)	580 (4.0)

Overall analyses were conducted for reaction times and error rates with prime type as a within-subject factor and sub-experiment as a between-subject factor In the analyses of reaction times, the main effect of prime type was highly significant [$F_1(2,118) = 47.41$, $P < .001$, [$F_2(2,84) = 27.85$, $P < .001$], indicating that targets were responded to faster when they were preceded by MORPH and SEM primes than by unrelated control primes. Post hoc Newman-Keuls tests showed that the mean reaction times to targets were significantly shorter ($P < .01$) for morphological primes (533 ms) than for semantic prime (557 ms) or control primes (582 ms). The difference between semantic and control primes was also significant ($P < .01$). The interaction between prime type and sub-experiment was significant by subjects [$F_1(2,118) = 4.32$, $P < .05$, although not by items [$F_2(1,84) = 1.09$, $P > .1$].

Planned tests were conducted to compare morphological and semantic priming effects. In masked priming, the 36 ms difference between MORPH primes and SEM primes was significant [$t_1(28) = 5.99$, $P < .001$, $t_2(42) = 3.30$, $P < .01$]. Moreover, the 17 ms semantic priming effect, as assessed against control primes, was also significant [$t_1(28) = 2.23$, $P < .05$, $t_2(42) = 2.65$, $P < .05$]. In visual-visual priming, the difference between MORPH primes and SEM primes (12 ms) was in the same direction as in masked priming, although it did not reach statistical significance [$t_1(31) = 1.19$, $P > .1$, $t_2(42) = 1.72$, $.05 < P < .01$]. The 32 ms semantic priming effect, against control primes, was highly significant [$t_1(31) = 5.96$, $P < .001$, $t_2(42) = 4.22$, $P < .001$].

The analyses of error rates found only a significant main effect of prime type [$F_1(2,118) = 5.14$, $P < .01$, $F_2(2,84) = 5.12$, $P < .01$]. Post hoc tests showed that while the error rates in both MORPH and SEM conditions were significantly lower than the rate in the control condition ($P < .05$ or $.01$), the difference between morphological priming and semantic priming was not significant ($P > .1$). No other effects were significant.

Discussion

The message from the experiment is clear. There is in general more than "pure" semantic priming between words sharing common morphemes. The additional priming effect, based on morphemic processing in reading compounds, is most obvious in masked priming. It can be argued that repeated access to form and semantic representations of critical morphemes in primes and targets leads to higher activation of semantic representations of target words. Although MORPH primes and SEM primes were well matched in their semantic relatedness to targets and, presumably, in the degree of semantic overlap between primes and targets, repeated activation of morphemic form and semantic properties not shared between SEM primes and targets led to larger priming effects for MORPH primes. The larger priming effect in masked priming was likely due to the larger contribution from orthographic and spatial overlap between primes and targets.

GENERAL DISCUSSION

The main purpose of this study was to investigate the interaction between morphological, orthographic, and phonological information in reading Chinese compound words. Results from the five sets of experiments can be summarised as follows. For words having common morphemes, significant priming effects were consistently found in masked and visual-visual priming (Experiments 1, 2, 3, and 5). The effects, however, were reduced in masked priming when the shared morphemes did not occupy the same spatial position (Experiment 3). The morphological priming effects were in general much stronger than the effects between words sharing homographic-homophonic characters or having homophonic morphemes. These effects were also larger than effects between semantically related words not sharing morphemes, although the advantage was reduced in visual-visual priming with a relatively long SOA (Experiment 5). Consistent priming effects were found for words having homographic-homophonic characters (Experiments 1, 2, 3, and 4A), although such words tended to inhibit each other in visual-visual priming with a long SOA when the critical characters were the initial morphemes of both primes and targets (Experiment 1). When the shared homographic characters were not homophones (Experiment 4B), the priming effects between words having these characters as initial morphemes were shifted (Figure 6), with a significant inhibitory effect in masked priming. Throughout the priming tasks and the SOAs between primes and targets, no significant priming effects were found for words having visually different homophonic morphemes (Experiments 1, 2, 3, and 4A).

Morphological priming and morphological structure in the lexicon

Clearly, the priming effects between words sharing morphemes cannot be reduced to just semantic or form-based priming. Instead, they point to a morphological dimension of lexical processing and representation. The prototypical model sketched in Fig. 1 captures this morphological dimension by dynamic *interactions* between form and semantic processing. It is assumed that the orthographic and phonological representations of compound words are composed of the forms of their constituent morphemes. The boundaries of the orthographic and phonological forms of constituent morphemes are clearly marked, partly due to the orthographic and phonological characteristics of the Chinese language and its writing system.[8] At the semantic level, both compound words and their constituent morphemes have representations composed of semantic features, with much overlap between whole-word and morpheme semantic representations. The degree of semantic overlap between whole words and constituent morphemes reflects the semantic transparency of the compounds (Zhou & Marslen-Wilson, 1999c; Zwitserlood, 1994). The initial morphological (or orthographic) decomposition in mapping visual input onto the lexicon and the activation of orthographic, phonological, and semantic representations of constituent morphemes are part of the processes of activating the semantic and form properties of compound words. The interactions between form and semantic processing of constituent morphemes and between processing of constituent morphemes and whole words result in the observed morphological effects in lexical processing.

The morphological priming effects between words sharing morphemes, summarised across experiments in Fig. 7, are joint effects of semantic priming based on general semantic overlap between primes and targets, semantic priming based on morphemic meanings, and form priming based on orthographic and phonological activation. However, the effects from different sources are not necessarily additive, but interactive in forming morphological priming. The form-based priming effects can be elevated by the masked priming technique (see Forster & Davis, 1991; Forster et al., 1987). The contribution of form priming to morphological priming can be clearly identified in Experiments 3 and 5. In Experiment 5, morphologically related words produced significantly larger priming effects than "pure" semantically related words in masked priming, although the advantage was reduced in visual-visual priming. In Experiment 3, the shift of spatial position of critical morphemes reduced the morphological priming effect in masked priming, compared with the effects in

[8] For Chinese two-character words, one might argue that this boundary marking is not morphological but orthographic and phonological, since representations for two-character monomorphemic words are probably also marked in the same way. However, there are only a small amount of such two-character monomorphemic words and many of them can be treated as semantically opaque compounds anyway. Thus in Chinese, calling this boundary marking "morphological" or "form-based" does not make much difference. For other languages like English, however, this boundary marking of polymorphemic words could be either explicit, as in many traditional theories of morphological processing (Taft & Forster, 1975, 1976), or implicit, as in connectionist theories of morphological processing (Rueckl, Mikolinski, Raven, Miner, & Mars, 1997; Seidenberg & McClelland, 1989; Zhou & Marslen-Wilson, 1999c). Whether boundaries between constituent morphemes are explicitly marked and whether this boundary marking is "morphological" or "formed-based" are fundamental to the issue of how morphological structure is represented in the lexicon (Rueckl et al., 1997; Zhou & Marslen-Wilson, 1999c).

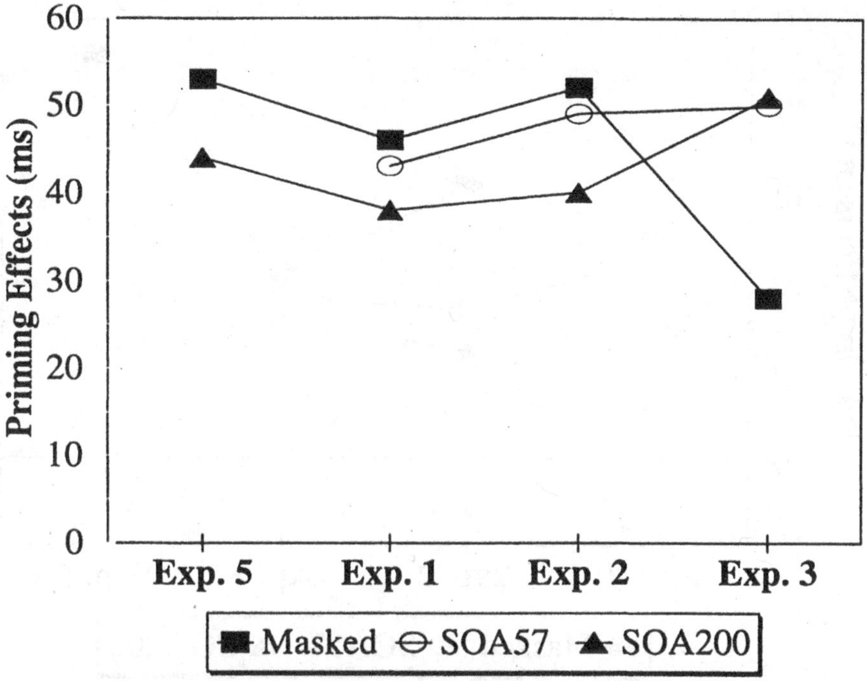

FIG. 7. Priming effects (ms) for MORPH primes in Experiments 1, 2, 3, and 5.

Experiments 1 and 2 and with the effects for the same words in visual-visual priming in Experiment 3. The contribution of the form processing of shared morphemes in masked priming may take the form of either activating constituent semantic representations more quickly or sending positive signals directly to the lexical decision mechanisms.

Character priming and access to semantics of constituent morphemes

Although the priming effects between words having homographic morphemes may be attributed to orthographically based activation of the target words, the variation in priming effects across experiments (Figs 5, 6, and 8) indicates that more detailed analyses of the processes involved in producing the effects are needed. The model sketched in Fig. 1 provides a good account for the results. This account, based on semantic and form activation of constituent morphemes, attributes the priming effects to parallel semantic activation of the homographic constituent morphemes and to interaction between semantic activation of constituent morphemes and whole words.

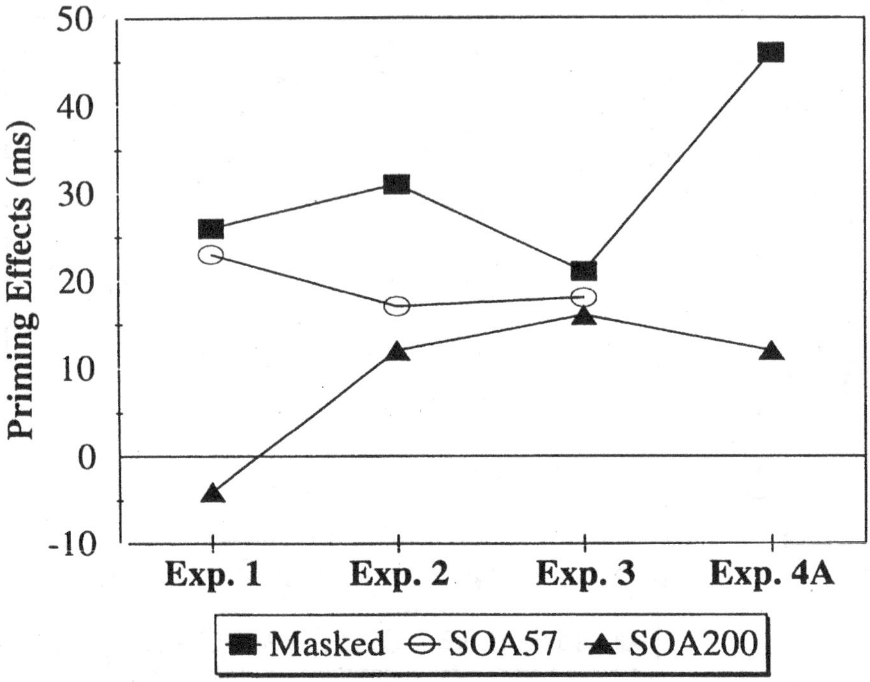

FIG. 8. Priming effects (ms) for CHAR primes in Experiments 1, 2, 3, and 4A.

The presentation of the critical morphemes in the primes activates the orthographic and phonological representations of these morphemes. Semantic representations of these morphemes are also activated, mainly through direct computation from orthography to semantics (see Zhou, 1997; Zhou & Marslen-Wilson, in press b). The alternative semantic representations of homographic morphemes are also activated, leading to facilitation in the recognition of target words. Semantic representations of homographic-homophonic morphemes also compete with each other and their activation interacts with semantic activation of whole words. As the SOA increases, this competition becomes stronger and the magnitude of priming effects decreases. Figure 8 summarises the priming effects at different SOAs across experiments 1 to 4.

The morphemic semantic competition is influenced by interaction between morphemic and whole-word semantic activation, which is in turn influenced by constituent positions of critical characters in primes and targets (see also Zhou & Marslen-Wilson, 1995). Because of a tendency to left-to-right processing in reading Chinese, the competition is stronger when the critical characters are at the initial constituent position. At the second constituent position, however, the competition is weaker, due to the contextual constraint from the processing of the initial morphemes. The processing of the initial morphemes activates the semantic representations of whole words. This semantic activation serves as contextual constraint in interpreting the ambiguous second character and there is less competition between the critical morphemes in these words and the semantic activation of the alternative morphemes. The negative priming effects between words having initial homographic-homophonic morphemes (Experiment 1) can be accommodated by the assumption that the visual input of the initial characters of targets are initially used to support further semantic activation of the critical morphemes in primes. Only when the second constituent of the target enters into semantic processing does the semantic representation of the initial critical character in the target become activated, due to interaction with semantic activation of the whole words.[9]

This semantic account of character priming is supported further by the comparison of priming effects between Experiments 1 and 4A (Figure 5). Because the critical characters do not represent alternative morphemes in monomorphemic words, competition between semantic interpretations of initial homographic morphemes is minimised. Consequently, the processing of monomorphemic targets is more likely to be facilitated by character primes than the processing of compound targets.

Phonology in reading Chinese compound words

In neither masked nor visual-visual priming did we observe significant priming effects between words having homophonic but non-homographic morphemes. This result suggests either that phonological information about constituent morphemes is not activated or that morphemic phonological activation by itself has no significant influence on semantic activation of morphemes and whole words.

[9] The significant inhibitory priming effect between Italian inflected words having homographic (and homophonic) stems (Laudanna et al., 1989, 1992) can be accounted for in the same way. The fact that inhibitory effects were not significant for Chinese compounds or for Italian derived words may be due to the degree of semantic contribution from homographic morphemes to whole words. Semantic properties of inflected words are mostly specified by semantic properties of their stems, while semantic properties of compound words and derived words are determined to a less extent by semantic properties of individual constituents or stems. Semantic competition between homographic morphemes thus exerts a larger influence on the processing of inflected words than on the processing of compounds or derived words.

There is evidence that the phonological properties of single-character words or morphemes are automatically activated in reading Chinese (e.g., Perfetti & Zhang, 1995, Zhou, 1997; Zhou & Marslen-Wilson, in press a). There is also evidence that phonological properties of constituent morphemes of compound words are activated, subject to task demands (see Footnote 4). Data from other studies support the proposition of automatic phonological activation of constituent morphemes in reading compound words. Zhou and Marslen-Wilson (1999) found that pseudohomophones created from compound words by replacing one constituent with orthographically dissimilar homophonic characters were more difficult to reject in lexical decision than matched control nonwords (see also Sakuma et al., 1988 for a similar finding for Japanese kanji compounds in a semantic categorisation task). Since lexical decision to pseudohomophones can be made on the basis of orthographic information, this phonologically based pseudohomophone effect can only indicate the automatic activation of phonological information, which interferes with the lexical decision response, either directly or through semantic activation.

Given these and other results, the null effect of phonological overlap between primes and targets in the current series of experiments can only be interpreted as suggesting that, although phonology of constituent morphemes is automatically activated in reading, it does not in general play a significant role in constraining the semantic activation of constituent morphemes and whole words. This conclusion is consistent with the finding that orthographically dissimilar homophonic compounds (e.g. 洁净 jie[2] jing[4], *hygienic;* 捷径 *jie[2] jing[4], shortcut*) do not significantly prime each other in lexical decision (Zhou, 1997; Zhou & Marslen-Wilson, in press a).

However, phonological information does play a significant role in constraining semantic activation when it interacts with appropriate orthographic information (Zhou & Marslen-Wilson, in press b). In this study, this point is clear from the comparison of priming effects between words having homographic characters, which were either homophonic or not (see Fig. 6). These priming effects decreased by about 30 ms in both masked and visual-visual priming when the critical characters were changed from homophonic to non-homophonic. This decrease of priming effects indicates that phonological information of constituent morphemes is automatically activated and this phonological activation influences semantic activation of constituent morphemes and compounds and hence lexical decision to compounds.

There are two possible ways for phonological activation to influence the CHAR priming effects. One is that morphemic semantic activation is constrained both by direct computation from orthography and by phonological mediation. These two routes to semantics operate in interaction with direct access plays a dominant role (Zhou, 1997; Zhou & Marslen-Wilson, in press a, b). The morphemic semantic competition between homographic but not homophonic morphemes is stronger than the competition between homographic-homophonic morphemes. The former types of homographic morphemes compete not only at the semantic level, but also at the phonological level. This phonological competition, acting in conjunction with direct visual access to morphemic semantics, intensifies semantic competition, leading to more negative priming. Another way to account for the phonological effect is to assume that the lexical decision task is sensitive to phonological activation as well as to semantic activation. If semantic activation leads the lexical decision mechanisms to make positive responses but the activation in the phonological system leads the mechanisms to make negative responses, the conflict delays lexical decision. This is the case for the inhibitory priming effects between words having homographic but non-homophonic characters (Experiment 4B). After the recognition of a CHAR prime (e.g., 重复 chong[2] fu[4], *repeat*), the phonological representation of the critical character (e.g., 重 chong[2]) is highly activated. When the target (e.g., 重量 zhong[4] liang[4], *weight*) is presented, the phonological representation of "chong(2)" is initially activated further while the phonological representation of "zhong[4]" is either not activated or inhibited. The combination of "chong[2]" with the second morpheme of the target (i.e., liang[4]) forms a nonword at the phonological level. This will inform the lexical decision mechanisms to make a "no" response, delaying the recognition of target words.

To summarise, this research demonstrates that morphological, orthographic, and phonological information interact with each other in the lexical processing of Chinese compound words. Morphological processing is exhibited through interaction between orthographic, phonological, and semantic processing of constituent morphemes and through interaction between semantic activation of morphemes and whole words. Semantic activation of constituent morphemes is constrained by both orthographic and phonological activation although phonology by itself has no significant influences on morphemic semantic activation. The prototypical representation model sketched in Fig. 1 captures the fundamental relations between morphology, semantics, orthography, and phonology in reading Chinese compound words and provides perhaps a new way to think of morphological processing.

REFERENCES

Bybee, J.L. (1985). *Morphology: A study of the relation between meaning and form.* Philadelphia: Benjamins.

Chen, H.-C., Cheung, S.L., & Flores d'Arcais, G.B. (1995). Orthographic and phonological activation in recognizing Chinese characters. *Psychological Research, 58*, 144–153.

Chen, H.-C., & Cutler, A. (1997). Auditory priming in spoken and printed word recognition. In H.-C. Chen (Ed.), *Cognitive processing of Chinese and other Asian languages* (pp.77–81). Hong Kong: The Chinese University Press.

Chen, H.-C., & Shu, H. (1997). *Lexical activation during the recognition of Chinese characters.* Manuscript, The Chinese University of Hong Kong.

Forster, K.I., & Davis, C. (1991). The density constraint on form-priming in the naming task: Interference effects from a masked prime. *Journal of Memory and Language, 30*, 1–25.

Forster, K.I., Davis, C., Schoknecht, C., & Carter, R. (1987). Masked priming with graphemically related forms: Repetition or partial activation? *Quarterly Journal of Experimental Psychology, 39A*, 211–251.

Institute of Language Teaching and Research (1986). *Modern Chinese frequency dictionary.* Beijing: Beijing Language Institute Press.

Laudanna, A., Bedecker, W., & Caramazza, A. (1989). Priming homographic stems. *Journal of Memory and Language, 28*, 531–546.

Laudanna, A., Bedecker, W., & Caramazza, A. (1992). Processing inflectional and derivational morphology. *Journal of Memory and Language, 31*, 334–348.

Leck, K.J., Weekes, B.S., & Chen, M.J. (1995). Visual and phonological pathways to the lexicon: Evidence from Chinese readers. *Memory and Cognition, 23*, 468–476

Perfetti, C.A., & Tan, L.H. (1998). The time course of graphic, phonological, and semantic activation in Chinese character identification. *Journal of Experimental Psychology: Learning, Memory, and Cognition, 24*, 101–118.

Perfetti, C.A., & Zhang, S. (1991). Phonological processes in reading Chinese words. *Journal of Experimental Psychology: Learning, Memory, and Cognition, 17*, 633–643.

Perfetti, C.A., & Zhang, S. (1995). Very early phonological activation in Chinese reading. *Journal of Experimental Psychology: Learning, Memory, and Cognition, 21*, 24–33.

Rueckl, J.G., Mikolinski, M., Raven, M., Miner, C., & Mars, F. (1997). Morphological priming, fragment completion, and connectionist networks. *Journal of Memory and Language, 36*, 382–405.

Sakuma, N., Sasanuma, S., Tatsumi, I.F., & Masaki, S. (1998). Orthography and phonology in reading Japanese Kanji words: Evidence from the semantic decision task with homophones. *Memory and Cognition, 26*, 75–87.

Seidenberg, M.S., & McClelland, J.L. (1989). A distributed, developmental model of visual word recognition and naming. *Psychological Review, 96*, 523–568.

Shen, D., & Forster, K.I. (1999). Masked phonological priming in reading Chinese words depends on the task. *Language and Cognitive Processes.*

Taft, M., & Forster, K. (1975). Lexical storage and retrieval of prefixed words. *Journal of Verbal Learning and Verbal Behavior, 14*, 638–647.

Taft, M., & Forster, K.I. (1976). Lexical storage and retrieval of polymorphemic and polysyllabic words. *Journal of Verbal Learning and Verbal Behavior, 15*, 607–620.

Taft, M., & Zhu, X. (1995). The representation of bound morphemes in the lexicon: A Chinese study. In L.B. Feldman (Ed.), *Morphological aspects of language processing* (pp.293–316). Hillsdale, NJ: Lawrence Erlbaum Associates Inc.

Taft, M., & Zhu, X. (1997). The model of lexicon processing: Orthography, phonology, and morpheme. In D.-L. Peng, H. Shu, & H.-C. Chen (Eds), *The cognitive research of Chinese* (pp.85–99). Shandong: Shandong Educational Publisher.

Wydell, T.N., Patterson, K.E., & Humphreys, G.W. (1993). Phonologically mediated access to meaning for Kanji: Is a ROWS still a ROSE in Japanese Kanji? *Journal of Experimental Psychology: Learning, Memory, and Cognition*, *19*, 491–514.

Xu, Y., Pollatsek, A., & Potter, M. (1999). The activation of phonology during silent Chinese word reading. *Journal of Experimental Psychology: Learning, Memory, and Cognition.*

Zhang, B.Y., & Peng, D.-L. (1992). Decomposed storage in the Chinese lexicon. In H.-C. Chen, & O.J.L. Tzeng (Eds), *Language processing in Chinese.* Amsterdam: North-Holland.

Zhou, X. (1997). The limited effect of phonology on access to meaning in reading Chinese. In D.-L. Peng, H. Shu, & H.-C. Chen (Eds), *The cognitive research of Chinese* (pp.159–184). Shandong: Shandong Educational Publisher.

Zhou, X., & Marslen-Wilson, W. (1994). Words, morphemes and syllables in the Chinese mental lexicon. *Language and Cognitive Processes*, **9**, 393–422.

Zhou, X., & Marslen-Wilson, W. (1995). Morphological structure in the Chinese mental lexicon. *Language and Cognitive Processes*, **10**, 545–600.

Zhou, X., & Marslen-Wilson, W. (1997). The abstractness of phonological representation in the Chinese mental lexicon. In H.-C. Chen (Ed.), *Cognitive Processing of Chinese and other Asian languages* (pp.3–26). Hong Kong: The Chinese University Press.

Zhou, X., & Marslen-Wilson, W. (1999a). *Pseudohomophone effects and lexical processing in reading Chinese.* Manuscript submitted for publication.

Zhou, X., & Marslen-Wilson, W. (1999b). The nature of sublexical processing in reading Chinese characters. *Journal of Experimental Psychology: Learning, Memory, and Cognition*, *25*, 1–19.

Zhou, X., & Marslen-Wilson, W. (1999c). *Lexical representation of compound words: Cross-linguistic evidence.* Manuscript submitted for publication.

Zhou, X., & Marslen-Wilson, W. (in press a). The relative time course of semantic and phonological activation in reading Chinese. *Journal of Experimental Psychology: Learning, Memory, and Cognition.*

Zhou, X., & Marslen-Wilson, W. (in press b). Phonology, orthography, and lexical semantic activation in reading Chinese. *Journal of Memory and Language.*

Zhou, X. Pollatsek, A., & Marslen-Wilson, M. (1999). *Orthographic and phonological constraints on semantic activation in reading Chinese.* Manuscript submitted for publication.

Zwitserlood, P. (1994). The role of semantic transparency in the processing and representation of Dutch compounds. *Language and Cognitive Processes*, *9*, 341–368.

LANGUAGE AND COGNITIVE PROCESSES, 1999, *14* (5/6), 567–607

The Cost of Switching between Kanji and Kana while Reading Japanese

Mohammed Shafiullah and Stephen Monsell
University of Cambridge, Cambridge, UK

Readers of Japanese must constantly switch between decoding two types of script, Kana and Kanji. Does this incur a measurable processing cost? In four discrete-trial reaction time experiments, with an inter-trial interval of 1 s or 2 s, Japanese readers had to switch predictably, every second trial, between reading words in Kanji and Kana (Hiragana in three experiments, Katakana in the fourth). The task was naming in two experiments, and semantic categorisation in two. In every case performance was significantly slower, by about 13 ms on average, and less accurate, on the trials following a change of script. In these and three further experiments we show that the cost does not arise from changes in spatial extent, number of characters, or the familiarity of words written in the two scripts, that neither the task nor the direction of switching have much impact on the cost, and that there is no cost for switching between naming words in the two Kana scripts, Hiragana and Katakana. We conclude that to decode Kana and Kanji draws on somewhat different resources, and speculate on the source of the switch cost.

INTRODUCTION

Written Japanese simultaneously uses two distinct types of script: the logographic Kanji characters and the two slightly different forms of moraic Kana character, Hiragana and Katakana. Kanji and Kana differ in a number of ways. Kana are relatively simple visual forms, which come from

---

Requests for reprints should be addressed to Stephen Monsell, School of Psychology, University of Exeter, Exeter EX4 4QG, UK; Email: S.Monsell@exeter.ac.uk.

Mohammed Shafiullah is now at the School of Social Sciences, University of Teesside, Borough Road, Middlesbrough TS1 3BA, UK; Email: M.Shafiullah@tees.ac.uk. This paper reports research conducted as part of a PhD dissertation under the supervision of the second author, and with the financial support of Naniwaya Co. Ltd., and Mr and Mrs Murayama. We thank Karalyn Patterson and John Duncan for their extensive advice and support, and Hsuan-Chih Chen, Insup Taylor, Marcus Taft, and an anonymous reviewer for their comments on a previous version. We thank Naomi Cross and Rayna Azuma for their careful application of native-speaker expertise to our materials.

a small and closed set. Each Kana character stands for a mora (one of the elementary syllabic units of spoken Japanese). To a skilled reader, the pronunciation of a Kana word is completely transparent, regardless of its familiarity. In contrast, Kanji are visually complex characters from a large and open set originally derived from Chinese. They correspond to morphemes. A single Kanji character in isolation typically has several possible pronunciations. In compounds and in derived and inflected forms their pronunciation is highly context-dependent. Words written in Kanji are largely phonologically opaque. The reader must learn a large set of single Kanji and their alternative readings, and an even larger set of compound Kanji, to be able to decode either their meaning or their pronunciation.

The two types of script are mixed in continuous text. The stems of most familiar content words are written as a single Kanji character or as a compound of two or more. Function words and the inflectional and derivational particles required for most words are written in Hiragana: for example, the honorific form of some nouns has a Hiragana prefix (e.g. お電話, Odenwa). Nouns, some pronouns (e.g. 私, watakushi; 何, nani), one class of adjectives in their predicative form (e.g. 親切, shinsetsu) and some adverbs (e.g. 大変, taihen in 大変暑い, taihen atsui) can occur in Kanji without modification by any Kana. Some content words are not written in Kanji. The many foreign loan words used in contemporary Japanese are written in Katakana, as are non-Japanese proper names. Katakana can also be used for emphasis (cf. italics in English). As well as for function words, including most pronouns, Hiragana is used in standard text for a few common indigenous content words whose Kanji are obscure, and there are a few Hiragana words without Kanji equivalents (e.g. ぶらぶら, burabura; おちゃっぴい, ochappii). A small number of compound words have constituent morphemes in different scripts (e.g. 板チョコ, itachoko (Kanji-Katakana); ガラス工場, garasukōjō (Katakana-Kanji)). In principle, any word can be "spelled out" in Hiragana, and will be if the author anticipates that the Kanji form will be unfamiliar to the reader. Children's texts and the comic books called "Manga" use a form of parallel transcription (furigana) in which a Hiragana or a Katakana transcription is written above or next to the Kanji.

Skilled adult readers of Japanese text must thus frequently switch between processing Kanji and Kana characters. Because grammatical morphemes are written in Hiragana, and because the majority of content word stems are written in Kanji, the reader can to some extent use sentence structure to anticipate a script switch, and also use script as a cue to sentence structure. It has been argued (Taylor, 1997; Taylor & Park, 1995) that the mixture of scripts is positively advantageous in this respect. But there is also a large literature suggesting that somewhat different mechanisms or pathways are used for decoding Kana and Kanji, and this motivates us to ask whether the need to switch between decoding the two different kinds of orthography may also incur a significant processing cost.

The general association in normal text between script switching and a change in syntactic class, together with the possibility that script serves as a cue to sentence structure, makes it extremely difficult to isolate experimentally from measures of the reading of normal sentences any cost specific to switching scripts. Hence the experiments reported in this paper used discrete-trial single-word reading tasks to probe for a cost of script switching unconfounded by changes in syntactic class, and without the overlay of sentence-level processes that might exploit script as a cue. The experiments establish first that there is such a cost, and second that it is attributable to the need to switch between scripts *per se*, not to correlated changes in other properties of the word-forms, such as visual complexity, spatial extent or familiarity. We begin by reviewing the evidence for distinct mechanisms, and the methodology of measuring switch costs.

Distinct mechanisms for processing Kanji and Kana?

Kana directly and transparently represents the phonology of Japanese, while Kanji characters correspond to units of meaning—morphemes—and have their origins in a depictive code. This suggests that these characters may be mapped to meaning and sound in different ways. The simplest hypothesis is that Kanji characters are translated directly to meaning, and only indirectly, via meaning, to phonology, while Kana characters are mapped directly to phonology, and only indirectly, via phonology, to meaning. A number of authors have maintained that (a) phonological mediation is necessary for access to meaning from words written in Kana (e.g., Allport, 1979; Kimura, 1984; McCusker, Hillinger, & Bias, 1981; Morton & Sasanuma, 1984; Sasanuma, 1984); (b) naming of Kana is accomplished by direct translation to phonology, without any semantic mediation (e.g., Feldman & Turvey, 1980; Goryo, 1987; Nomura, 1981) and by means of a non-lexical assembly process (Saito, 1981; Saito, Inoe, & Nomura, 1979); (c) phonological mediation is not necessary for access to meaning from words written in Kanji (e.g., Kaiho, 1976; Kimura, 1984; McCusker et al., 1981; Morton & Sasanuma, 1984; Sasanuma, 1984); (d) naming of Kanji words is necessarily mediated by meaning (e.g., Feldman & Turvey, 1980; Goryo, 1987; Nomura, 1981).

One kind of evidence appealed to has been faster semantic categorisation decisions for Kanji than for Kana words. However in the majority of such experiments, the Kana word-forms were visually unfamiliar transcriptions of Kanji words; the greater familiarity of the Kanji forms could have been responsible for their RT advantage. Hirose (1984) used visually familiar Katakana words along with visually unfamiliar Katakana transcriptions of Kanji words, and Kanji words, in a semantic categorisation experiment. RTs for Kanji words were shorter than those for visually familiar Katakana words, while the RTs for the visually unfamiliar Katakana transcriptions of Kanji words were the longest. He argued that access to meaning could be achieved via a direct orthography-to-meaning route not only for Kanji, but also for visually familiar Kana words. Of course, this still leaves unexplained the shorter RT for Kanji than for familiar Katakana words. Perhaps familiar Kana forms become more weakly associated to their meanings than Kanji forms because semantic access for the former receives additional support from access via the phonological route.

Wydell, Patterson, and Humphreys (1993) argued that access to meaning for Kanji words does involve phonological mediation. Their subjects saw a category label and then a target word, and had to decide whether the target word named an exemplar of the category. RTs for Kanji that were homophones of category members were longer than for control words. RTs for words that were visually similar to category members were also longer than for control words. They concluded that Kanji words have both direct access to meaning and phonologically mediated access, in parallel. Note that the phonological mediation for Kanji must be via retrieved phonology[1] rather than the piece by piece assembly of phonology afforded by Kana.

Most studies comparing the naming of Kana and Kanji words have, like the majority of categorisation studies, failed to control for visual familiarity. When naming visually unfamiliar Kana words, subjects must necessarily assemble a pronunciation "non-lexically". For familiar Kana words the subject could also use "lexical" retrieval of learned pronunciations—whether through direct retrieval of the whole word-form's pronunciation, or via semantic mediation, or both. Besner and Hildebrandt (1987) compared naming RTs for words normally written in Katakana, Katakana transcriptions of Kanji words and Katakana non-words. RTs for visually familiar Katakana words were shorter than those for Katakana

[1] Complex Kanji have two components: a semantic radical which normally indicates the meaning, and a phonetic radical which normally supplies the phonological information. Flores d'Acrais, Saito, and Kawakami (1995) demonstrated that precueing the naming of complex Kanji by their phonetic radicals (60 ms and 180 ms SOA) reduced the naming RTs. However the phonological information supplied by the phonetic radical is not reliable. It remains to be tested whether semantic radicals facilitate semantic categorisation RTs.

transcriptions of Kanji words. They argued that the reader attempts to retrieve a stored phonological description of the whole word ("addressed phonology") in addition to assembling phonology when naming visually familiar Katakana words. The distinction between addressed phonology and assembled phonology is reified in separate pathways in the dual route model (Coltheart, Curtis, Atkins, & Haller, 1993; Patterson & Morton, 1985). In recent connectionist models (e.g., Plaut, McClelland, Seidenberg, & Patterson, 1996; Van Orden & Goldinger, 1994) the distinction is blurred because the sub-lexical correspondences that enable the "assembled" pronunciations of non-words and the higher-level correspondences that permit "retrieval" of the pronunciation of exception words are superimposed and distributed across the same set of connection weights. The same could be true of Japanese, but one presumes that there would at least have to be distinct populations of input units for representing Kanji and Kana (see Patterson, Suzuki, & Wydell, 1996; Patterson, Suzuki, Wydell, & Sasanuma, 1995).

Hence, contrary to the simple hypothesis that only Kanji words map directly to meaning, and only Kana words map directly to pronunciation, there is evidence that, once learned, Kanji words directly evoke pronunciations as well as meanings, and that familiar Kana words evoke learned meanings and pronunciations, as well as the assembly of a pronunciation. This may seem to weaken the proposal that Kanji and Kana are processed in different ways. However, it remains that only words written in Kana afford the option of mora-by-mora assembly of phonology. There are, moreover, a number of neuropsychological studies showing impaired naming of Kanji words while the naming of Hiragana words remains largely unaffected (e.g., Imura, 1943; Kato, 1912; Kurachi, Endo, Yamaguchi, & Enokido, 1978; Ohashi, 1965; Patterson et al., 1995; Sasanuma & Monoi, 1975). Selective impairment of the naming of Kana words has also been reported (e.g., Anzai, Okuse, & Aizawara, 1965; Kotani, 1935; Miura, 1934; Nishikawa, 1973; Sasanuma, 1980). At least one study has shown impaired comprehension of Kanji while the comprehension of words written in Kana was relatively unaffected (Imura, 1943). Selectively impaired comprehension of Kana has also been reported (e.g., Anzai et al., 1965; Kotani, 1935). The apparent double dissociation suggests that computing phonology and meaning from the two kinds of script depends on mechanisms and pathways that are not just functionally but also anatomically distinct. The difference could be at the level of visual analysis, as the two kinds of character differ in their features and spatial organisation, Kana being relatively simple characters arranged in a row (or column) while Kanji are more complex assemblies of radicals. Or it could be the case that the hypothesis of mediated versus non-mediated translation is partially correct, in that the Kanji-to-meaning and Kana-to-pronunciation links are stronger and less vulnerable than Kanji-to-pronunciation and Kana-to-meaning links.

Cost of script switching?

If Kana and Kanji words were processed by the same mechanism, there would be no reason to expect that reading a Kanji word after reading a Kana word would be any harder than after a word written in the same script—provided that semantic, phonological and visual similarities known to influence performance are controlled. Hence observation of a switch cost would supplement the evidence reviewed above suggesting that separate mechanisms are involved. However, the hypothesis of distinct mechanisms—we may speak loosely of Kanji and Kana "input modules"—does not necessarily predict a cost of switching between the scripts. A priori, we can image at least three ways in which the requirement to switch scripts *might* impose a processing cost, but none seems obligatory:

1. Some control operation might be required to activate the connection(s) between the appropriate input module (Kana or Kanji) and the target domain (meaning or pronunciation). But it is not obvious, a priori, why *both* input modules should not be left connected to the target domain.
2. There could be a passive priming effect. If the Kanji module has not been used for a few seconds it may take longer to activate than if it has been activated by the immediately preceding word. But one might just as easily argue that giving an input module time to recover from processing a previous word would allow activation from competing words to decline (see, for example, Wheeldon & Monsell, 1994).
3. Processing resources may need to be reallocated between the Kanji and the Kana modules. Activation of meaning by a written word is often said to be "automatic", and this may seem to imply no demand on non-specific resources. But the characterisation of word recognition as automatic usually refers to freedom from intentional control, as in "automatic" semantic priming (Neely, 1977, but see Stolz & Besner, 1996), or resistance to intentional control, as in the Stroop effect (MacLeod, 1991, but see Besner, Stolz & Boutilier, 1997), or happening without awareness or intention (e.g., Marcel, 1983), none of which senses is necessarily correlated with lack of resource demand. Several authors have argued that access to meaning or pronunciation for a familiar word requires, or is at least rendered more efficient, by the focusing of attention in the posterior attentional system (Carr, 1992), or by the allocation of a "resource"

also used by other processes, such as maintaining a visual pattern in working memory or tone detection (e.g., Herdman & Beckett, 1996). If this is the case then allocating this resource to the Kana "module" may withdraw it to some degree from the Kanji "module", and vice versa.

We return to these ideas in the final discussion. For now, they merely license speculations, not strong expectations, about whether switching between reading Kanji and Kana should incur a measurable cost. The question of whether it does is of both theoretical and practical importance. The theoretical issue may be understood by reference to the literature on divided attention. Several decades ago, it would have been possible to speculate in an unrestrained manner, much as we have above, whether there should be a cost in switching between processing stimuli from two different regions or objects in the visual field, or auditory sources. There is now a large literature on this question, as a result of which we have learned a good deal about spatial attention and processing limitations. If Japanese readers, for all their years of practice, suffer a measurable cost in switching between scripts, that would suggest a limitation, no less important, in the ability to divide attention or resources between two different types of input code connected to the same lexical and phonological representations.

The practical question is whether the need to alternate frequently between decoding two types of script imposes a processing burden during the reading of continuous text in Japanese. Cultures rightly take pride in their writing systems, both as artefacts defining the culture, and because of the literature and records accessible through them. But they also occasionally take into account questions of efficiency when deciding whether to modify them or their usage: consider the occasional suggestions that the spelling of English should be made phonetically transparent, or the Chinese decision to use the pinyin Roman alphabet in schools as a bridge to the reading of Chinese characters. Even if, as Taylor and Park (1995) have argued, there are benefits gained from the mixture of scripts, it is no less important to be aware of any costs. Of course, as the studies reported in this paper clearly involve an unnatural form of script switching, different in several ways from that required in the reading of continuous text, any positive evidence for a switch cost can only raise the question of what the consequences for normal reading may be, not answer it.

Measurement of switch costs

The methodology we use to probe for a cost of switching between scripts derives from recent research on "task-switching". We refer to experiments in which, on each of a series of trials, a stimulus is presented that affords a response in one of two (or more) tasks. For example, the stimulus on each trial might be a digit, and the subject has to classify it either as odd or even (Task A), or as greater or less than five (Task B). The aim is to compare reaction time and errors for trials on which the subject switches from one task to the other, and trials on which they perform the same task as on the previous trial, all other things being equal, to yield a measure of "switch cost". Jersild (1927) pioneered one method, later revived by Spector and Biederman (1976) and Allport, Styles, and Hsieh (1994): Performance is compared between blocks of trials in which the subjects alternate between two tasks, and blocks in which they perform just one task. However, as Rogers and Monsell (1995) point out, the switch cost measured by this comparison may index not only the processing overhead incurred by switching tasks, but also the burden of maintaining two task-sets in a state of readiness rather than one. In addition, the comparison may be contaminated by the subjects' perception that the alternating blocks are more difficult, leading them to exert more effort on those blocks. Rogers and Monsell developed a purer measure of switch costs—the "alternating runs" paradigm. Subjects alternate on a predictable schedule between runs of n trials in the two tasks. If $n = 2$, the task sequence would be AABBAABB . . . so that the task alternates every two trials. Cues such as position on the screen, or background colour, help subjects keep track of the task required and position in the run. Comparison of reaction time and errors between switch trials (AB, BA) and non-switch trials (AA, BB) provides a measure of the cost in processing time and errors of a task switch.

The present experiments applied the alternating runs paradigm to script-switching. Subjects performed the same task—semantic categorisation in some experiments, naming in others—on every trial. A new stimulus was presented on every trial. The script changed every second trial, in most of the experiments between Kanji and Kana. We used a long response-stimulus interval—1 s or 2 s, and the script switch was predictable, so that the subject had the opportunity to prepare for each change of script. In the case of task-switching, a long preparation interval has been observed to reduce, but not eliminate switch costs (Meiran, 1996; Rogers & Monsell, 1995). Hence in one sense we are minimising our chance of detecting a cost of switching scripts, and any cost we detect will set a lower bound to the cost suffered in fluent reading, where the rapid rate of processing allows little opportunity to prepare actively for a script switch. On the other hand, presenting each stimulus as soon as the previous response is detected would have introduced obvious practical difficulties in the measurement of naming responses, not to mention allowing the subject no time to breathe.

Although we borrow a methodology from task-switching studies, the case of script-switching is quite different theoretically. Task switching involves a shift between two different kinds of *output* to the same input—two different S–R mappings. In the case of script switching the shift is between two kinds of input (different scripts) mapped to the same output. In natural reading for meaning the output is activation of meanings (and syntactic properties, etc.). When reading aloud, it is activation of phonology. In the present experiments we use a semantic categorisation task to index access to meaning, and reading aloud to index access to phonology, but only one of these tasks per experiment. As already noted, it is not obvious that shifts between two different kinds of script mapped to the same output should cause any difficulty at all.

Another case of input switching is language switching. Meyer and Ruddy (1974) presented English–German bilinguals with pairs of visual items for lexical decision. The subjects had to say "yes" when both items were words. RTs were longer when one word was English and one German, then when both were in the same language. Meyer and Ruddy attribute this to a need to switch between distinct language pathways. However, lexical decision poses the problem that a letter string that is a word in one language may be a non-word in another, and this may prevent the subject from keeping both language pathways "open". This problem can be avoided by using semantic judgement tasks. Several studies have found no cost of language switching in such tasks (Caramazza & Brones, 1980; Colleta, in McCormack, 1977; Hines, 1978). Meyer and Ruddy argued that this was because relatively few stimuli were used, allowing the subject to develop direct S–R connections by-passing normal lexical access. However, a recent study in our lab, using semantic categorisation and a large set of words found no evidence for any cost of switching between French and English, even at very short response stimulus intervals. In other lexical decision studies smaller switch costs have been observed with languages distinguished by physical or orthographic cues (Grainger & Beauvillian, 1987; MacNamara & Kushnir, 1971). This differentiation makes it unlikely that a non-word in one language will look like a word in the other, and appears to allow the subject to, as it were, keep the "gate" from each language open.

In testing for a cost of switching between Kanji and Kana, we must be alert to several potential hazards. We must not attribute to switching between scripts what is in fact a cost of switching attention between visual analysis at different grains, or between different spatial extents of visual object. We deal with this by means of control experiments. A second potential pitfall is that when "easy" and "hard" stimuli are mixed in a block, reaction times tend to homogenise Los (1996). Responses to the easier stimuli slow down, and responses to the more difficult stimuli speed up, compared to the same stimuli in unmixed blocks. For example, Lupker and Brown (1997) found that non-words were named faster when mixed with high frequency exception words than when named in a block of non-words only, and attribute this to subjects adopting a single response criterion for a block, but varying it between blocks. We must thus be alert to possible trade-offs between accuracy and speed that might suggest a more cautious response criterion on switch trials.

OVERVIEW OF THE EXPERIMENTS

In each experiment we tested subjects' ability to switch between reading two types of word while performing just one task. In four experiments, the types were words written in Kanji and Kana (Hiragana in three cases, Katakana in Experiment 6). In Experiments 3 and 4, the input switched between two types of Kanji, and in Experiment 7 between Hiragana and Katakana words. In Experiments 1, 4 and 6, the task was a binary semantic classification. In the remaining experiments, the subject simply named each word aloud. The first four experiments used for the Kana items Hiragana transcriptions of words normally written in Kanji. For Japanese adult readers these are necessarily unfamiliar forms which do not afford direct access to meaning or pronunciation, but they allow us to use a large vocabulary, to avoid repetition of the items, and to use the same words in both scripts. The last three experiments sacrifice these advantages in order to demonstrate that the phenomenon extends to words normally written in Hiragana and Katakana.

In every experiment, there were two kinds of block. In "mixed" blocks, the type of word alternated predictably every second trial. In "pure" blocks, there was only one type of word. The order of mixed and the two types of pure blocks was counterbalanced over subjects. In both pure and mixed blocks there was an interval of one or two seconds between each response and the next trial, so that there was time to prepare for the next item, including any change in word type. Experiments 1 (semantic categorisation) and Experiment 2 (naming) establish the basic designs and procedures which were then used with little modification in the remaining experiments.

The analysis strategy is also the same for all the experiments, and we describe it here to avoid repetition. Consider the case where the two types of word are in different scripts, Kanji and Hiragana. For each subject we have equal numbers of trials in the six combinations of two scripts and three trial types: switch trials in the mixed blocks, non-switch trials in the mixed blocks, and trials in the pure blocks. Our primary interest is whether there is a cost of switching between scripts. Our favoured measure of the cost is the difference between mean RT and error rate on switch and non-switch trials in the mixed blocks (the within-block measure of Rogers and

Monsell, 1995). This we test in an analysis of variance on the data from mixed blocks only, with the factors trial type (switch, non-switch) and word type (the two scripts), testing the simple main effects of switching to explore any interaction between switching and script.

The pure blocks provide a baseline measure of performance without switching. It is of some interest to consider an alternative measure of the cost of switching, and that is the difference between performance on switch trials in the mixed blocks, and performance in the pure blocks. (This is the measure closest to Jersild's (1927) contrast of performance in pure and alternating blocks.) To assess this measure, we report analyses of variance with type (switch, pure) and script as the factors.

Finally, to compare performance on the two scripts we report a main effect of script from an analysis of variance using all the data, with script as one factor, and trial type (switch, non-switch, and pure) as the other.

Ideally, we would have liked to present each stimulus just once, so that there would be no possibility of repetition priming, or learning of responses to stimuli, which might interact with switch costs. However in all but Experiments 1a and 2a, limitations on the size of the stimulus sets made it necessary to present the same stimuli several times. We constructed the stimulus sequences so that the repetitions of the same item were as far apart as possible. We will report in the final discussion section an analysis of the effects of practice and repetition.

Subjects

In every experiment we tested 18 paid volunteers. All were native speakers and skilled readers of Japanese, with normal or corrected-to-normal vision. All had received formal education in Japan at least to the level of high school graduation. In Experiment 1 the subjects were research students or postdoctoral researchers at Cambridge University, aged between 27 and 40. In Experiment 6, the subjects were Oxford undergraduates. In all other experiments the subjects were undergraduates at Japanese universities (Nihon, Seiko, Ueno Gakuen Junior College, Osaka Gakuen University) aged between 18 and 26, attending summer schools in England at Oxford or Cambridge colleges, except in the case of Experiment 3, where five of the subjects were learning English at a language school in Cambridge. For the semantic categorisation experiments, only right-handed subjects were tested. The ratio of men to women varied from 50:50 to 0:100. For several experiments words were selected on the basis of familiarity ratings by groups of subjects from the same populations as in the experiments. A new group of subjects was tested in every experiment, and no subject was tested on words he or she had previously rated.

EXPERIMENT 1

The experiment was divided into two parts. In part (a) the stimuli were words represented by two or more Kanji, which we shall call *multiple Kanji*, and their Hiragana transcriptions. In part (b) the stimuli were *single Kanji* words and their Hiragana transcriptions. There are fewer single Kanji stimuli available.

Kanji were adopted from written Chinese to write indigenous Japanese words as well as borrowed Chinese words. This has resulted in the majority of single Kanji having two readings: the 'On' reading (an approximation to the original Chinese pronunciation) and the 'Kun' reading (the indigenous Japanese word). The On reading normally has a smaller number of phonemes. The loss of the tonal distinctions in the original Chinese means that the number of characters homophonous in their On readings is often large. Though there are many exceptions, the general rule is that the Kun reading is used for isolated single Kanji (i.e., free morphemes), and the On reading for compound Kanji (i.e., bound morphemes). For example, 人間; [ningen] (human), deriving from Chinese [rén jian], is a multiple Kanji word with both Kanji 人 [nin] and 間 [gen] receiving the On reading. The Kun readings of these Kanji are 人 [hito] (person) and 間 [aida] (between). According to Paradis, Hagiwara, and Hildebrandt (1985), 38% of the 2000 most common Kanji have no Kun reading. Most Kanji are homographs for several morphemes. Some Kanji have more than one On-reading (deriving from different periods of borrowing from the Chinese) the pre-Tang pronunciation, i.e., Go-on, and the Tang pronunciation, i.e., Kan-on. The assignment of different Japanese words to the same Chinese characters moreover produced more than one Kun reading for some Kanji. Kanji with more than one Kun reading are less common than Kanji with more than one On reading.

Some multiple Kanji words convey the meaning of their constituent Kanji in the same way as English compounds like bookshelf (e.g., 本棚, hondana), but others (e.g., 独仏, dokufutsu) convey meanings other than a combination of the meanings of their constituents. Typically each constituent Kanji represents part of the pronunciation of the whole word (as in 大学, diagaku), but in some multiple-Kanji words (e.g., 大和, yamato) the pronunciation of the whole word is completely arbitrary. Although the On-reading of the character is used in pronouncing most multiple-Kanji words, some compound Kanji words contain morphemes in both On and Kun readings (e.g., 本棚, hondana). The Kana transcription of a multiple-Kanji word has on average fewer Kana characters per Kanji character than the Kana transcription of a single-Kanji word. Some authors have gone as far as to claim that multiple-Kanji words are, along with Kana words, processed predominantly in the left hemisphere while single-Kanji words are processed predominantly in the right hemisphere (Hatta, 1978; Nakagawa, 1994). Given these various differences between multiple- and single-Kanji words, it seemed sensible to test them in separate sub-experiments.

Method

Materials. Multiple-Kanji words were selected for Experiment 1a subject to the following constraints.[2] They were multiple character nouns, without Kana inflections (suffixes and prefixes), without homophones, written as two (75%) or three (25%) Kanji characters. We attempted to include only items familiar to adult readers and unambiguously classifiable as animate or inanimate. The Kanji and their transcriptions were checked for accuracy by native Japanese speakers. An additional list was created for practice trials and warm-up trials. The Hiragana transcriptions had between 2 to 6 characters per word. The 600 experimental Kanji were divided into 12 sublists and their Hiragana transcriptions were similarly subdivided, so that sublists were roughly matched in terms of the average frequency and the number of characters per word.

Single-Kanji words for Experiment 1b were selected subject to the same constraints, except that each had to be a single character with an independent and single Kun reading. Enough such words were available to generate a usable set of 60, half signifying animate objects while the other half signify inanimate objects. An additional list of less suitable characters was used for practice trials and warm-up trials. The average number of characters for the Hiragana transcriptions (i.e. the number of morae) was three. Twenty-three of the single-Kanji characters were constitutents of multiple-Kanji words in the experiment.

A frequency table published by the National Research Institute for the Japanese Language (1982) was used to help select items familiar to adult Japanese readers. But the number of words in this table is limited, and the frequency, especially of single Kanji words, is not well documented. In later experiments we relied upon ratings of familiarity.

The fonts were chosen to minimise the difference in average horizontal extent between the Kanji and their Hiragana transcription: a 36-point Honmincho font was used for the Kanji words, and a 24-point Honmincho font for their Hiragana equivalents. (Examples of the stimuli are shown in Fig. 1.) The horizontal visual angle for a Hiragana word was in the range of about 0.5° (one character) to 5° (six characters) for Hiragana words and

---

[2] Lists of all the materials are available from the first author.

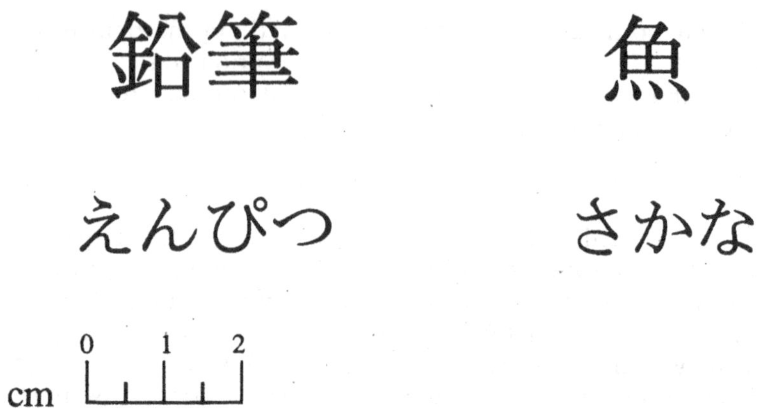

FIG. 1. An example of a multiple-Kanji word (on the left), and of a single-Kanji word (on the right), with Hiragana transcriptions below, in the sizes at which they were displayed in the experiment.

about 0.75° (one character) to 4° (three characters) for Kanji words. The vertical visual angle was about 1.75° for Hiragana and 2.5° for Kanji.

Procedure. The experiment was run using SuperLab (Haxby, Parasuraman, Lalonde, & Abboud, 1993) on a Macintosh IIci. Each word was displayed, black on white, in the centre of a monitor about 50 cm in front of the subjects. The software displayed the characters within one refresh cycle and synchronised with the refresh cycle. Response timing was accomplished via a six finger keyboard interfaced to give 1 ms resolution.

The subjects were first instructed orally in Japanese, then with written instructions presented on the monitor, and questions were invited. Subjects were asked to judge whether each stimulus signified an animate or an inanimate object, pressing the right index key for "animate", or the left index key for "inanimate", as quickly as possible while trying to avoid errors. The stimulus remained visible on the screen until the subjects pressed a key. A beep sounded immediately after an incorrect response. The response-stimulus interval was 1000 ms. A fixation cross (a small plus sign) appeared in the centre of the screen after each response, and remained until it was replaced by the following stimulus. The stimulus type was not explicitly precued.

All subjects were tested first with multiple-Kanji (Experiment 1a) and then with single-Kanji words (Experiment 1b). Subjects were told what script would be used before each pure block, or the order of scripts before each mixed block. Each new type of block began with 24 practice trials, and there were four warm-up trials at the beginning of each subsequent block. The subjects were informed orally about their speed and accuracy after each block, and rested briefly.[3]

Design. There were six trial sequences in each part of the experiment, two each for pure Kanji, pure Hiragana and mixed scripts. The order of presentation of pure and mixed sequences was counter-balanced over six subjects, by giving each subject one of the possible orders of Pure (Script 1), Pure (Script 2) and Mixed blocks, followed by the same order reversed.

For the multiple-Kanji words of Experiment 1a, there were 50 in each sequence of trials for the pure Kanji and Kana conditions, each presented as a single block. The corresponding mixed sequence of 200 trials (50 each of Hiragana/Katakana × switch/non-switch) was split into four blocks of 50 trials. Odd blocks began with Kanji and even blocks began with Hiragana. There were thus 12 blocks in total, with each word occurring just once per subject. The assignment of the six matched sublists of animate and inanimate items to condition (Kanji/Hiragana × switch/non-switch/pure) was rotated over six subjects so that each item occurred equally often in each condition without any repetition of a word within an experimental session. The order of items in each sublist was randomised anew for every subject.

Given the much smaller set of single-Kanji words in Experiment 1b, repetitions were unavoidable. Each sequence of trials for the pure conditions was presented as a single block of 30 trials. The corresponding sequences of mixed trials were divided into four blocks of 30. Different subsets of stimuli were presented in alternate blocks so that no item was repeated at a lag of less than one intervening block. In the course of a session, each item occurred once in each combination of switch/non-switch/pure × Kanji/Hiragana. The order of presentation was counter-balanced as for the multiple-Kanji words.

Results

The error rates were higher than anticipated (multiple Kanji experiment: 17.5% for Hiragana, 13% for Kanji; single Kanji experiment: 10.5% for both Kanji and Hiragana). In the effort to achieve a vocabulary of 600 items that were non-homophonic multi-character Kanji words with referents that were readily classifiable, we had clearly included some items that were, with respect to the age and cultural cohort we were testing, archaic or had shifted their connotations. We completely excluded

[3] Superlab regrettably lacks functions for displaying the average RT and error rates at the end of each block. Thus each block was run as a separate Superlab session, and an Excel macro was used to compute and display the average RTs and error rates after each block.

from further analysis all trials on items with a per-item error rate greater than 40%.[4] Each Kanji word and its Hiragana transcription were considered as two versions of the same item, so that error-prone items were equally excluded from both Kanji and Hiragana data. This resulted in the exclusion of 15% of the multiple-Kanji words and their Hiragana transcriptions, and 10% of the single-Kanji words and their Hiragana transcriptions.

We also had the items rechecked with respect to current familiarity and classification by two expert native speakers, including one from the same cohort as the subjects, and excluded any that they found problematic. We note that every item occurred with the same frequency in all conditions.

The mean correct RT and error rate for the six conditions of this and the other experiments are summarised in the Appendix. Two measures of switch cost are shown: the difference between mean RTs for switch and non-switch trials in the mixed blocks, and the difference between mean RTs on switch trials in the mixed blocks and the pure blocks.

(a) Multiple-Kanji words. Mean correct RTs for switch and non-switch trials indicate an average switch cost of 9 ms for Kanji (i.e., for switching from Hiragana to Kanji) and 7 ms for Hiragana. The effect of switching, though small, is reliable [$F(1,17) = 7.04$, $P < .02$]; the script by switch interaction was not significant ($F < 1$).[5] Given the small size of these effects on mean RT and possible concern that a few remaining problematic items were responsible for the switch costs through some interaction between difficulty and switching, we repeated the analysis with median

[4] Most problematic items were clustered above the 40% cut-off points. A further 3% of items in Experiment 1a and one additional item in Experiment 1b fell between the 25% and 40% cut-off points. A further analysis was conducted on the data from Experiment 1a using a 25% cut-off point. The pattern of results remained unchanged. The mean RTs in switch, non-switch and pure conditions were 600, 590 and 554 ms for the multiple Kanji and 690, 682 and 681 ms for the Hiragana transcriptions. The latency differences between switch and non-switch blocks [$F(1,17) = 8.9$, $P < .01$], switch and pure blocks [$F(1,17) = 9$, $P < .01$] were significant. The error rates in switch, non-switch and pure conditions were 6.5%, 5.8% and 4.4% for the multiple Kanji words and 7.3%, 6.1% and 5.9% for the Hiragana transcriptions. The main effects of switching were significant: [$F(1,17) = 5.7$, $P = .03$] for mixed blocks and [$F(1,17) = 12.2$, $P < .01$] for switch versus pure conditions.

[5] For several reasons we do not report by-item analyses. We either have word sets so much larger (600) than the number of subjects (18) that it is clearly in our ability to generalise outcomes over subjects rather than over materials that power is limited: each group of 3 subjects also has a different assignment of items to the 6 conditions, so that the effect × subjects interactions estimating mean square error to some extent include effect × item variability. Or we have smaller sets of 60 (or in one case 30) words, whose selection so exhausts the words of that type available in Japanese that the ability to generalise to other words of that type is moot. Most of the effects we shall report are within-item effects, and the critical effects are replicated over several experiments with different word sets.

RT, yielding a mean of the median costs of 13 ms for Kanji and 7 ms for Hiragana—again a reliable main effect [$F(1,17) = 6.89$, $P < .02$], and no reliable interaction ($F < 1$). There were also more errors on switch than on non-switch trials. An ANOVA on the arc-sine transformed scores of the error proportions showed that the effect of switching was marginally reliable [$F(1,17) = 3.94$, $P = .063$].

If, instead, we assess switch costs by comparing performance on switch trials to performance in the pure blocks, the cost of a switch on mean RT was 41 ms for Kanji and 5 ms for Hiragana [$F(1,17) = 6.72$, $P = .02$], and the interaction was reliable [$F(1,17) = 12.65$, $P = .02$]. The simple main effect for Hiragana was not significant ($F < 1$). The comparable figure for median RTs were 49 ms switch cost for Kanji and a 21 ms switch cost for Hiragana. In this case the main effect of switching was marginally significant [$F(1,17) = 4.38$, $P = .052$], as was the interaction [$F(1,17) = 4.12$, $P = .058$]. The error rates differ in the same direction as the RTs [$F(1,17) = 8.15$, $P = .01$].

Mean RT was shorter [$F(1,17) = 159.1$, $P < .0001$], and the error rate lower [$F(1,17) = 49.3$, $P < .0001$], for Kanji than for Hiragana words.

(b) Single-Kanji words. A comparison of correct mean RTs on switch and non-switch trials yields a switch cost of 14 ms for Kanji and 7.5 ms for Hiragana [$F(1,17) = 35.85$, $P < .0001$], but no reliable interaction [$F(1,17) = 1.71$]. For median correct RTs the corresponding figures are 10 ms for Kanji and 11 ms for Hiragana [$F(1,17) = 12.05$, $P = .0029$]. The interaction was not reliable, $F < 1$. For both scripts more errors occurred on switch than non-switch trials [$F(1,17) = 10.10$, $P = .0055$].

If we compare switch trials to the pure block, the mean RTs indicated a switch cost of 20 ms for Kanji and 11 ms for Hiragana—a marginally significant effect [$F(1,17) = 3.69$, $P = .0718$]; the script × switch interaction was not significant [$F(1,17) = 1.89$]. Means of the median correct RTs indicated a switch cost of 21 ms for Kanji and 3 ms for Hiragana ($F = 1$). The interaction was also not significant, ($F < 1$). Subjects made more errors on switch trials than in pure blocks [$F(1,17) = 8.12$, $P = .011$].

Mean RT was shorter [$F(1,17) = 52.50$, $P < .001$], and errors less frequent [$F(1,17) = 98.57$, $P < .0001$], for single Kanji words than for their Hiragana transcriptions.

Discussion

There was a small but significant cost of switching script for both multiple and single-Kanji words. Responses on switch trials were slower and more error-prone than on non-switch trials in the mixed blocks. That the pattern of results is similar for mean and median RTs suggests that the cost does not arise from slow responses on just a few switch trials. The costs are certainly small in size, especially if we compare them to costs observed in task-switching experiments and we clearly need replications with other tasks and materials to be sure that the costs are robust. However, given that these subjects had been switching between scripts whenever they read for many years, we were surprised to observe any switch cost at all.

Hiragana transcriptions of Kanji words are of course unfamiliar to the adult reader, and enforce access to meaning via phonological assembly. It is not in the least surprising that reaction times to these items are slower than to the Kanji, nor that mixing the Kanji with Hiragana transcriptions slows them down (hence the large difference between Kanji in mixed and pure blocks)—suggesting the sort of homogenisation effect of mixing difficult and easy items described by Los (1996). However, the switch costs *within* the mixed blocks do not appear to arise merely as a by-product of difficulty, or a homogenisation effect: there is a cost for switching to the (easy) Kanji just as there is a cost of switching to the (hard) Hiragana. And even though the Hiragana transcriptions are unnatural stimuli which must be decoded by phonological assembly, it is of theoretical interest that, even with time to "reorient" between trials, readers suffer a measurable cost in dividing their attention between two input pathways converging on the same semantic representations.

EXPERIMENT 2

As a first step towards understanding the switch cost, we tested its generality by having subjects switch between naming Kanji items and their Hiragana transcriptions. Because of the phonological transparency of Hiragana, we now expect the Hiragana words to enjoy an overall advantage. Although the Hiragana transcriptions are unfamiliar patterns, it is agreed that assembly is the normal mode of decoding Hiragana (the only mode, according to some). Thus we were not now asking subjects to switch between an "unnatural" translation and a natural one. Apart from the change of task, the experiment was essentially the same as the previous one, except that different groups of 18 subjects were tested on the multiple-Kanji and single-Kanji items.

Method

The materials, procedure and design were identical to Experiment 1 with the following exceptions. A microphone connected to a voice key interfaced to the computer was used to detect speech onsets. The response-stimulus interval was now two seconds, instead of one. This allowed the experimenter to code errors on line by pressing a key to denote one of: a correct response, a correct response with dubious voice-key triggering (excluded from the RT analysis), a wrong pronunciation or a dysfluent response (both counted as errors), or a trial to be discarded (e.g. subject coughs). Errors were also recorded in writing. Subjects were instructed to say the word clearly and as quickly as possible.

Results

All items with an error rate of 40% or more in Experiment 1 were excluded from the present analyses. Of course, the error rates were much lower in the naming task, especially on the Hiragana words.

(a) Multiple Kanji words. The mixed blocks yielded a switch cost in correct mean RT of 15.6 ms for Kanji and 13.5 ms for Kana [$F(1,17) = 66.93$, $P < .0001$]; the interaction with script was not significant [$F(1,17) = 2.37$, $P = .14$]. For median RTs the average switch costs were 7 ms for Kanji and 5 ms for Hiragana [$F(1,17) = 9.30$, $P = .0072$]; the interaction was not reliable ($F < 1$). More errors were made on switch than on non-switch trials [$F(1,17) = 59.60$, $P < .0001$].

Comparing performance on switch trials and in the pure blocks, mean correct RTs showed a switch cost of 24 ms for Kanji and 36 ms for Hiragana [$F(1,17) = 105.50$, $P < .0001$]; the interaction was just significant too [$F(1,17) = 4.67$, $P = .045$]. For median correct RTs the mean cost was 28 ms for Kanji and 25 ms for Hiragana [$F(1,17) = 5.30$, $P = .0342$]; the interaction was not reliable ($F < 1$). More errors occurred on the switch trials than in pure blocks [$F(1,17) = 44.04$, $P < .0001$].

Correct naming responses to Kanji were slower than to Hiragana [$F(1,17) = 493.39$, $P < .0001$], and more errors were made, [$F(1,17) = 663.48$, $P < .0001$].

(b) Single Kanji words. Comparison of mean correct RTs for switch and non-switch trials yielded a switch cost of 21 ms for Kanji and 19 ms for Hiragana [$F(1,17) = 54.99$, $P < .0001$]; the switch × script interaction was non-significant ($F < 1$). The costs assessed from median correct RTs were 12 ms for Kanji and 16 ms for Hiragana [$F(1,17) = 15.74$, $P < .001$]; the interaction was not reliable ($F < 1$). More errors occurred on switch than on non-switch trials [$F(1,17) = 21.31$, $P < .001$].

If we use performance in the pure blocks as the baseline instead, the mean correct RTs yield a reliable main effect of switching [$F(1,17) = 15.39$, $P < .01$], with switch costs of 11 ms for Kanji and 32.5 ms for Hiragana. In this case the interaction was significant [$F(1,17) = 11.67$, $P = .003$], and the simple main effect for Kanji was not [$F(1,17) = 2.83$, $P = .11$]. For median correct RT the costs were 11 ms for Kanji and 40 ms for Hiragana. The switching effect was marginally significant [$F(1,17) = 3.29$, $P < .1$], and the interaction was reliable [$F(1,17) = 4.69$, $P = .045$]. More errors occurred on switch trials than in the pure blocks [$F(1,17) = 8.16$, $P = .0109$].

The mean correct RTs for Hiragana were shorter than those for Kanji [$F(1,17) = 384.83$, $P < .0001$], and the error rates were lower [$F(1,17) = 478.24$, $P < .0001$].

Discussion

Performance in the simple naming task used in Experiment 2 showed at least as large and statistically robust a cost of switching as in the semantic categorisation task used in Experiment 1. It would appear that the cost of switching scripts is not restricted to the somewhat artificial categorisation task. Nor is it restricted to the situation of having to switch between an unfamiliar decoding of a familiar word (Hiragana to meaning) and a familiar one (Kanji to meaning). Of course the present experiment involves switching between assembly- and retrieval-based access to phonology, and that could be the source of the switch cost. It is notable too that the costs do not seem proportionate to the level of difficulty on switch trials; although Kanji were slower to pronounce than their Hiragana transcriptions, there was little difference in the cost of switching from one to the other.

Responses to single-Kanji words were generally faster than responses to multiple-Kanji words. There may be many reasons for this. There were different numbers of trials in the single- and multiple-Kanji experiments. Single-Kanji words were repeated six times (three times in each script) while multiple Kanji were presented just once. Single-Kanji words and their transcriptions are visually less complex and extend less into the parafovea than the multiple Kanji words. In the categorisation task the semantic radical may be more likely to provide a useful cue to categorisation for single than for multiple-Kanji words. (For example, 猫, neko (cat) and 猪, inoshishi (wild boar) have the radical frequently used for Kanji signifying animals.) Although the Kanji characters used in some multiple-Kanji words clearly indicate whether the word signifies an animate object or not, this was not the case for most of the multiple-Kanji items. In the naming task, the average number of morae is greater for the multiple-Kanji than for the single-Kanji words, which may also influence the latency. However, regardless of its origins, the performance advantage for single-Kanji words and their Hiragana transcriptions was not accompanied by a marked difference in the switch costs observed, either for single- or for multiple-Kanji words.

Thus far, then, we seem to have demonstrated a numerically small but robust cost of switching from reading a Kanji word to reading a Hiragana transcription of a word normally written in Kanji, and vice versa. The cost does not seem to depend strongly on the direction of switching, nor on other factors (such as single versus multiple Kanji, or the interaction between task and script) which have marked effects on baseline performance. And switch costs assessed using the subtraction recommended by Rogers and Monsell (1995) are generally a little smaller than those based on the Jersild-like comparison of switch trials to trials in pure blocks, suggesting that the former is perhaps a less inclusive measure.

The remaining experiments followed up this initial finding with four purposes in mind: to replicate the effect with other sets of materials (Experiments 5, 6); to address the concern that the switch costs might arise from differences in the visual properties of Hiragana and Kanji words (Experiments 3–5); to address the concern that the finding of switch costs might depend somehow on the unfamiliarity of Hiragana transcriptions of Kanji words (Experiments 5, 6); to inquire whether there is also a cost of switching between Hiragana and Katakana (Experiment 7).

EXPERIMENT 3

Kanji characters have up to 30 strokes while the number of strokes in Kana characters does not exceed four.[6] Although the number of characters in Kana transcriptions is normally higher than that of the corresponding Kanji, on average the total number of strokes per Kanji word is higher than the total number of strokes in its Hiragana transcription. Hence, by this measure, and doubtless by many others, such as the amount of contour per unit area, or the spatial frequency, words written in Kanji tend to be visually more complex than words written in Kana; they have more intricate pattern information packed into the same visual angle. Could it be the case that shifts (whether stimulus-driven or anticipated) in the visual analysis mechanisms engaged—e.g., different spatial frequency channels—are responsible for the switch costs we have observed? In the present experiment, we attempted to test this by having subjects switch between markedly different levels of visual complexity without changing scripts, in the same way as they previously switched scripts. We used the naming task.

[6] However, if we include diacritics (e.g., ぶ [bu]) then the maximum number of strokes in Kana is six.

Method

This experiment used two lists of 60 single-Kanji words. One was of visually simple Kanji containing one to six strokes. The other was a list of visually complex Kanji containing more than 12 strokes. The visual familiarity of a larger set of stimuli was first rated by 30 undergraduate native Japanese speakers on a five-point scale (i.e., unfamiliar = 1, very familiar = 5). Only words obtaining average (2.9) or above average scores were used and the two lists were matched for familiarity. All the Kanji used were free morphemes with no Kana inflection. They were displayed in a 36 point Honmincho font. The design was identical to that of Experiments 1b and 2b, except that the Kanji and Hiragana stimuli used in those experiments were replaced by the new lists of visually simple and visually complex Kanji.

Results and Discussion

Responses to visually complex Kanji were 34 ms slower than those to visually simple Kanji. An analysis of variance with the factors complexity and trial type (switch, non-switch and pure) showed a highly reliable effect of complexity [$F(1,17) = 69.44$, $P < .0001$], but neither the effect of trial type nor the interaction between trial type and complexity was reliable (Fs < 1). Similarly the error rates for complex Kanji were higher than those for simple Kanji [$F(1,17) = 21.32$, $P < .001$], but no other effects were reliable.

Performance on switch and non-switch trials in mixed blocks was very similar, with a switch cost indicated by mean correct RT of −0.5 ms ($F < 1$). There were actually reliably more errors in the non-switch condition than in the switch condition [$F(1,17) = 10.38$, $P = .005$].

A similar lack of evidence for any cost of switching between complex and simple Kanji is evident if we compare switch trials in mixed blocks to trials in pure blocks. This estimate of cost was 4.5 ms for mean RT ($F \approx 1$). There was no reliable difference in error ($F < 1$).

There was thus no evidence of a cost when subjects had to switch between processing visually complex and visually simple Kanji characters, even though the difference in complexity was marked and had a substantial effect on performance.[7] This implies that the costs of switching between

[7] Of course, there might be other differences confounded with complexity. For example, one referee who examined our materials suggested that the complex characters might have more competing readings. However, another native speaker assessor detected more phonological ambiguities among the simple items. In fact Wydell, Butterworth, and Patterson (1995) demonstrated that the naming latencies of phonologically ambiguous Kanji are not longer than those of non-ambiguous ones.

Kanji and Hiragana in Experiments 1 and 2 could not have resulted from a difference in average visual complexity between the two scripts.

EXPERIMENT 4

Another difference in the visual properties of Kanji words and their Hiragana transcriptions is in their average spatial extent. In most cases a larger number of Hiragana characters is required to represent a Kanji word than the number of Kanji characters it contains. If characters of the same size are used, the Hiragana words will on average have a greater lateral extent. We attempted to minimise the difference by using a 36 point Kanji font and a 24 point font for the Hiragana words, but this trades a difference in vertical extent for the difference in lateral extent.

There is evidence that the size of the "attentional spotlight" in vision changes as a function of task demands. LaBerge (1983) presented five-letter strings or words, and required the subject to categorise the central letter, or classify the whole item as word or non-word, while also detecting a digit in any position. For the letter task, responses to the digit declined in speed the further they were from the centre, but in the lexical decision task, there was no effect of eccentricity on digit detection. Eriksen and St. James (1986) and Eriksen and Yeh (1985) suggested that visual attention, though not sharply bounded, behaves like a "spotlight" of variable extent: the size can vary continuously between the entire visual field and an area of about 1°; processing efficiency is inversely related to the size of the attended area; a change in size of the attentional field ("zooming") has a measurable time duration.

LaBerge's result suggests endogenous control of the size of the attentional field. But, if we assume that the spotlight size is also exogenously driven by the stimulus size (when there is a single central stimulus) then the switch costs observed in Experiments 1 and 2 might be attributable to time taken to "zoom" the field between the sizes (and perhaps shapes) of the Kanji words and the Hiragana transcriptions. The next two experiments test this possibility. In the first one we used the semantic categorisation task, and had subjects switch between two sizes of Kanji word.

Method

The experiment used essentially the same set of single-Kanji words as used in Experiments 1b and 2b, with a few error-prone items replaced. The design and procedure were identical to those of Experiment 1b, except that the Hiragana transcriptions were replaced with the Kanji words displayed in a 24 point font, so that, in the mixed blocks, the size of the stimuli changed, every second trial between the 24 point and 36 point fonts.

Results and discussion

The response to a small font was slightly slower than to a large font, but the effect was not reliable [$F(1,17) = 2.4$, $P < .14$]. On the other hand the small Kanji evoked significantly fewer errors than the large Kanji [$F(1,17) = 35.23$, $P < .0001$].

The difference between mean RT for switch and non-switch trials was a non-significant 4.5 ms [$F(1,17) = 2.25$]. However the interaction between trials and script size was significant [$F(1,17) = 7.40$, $P = .015$]. There was a reliable 13 ms cost of switching from small to large [$F(1,17) = 8.1$, $P = .011$], but an unreliable 4 ms benefit of switching in the opposite direction [$F(1,17) = 1.06$]. Moreover there were only about half as many errors on switch as on non-switch trials [$F(1,17) = 10.47$, $P = .0049$]. Hence, there is some suggestion that subjects threw caution to the winds when the font size did not change, which might account for the slightly, though not reliably, slower responses on switch trials. Interestingly, if we compare switch trials to pure blocks instead, there is no switch cost (unlike the pattern seen in Experiments 1 and 2): the difference was actually negative for both mean RT ($F < 1$), and errors ($F < 1$). This supports the notion that the small time cost of a switch observed within the mixed blocks is due to a dynamic adjustment in response criterion.

Hence there is little evidence that a change in size, and hence a need to change the size of the "attentional spotlight" is responsible for the cost of a script shift observed in Experiments 1 and 2. However, Experiment 5 provides a further test of the hypothesis.

EXPERIMENT 5

Experiments 1 and 2 had subjects switch between words normally written in Kanji and Hiragana transcriptions of the same words. As already noted, the latter are unfamiliar forms of the words in question. With respect to the theoretical significance of the switch cost, it is important to rule out the possibility that it results from a shift in the (average) familiarity of items between the Kana and Kanji trials, or that it results somehow from the mismatch between the unfamiliar form in which the word is presented and its normative form. With respect to the practical significance of the switch cost, it is obviously essential to show that the cost is not restricted to unnatural stimuli of a type rarely encountered. Hence the remaining experiments used words normally written in Kana, and a between-words design. Ideally, we would like to control both visual extent, by matching the number of characters in the Kana and Kanji words, and to use both semantic classification and naming tasks. However, matched Hiragana words describing objects suitable for a classification task are in very short supply. In the present experiment, subjects switched between naming two-character Kanji words and two-character words normally written in Hiragana. In Experiment 6 we exploited the larger pool of Katakana words to examine semantic classification, but without matching length.

Method

The size of the stimulus set was limited by the difficulty of finding words normally written in Hiragana that contained only two characters. A set of candidate words was rated for familiarity on a five-point scale by 36 Japanese undergraduates; only words without homophones and without prefixes or suffices were considered. We were able to find 30 two-character words normally written in Hiragana (familiarity M = 2.8, SD = 0.49). Japanese undergraduate students rated the Kanji of these words as too obscure for use, and preferred the Hiragana forms. A list of two-character Kanji words with only two morae were also selected (M = 3.3, SD = 0.40). For both Kanji and Hiragana words geminate consonants (e.g., 学校, gakko) and palatisation (e.g., 京都, kyōtō) were excluded. A 36 point Honmincho font was used to display both Kanji and Hiragana words. The presentation of stimuli and the design were as in Experiment 2b, except that there were only half the number of stimuli. It was thus necessary to repeat stimuli within a block. However, all the stimuli were used once in the first half of a block before being re-used, in a different random order, in the second half.

Results and Discussion

The comparison of switch to non-switch trials yielded a reliable cost for mean correct RT: [$F(1,17) = 31.26$, $P < .01$], and no reliable interaction ($F < 1$); the costs were 7 ms for Kanji and 13 ms for Hiragana. The cost estimated from median correct RTs was also reliable [$F(1,17) = 14.06$, $P < .0016$], and did not interact reliably with script [$F(1,17) = 1.23$]: a 5 ms cost for Kanji and a 10 ms cost for Hiragana. More errors were made on switch trials [$F(1,17) = 8.75$, $P = .008$].

Comparing switch trials to trials in pure blocks indicated a 17 ms switching cost for both Kanji and Hiragana [$F(1,17) = 7.79$, $P \leq .05$]. Median correct RTs showed an 11 ms cost for Kanji and a 17 ms switch cost for Hiragana, a reliable main effect [$F(1,17) = 6.50$, $P < .05$], but no reliable interaction [$F(1,17) = 2.15$]. There were more errors on the switch trials, but not reliably so [$F(1,17) = 2.19$]. Responses were slower [$F(1,17) = 239.82$, $P < .0001$], and less accurate [$F(1,17) = 256.34$, $P < .0001$], for the Kanji than for the Hiragana words.

The significant cost of switching between scripts is similar to that seen in Experiments 1 and 2. Hence, with respect to naming, at least, the switch does not derive from a difference in familiarity of the forms. Although the Hiragana words afford pronunciation by assembly, while the Kanji do not, both afford access to a learned pronunciation (and meaning). Moreover, the two kinds of words had the same spatial extent and number of characters. They differ in visual complexity, but Experiment 3 appears to have ruled that out as the source of the effect. The costs observed here were somewhat smaller than in the other two naming experiments, and the preferred measure of mean RT cost was significantly smaller than in Experiment 2b. However, the constrained stimulus selection meant that the words were repeated even more than in Experiment 2b, and were less representative of Japanese words. For example, the two-character Hiragana words used in this experiment avoided geminate consonants and palatalisation.

EXPERIMENT 6

Experiments 3 through 5 have manipulated or controlled visual complexity, spatial extent, number of characters and familiarity, and demonstrated that the costs of switching between naming Hiragana and Kanji words can be attributed to changes in none of these properties. We would like to check that the robustness of the effect, with these properties controlled, generalises to the semantic categorisation task with which we began. But there are simply not enough familiar words normally written in Hiragana suitable for use in a semantic categorisation task. So, in the present experiment, we looked at the consequence of switching between Kanji words and words normally written in Katakana, the set of Kana characters primarily used for foreign loan words, using a semantic categorisation task—this time a judgement of the size of the object designated by the word. However differences in the number of characters and morae in the Katakana and Kanji words could not be controlled due to lack of appropriate stimuli.

Method

Thirty undergraduates rated the visual familiarity of candidate stimuli. Lists of 60 Katakana words (familiarity M = 3.1, SD = 0.45) and 60 Kanji words (M = 2.9, SD = 0.48) were selected. The Kanji words all had two characters. There were not enough two-character Katakana words so 3 two-, 39 three-, and 18 four-character Katakana words were used. Twenty-nine words in each set denoted "large" objects—i.e., objects clearly larger than the outer border of the computer screen (34 × 28 cm) used in the experiment (e.g., a house, a bus)—while 31 signified "small" objects (e.g., a camera, a watch). The Kanji words were displayed in a 36 point Honmincho and the Katakana words in a 24 point Honmincho font.

Procedure and design were as in Experiment 1b, with the "large"/"small" classification replacing the "animate"/"inanimate" classification.

Results and Discussion

For correct mean RTs, the switch responses were slower than the non-switch responses [$F(1,17) = 5.74$, $P = .03$], by 12 ms for Kanji and 13 ms for Katakana. Median correct RTs showed a similar pattern, an 11 ms cost for Kanji and a 14 ms cost for Katakana [$F(1,17) = 8.92$, $P < .01$], and no reliable interaction ($F < 1$). There were more errors on switch than non-switch trials [$F(1,17) = 15.29$, $P < .01$].

The between blocks measure indicated a 23 ms switch cost for Kanji and an 18 ms switch cost for Katakana [$F(1,17) = 6.25$, $P < .05$], and no interaction with script ($F < 1$). Similarly a 20 ms switch cost for Kanji and a 17 ms cost for Katakana were found for the median correct RTs [$F(1,17) = 4.60$, $P < .05$], with no interaction ($F < 1$). More errors were made on switch trials than in the pure blocks [$F(1,17) = 23.46$, $P < .01$].

The mean response latencies for Kanji were slightly shorter than those for Katakana but not reliably so [$F(1,17) = 1.62$]. There were more errors on Katakana words [$F(1,17) = 70.05$, $P < .0001$]. Given the widespread assumption that the mapping of Kana to meaning is less direct than for Kanji, it is of some interest that semantic categorisation performance was so similar for the Kanji and Katakana words.

The results of this experiment extend the previous results in three ways. They demonstrate a reliable cost of switching between reading Kanji and Kana in another semantic categorisation task. They confirm that this happens even when words in the two scripts are matched for familiarity. They show for the first time a cost of switching between reading Katakana and Kanji, which supplements the previous demonstrations of a Hiragana–Kanji switch cost.

EXPERIMENT 7

We have now looked at switching between Hiragana and Kanji, and between Katakana and Kanji. The final experiment in the series looked at switching between Katakana and Hiragana. There are two reasons to do so. First, Katakana are used to represent a particular class of words—foreign loan words. The sceptic might therefore point out that the switch cost observed in the previous experiment could be attributable to shifting between two classes of words, not between scripts *per se*. More generally, it is important to establish whether the cost of switching that we have observed is associated with changing between scripts that operate according to different principles, not merely to any change in the population or type of characters. Hiragana and Katakana are different scripts, but they both use characters of similar design which map transparently onto phonological units. The two scripts should be processed by essentially the same mechanism, and we do not, therefore, expect to observe any cost of switching between them.

Method

A candidate set of three-character Hiragana and Katakana words were rated for familiarity by 36 Japanese undergraduate students. The Hiragana words were indigenous Japanese words whose Kanji were too obscure to be used by Japanese undergraduates. Some of the Hiragana words used in this experiment were included in Experiments 1b and 2b in both Hiragana and Kanji forms. However, visual familiarity was not controlled in those experiments. The Katakana words were foreign loan words. Sets of 30 visually familiar words of each type were selected on the basis of this judgement (for Katakana M = 3.2, SD = 0.44; for Hiragana M = 2.8, SD = 0.49). The selected words had no homophones, no geminate consonants, and no palatalisation. The words were displayed in a 36 point Honmincho font. The naming task was used, with procedure and design identical to those of Experiment 5.

Results and Discussion

Mean correct reaction times were 1.5 ms slower on switch than on switch trials [$F(1,17) = 2.73$, $P = .11$]; there was also no reliable interaction with script ($F < 1$). The difference in the error rates was not significant [$F(1,17) = 2.2$].

Performance in pure blocks was fractionally slower, by 1.5 ms, than that of switch trials in the mixed blocks ($F < 1$), and there were reliably more errors in pure blocks [$F(1,17) = 10.57$, $P = .004$], but this "benefit" of switching was confined to the Katakana words, so that the switch × script interaction was reliable [$F(1,17) = 8.18$, $P = .01$].

The subjects named Katakana words slightly faster than Hiragana words and this difference between Katakana and Hiragana words was significant [$F(1,17) = 10.18$, $P = .005$], and the error rates were also slightly lower for Katakana words [$F(1,17) = 19.35$, $P < .001$]. Nevertheless, these two sets of words did not differ greatly in difficulty. The naming latencies were as low as in any of the other experiments, even though these were all three-character words. It is tempting to suggest that this is because the subject in the present experiment can, in essence, focus entirely on the Kana "route". (Cf. Monsell, Patterson, Graham, Hughes, & Milroy, 1992, on naming pure versus mixed blocks of exception words and non-words in English.)

It is impossible to prove the null hypothesis, given that the costs of Kana/Kanji switching in the earlier experiments have always been numerically modest, but the present results suggest that switching between reading visually familiar Katakana and Hiragana words incurs no cost. The absence of any cost for switching between the two Kana scripts stands in marked contrast to the costs observed in each of the experiments on Kanji–Hiragana switching and the one experiment on Kanji–Katakana switching. The implication is that it is not merely switching between two symbol sets that generates those costs but switching between scripts whose processing depends on different mechanisms or combinations of routes. Note also that differences in category, part of speech etc. between the two sets of words were probably at least as great in this experiment as in the Kanji–Kana switching experiments.

GENERAL DISCUSSION

The Appendix summarises the switch costs observed in all nine experiments (counting the two parts of Experiments 1 and 2 separately). It is instructive to compare costs across experiments. First, it is clear that there are significant costs of switching in all the experiments in which subjects switched between Kanji and Kana words (first six columns), and no reliable or sizeable costs when the subjects switched either between the two types of Kana, or between sets of Kanji words differing in size or complexity (last three columns). The cost of switching between Kanji and Kana is not numerically large, but it is robust. The mean RT difference (and standard error of the difference) between switch and non-switch trials over all the Kanji/Kana experiments is 13.1 ± 1.8 ms, which is significantly different from zero by experiments [$t(5) = 7.3$, $P < .001$]. The difference between switch trials and trials in pure blocks is 21.7 ± 1.9 ms [$t(5) = 11.2$, $P < .001$]. The comparable error rate difference between switch and non-switch trials was 0.68 ± 0.1% [$t(5) = 6.7$, $P = .001$], and between switch trials and trials in pure blocks 0.68 ± 0.19% [$t(5) = 3.5$, $P < .017$].

Comparisons can be made between subsets of experiments; the means we report below weight each experiment by the number of trials it contributes.

Tasks. There is no evidence that average switch costs differ markedly for naming and semantic categorisation tasks: latencies on switch trials exceeded those on non-switch trials by an average of 10.5 ms for semantic categorisation, and 15.1 ms for naming. The mean difference between switch trials and trials in pure blocks was 20.6 ms for categorisation and 24.5 ms for naming.

Scripts. If we compare switch and non-switch trials averaged over task, switching to Kanji from Kana cost an average of 13.3 ms, while switching in the opposite direction cost 12.3 ms. If we compare switch trials to trials in pure blocks, the estimates are 24.6 ms and 20.5 ms respectively. However, given that naming is easier for Kana than for Kanji words, while semantic categorisation is harder, we might expect any asymmetry in switch costs between the two scripts to depend on the task. For the within-block difference between switch and non-switch trials, there was little evidence for this: when the task was categorisation, the switch cost was 11.7 ms for Kanji and 9.2 ms for Kana, but for naming, the costs were 14.9 ms for Kanji and 15.4 ms for Kana, only a slight trend in the direction of larger costs for the easier script for each task. In a by-experiments ANOVA (each experiment now weighted equally), the interaction was nowhere near reliable (F = 1). If, however, we compare switch trials to trials in pure blocks, the weighted mean cost to categorisation RT was 30.6 ms for Kanji and 10.5 ms for Kana, while for naming, the costs differed in the opposite direction: 18.5 ms for Kanji and 30.5 ms for Kana. In a by-experiments ANOVA, this interaction was marginal [$F(1,4)$ = 6.4, P = .06]. This modest asymmetry may remind cognoscenti of the task-switching literature of Allport et al.'s (1994) claim that it is harder to switch to the easier of two tasks afforded by the same stimulus because the dominant task requires more suppression to enable the weaker task, and this inhibition carries over to the next trial. It is, however, unclear how Allport et al.'s argument would apply to the case of input switching, where there is no logical need to suppress the processing of the other script.

The two measures of cost. In every Kanji/Kana experiment the within-block measure of the time cost of a switch (switch minus non-switch RT) yielded a smaller estimate of the cost than the between-blocks contrast between switch trials and trials in the pure blocks. This is compatible with the notion that the first measure excludes a component of cost attributable perhaps to the need not only to cope with transitions between scripts but also to maintain a readiness to process either script. It would appear to be this component that is the main source of the asymmetry in switch costs, such as it is. The contrast of mixed and pure blocks may also involve the homogenisation of RTs noted by Los (1996) when difficult and easy stimuli are mixed: this may account for the especially large difference between pure and mixed blocks for the Kanji words observed in Experiment 1.

Practice and repetition. In Experiments 1a and 2a, to avoid repetition of items we used large (and presumably representative) word sets, accepting differences in size, number of characters and familiarity between Kanji and Kana words. In the later experiments, we controlled for these differences, but paid the price of having to use smaller and less representative sets, and allowing subjects to see each word several times.

The fact that switch costs in the two sets of experiments were similar suggests that switch costs are resistant to amelioration by repetition.

We analysed effects of repetition and practice by dividing the mixed blocks in each experiment into four quarters, one successive pair of blocks per quarter. Figure 2 shows performance on switch and non-switch trials as a function of practice in Experiments 1a (categorisation) and 2a (naming), in which each item occurred only once; this is a test of practice unconfounded by repetition. In the categorisation experiment, there was a significant reduction in the time cost of a switch with practice [$F(3,51) = 2.9$, $P = .04$], while there was no such reduction for naming ($F < 1$). (For the error cost, $F < 1$ in both cases.) Figure 3 shows performance averaged over the other categorisation experiments (Experiments 1b and 6) and the other naming experiments (Experiments 2b and 5). In these experiments repetition is confounded with practice, in that each item occurs more than once, which probably explains why the slopes are steeper than in Figure 2. However, the picture is similar. On average the time cost of a switch reduced with practice in the categorisation experiments, though this interaction was reliable only for Experiment 1b [$F(3,51) = 7.74$, $P < .001$]; error costs showed no consistent pattern. For the naming experiments, the dominant pattern was again no decrease in either the time or the error cost

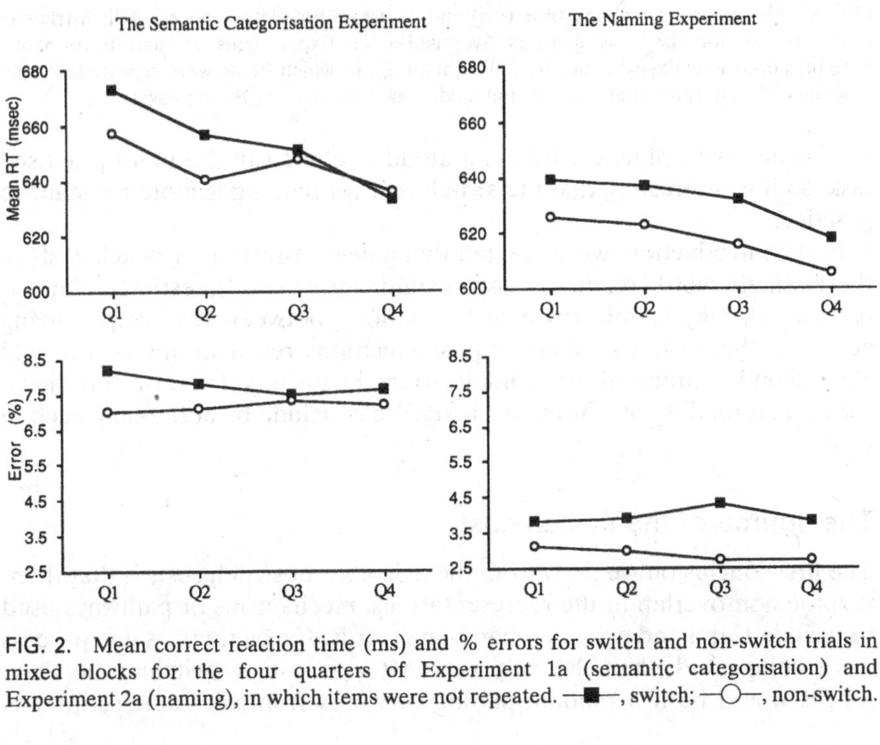

FIG. 2. Mean correct reaction time (ms) and % errors for switch and non-switch trials in mixed blocks for the four quarters of Experiment 1a (semantic categorisation) and Experiment 2a (naming), in which items were not repeated. —■—, switch; —O—, non-switch.

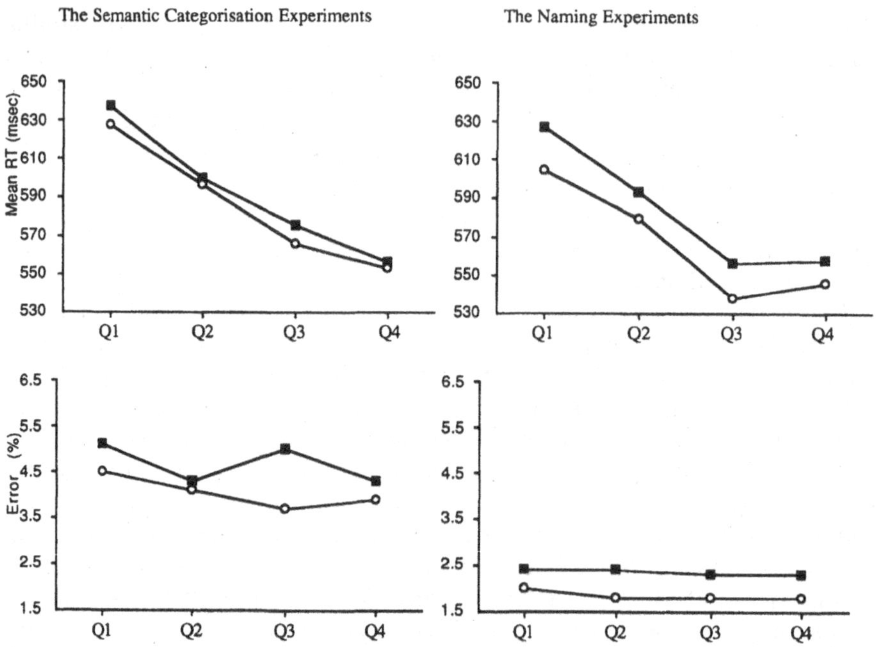

FIG. 3. Mean correct reaction time (ms) and % errors for switch and non-switch trials in mixed blocks for the four quarters averaged over Experiments 1b and 6 (semantic categorisation) and Experiments 2b and 5 (naming), in which items were repeated, so that practice and item repetition were confounded. —■—, switch; —○—, non-switch.

of a switch with practice. Reading aloud is obviously the more practised task, so it is interesting that the switch cost for naming is more resistant to practice.

In the introduction, we suggested that a demonstration of switch costs in these single-word reading tasks would raise two questions. One is theoretical: why should dividing "attention" between two scripts giving access to the same meanings or pronunciations result in any cost at all? The second is practical: what implications might this demonstration have for normal reading of continuous text? We conclude by addressing each in turn.

The source of the switch cost

The first conclusion we draw from the existence of switch costs is that there is some non-overlap in the representations, mechanisms or pathways used to decode Kanji and even familiar Kana words. If exactly the same process were being used, then the only reason for a cost of switching between scripts would be if a random pairing of words from the same script was more similar, in some way that influenced processing, than a random pairing across scripts. In many of our experiments the same words were used in the Kanji and Kana sets, so that we can rule out semantic, syntactic and phonological similarity. We cannot, however, rule out visual similarity, since Kanji and Kana words are intrinsically different in their visual properties. We have ruled out spatial extent, complexity and number of characters as effective differences in visual properties, but it is certainly possible that different populations of feature detectors, or word-form detectors, or detectors of intermediate units such as stroke patterns (Chen, Allport, & Marshall, 1996) are activated by Kanji and Kana words, and that switching between these incurs costs. There may also be differences between (familiar) Kana and Kanji words in the strengths of their associations to meaning and phonology, respectively. The costs may also reflect the fact that only Kana characters engage the phonological assembly process.

However, even if different mechanisms—in any of these senses—are used for reading Kana and Kanji words, it remains far from obvious why a switch between scripts should impair performance. We briefly suggested in the introduction three possible sources of switch costs. We expand on these suggestions here, but are as yet unable to decide between them.

Control operations? In the case of task-switching, switch costs have been attributed to the time taken by a control process that activates or inhibits particular input/output connections (Rogers & Monsell, 1995). These authors also suggest that only part of this control work can be carried out in advance of the stimulus, so that costs of a task switch are observed even with ample opportunity for preparation for a change of task. We acknowledge the possibility that the (much smaller) cost of switching we have observed in the present experiments—even with ample opportunity for preparation—derives from such control operations. But we are unable to see why any control operations should be required to switch scripts. Even if Kana and Kanji are processed by different pathways, or different populations of feature detectors, or with differential ease by different pathways, there would seem to be no logical reason not to leave both pathways or populations connected to semantic or phonological output—much as, when you anticipate successive visitors arriving at both the front and back doors of your house, you can leave both open, whereas if you must simultaneously exclude cats, hedgehogs and burglars, you should only open one at a time.

Passive priming? Repetition of orthographic elements in two closely successive stimuli sometimes facilitates processing of the second (e.g., Evett & Humphreys, 1981; Forster, Davis, Schoknecht, & Carter, 1987).

The standard assumption is that feature-, letter- or word-detectors already activated by the prime require less input to bring them to a critical level of activation. The costs of script switching could, perhaps, be a variant of this kind of priming effect. Inasmuch as Kanji and Kana activate different populations of detectors, then two words written in the same script should partially activate more feature detectors, and perhaps detectors for higher level units such as radicals and characters, in common. However, these sub-lexical facilitatory effects are typically observed at very short lags, and under masked priming conditions. Even under these conditions, inhibitory effects on lexical decisions of priming with a lexical neighbour are sometimes seen (Segui & Grainger, 1990) and with unmasked primes at a longer interval, there have been several reports of inhibitory priming by a lexical neighbour (e.g., Colombo, 1986; Segui & Grainger, 1990). Lexical identification is now standardly seen as being a competitive process: persisting activation of a primed competitor (a neighbour in stimulus space) means that it takes longer for the target to achieve a level of activation sufficiently higher than other members of a cohort of similar candidate word-forms partially activated by the target (cf. Monsell & Hirsh, 1998). Presumably Kanji and Kana word-forms are not competitors in this sense, since they contain different features. Hence we might expect that allowing a longer interval to elapse since the last encounter with another word from the same script would have the beneficial effect of allowing the activation of competitors to decay. The same could apply to any intermediate level—radical-detectors used in the recognition of Kanji words, or Kana detectors used in the recognition of Kana words.

Thus there are reasons to expect both positive and negative effects of a word immediately following another written in the same script. It could also be the case that, rather than reflecting the activation of common elements, the switch cost derives from a non-specific "warm-up" effect, with processing facilitated if a whole route is still "warm" from use on the previous trial. That the between-block measure of switch cost is only about 50% greater than the within-block cost would suggest that the major component of any such warm-up effect has a short time-course.

Competition for resources? Inasmuch as Kana and Kanji words are processed by non-overlapping mechanisms, there may be some resource that increases the efficiency of either Kanji and Kana processing, but has capacity so limited that it cannot be directed to both at once without impairing the efficiency of processing one. The switch cost could then arise from the time taken to attract this resource. At the level of the neural substrate, this resource could be as basic as the chemicals required for metabolism and synthesis of neurotransmitters. Modern neuro-imaging rests largely on the simple notion that the blood supply carrying these metabolites is selectively routed on demand to active regions. If Kana and Kanji word forms are represented in slightly different regions of cortex, or place differential demands on anatomically displaced neural networks representing different kinds of stimulus features, then switch costs could derive from the slightly less efficient processing that occurs during the lag before the shift in the locus of activation has been followed by a shift in the local distribution of metabolites. Frith and Friston (1997) cite an estimate of 5–8 s for this lag. At the functional level of analysis, spatial attention is an example of a limited resource. Focusing attention on a spatial locus makes processing of a stimulus at that locus more efficient and processing at others less efficient. Attention can be attracted to a region exogenously, by a stimulus onset, or endogenously, in a slower process of voluntary direction of attention. It takes time to shift attention from one locus to another (Posner, 1980). Kana and Kanji representations may act as channels in a similar way. Given that we have allowed a second or more of preparation, we have presumably allowed any endogenous orienting to take place already, and must be picking up an additional exogenous component.

Relevance to normal reading

We can see no reason why the slowed access to meaning and pronunciation from a word following a script change that we have demonstrated here with discrete RT tasks should not apply also during continuous reading. Many factors that affect single word reading tasks also influence, for example, fixation durations in fluent reading (Rayner & Pollatsek, 1989).

Of course the materials and tasks we have used here are unnatural in several ways. Hiragana transcriptions of Kanji words, especially when used for access to meaning, as in Experiment 1, are especially unnatural (albeit convenient in terms of experimental design). However, Experiments 5 and 6 demonstrated similar switch costs for semantic categorisation of familiar Katakana words and naming of familiar Hiragana words. We have not tested the grammatical words normally written in Hiragana, because of the problem of confounding script switching with changes in syntactic class and frequency. Moreover, we suspect that, having allowed long intervals for preparation between trials, we have measured only the lower bound of the mixing costs that may occur in reading continuous text. Task-switching costs are typically higher when the subject cannot prepare for a switch (Meiran, 1996; Rogers & Monsell, 1995) the same may be true for script-switching, and the high rate of continuous reading allows no time for preparation even if the next word's script can be detected parafoveally.

Taylor and Park (1995) and Taylor (1997) suggests that a mixed script helps Japanese readers to locate the content words, and that this makes comprehension more efficient. Taylor and Park (1995) demonstrated that English sentences were read faster when the content words were written in bold face. They argue that when reading Japanese, the correlation between script and syntactic role, although imperfect, may, in the same way, help direct attention to the content morphemes. They point to the existence of numerous studies showing that mixed Kanji–Hiragana texts are easier to read than all-Hiragana texts. Osaka (1989) found that the eye fixates more often on Kanji than on Hiragana, and that saccade magnitude for mixed Kana–Kanji sentences was significantly larger than that for Kana-only sentences (see also Sakamoto & Makita, 1973). However, the problem with these studies would appear to be that Hiragana-only words and sentences are generally less familiar to adult readers. That familiarity matters was demonstrated by Taylor and Park (1995) who compared the reading of three types of Korean sentences: 50% Chinese characters (the remainder being written in the Hangul alphabetic syllabary), 10% Chinese characters, and Hangul-only sentences. Reading was fastest for Hangul-only sentences. Korean readers are more familiar with Hangul-only text. When subjects were practised on reading the Chinese characters, these differences diminished or disappeared.

We certainly accept Taylor's (1997) argument that the association between different scripts and syntactic classes may be positively beneficial in mixed-script reading, providing visible cues to syntactic role and structure. This benefit could outweigh the cost in processing time for single words that switching scripts apparently induces, or it may not. To answer this question, we will have to be ingenious in thinking of ways to separate out, in measures of normal reading, the cost of switching between orthographies that we have identified, and the benefits of the cueing effect.

REFERENCES

Allport, D.A. (1979). Word recognition in reading: A tutorial review. In P.A. Kolers, H. Bouma, & M. Wrolstad (Eds), *Processing of visible language*, Vol. 1, pp.227–257. New York: Plenum Press.

Allport, D.A., Styles, E.A., & Hsieh, S. (1994). Shifting intention set—exploring the dynamic control of tasks. In C. Umilta & M. Moscovitch (Eds), *Attention and Performance: XV*, pp.421–452. Hillsdale, NJ: Lawrence Erlbaum Associates Inc.

Anzai, S., Okuse, T., & Aizawara, H. (1965). Iwayuru jungomōchō ni kansuru kōsatsu, tokuni kokugo no tokushusei ni kansura mondai [Pure word blindness: Characteristic features in Japanese language]. *Naika [Internal Medicine]*, *15*, 187–192.

Besner, D., & Hildebrandt, N. (1987). Orthographic and phonological codes in the oral reading of Japanese Kana. *Journal of Experimental Psychology: Learning, Memory, and Cognition*, *13*, 335–343.

Besner, D., Stolz, J.A., & Boutilier, C. (1997). The Stroop effect and the myth of automaticity. *Psychonomic Bulletin and Review*, *4*, 221–225.

Caramazza, A., & Brones, E. (1980). Semantic classification by bilinguals. *Canadian Journal of Psychology*, *34*, 77–81.

Carr, T.H. (1992). Automaticity and cognitive anatomy: Is word recognition "automatic"? *American Journal of Psychology*, *105*, 201–238.

Chen, Y-P, Allport, D.A., & Marshall, J.C. (1996). What are the fundamental orthographic units in Chinese word recognition: the stroke or the stroke pattern? *Quarterly Journal of Experimental Psychology*, *49A*, 1024–1043.

Colombo, L. (1986). Activation and inhibition with orthographically similar words. *Journal of Experimental Psychology: Human Perception and Performance*, *12*, 226–234.

Coltheart, M., Curtis, B., Atkins, P., & Haller, M. (1993). Models of reading aloud: Dual-route and parallel-distributed-processing approaches. *Psychological Review*, *100*, 589–608.

Eriksen, C.W., & St. James, J.D. (1986). Visual attention within and around the field of focal attention: A zoom lens model. *Perception and Psychophysics*, *40*, 225–240.

Eriksen, C.W., & Yeh, Y.Y. (1985). Allocation of attention in the visual field. *Journal of Experimental Psychology: Human Perception and Performance*, *11*, 583–597.

Evett, L.J., & Humphreys, G.W. (1981). The use of abstract graphemic information in lexical access. *Quarterly Journal of Experimental Psychology*, *33A*, 325–350.

Feldman, L.B., & Turvey, M.T. (1980). Words written in Kana are named faster than the same words written in Kanji. *Language and Speech*, *23*, 141–147.

Flores d'Arcais, G.B., Saito, H., & Kawakami, M. (1995). Phonological and semantic activation in reading Kanji characters. *Journal of Experimental Psychology: Learning, Memory, and Cognition*, *21*, 34–42.

Forster, K.I., Davis, C., Schoknecht, C., & Carter, R. (1987). Masked priming with graphemically related forms—repetition or partial activation. *Quarterly Journal of Experimental Psychology*, *39*, 211–251.

Frith, C., & Friston, K.J. (1997). Studying brain function with neuroimaging. In M.D. Rugg (Ed.), *Cognitive Neuroscience*, pp.169–195. Hove, UK: Psychology Press.

Goryo S. (1987). *Yomu to iu koto: ninchi kagaku sensho 5 [The facts about reading: selected readings in Cognitive Sciences 5]*. Tokyo: Tokyo University Press.

Grainger, J. & Beauvillain, C. (1987). Language blocking and lexical access in bilinguals. *Quarterly Journal of Experimental Psychology*, *39A*, 295–319.

Hatta, T. (1978). Recognition of Japanese Kanji and Hiragana in the left and right visual fields. *Japanese Psychological Research*, *20*, 51–59.

Haxby, J.V., Parasuraman, R., Lalonde, F., & Abboud, H. (1993). SuperLab: General-purpose Macintosh software for human experimental psychology and psychological testing. *Behaviour Research Methods, Instruments, & Computers*, *25*, 400–405.

Herdman, C.M., & Beckett, B.L. (1996). Code-specific processing in word naming—evidence supporting a dual route model of word recognition. *Journal of Experimental Psychology: Human Perception and Performance*, *22*, 1149–1165.

Hines, T.M. (1978). The independence of languages in bilingual memory. *Dissertation Abstracts International*, *39*, 1012-B. (University Microfilm No. 78-14, 314).

Hirose, T. (1984). The effects of script frequency on semantic processing of Kanji and Kana (in Japanese). *Japanese Journal of Psychology*, *55*, 173–176.

Imura, T. (1943). Shitsugoshō, nihongo ni okeru tokusei [Aphasia: Characteristic symptoms in Japanese]. *[Psychiatria et Neurologia Japonica]*, *47*, 196–218.

Jersild, A.T. (1927). Mental set and shift. *Archives of Psychology, whole no. 89*.

Kaiho, H. (1976). Kanji imi jōhō shōri katei II [Semantic processing of Kanji II]. *Nihon shinri gakkai dai 40 kai taikai happyō ronbunshū [The proceedings of the 40th conference of the Japanese Psychological Association]*, *40*, 417–418.

Kato, Y. (1912). Migigawa hanmōshō o heihatsuseru shitsudokushō no ichi rei. [A case of dyslexia accompanied by right homonymous hemianopia]. *Seishin Shinkeigaku Zasshi [Psychiatria et Neurologia Japonica]*, *11*, 57–70.

Kimura, Y. (1984). Concurrent vocal interference: Its effects on Kana and Kanji. *Quarterly Journal of Experimental Psychology*, *36A*, 117–131.

Kotani, S. (1935). Shitsudoku shisshō no ichirei [A case of alexia with agraphia]. *Jikken Shinrigaku Kenkyuu [Japanese Journal of Experimental Psychology]*, *2*, 333–348.

Kurachi, M., Endo, M., Yamaguchi, N., & Enokido, H. (1978). Nōkenssen ni yoru kankaku shitsugo no byōjō ni tsuite—jūni shōrei no kentō [Clinical picture of sensory aphasia due to cerebral infarction: Observation of twelve cases]. *Kanazawa Daigaku Jūzen Igakukai Zasshi [Kanazawa University Journal of Medicine]*, *87*, 104–121.

LaBerge, D. (1983). Spatial extent of attention to letters and words. *Journal of Experimental Psychology: Human Perception and Performance*, *9*, 371–379.

Los, S.A. (1996). On the origin of mixing costs: exploring information in pure and mixed blocks of trials. *Acta Psychologica*, *94*, 145–188.

Lupker, S.J., & Brown, P. (1997). Strategic control in a naming task: Changing routes or changing deadlines? *Journal of Experimental Psychology: Learning, Memory, and Cognition*, *23*, 570–590.

McCormack, P.D. (1977). Bilingual linguistic memory: The independence–interdependence issue revisited. In P.A. Hornby (Ed.), *Bilingualism: Psychology, social and educational implications*, pp.57–66. New York: Academic Press.

McCusker, L.X., Hillinger, M.A., & Bias, R.G. (1981). Phonological recoding and reading. *Psychological Bulletin*, *81*, 217–245.

MacLeod, C.M. (1991). Half a century of research on the Stroop effect: An integrative review. *Psychological Bulletin*, *109*, 163–203.

Macnamara, J., & Kushnir, S. (1971). Linguistic independence of bilinguals: The input switch. *Journal of Verbal Learning and Verbal Behaviour*, *10*, 480–487.

Marcel, A.J. (1983). Conscious and unconscious perception: Experiments on visual masking and word recognition. *Cognitive Psychology*, *15*, 197–237.

Meiran, N. (1996). Reconfiguration of processing mode prior to task performance. *Journal of Experimental Psychology: Learning, Memory, and Cognition*, 22, 1423–1442.

Meyer, D.E., & Ruddy, M.G. (1974). *Bilingual word-recognition: Organisation and retrieval of alternative lexical codes.* Paper presented to the Eastern Psychological Association, Philadelphia.

Miura, T. (1934). Chōhihitsusei shitsugoshō no chiken hoi [Transcortical aphasia]. *Seishin Shinkeigaku Zasshi [Psychiatria et Neurologia Japonica]*, *37*, 757–793.

Monsell, S., & Hirsh, K.W. (1998). Competitor priming in auditory word recognition. *Journal of Experimental Psychology: Learning, Memory, and Cognition*, *24*, 1495–1520.

Monsell, S., Patterson, K.E., Graham, A., Hughes, C.H., & Milroy, R. (1992). Lexical and sub-lexical translation of spelling to sound: Strategic anticipation of lexical status. *Journal of Experimental Psychology: Learning, Memory, & Cognition*, *18*, 452–467.

Morton, J., & Sasanuma, S. (1984). Lexical access in Japanese. In L. Henderson (Ed.), *Orthographies and Reading: Perspectives from Cognitive Psychology, Neuropsychology and Linguistics.* Hove, UK: Lawrence Erlbaum Associates Ltd.

Nakagawa, A. (1994). Visual and semantic processing in reading Kanji. *Journal of Experimental Psychology: Human Perception and Performance*, *20*, 864–875.

National Research Institute for the Japanese Language. (1982). *Kokuritsu Kokugo Kenkyūjo, Hokoku 62 [The National Language Research Institute, Report 62].* Tokyo: Shuei Shuppan.

Neely, J.H. (1977). Semantic priming and retireval from lexical memory: roles of inhibitionless spreading activation and limited-capacity attention. *Journal of Experimental Psychology: General*, *106*, 226–254.

Nishikawa, K. (1973). Nihon nōen wakuchin chūshago hasshōshita shajishōgai no chomei na junsui shitsudokushō no ichirei [A case of alexia with copy disturbance appearing after a vaccination for Japanese encephalitis]. *Seishin Igaku [Clinical Psychiatry]*, *15*, 649–657.

Nomura, Y. (1981). Data-driven and conceptually-driven processing in the reading of Kanji and Kana scripts. *Psychologia*, *24*, 65–74.

Ohashi, H. (1965). *Rinshō no byōrigaku [Clinical cerebral pathology]*. Tokyo: Igaku Shoin.

Osaka, N. (1989). Eye fixation and saccade during Kana and Kanji text reading: Comparison of English and Japanese text processing. *Bulletin of the Psychonomic Society*, *27*, 548–550.

Paradis, M., Hagiwara, H., & Hildebrandt, N. (1985). *Neurological aspects of the Japanese writing system*. Orlando: Academic Press.

Patterson, K.E., & Morton, J. (1985). From orthography to phonology: An attempt at an old interpretation. In K.E. Patterson, J.C. Marshall, & M. Coltheart (Eds), *Surface dyslexia: Neuropsychological and Cognitive Studies of Phonological Reading*, pp.335–359. Hove, UK: Lawrence Erlbaum Associates Ltd.

Patterson, K., Suzuki, T., & Wydell, T. (1996). Interpreting a case of Japanese alexia: the key is in phonology. *Cognitive Neuropsychology*, *13*, 803–822.

Patterson, K., Suzuki, T., Wydell, T., & Sasanuma, S. (1995). Progressive aphasia and surface alexia in Japanese. *Neurocase*, *1*, 155–165.

Plaut, D.C., McClelland, J.L., Seidenberg, M.S., & Patterson, K. (1996). Understanding normal and impaired word reading—computational principles in quasi-regular domains. *Psychological Review*, *105*, 56–115.

Posner, M.I. (1980). Orienting of attention. *Quarterly Journal of Experimental Psychology*, *32*, 3–25.

Rayner, K., & Pollatsek, A. (1989). *The psychology of reading*. NJ: Prentice Hall.

Rogers, R.D., & Monsell, S. (1995). Costs of a predictable switch between simple cognitive tasks. *Journal of Experimental Psychology: General*, *124*, 207–231.

Saito, H. (1981). Kanji to Kana no yomi ni okeru keitaiteki fugōka oyobi onintekifugōka on kentō. [Orthographic and phonological processing in the reading of Kanji and Kana]. *Shinrigaku Kenkyuu. [Psychological Research]*, *52*, 266–272.

Saito, H., Inoue, M., & Nomura, Y. (1979). Information processing of Kanji and Kana: The close relationship among graphemic, phonemic and semantic aspects. *Psychologia*, *22*, 195–206.

Sakamoto, T., & Makita, K. (1973). Japan. In J. Downing (Ed.), *Comparative reading*. New York: Macmillan.

Sasanuma, S. (1980). Acquired dyslexia in Japanese: Clinical features and underlying mechanisms. In M. Coltheart, K. Patterson, & J.C. Marshall (Eds), *Deep dyslexia*, pp.48–90. London: Routledge and Kegan Paul.

Sasanuma, S. (1984). Can surface dyslexia occur in Japanese? In L. Henderson (Ed.), *Orthographies and Reading: Perspectives from cognitive psychology, neuropsychology, and linguistics* (pp.43–56). Hove, UK: Lawrence Erlbaum Associates Ltd.

Sasanuma, S., & Monoi, H. (1975). The syndrome of gogi (word-meaning) aphasia: Selective impairment of Kanji processing. *Neurology*, *25*, 627–632.

Segui, J., & Grainger, J. (1990). Priming word recognition with orthographic neighbours—effects of relative prime target frequency. *Journal of Experimental Psychology: Human Perception and Performance*, *16*, 65–76.

Spector, A., & Biederman, I. (1976). Mental set and mental shift revisited. *American Journal of Psychology*, *89*, 669–679.

Stolz, J.A., & Besner, D. (1996). Role of set in visual word recognition—activation and activation blocking as nonautomatic processes. *Journal of Experimental Psychology: Human Perception and Performance*, *22*, 1166–1177.

Taylor, I. (1997). Psycholinguistic reasons for keeping Chinese characters in Korean and Japanese. In H-C. Chen (Ed.), *Cognitive processing of Chinese and related Asian languages*, pp.299–319. Hong Kong: The Chinese University Press.

Taylor, I., & Park, K.-S. (1995). Differential processing of content words and function words: Chinese characters and phonetic scripts. In I. Taylor, & D.R. Olson (Eds), *Scripts and literacy: Reading and learning to read alphabets, syllabaries, and Chinese characters*. Dordrecht: Kluwer Academic Publishers.

Van Orden, G.C., & Goldinger, S.D. (1994). Interdependence of form and function in cognitive systems explains perception of printed words. *Journal of Experimental Psychology: Human Perception and Performance*, *20*, 1269–1291.

Wheeldon, L.R., & Monsell, S. (1994). Inhibition of spoken word production by priming a semantic competitor. *Journal of Memory and Language*, *33*, 332–356.

Wydell, T.N., Butterworth, B., & Patterson, K. (1995). The inconsistency of consistency effects in reading: The case of Japanese Kanji. *Journal of Experimental Psychology: Learning, Memory, and Cognition*, *21*, 1155–1168.

Wydell, T.N., Patterson, K.E., & Humphreys, G.W. (1993). Phonologically mediated access to meaning for Kanji: Is a Rows still a Rose in Japanese Kanji? *Journal of Experimental Psychology: Learning, Memory, and Cognition*, *19*, 419–514.

APPENDIX

Mean correct RT (ms), mean standard deviation of the correct RT (ms), and error rate (%) for each combination of word type and trial type, and two estimates of switch cost: the difference between mean RT on switch and non-switch trials, and the difference between mean RT on switch trials in the mixed blocks and on trials in the pure blocks.

	Exp. 1a Sem. Cat.	*Exp. 1b Sem. Cat.*	*Exp. 6 Sem. Cat.*	*Exp. 2a Naming*	*Exp. 2b Naming*	*Exp. 5 Naming*	*Exp. 4 Sem. Cat.*	*Exp. 3 Naming*	*Exp. 7 Naming*
	Kanji						*Large*	*Complex*	*Katakana*
Switch	607 (67) 7.4	530 (53) 4.6	637 (87) 3.8	661 (61) 6.3	568 (67) 3.2	584 (73) 3.5	581 (63) 3.4	634 (52) 6.4	441 (40) 1.1
Non-switch	598 (61) 6.9	515 (50) 3.8	624 (77) 3.3	645 (58) 5.2	547 (64) 2.3	577 (76) 3.2	568 (56) 5.3	637 (71) 7.6	438 (36) 1.0
Pure blocks	566 (51) 5.8	509 (41) 4.1	614 (65) 2.9	637 (60) 4.7	557 (62) 2.6	567 (62) 3.4	578 (60) 2.3	633 (35) 5.1	440 (45) 1.9
Switch minus non-switch	9	15	13	16	21	7	13	−3	3
Switch minus pure	41	21	23	24	11	17	3	1	1
	Kana						*Small*	*Simple*	*Hiragana*
Switch	698 (75) 8.2	560 (58) 6.3	641 (78) 4.0	603 (64) 1.7	487 (69) 0.9	486 (52) 1.7	577 (59) 1.9	604 (53) 3.7	451 (43) 1.8
Non-switch	691 (76) 7.3	552 (60) 5.7	627 (73) 3.4	589 (61) 0.6	467 (67) 0.5	473 (47) 1.3	581 (59) 3.8	602 (46) 4.7	451 (46) 1.3
Pure blocks	693 (54) 6.9	548 (35) 5.6	623 (60) 3.7	567 (58) 1.5	454 (62) 0.6	467 (49) 1.7	585 (75) 3.5	596 (55) 3.8	455 (49) 1.6
Switch minus non-switch	7	8	14	14	20	13	−4	2	0
Switch minus pure	5	12	18	36	33	19	−8	8	−4
Mean switch minus non-switch	8*	11.5**	13.5*	15**	20.5**	10**	4.5	−0.5	1.5
Mean switch minus pure	23*	16.5	20.5**	30**	22**	18**	−2.5	4.5	−1.5

* $P < .05$, ** $P < .01$.

LANGUAGE AND COGNITIVE PROCESSES, 1999, *14* (5/6), 609–630

Processing Spoken Chinese: The Role of Tone Information

Yun Ye and Cynthia M. Connine
State University of New York at Binghamton

Vowel and tone monitoring tasks were used to investigate the role of tone information in processing Mandarin. In Experiment 1, participants monitored for a tone-plus-vowel combination (tone 2-/a/). Both existent (known) and non-existent syllables contained targets and monitoring reaction times showed faster monitoring times for existent syllable carriers. Non-target bearing existent syllables mismatched on either the vowel or the tone and showed faster responses for vowel mismatch stimuli. This finding supports a perceptual advantage for vowel information. In Experiment 2, separate vowel and tone monitoring tasks were used for target syllables that occurred phrase-finally in idiomatic (highly constraining) phrases or neutral semantic context. In the neutral context, vowel monitoring was faster than tone monitoring. In contrast, highly predictive contexts showed a tone advantage. Experiment 3 used idiomatic contexts that did or did not contain a mismatching tone in the penultimate syllable. Mismatching tones were very similar to or highly distinct from the intended tone and both tone and vowel monitoring reaction times showed graded effects based on similarity of the mismatch. A modified version of the TRACE model for tone languages that includes a separate level or representation for tones that permit graded activation and highly interconnected syllable representations is discussed.

Requests for reprints should be addressed to Cynthia M. Connine, Psychology Department, State University of New York at Binghamton, Binghamton, N.Y. 13901.
Email: connine@binghamton.edu

The research was supported by NIDCD Grant R01 DC02134 to the second author. Additional support was provided by the Center for Cognitive and Psycholinguistic Science. Portions of this research were presented at the 1998 Meeting of the Acoustical Society of America. We thank Albrecht Inhoff, Celia Klin, Dick Pastore, Brian Lang, and Paul LoCasto for their helpful comments and discussion. The first author also thanks Peter M. Luca and Datong Chen for their help on the manuscript.

INTRODUCTION

The languages of the world can be divided into two categories based on whether tone functions distinctively. Non-tonal languages include English and French whereas tonal languages include languages such as Chinese and Vietnamese (south-east Asia), Sudanese and Bantu (Africa) and Trique (south-western Mexico). Pike (1948) defined a tone language as "having lexically significant, contrastive, but relative pitch on each syllable". This definition highlights three important features of tone languages. First, tone information is lexically significant in that it is used to distinguish the meaning of words. Second, tones are contrastive in that listeners extract physical dimensions that permit the categorisation of lexically significant tones into functional categories. Third, in language processing, it is the relative pitch height which accounts for lexical identity, not the actual pitch. The present experiments focus on the contribution of tone information to processing spoken Mandarin.

According to Chao (1948), there are four stressed syllable types in Mandarin that correspond to characteristic pitch patterns. The pitch patterns are described by a 5-point scale with 1 representing the lowest value and 5 representing the highest level. Each tone can be labelled by giving its starting and ending pitch. The first tone is high-level [55]; the second tone is high-rising [35]; the third tone is low-dipping [214]; and the fourth tone is high-falling [51].

A number of studies have investigated tone perception in spoken word recognition of tone languages. Despite different stimuli, subjects, and experimental tasks, a consistent result is that fundamental frequency is the primary carrier of tone information (Howie, 1976; Hombert, 1976, cited in Gandour, 1981; Gandour, 1978, 1983; Repp & Lin, 1990). It is clear that a change in fundamental frequency or some other acoustic attribute determines the expression of and perception of tones. What is less clear is the contribution of tone information to on-going language processing. Some studies have sought to establish hemispheric specialisation for tonal processing in arguing for an important linguistic role for tone. For example, Van Lancker and Fromkin (1973) used a dichotic-listening task in native speakers of Thai and found a right ear advantage for tone words while hummed stimuli (the five Thai tones hummed without any segmental information) did not show any right ear advantage. They concluded that left-hemisphere specialisation occurs for pitch when it is used linguistically (see also Yang, 1991). Other evidence comes from Gandour (1981, 1988) who examined the extent and nature of the impairment in the perception of tones by aphasic patients. Patients were asked to identify three sets of stimuli, each set containing five Thai words minimally distinguished by tone. The results indicated that the performance of left brain-damaged aphasics differed significantly from normal subjects, while the performance of the right brain-damaged non-aphasics did not.

Other experiments have used established psycholinguistic methods to investigate processing of tone information. Fox and Unkefer (1985) used a tone identification task for stimulus continua where a tone manipulation resulted in a lexical bias. They found that tone category identification was biased toward forming a word response. More recently, Lee et al. (1996) presented lexical and non-lexical tones in Cantonese to Cantonese speakers and found a lexical effect for same/different judgements. The lexical effect disappeared when the same materials were presented to native English and to Mandarin speakers.

These experiments suggest that tone information is used linguistically to establish lexical identity in tone languages. However, many questions remain concerning the role of tonal information in word recognition and other work provides less clear support. For example, Yang (1991) failed to find the typical right ear advantage for linguistic information when the task focused on tone identification. More recently, Cutler and Chen (1997) examined processing of lexical tone in Cantonese using both lexical decision and same-different judgements. They found comparable performance on non-words created by altering an onset, vowel, tone or their combination for native speakers of Cantonese and from listeners with no knowledge of Cantonese. These results suggest that tone perception is a simple perceptual process that does not necessarily involve the lexicon.

The purpose of the current experiments was to investigate the mapping of tone information during on-going spoken Chinese processing. In order to accomplish this goal, a preliminary issue must be addressed related to research by Cutler and Chen (1997). In their experiments, it was found that there were more errors in lexical decision when non-words mismatched real words in tone information compared with a mismatch in segmental information. The interpretation offered for these results was that tones and vowels differ in their availability in the signal with tone information available relatively later. The consequence of this is a perceptual disadvantage for tone information. This raises the possibility that the contribution of tone information in spoken Chinese may be obscured by its temporal characteristics and therefore difficult to establish. In order to investigate the contribution of tone, experimental designs and methods must be developed in light of the potential temporal disparity in the availability of tone information.

Experiments 1 and 2 were designed with this concern in mind. The primary goal of Experiment 1 was to provide converging evidence for delayed availability of tone information. The purpose of Experiment 2 was to develop a methodology able to neutralise the temporal disadvantage for tone information and reveal its contribution to lexical processing. The final experiment, Experiment 3, extends the results of Experiment 2 to address the central question of how tone information is mapped on to lexical representations.

EXPERIMENT 1

Experiment 1 was designed to systematically investigate the possible temporal asymmetry in vowel and tone processing suggested by Cutler and Chen (1997). A tone-vowel detection task was used where subjects were required to detect a tone-vowel combination. The task was designed to encourage processing of both vowel and tone information and as a result, be sensitive to both dimensions. Target-bearing stimuli included both existent (known) syllables and non-existent (unknown) sellable carriers (see Table 1). Non-target bearing existent syllable carriers were created in order to address the issue of the relative availability of vowel and tone information. Non-target bearing stimuli mismatched the tone (but not the vowel) dimension or the vowel (but not the tone) dimension of the target combination.

Neither non-target stimulus type contained the required tone-vowel combination and require a 'no target' response. However, the stimuli differ in the temporal availability of information for making the correct 'no-target' response. If tone information is available subsequent to vowel information, then listeners must wait to determine if the tone matches the target combination. This predicts that tone-mismatch stimuli should be responded to more slowly than vowel-mismatch stimuli.

Method

Participants. A group of 30 students (15 males and 15 females) were recruited as subjects from State University of New York at Binghamton. All subjects were native speakers of Mandarin and were paid for their participation. No participant reported a history of hearing impairment or speech disorder.

Materials. A group of 30 existent syllable stimuli were selected that contained a main vowel /a/ and a tone 2 to serve as target bearing items

TABLE 1
Example Stimuli, Experiment 1

Target Bearing Stimuli		*No-target Stimuli*	
Existent Syllable Target	*Non-existent Syllable Target*	*Vowel Changed Filler*	*Tone Changed Filler*
/ba/ with Tone 2	/ra/ with Tone 2	/bi/ with Tone 2	/ba/ with Tone 4

(yes response). The phonetic qualities of the main vowel /a/ vary considerably in different syllables but /a/ was selected because this vowel permitted the largest pool of syllables (see Norman, 1988, for a discussion of the context dependency of vowels). A second set of 30 non-existent syllables were created from the existent syllables stimuli by changing the initial consonant. Both of the two groups served as target-bearing stimuli. For example, the existent syllable /ba/ with a tone 2 means "pull"; the corresponding non-existent syllable is /ra 2/.

A set of 60 existent syllable stimuli served as non-target bearing items. Half of the stimuli contained the vowel /a/ and a tone 4. Tone 4 was chosen as the non-target tone because it is implemented with very different physical features relative to the target tone (tone 2) (Fox & Qi, 1990; Moore, 1993). The remaining 30 stimuli contained the vowel /i/ and a tone 2. The vowel /i/ was selected as a non-target vowel because its acoustic-phonetic features are very different from vowel /a/ (Howie, 1976). The full stimulus set is shown in Appendix A.

The set of 120 stimuli were recorded by a female native speaker of Mandarin Chinese in a sound damped room. Stimuli were digitised at 10 kHz (12 bit resolution) and timing marks (inaudible to participants) were placed at the onset of each stimulus.

Experimental design. Two lists of stimuli were created. Each list contained 30 target items (half existent syllable; half non-existent syllable) as well as 30 no-target items (half change tone; half change vowel). The lists were counterbalanced across condition but each participant heard each list. Order of list presentation was counterbalanced across subjects. The completely within-subjects design was necessary due to the small number of native Chinese speakers available. Each list was preceded by a set of practice trials.

Procedure. Participants were asked to indicate whether a stimulus did or did not contain the target tone-vowel combination by pressing an appropriately labelled response button. The instructions emphasised that the 'yes' button should be pressed only when the syllable contained a vowel /a/ and tone 2. Otherwise the 'no' button should be pressed. Both speed and accuracy were emphasised. The following is a translation of the instructions (the instructions were read to participants in Chinese):

> In this experiment, you will hear a single syllable each time. It may or may not be a meaningful syllable. You need not pay attention to its meaning, your task is to detect a vowel /a/ and a tone 2 combination. That is, when you feel that the syllable contains a vowel /a/ and a tone 2, please press the "Yes" button; if it only contains a vowel /a/ but not with a tone 2 or with a tone 2 but does not contain a vowel /a/, or any other case, you should press the "No"

button. For example, when you hear syllables like "an2, ang2, ian2, ai2", you should press "Yes"; if you hear syllables like "an4, ang4" or "ing2, ong2" you should press "No". You will do a practice set first. The computer will record your reaction time and error rate. Please respond as quickly and as accurately as possible.

Results and Discussion

Reaction times less than 200 ms or greater than 2000 ms were excluded from both subject and item analyses (9.4%). The mean reaction time from stimulus onset and from stimulus offset, along with the percentage of correct responses for non-target bearing and target-bearing stimuli are presented in Table 2. A preliminary analysis conducted with list presentation as a factor showed no significant effects of or interactions with this variable.

Reaction time data from both onset and offset of the stimuli were analysed. As is clear from Table 2, the data patterns were identical and the outcome of statistical tests permitted identical conclusions. We report here the statistics for reaction time data timed from stimulus onset. Consider, first, non-target bearing stimuli. Vowel-mismatch stimuli were faster (93 ms) than the tone-mismatch stimuli [$t_1(29) = -4.08$, $P < .01$; $t_2(58) = -3.89$, $P < .01$]. The results also showed a higher percentage (4%) of correct 'no' responses for the vowel-mismatch compared to the tone-mismatch stimuli. However, this difference was not significant.

As is shown in Table 2, the results also showed a clear advantage for existent syllables (104 ms) [$t_1(29) = -5.5$, $P < .01$; $t_2(58) = -3.4$, $P < .01$]. A similar comparison of percentage correct showed a small increase in accuracy for existent stimuli (4%) that was not significant [$t_1(29) = 1.7$, $P = .1$; $t_2(58) = 1.6$, $P = .11$].

TABLE 2
Experiment 1. Mean Reaction Time and Percentage Correct (in Parentheses) for Target-bearing as a Function of Syllable Status (Existent and Non-existent) and Non-target Bearing Stimuli as a Function of Mis-match Dimension. Reaction Times Measured from Stimulus Onset and Offset are Displayed.

	Measured from Onset	*Measured from Offset*
Target-bearing		
Existent syllable	1150 (93)	744 (93)
Non-existent syllable	1254 (90)	830 (91)
Non-target-bearing		
Vowel-mismatch	1057 (94)	650 (93)
Tone-mismatch	1150 (90)	739 (90)

The reaction time results are consistent with the claim of Cutler and Chen (1997) concerning the relatively late availability of tone compared with vowel information. For single syllable stimuli, the perceptual acquisition of tone information lags behind that of vowel information. Although tones are an important information source for disambiguating the semantic interpretation of Chinese syllables, the results support the counter-intuitive conclusion that their perceptual disadvantage prevents an early role. These results raise two related issues. The first issue is methodological in that investigations concerning the role of tone information must be cognisant of its apparent perceptual disadvantage. The second issue concerns the emergence of the tone disadvantage found in Experiment 1 (and by Cutler & Chen, 1997) to processing Chinese syllables in context. Characteristic of Chinese is that it has relatively few distinct syllables (cf. Forrest, 1948). The large degree of ambiguity that is a consequence of this language configuration may have contributed to the extensive use of fixed word order in Chinese (Forrest, 1948). This latter characteristic of the language may have consequences for the organisation and access of Chinese syllables in context. The perceptual disadvantage for tones found in Experiment 1 and the claim that tone information becomes available relatively late may not obtain for a more realistic processing environment.

In Experiment 2, we sought to investigate whether a tone disadvantage persists for syllables processed in a meaningful context. To accomplish this goal, we developed materials that provided a highly constraining context prior to a target. An extreme case of highly constraining contexts, idiomatic contexts, were selected in order to capitalise on potential lexical connections. Connine, Blasko, Brandt, and Layer (1992) have argued that lexicalised idioms provide a means for a powerful, localised, contextual constraint. Activation of a lexicalised phrase in memory permits pre-activation of phonological information occurring late in the expression. Similarly in Mandarin, the highly constraining context provided by lexicalised expressions may serve to pre-activate the anticipated syllable (both segments and tone) prior to being heard by the listener and, if so, the advantage for vowel information may be offset by pre-activation of stored tones. In the absence of pre-activation, the perceptual advantage for vowels should dominate and the vowel advantage should still be evident.

Experiment 2 used a three syllable idiom context to pre-activate the lexical representation of the fourth syllable and a three syllable neutral context to serve as a control. Both vowel and tone monitoring tasks were used (see Connine & Titone, 1996 for a discussion of a phoneme monitoring). For both tasks, pre-activation of the target (final) syllable should result in faster monitoring times in the idiom compared with the neutral context. Across tasks, neutral contexts are predicted to show an

TABLE 3
Example Stimuli, Experiment 2

Vowel Monitoring Task		Tone Monitoring Task	
Target	*Filler*	*Target*	*Filler*
lai2 ri4 fang1	shan1 si1 er2	lai2 ri4 fang1	da4 shi1 shuo3
chang2 xia2 mian4	*xing2* xia1 mian1	*chang2* xia2 mian4	*wang4* xia4 mian1
shi1 *chang2*	shi2 *xing2*	shi1 *chang2*	shi3 *wang4*

advantage for vowel monitoring compared with tone monitoring. A final comparison across tasks for the idiomatic contexts provides the critical comparison for the emergence of a significant role for tones. If, as hypothesised above, the structure of Chinese results in lexical organisation that gives priority to tones, then conditions of maximum lexical involvement would permit the emergence of a tone advantage. Example stimuli are shown in Table 3 (see Appendix B for the full stimulus set).

EXPERIMENT 2

Method

Participants. A group of 10 students were recruited to serve as participants. All participants were native speakers of Mandarin and were paid $5.00 per hour of participation.

Materials. A set of 30 three-syllable idioms and a set of 30 neutral three-syllable phrases served as contexts for the final target stimuli. The fourth syllable in each stimulus contained the vowel /a/ (the vowel target) and a tone 2 (the tone target). In order to provide comparable targets for a given idiom/neutral context set, the identical target stimulus was cross-spliced into the contexts. Two versions of each stimulus were recorded so that one version was used as the context and one version was used to excise the final target stimulus. The identical target was cross-spliced into the idiom and its neutral context. This ensured that any differences found were due to differences in the contexts, not idiosyncratic differences between recordings. For half of the stimuli, the target stimulus was excised from the idiom context and for the remaining stimuli, the target was excised from the neutral context. The resulting stimuli sounded completely natural and contained no disfluencies as a consequence of the cross-splicing. Stimuli were digitised at 10 kHz (12 bit resolution) and timing marks (inaudible to participants) were placed at the onset of each stimulus. The stimuli were recorded by a female native speaker of Mandarin.

A separate set of 30 fillers each were selected and recorded for the vowel and tone tasks to serve as 'no target' stimuli. The 'no target' vowel fillers contained a final syllable with a /i/ vowel-tone 2 combination. The 'no target' tone fillers contained a final syllable with an /a/ vowel-tone 4 combination. Half of each set of fillers were idioms and half were neutral phrases.

In order to verify that the experimental idioms provided sufficient constraint, a pretest was conducted. A group of four native Mandarin speakers were presented with 210 four-syllable-phrases which contained 90 idioms and 120 filler control four-syllable-phrases with the last syllable of each phrase omitted. Participants were asked to complete the phrase with the first syllable that came to mind. Based on the pretest, two idioms were replaced with an idiom that provided a more constraining context. The final set of idioms had only a single possible fourth syllable that would produce a meaningful phrase.

Experimental design. Because of the limited pool of native Mandarin speakers, each participant performed both the vowel and the tone monitoring tasks. Task presentation order was counterbalanced across participants. For each task, two lists were created containing 15 idiom and 15 neutral contexts. Items were counterbalanced across lists. Each list contained a different set of no-target fillers. Each participant heard each of the four lists, blocked by task on two separate days of testing. Test days were separated by at least one day. Prior to hearing each experimental list, a practice set of 12 items was presented (six with-target trials and six no-target trials).

Procedure. For the vowel monitoring task, participants were instructed to listen to each stimulus and to press a button as quickly and accurately as possible if the last syllable in the phrase contained the vowel /a/.

The tone monitoring task required participants to attend to the tone information of the last syllable and press the button marked "Yes" as quickly and accurately as possible for Tone 2 syllables. In both tasks, participants were instructed to press the "No" key if no target was present on that trial.

Results and Discussion

Table 4 shows mean reaction times as a function of monitoring task (vowel monitoring *vs.* tone monitoring) and context type (idiom *vs.* neutral) along with the percentage correct for each condition. Reaction times less than 200 ms and greater than 2000 ms were discarded from all analyses (3.5% of the responses).

An initial analysis which included task presentation order (tone first *vs.* vowel first) and list as variables showed no significant main effects of these

TABLE 4
Experiment 2. Mean Reaction Time as a Function of Context (Idiom *vs.* Neutral) and Monitoring Task (Vowel Monitoring *vs.* Tone Monitoring). The Percentage Correct are Shown in Parentheses.

	Vowel Monitoring Task	*Tone Monitoring Task*
Idiom	654 (92)	589 (98)
Neutral	720 (93)	787 (98)

factors nor interactions with the experimental variables. A two-way ANOVA with monitoring task (tone or vowel monitoring) and context (idiom *vs.* neutral phrase) was conducted on the reaction time data. Overall, monitoring times for the idiom context were faster than the neutral context (621 ms and 753 ms, respectively). The 132 ms effect of context was significant [$F_1(1,9) = 48.45$, $P < .01$; $F_2(1,29) = 92.23$, $P < .01$]. The main effect of monitoring task was not significant (F_1 and $F_2 < 1$) indicating no overall speed difference between the two tasks.

The pattern of main effects was accompanied by a significant interaction [$F_1(1,9) = 19.99$, $P < .01$; $F_2(1,29) = 10.81$, $P < .01$]. A series of planned comparisons were performed to explore the interaction. Consider, first, comparisons across tasks for the two contexts. The neutral context showed faster vowel monitoring compared to tone monitoring (720 ms and 787 ms, respectively [$t_1(9) = -2.44$, $P < .05$; $t_2(29) = 2.16$, $P < .05$]. This is consistent with the evidence of an advantage for detecting vowel information found in Experiment 1.

A very different pattern of results was found for the idiom contexts where vowels were detected more slowly (65 ms) than tones [$t_1(9) = 2.3$, $P < .05$; $t_2(29) = -2.58$, $P < .05$]. The presence of a highly constraining context renders the tone information relatively more accessible compared with the vowel information.

An ANOVA on percentage correct responses showed only a main effect of task with a small (6%) decrease in accuracy for the vowel monitoring task [$F_1(1,9) = 7.22$, $P < .05$; $F_2(1,29) = 8.99$, $P < .05$].

To summarise, the results from Experiment 2 suggest that pre-activation of tone and vowel information can disrupt the vowel advantage. In fact, the results show that pre-activation induces a processing advantage for tone information relative to vowels. Processing of the target syllable in a meaningful context permits the privileged role of tone information to emerge.

Comparison of the results of Experiments 1 and 2 makes clear the strong influence of context information on tone perception. The tone advantage suggests that the present and previous demonstrations for a vowel advantage is applicable only in environments where context is minimal. Given a realistic processing environment that includes a highly constraining context, the perceptual advantage for vowels is compensated for by the processing architecture of spoken word recognition. One influential model used to account for the effects of context on speech perception is the TRACE model (McClelland & Elman, 1986). The TRACE model posits a three level architecture (feature, phoneme and lexical nodes) with excitatory connections between levels. The excitatory connections from lexical nodes to constituent phonemes permit contextual information to contribute directly to their activation. Figure 1 shows a modified version of the TRACE model that incorporates the unique properties of tone languages. We assume that tone information is a separate level of representation during speech processing and is indicated in Figure 1 (toneme). Excitatory links exist from tone nodes to existent sellable representations and to segments that co-occur with that tone. As in TRACE, we assume that the degree of toneme (and phoneme) activation is based on the goodness of the input signal and the lexical feedback connections where the level of lexical feedback is a function of its activation. As in our other work (Connine, Blasko, & Titone, 1993; Connine, Titone, Deelman, & Blasko, 1997) we assume that goodness of fit activation is based on a featural description where common features computed from the signal (or activated as a byproduct of character recognition, see Zhou & Marslen-Wilson, 1999) map onto compatible representations. The pervasive homophone phenomena resulted in only weak feedback from lexical representations to the tonemes for the single syllables used in Experiment 1. The resulting activation was insufficient to diffuse the temporal disadvantage for tone information. In Experiment 2, a similar state of affairs existed for target syllables in the neutral context. Tonemes in the neutral context did not receive the strong feedback from the lexicon-toneme connections, and as a result, the temporal advantage for vowels dominated. In contrast, the highly constraining context provided robust lexical activation for the target syllable tones and segments. Given robust lexical activation, tonemes were activated not only via the phoneme-toneme connections but also strongly activated via the lexicon-toneme connection.

Note, in Figure 1 an additional assumption of the proposed model related to the configuration of tones and lexical representations. We assume that the feedback connections from lexical representations to tonemes have larger weights (symbolised by the larger arrow) than to phonemes. The theoretical advantage to this assumption is that it accurately captures the importance of tone information in discriminating among otherwise homophonic sequences and is consistent with the tone

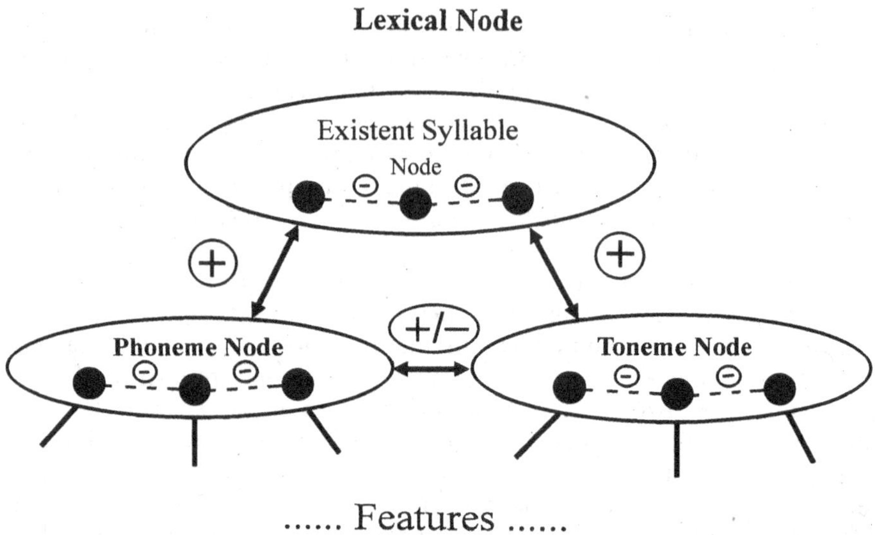

FIG. 1. Phoneme, toneme, and syllable nodes and connections. Larger arrows indicate greater connection strength.

advantage in highly constraining contexts. It should be noted that the proposed model is intended to account for access and representation of tone information for spoken language. The time-course of tone activation may be quite different for processing visual Chinese characters. For example, Taft and Chen (1992) have shown that same/different pronunciation judgments were made more slowly for single characters differing in tones than for characters differing in vowels. These results suggest heightened accessibility for vowel information compared to tone information in processing visual characters. It would be of interest to determine whether the same results obtained when a constraining context is available.

Experiment 3 was designed to investigate further the hypotheses described above. The TRACE model, as well as other influential models of spoken word recognition (see Norris, 1994) assume that activation is modulated by the degree of similarity between a target representation and the input information based on overlap of featural values (see Connine, Titone, Deelman, & Blasko, 1997, for evidence supporting this assumption for English consonants). If so, the extension of this architecture to tone languages predicts that lexical activation will be modulated by the similarity between the tone input and the stored lexical representation based on tonal features. Experiment 3 used highly constraining idiomatic phrases similar to those used in Experiment 2. Similarity of the input to a lexical representation was manipulated by including two mismatching tone conditions. The tone mismatch conditions were accomplished by altering

TABLE 5
Example Stimuli, Experiment 3

Vowel Monitoring Task			*Tone Monitoring Task*		
Idiom	*Close Mismatch*	*Far Mismatch*	*Idiom*	*Close Mismatch*	*Far Mismatch*
jin1 yu4 *liang2* *yuan2*	jin1 yu4 *liang3* *yuan2*	jin1 yu4 *liang4* *yuan2*	jin1 yu4 *liang2* *yuan2*	jin1 yu4 *liang3* *yuan2*	jin1 yu4 *liang4* *yuan2*

the tone of the penultimate syllable to create a close (a tone 2 was pronounced as a tone 3) mismatch or a far (a tone 2 was pronounced as a tone 4) mismatch.

Table 5 shows example stimuli for the tone and vowel monitoring tasks. As in Experiment 2, participants monitored for a vowel or tone on the final syllable of the phrase. Unaltered idiom contexts were included to serve as a control against which to compare the close and far mismatch conditions. If tone information in the penultimate syllable contributes to activation of the target syllable in a graded fashion, then target reaction time should be faster for close compared to far mismatch conditions. Unaltered idiom contexts should show fastest overall reaction times. Further, decreased activation of the target syllable from the context (via mismatching tones) should decrease the tone advantage.

EXPERIMENT 3

Method

Participants. A group of 10 students were recruited as participants from the State University of New York at Binghamton.[1] All subjects were native speakers of Mandarin and were paid $5.00 per hour of participation.

Materials. A set of 30, four-syllable idioms were selected where the third and fourth syllable both contained a second tone and the final (target) syllable contained the vowel /a/. Two sets of tone mismatch stimuli were created. In the first (close mismatch), the idioms were recorded with the third syllable tone 2 mispronounced as a tone 4; in a second set (far mismatch), the third syllable was mispronounced as a tone 3.

[1] Due to the restricted availability of native Mandarin speakers, two of the participants in Experiment 2 and all (ten) of the participants in Experiment 3 had served in other experiments involving tone/vowel detection tasks. This may account for the increased speed in responding to Experiment 3.

The identical set of idioms served as target stimuli for the tone and vowel monitoring tasks. As in Experiment 2, all the idioms used were screened by a pretest to ensure that the idiom contexts were highly constraining (there was only one possible fourth syllable to form a meaningful phrase). The complete stimulus set is listed in Appendix C.

Experimental design. Because of the limited pool of native Mandarin speakers, each participant performed both the vowel monitoring task and the tone monitoring task. In the vowel monitoring task, three lists of 30 items containing the target vowel /a/ were arranged. Each list contained ten idiom items, ten close tone mismatched items and ten far tone mismatched items. The conditions (idiom, close tone mismatch and far tone mismatch) and items were counterbalanced across the lists. Each subject heard all the lists. Similarly, in the tone monitoring task, the 30 target bearing items were arranged into three lists. A comparable set of no-target fillers was created for each list. All other design aspects were the same as Experiment 2.

Procedure. The procedure was identical to Experiment 2.

Results and Discussion

Mean reaction times as a function of monitoring task (vowel monitoring *vs.* tone monitoring) and context type (idiom *vs.* close tone mismatch *vs.* far tone mismatch) are shown in Table 6 along with percentage correct. Reaction times less than 200 ms and greater than 2000 ms were excluded (8.6% of responses).

As is clear from Table 6, vowel and tone monitoring was faster in the idiom context compared to the close mismatch condition. More

TABLE 6
Experiment 3. Mean Reaction Time as a Function of Context (Idiom *vs.* Close Mismatch *vs.* Far Mismatch) and Detection Task (Vowel Detection *vs.* Tone Detection). The Percentage Correct are Shown in Parentheses

	Vowel Monitoring	*Tone Monitoring*
Idiom	442 (98)	408 (99)
Close Mismatch	464 (98)	445 (97)
Far Mismatch	543 (97)	531 (98)

importantly, both tasks showed a further increase in monitoring time for the far mismatch condition. A two-way ANOVA with task and context type as factors showed a main effect of context type [$F_1(2,18) = 64.18$, $P < .01$; $F_2(2,58) = 13.21$, $P < .05$]. A series of planned comparisons showed the following effects. For the vowel monitoring task, the reaction time difference between close tone mismatch and far tone mismatch was significant [$t_1(9) = -4.5$, $P < .01$; $t_2(29) = -2.65$, $P < .05$]. The two mismatch conditions showed markedly different effects in that the far mismatch effect was larger than the close mismatch effect (101 ms and 22 ms, respectively) and a *t*-test on the difference scores was significant [$t_1(9) = -4.5$, $P < .01$; $t_2(29) = -2.65$, $P < .05$].

For the tone monitoring task, the reaction time difference between close *vs.* far tone mismatch conditions (86 ms) was significant [$t_1(9) = -4.9$, $P < .01$; $t_2(29) = -3.5$, $P < .01$] as was the *t*-test on the difference scores for these conditions relative to the idiom baseline [37 ms and 123 ms, close and far mismatch, respectively; $t_1(9) = -4.9$, $P < .01$; $t_2(29) = -3.51$, $P < .01$].

A set of *t*-tests performed on percentage correct showed no significant differences in either task. Across both tasks, manipulation of tone information in terms of the degree of similarity between the stimulus and the lexical tone modulated monitoring performance. These results are consistent with two major conclusions. First, decreased activation of the final syllable via a mismatching context tone supports a crucial role for tone information in establishing lexical hypotheses in continuous, spoken Chinese. Second, the differential effects of close and far tone mismatches suggest that tone information is not mapped onto a lexical representation in a categorical fashion. Rather, tone information extracted from the speech signal serves to establish a tonal hypothesis that is graded in activation (Connine & Ye, 1997). Note that the far mismatch context does not functionally reduce to a neutral context—in contrast to the neutral condition of Experiment 2 (where a vowel advantage was found), the far mismatch context still shows a small tone advantage. This indicates that the effectiveness of the context is drastically reduced but not neutralised to where a vowel-advantage can re-emerge.

GENERAL DISCUSSION

The three experiments reported here examined processing of lexical tone information in Mandarin. Experiment 1 began by addressing the issue of perceptual differences in processing tones and vowels. The results were consistent with Cutler and Chen's (1997) results showing a disadvantage for tone processing. Experiment 2 demonstrated that the vowel advantage disappears when syllables are processed in context. A perceptual advantage for vowels may describe processing with minimal context but in more realistic language processing environments, the perceptual advantage is compensated for by the architecture of spoken word recognition. More importantly, Experiment 2 showed a tone advantage when the target occurred in a pre-activated syllable providing strong support for a modified TRACE model adapted for tone languages. There are three basic assumptions of the modified model. First, tone processing is not just a simple perceptual process void of lexical involvement but is highly lexically involved. The toneme-lexicon connection is a bi-directional route where activation of the toneme influences activation of the lexical representations and the activation of lexical representation can, in turn, contribute to the activation of tonemes. The lexical architecture in Figure 1 deliberately assigns tone and segmental information to separate representations. The separate representation of segmental and prosodic information is consistent with current views in linguistics (Selkirk, 1986) and with psycholinguistic investigations (Speer, Shi, & Slowiaczek, 1989).

A final crucial aspects of the toneme hypothesis is that activation of lexical tone is not an all-or-none process. Considerable mismatch can be tolerated with mismatching information accommodated via partial match of the compatible information. Experiment 3 provided clear support for this assumption and cross-language support for similar effects based on consonant mismatch in English (Connine et al., 1993, 1997; see also Allopenna, Magnuson, & Tanenhaus, 1998). The parallel findings for tone and non-tone languages reflect the fundamental principles underlying spoken language processing.

REFERENCES

Allopenna, P.D., Magnuson, J.S., & Tanenhaus, M.K. (1998). Tracking the time course of spoken word recognition using eye movements: Evidence for continuous mapping models. *Journal of Memory and Language*, *38*, 419–439.

Chao, Y.R. (1948). *Mandarin primer*. Cambridge: Harvard University Press.

Connine, C.M., Blasko, D.M., Brandt, R., & Layer, J.K. (1992). Idiomatic processing: Syntactic frozenness and subjective familiarity. *Psychological Research*, *54*, 225–232.

Connine, C.M., Blasko, D.M., & Titone, D.A. (1993). Do the beginnings of spoken words have a special status in auditory word recognition? *Journal of Memory and Language*, *32*, 193–210.

Connine, C.M., Titone, D., Deelman, T., & Blasko, D. (1997). Similarity mapping in spoken word recognition. *Journal of Memory and Language*, *37*, 463–480.

Connine, C.M., & Titone, D. (1996). Phoneme monitoring. *Language and Cognitive Processes*, *11*, 635–646.

Connine, C.M., & Ye, Y. (1997). Spoken word recognition: A view from Chinese. In D. Peng, H. Shu, & H. Chen (Eds), *Language Processing in Chinese*, pp.195–216. People's Republic of China. Shangdong Education Press.

Cutler, A., & Chen, H.-C. (1997). Lexical tone in Cantonese spoken-word processing. *Perception and Psychophysics*, *59*, 165–179.

Forrest, R.A.D. (1948). *The Chinese language*. London: Faber and Faber.

Fox, R.A., & Unkefer, J. (1985). The effect of lexical status on the perception of tone. *Journal of Chinese Linguistics*, *13*, 69–90.

Fox, R.A., & Qi, Y.Y. (1990). Context effects in the perception of lexical tone. *Journal of Chinese Linguistics*, *18*, 261–283.

Gandour, J. (1978). The perception of tone. In V.A. Fromkin (Ed.), *Tone, a linguistic survey*, pp.41–76. New York: Academic Press.

Gandour, J. (1981). Perceptual dimensions of tone: evidence from Cantonese. *Journal of Chinese Linguistics*, *9*, 20–36.

Gandour, J. (1983). Tone perception in far eastern languages. *Journal of Phonetics*, *11*, 149–175.

Gandour, J. (1988). Perception and production of tone in aphasia. *Brain and Language*, *35*, 201–240.

Howie, J.M. (1976). *Acoustic studies of Mandarin vowels and tones*. Cambridge: Cambridge University Press.

Lee, Y.-S., Vakock, D.A., & Wurm, L.H. (1996). Tone perception in Cantonese and Mandarin: a cross-linguistic comparison. *Journal of Psycholinguistic Research*, *125*, 527–542.

McClelland, J., & Elman, J. (1986). The TRACE model of speech perception. *Cognitive Psychology*, *18*, 1–86.

Moore, C.B. (1993). Phonetic observations on stress and tones in Mandarin Chinese. *Working Papers of the Cornell Phonetics Laboratory*, *8*, 87–117.

Norman, J. (1988). *Chinese*. Cambridge: Cambridge University Press.

Norris, D. (1994). Shortlist: A connectionist model of continuous speech recognition. *Cognition*, *52*, 189–234.

Pike, K.L. (1948). *Tone languages*. Ann Arbor, MI: University of Michigan Press.

Repp, B.H., & Lin, H.-B. (1990). Integration of segmental and tonal information in speech perception: a cross-linguistic study. *Journal of Phonetics*, *18*, 481–495.

Selkirk, E.O. (1986). *Phonology and syntax*. Cambridge, MA: MIT Press.

Speer, S., Shi, C., & Slowiaczek, M.L. (1989). Prosodic structure in language understanding: Evidence from tone sandhi in Mandarin. *Language and Speech*, *32*, 337–354.

Taft, M., & Chen, H-C. (1992). Judging homophony in Chinese: The influence of tones. In H.-C. Chen & O.J.L. Tzeng (Eds), *Language processing in Chinese*, pp.151–172. Amsterdam: Elsevier.

Van Lancker, D., & Fromkin, V.A. (1973). Hemispheric specialization for pitch and tone: Evidence from Thai. *Journal of Phonetics*, *1*, 101–109.

Yang, Y.-F. (1991). Ear differences in distinguishing consonant features and lexical tones. *Acta Psychologica Sinica*, *2*, 131–137.

Zhou, X., & Marslen-Wilson, W. (1999). Processing lexical tones in visual recognition of Chinese characters. Birkbeck College, University of London, Manuscript in preparation.

APPENDIX A

Experimental Items in Experiment 1

"Yes" Response Stimuli				*"No" Response Stimuli*			
Base Syllable		*Non-existent Syllable*		*Vowel Changed Existent Syllable*		*Tone Changed Existent Syllable*	
ba	2	ra	2	bi	2	ba	4
bai	2	fai	2	bin	2	bai	4
cai	2	jai	2	ci	2	cai	4
hai	2	qai	2	ni	2	hai	4
lai	2	rai	2	ling	2	lai	4
mai	2	xai	2	mi	2	mai	4
pai	2	yai	2	pei	2	pai	4
bao	2	fao	2	bie	2	bao	4
tao	2	wao	2	di	2	tao	4
jiao	2	fiao	2	ji	2	jiao	4
liao	2	giao	2	li	2	liao	4
miao	2	hiao	2	ming	2	miao	4
piao	2	siao	2	ping	2	piao	4
tiao	2	ziao	2	xi	2	tiao	4
xiao	2	ciao	2	xing	2	xiao	4
qiao	2	kiao	2	qi	2	qiao	4
lian	2	cian	2	lei	2	lian	4
mian	2	fian	2	mie	2	mian	4
nian	2	gian	2	ning	2	nian	4
pian	2	hian	2	pi	2	pian	4
qian	2	kian	2	qie	2	qian	4
tian	2	rian	2	ti	2	tian	4
xian	2	sian	2	xie	2	xian	4
yan	2	zian	2	ye	2	ian	4
huan	2	buan	2	yi	2	huan	4
luan	2	fuan	2	liu	2	luan	4
quan	2	muan	2	qing	2	quan	4
xuan	2	puan	2	xie	2	xuan	4
jia	2	pia	2	jing	2	jia	4
xia	2	tia	2	ting	2	xia	4

APPENDIX B

Experimental Items in Experiment 2

Lexical Status	*1st Syllable*	*1st Tone*	*2nd Syllable*	*3rd Tone*	*3rd Syllable*	*3rd Tone*	*Target Syllable*	*Target Tone*
Idiom	chou	4	ming	2	yuan	3	yang	2
Neutral	xia	4	mian	2	shi	3	yang	2
Idiom	bai	3	zhe	2	bu	4	nao	2
Neutral	xia	3	mian	2	shi	4	nao	2
Idiom	bian	4	hua	4	wu	2	chang	2
Neutral	xia	4	mian	4	shi	2	chang	2
Idiom	bie	2	chu	1	xin	1	cai	2
Neutral	xia	2	mian	1	shi	1	cai	2
Idiom	bu	2	neng	2	zi	1	ba	2
Neutral	xia	2	mian	2	shi	1	ba	2
Idiom	bu	4	yi	3	wei	2	ran	2
Neutral	xia	4	mian	3	shi	2	ran	2
Idiom	cang	1	hai	3	sang	1	tian	2
Neutral	xia	1	mian	3	shi	1	tian	2
Idiom	bu	4	yi	3	wei	2	ran	2
Neutral	xia	4	mian	3	shi	2	ran	2
Idiom	chi	4	shou	3	kong	1	quan	2
Neutral	xia	4	mian	3	shi	1	quan	2
Idiom	du	4	ri	4	ru	2	nian	2
Neutral	xia	4	mian	4	shi	2	nian	2
Idiom	fa	1	fen	4	tu	2	qiang	2
Neutral	xia	1	mian	4	shi	2	qiang	2
Idiom	cuo	4	zong	1	fu	4	za	2
Neutral	xia	4	mian	1	shi	4	za	2
Idiom	da	4	yan	2	bu	4	can	2
Neutral	xia	4	mian	2	shi	4	can	2
Idiom	dong	4	ren	2	xin	1	xian	2
Neutral	xia	4	mian	2	shi	1	xian	2
Idiom	gu	3	wang	3	jin	1	lai	2
Neutral	xia	3	mian	3	shi	1	lai	2
Idiom	gui	3	ku	1	lang	2	hao	2
Neutral	xia	3	mian	1	shi	2	hao	2
Idiom	hua	1	hao	3	yue	4	yuan	2
Neutral	xia	1	mian	3	shi	4	yuan	2
Idiom	guan	1	mian	3	tang	2	huang	2
Neutral	xia	1	mian	3	shi	2	huang	2
Idiom	hao	4	yi	4	wu	4	lao	2
Neutral	xia	4	mian	4	shi	4	lao	2
Idiom	jia	1	po	4	ren	2	wang	2
Neutral	xia	1	mian	4	shi	2	wang	2
Idiom	lao	3	jian	1	ju	4	hua	2
Neutral	xia	3	mian	1	shi	4	hua	2
Idiom	lao	3	sheng	1	chang	2	tan	2
Neutral	xia	3	mian	1	shi	2	tan	2
Idiom	zheng	4	zhong	4	xia	4	huai	2

Experimental Items in Experiment 2—*cont.*

Lexical Status	*1st Syllable*	*1st Tone*	*2nd Syllable*	*3rd Tone*	*3rd Syllable*	*3rd Tone*	*Target Syllable*	*Target Tone*
Neutral	xia	4	mian	4	shi	4	huai	2
Idiom	li	4	wan	3	kuang	2	lan	2
Neutral	xia	4	mian	3	shi	2	lan	2
Idiom	jin	1	yu	2	liang	2	yan	2
Neutral	xia	1	mian	2	shi	2	yan	2
Idiom	zai	4	jie	2	nan	2	tao	2
Neutral	xia	4	mian	2	shi	2	tao	2
Idiom	kang	1	kai	3	ji	1	ang	2
Neutral	xia	1	mian	3	shi	1	ang	2
Idiom	hai	3	jiao	3	tian	1	ya	2
Neutral	xia	3	mian	3	shi	1	ya	2
Idiom	guo	4	he	2	chai	1	qiao	2
Neutral	xia	4	mian	2	shi	1	qiao	2
Idiom	huo	3	shao	1	mei	2	mao	2
Neutral	xia	3	mian	1	shi	2	mao	2

APPENDIX C

Experimental Items in Experiment 3

Lexical Status	*1st Syllable*	*1st Tone*	*2nd Syllable*	*3rd Tone*	*3rd Syllable*	*3rd Tone*	*Target Syllable*	*Target Tone*
Idiom	yi	1	pu	4	shi	2	han	2
Close	yi	1	pu	4	shi	3	han	2
Far	yi	1	pu	4	shi	4	han	2
Idiom	li	4	wan	3	kuang	2	lang	2
Close	li	4	wan	3	kuang	3	lang	2
Far	li	4	wan	3	kuang	4	lang	2
Idiom	yi	4	zheng	4	ci	2	yan	2
Close	yi	4	zheng	4	ci	3	yan	2
Far	yi	4	zheng	4	ci	4	yan	2
Idiom	fei	1	huang	2	teng	2	da	2
Close	fei	1	huang	2	teng	3	da	2
Far	fei	1	huang	2	teng	4	da	2
Idiom	bu	4	yi	3	wei	2	ran	2
Close	bu	4	yi	3	wei	3	ran	2
Far	bu	4	yi	3	wei	4	ran	2
Idiom	bu	4	yan	4	qi	2	fan	2
Close	bu	4	yan	4	qi	3	fan	2
Far	bu	4	yan	4	qi	4	fan	2
Idiom	fan	3	fu	4	wu	2	chang	2
Close	fan	3	fu	4	wu	3	chang	2
Far	fan	3	fu	4	wu	4	chang	2
Idiom	feng	1	zhu	2	can	2	nian	2
Close	feng	1	zhu	2	can	3	nian	2
Far	feng	1	zhu	2	can	4	nian	2
Idiom	dou	4	zhi	4	ang	2	yang	2
Close	dou	4	zhi	4	ang	3	yang	2
Far	dou	4	zhi	4	ang	4	yang	2
Idiom	xin	1	luan	4	ru	2	ma	2
Close	xin	1	luan	4	ru	3	ma	2
Far	xin	1	luan	4	ru	4	ma	2
Idiom	yi	3	ya	2	huan	2	ya	2
Close	yi	3	ya	2	huan	3	ya	2
Far	yi	3	ya	2	huan	4	ya	2
Idiom	chu	1	mo	4	wu	2	chang	2
Close	chu	1	mo	4	wu	3	chang	2
Far	chu	1	mo	4	wu	4	chang	2
Idiom	fa	1	fen	4	tu	2	qiang	2
Close	fa	1	fen	4	tu	3	qiang	2
Far	fa	1	fen	4	tu	4	qiang	2
Idiom	lao	3	sheng	1	chang	2	tan	2
Close	lao	3	sheng	1	chang	3	tan	2
Far	lao	3	sheng	1	chang	4	tan	2
Idiom	kua	1	kua	1	qi	2	tan	2
Close	kua	1	kua	1	qi	3	tan	2
Far	kua	1	kua	1	qi	4	tan	2

Experimental Items in Experiment 3—*cont.*

Lexical Status	*1st Syllable*	*1st Tone*	*2nd Syllable*	*3rd Tone*	*3rd Syllable*	*3rd Tone*	*Target Syllable*	*Target Tone*
Idiom	zhi	4	li	3	ming	2	yan	2
Close	zhi	4	li	3	ming	3	yan	2
Far	zhi	4	li	3	ming	4	yan	2
Idiom	ming	2	lie	4	qian	2	mao	2
Close	ming	2	lie	4	qian	3	mao	2
Far	ming	2	lie	4	qian	4	mao	2
Idiom	wua	4	di	4	wei	2	lao	2
Close	wua	4	di	4	wei	3	lao	2
Far	wua	4	di	4	wei	4	lao	2
Idiom	feng	4	fa	1	tu	2	qiang	2
Close	feng	4	fa	1	tu	3	qiang	2
Far	feng	4	fa	1	tu	4	qiang	2
Idiom	kan	3	kan	3	er	2	tan	2
Close	kan	3	kan	3	er	3	tan	2
Far	kan	3	kan	3	er	4	tan	2
Idiom	jin	1	yu	4	liang	2	yuan	2
Close	jin	1	yu	4	liang	3	yuan	2
Far	jin	1	yu	4	liang	4	yuan	2
Idiom	juan	3	tu	2	chong	2	lai	2
Close	juan	3	tu	2	chong	3	lai	2
Far	juan	3	tu	2	chong	4	lai	2
Idiom	ya	3	ko	3	wu	2	yan	2
Close	ya	3	ko	3	wu	3	yan	2
Far	ya	3	ko	3	wu	4	yan	2
Idiom	du	4	ri	4	ru	2	nian	2
Close	du	4	ri	4	ru	3	nian	2
Far	du	4	ri	4	ru	4	nian	2
Idiom	tu	1	ru	2	qi	2	lai	2
Close	tu	1	ru	2	qi	3	lai	2
Far	tu	1	ru	2	qi	4	lai	2
Idiom	yong	3	wang	3	zhi	2	qian	2
Close	yong	3	wang	3	zhi	3	qian	2
Far	yong	3	wang	3	zhi	4	qian	2
Idiom	po	4	jing	4	chong	2	yuan	2
Close	po	4	jing	4	chong	3	yuan	2
Far	po	4	jing	4	chong	4	yuan	2
Idiom	cheng	2	xing	4	er	2	lai	2
Close	cheng	2	xing	4	er	3	lai	2
Far	cheng	2	xing	4	er	4	lai	2
Idiom	de	2	sheng	4	huan	2	chao	2
Close	de	2	sheng	4	huan	3	chao	2
Far	de	2	sheng	4	huan	4	chao	2
Idiom	can	3	jue	2	ren	2	huan	2
Close	can	3	jue	2	ren	3	huan	2
Far	can	3	jue	2	ren	4	huan	2

LANGUAGE AND COGNITIVE PROCESSES, 1999, *14* (5/6), 631–662

Incremental Pré-head Attachment in Japanese Parsing

Yuki Kamide
Department of Psychology, University of York, UK

Don C. Mitchell
School of Psychology, University of Exeter, UK

The present study addresses the question of whether structural analyses of verb-arguments are postponed up until the head verb has been processed (head-driven parsing accounts) or initiated prior to the appearance of the verb (pre-head attachment accounts). To explore this question in relation to a head-final language, a Japanese dative argument attachment ambiguity was examined in both a questionnaire study (Experiment 1) and a self-paced reading test (Experiment 2). The data suggested that the dative argument attachment ambiguity is resolved in the manner predicted by pre-head attachment accounts. The results were incompatible with most variants of the head-driven parsing model, and were not of the form currently predicted by constraint-satisfaction models. We end by discussing the general theoretical implications of the findings.

INTRODUCTION

Head-driven Parsing

The question of what types of information guide initial parsing decisions has been the focus of a great deal of attention in the psycholinguistic literature. Factors that have been examined include the effects of proximity and structural simplicity (Frazier, 1987), the effects of discourse context (Altmann & Steedman, 1988), effects of intonation and prosody

Requests for reprints should be addressed to Yuki Kamide, Department of Psychology, University of York, Heslington, York, YO10 5DD, UK. Email: y.kamide@psych.york.ac.uk

The experiments in the present paper were conducted as part of the first author's PhD work at the University of Exeter.

We are grateful to Gerry Altmann, Chuck Clifton, Gerard Kempen, Christoph Scheepers, Patrick Sturt, and two anonymous reviewers for their very thoughtful comments on an earlier draft of the paper.

(Fodor, 1998), effects of prior exposure to language (Cuetos, Mitchell, & Corley, 1996), and the effects of detailed lexical information (Ford, Bresnan, & Kaplan, 1982; MacDonald, Pearlmutter, & Seidenberg, 1994; Trueswell & Tanenhaus, 1994).

The present paper focuses on the last of these classes of information that potentially influence the course of parsing. In particular, it is primarily concerned with the role of "head information" in the early stage of parsing—an issue that has previously been explored by numerous investigators (Ford et al., 1982; Pritchett, 1991, 1992; MacDonald et al., 1994; Trueswell & Tanenhaus, 1994; Konieczny, Hemforth, Scheepers, & Strube, 1997). The "head" of a phrase or clause can be characterised as the "core" word in the constituent. For example, the head of a noun phrase (NP) (e.g., "the pretty cat") is the noun itself ("cat", in this example). Similarly, the head of a verb phrase (VP) (e.g., "(The pretty cat) likes cheese very much") is the verb ("likes"). According to certain linguistic theories (Chomsky, 1981; Fillmore, 1968; Jackendoff, 1972, Grimshaw, 1990; Pollard and Sag, 1987, 1994), each and every head is associated with certain types of item-specific information ("head information") that dictates or at least constrains the kinds of relationship it can enter into with other constituents within the sentence. If the head is a verb, for instance, this head information might include a list of permissible "argument structures" of the head (i.e., types of constituent it can be interlinked with). As an illustration, the verb "put" in Sentence (1) links with three structures.

(1) The man put the book onto the table.

One of these structures represents a person doing the "putting", a second, the object being moved and the third the destination of the action (see Fillmore, 1968; Grimshaw, 1990; MacDonald et al., 1994, for detailed analysis of verb-argument structures).

A central concern of recent psycholinguistic research has been to assess the importance of such head information in parsing relative to other possible types of information or constraints. One, admittedly extreme, possibility is that the human parser makes use of such information to the exclusion of all other potential sources of guidance.

A system that is constrained by grammatical information stored with only heads may be referred to as a "head-driven" parser. Pritchett (1991) has proposed such a parser (see also Pritchett, 1987, 1988, 1992). This system is governed by Principle (2) as given below:

(2) A node cannot be projected before the occurrence of its head, since the relevant features which determine its categorical identity and

license both its own and its arguments' attachment are theretofore undetermined (Pritchett, 1991; p.252).

Hence the crucial characteristic of head-driven parsing is that the parser does not make attachment decisions prior to a head. Thus, in sentences like (1), the claim is that the first Noun Phrase (NP) ("The man") temporarily remains unattached to any other linguistic structure awaiting the arrival of the head-verb "put". Once the verb materialises it provides "docking points" not only for the free-floating NP but also for the two other constructions to follow. Furthermore, based on the Theta Criterion (Chomsky, 1981, 1986), Pritchett (1991, 1992) argues that the head-driven parser is dominated by information stored with heads in attachment decision-making during the course of parsing. This is represented as the "Generalized Theta Attachment" principle in Pritchett (1992):

(3) Generalized Theta Attachment:
Every principle of the Syntax attempts to be maximally satisfied at every point during processing (Pritchett, 1992; p.138).

Note, however, that immediate satisfaction of licensing requirements (i.e., GTA) is not a mandatory property of a head-driven parser. For instance, one could posit a parser (a) that does not make attachment decisions until a potential head appears *and* (b) that does not follow the GTA principle at the head. Such a parser could still be referred to as head-driven. Thus, not every possible head-driven parser has to be governed by licensing information. On the other hand, it is also important to note here that Pritchett's theory is rather radical compared with other licensing parsing theories (Abney, 1989; Gorrell, 1995; Weinberg, 1995) and also with constraint-satisfaction (or constraint-based) models (MacDonald et al., 1994; Trueswell & Tanenhaus, 1994), in the sense that Pritchett (1991, 1992) rules out the use of any information other than that stored with heads, typically licensing relations. In contrast, the other theories mentioned above posit the use of several different kinds of information often on a weighted parallel basis (e.g., head information, discourse information for constraint-satisfaction models). Alternatively, they use a hierarchy of prioritised types of information (e.g., complementary attachment principles (the Verb Attachment and Low Attachment principles) are included in the account presented by Abney, 1989). Hereafter, however, we shall concentrate our discussion of head-driven parsing on parsers with both head-driven and licensing-driven properties, namely, parsers (a) that make no attachment decision until the head arrives *and* (b) that are governed exclusively by the premise that they have to fill licensing requirements *maximally* (i.e., whenever possible) *as soon* as they can (e.g., the head-driven parser proposed by Pritchett, 1991). Note that such parsers attempt to fill even optional licensing requirements (e.g., optional thematic roles) in order to accomplish maximal licensing.

Some crucial features of a strictly head-driven account are set out clearly in a computational model of parsing developed by Vosse and Kempen (submitted). In this account (the Unification-Space, or U-Space, model) the arrival of successive words of a sentence causes their associated "lexical frames" to be copied in turn into a working space ("Unification Space") that is then used as a medium for computing syntactic links between frames. Upon entering U-Space, each form is immediately linked with others already present, using sets of connections whose strengths vary over time depending on a complex set of inhibitions, and constraints designed to ensure that the links conform to a variety of types of semantic and syntactic agreement. The details of the "unification" or constraint-satisfaction procedure are critical to the workings of the implementation, but need not be spelt out for the present purpose—which is to outline an explicit head-driven model.

In the U-Space model, the structured representation of (part of) a sentence comes exclusively from (a) the lexical frames copied into U-Space as the successive words arrive and (b) the computed links between these frames. Crucially, the top-level S node is construed within the theory as being part of the lexical form for verbs (and verbs alone). It follows that before the verb arrives, nothing at all can be linked to the S node (or its constituent V node)—for the simple reason that neither yet exists at this point within the system. Because of this, the structuring of the NP must await the arrival of the verb itself. When the verb does appear and its frame joins the others in U-Space, its numerous unification constraints can finally exert their influences on the structural linkages. In a later section of the paper we shall use the explicit nature of the Vosse/Kempen statement to derive predictions for strictly head-driven parsing models of this kind. The predictions are particularly stark for head-final languages (like Japanese and Korean), but important, too, in languages with head-final subconstituents (e.g., Dutch and German). For example, consider the following Japanese sentence (Sentence 4):

(4) Chika-ga Kayo-ni koneko-o ageta.
Chika-Nom Kayo-Dat kitten-Acc gave.
"Chika gave a kitten to Kayo."

This sentence features three pre-verbal arguments: "Chika-ga" (Chika-Nom), "Kayo-ni" (Kayo-Dat) and "koneko-o" (kitten-Acc). According to strictly head-driven models, the three arguments are left unattached until the head verb "ageta" appears at the end of the sentence. Hence the model posits the steady accumulation of structurally unattached constituents as the reader or listener progresses through the sentence. A system of this kind would be expected to impose considerable demands on short-term memory.

Pre-head Attachment

Such memory demands could be held in check if, contrary to the assumptions of head-driven parsing, structural analysis is initiated *before* the head is heard or read. In the remainder of the present paper, we shall refer to such devices as "pre-head attachment parsers". Pre-head attachment accounts contrast with head-driven parsers in that they impose fewer constrains on the starting point for computing structural relations. In the Japanese sentence (4) above, for example, arguments might be assigned to the as-yet-unprocessed verb as soon as each argument phrase is encountered in the sentence. Such incremental pre-head attachment parsing is premised on the assumption that representational features typically associated with heads (e.g., VPs for verbs) can be postulated before the head words themselves appear.

There are numerous different ways in which such models can be formulated. For instance, borrowing the theoretical language of the Vosse/Kempen U-Space model, one could posit a parsing system which, unlike the "official" version of the theory, allows certain kinds of *non*-lexical frames to be inserted into unification space in the course of sentence processing. In particular, a pre-head variant of the U-Space model might allow (say) a "generic sentence-structure frame" to be injected either just before or just after the first lexical frame is loaded. A "generic sentence-structure frame" is envisaged as being something like a standard verb-frame but lacking the lowest level information which instantiates the frame as the product of a particular verb.[1] If this new, non-lexical frame were handled in the same way as the standard bottom-up units, this would open the way for the establishment of NP-V node links immediately after the arrival of Word 1. For example, an early NP might be marked as a potential argument for a verb slot even though the verb destined to occupy that slot had not yet made its appearance. In such a variant of pre-head attachment accounts, the exact trajectory of the build-up of link strengths would depend on the precise assumptions made about the "generic frame" and its inherent constraints. However, the broad description above is sufficient to give a flavour of models of this kind. There are several different theories that share the premise that verb-centred processes can precede the verb itself (Inoue & Fodor, 1995; Konieczny, 1996; Mazuka &

[1] Loading the generic frame *before* the first word might be feasible for a reader who used the full-stop at the end of the preceding sentence to infer that a new one was about to start. In spoken comprehension, a change of speaker might provide comparable information.

Itoh, 1995). Rather than examining the details of these theories, we shall refer to the general account as the pre-head attachment hypothesis. In our discussion, the pre-head attachment hypothesis is taken to cover any account that allows pre-head attachment in at least some linguistic circumstances.

The major aim of the present paper is to explore the issue of head-driven/pre-head attachment. To recap, we have defined head-driven parsers as making no attachment decisions prior to heads, and then trying to satisfy head-derived constraints as soon as heads arrive. In contrast, our definition of pre-head attachment parsers suggests that the parser does make attachment decisions before heads arrive. As already mentioned, head-final languages provide an important arena for investigating this question. In the present paper we shall concentrate upon an attachment ambiguity that occurs in the Japanese language. Before moving onto the sentence structure, we shall review one or two previous empirical studies dealing with the issue.

Empirical Studies on Head-driven/Pre-head-driven Parsing in Head-final Structures

In the past, the majority of studies of head-awaiting have been carried out in the German language (Bader & Lasser, 1994; Hemforth, 1993; Konieczny, 1996; Konieczny et al., 1997; Scheepers, Hemforth, & Konieczny, 1994). For instance, Bader and Lasser (1994) conducted a self-paced reading task using the following ambiguity in German subordinate clauses:

(5a) daß sie $_{(\text{Nom/Acc})}$ nach dem Ergebnis zu fragen tatsächlich erlaubt hat
that she/her for the result to ask indeed permitted has
"that she indeed has permitted to ask for the result"

(5b) daß sie $_{(\text{Nom/Acc})}$ nach dem Ergebnis zu fragen tatsächlich erlaubt worden ist
that she/her for the result to ask indeed permitted has been
"that to ask her for the result has been permitted"

The sentences in (5) contain a female singular pronoun "sie" that is ambiguous between nominative ("she" for English) and accusative case ("her" for English). Permissible argument structures of the first verb "fragen" include "fragen [NP-Nom <Agent>, NP-Acc <Goal>, nach-PP <Theme>]" and "fragen [NP-Nom <Agent>, nach-PP <Theme>]". The temporary ambiguity in (5) is whether the ambiguously case-marked "sie" is analysed as the object of the first verb "fragen" (accusative reading), or as the subject of the second verb "erlaubt" (nominative reading). The ambiguity can be resolved by the appearance of an auxiliary word at the end of the clause. If "hat" (has) follows, as in (5a), the nominative analysis turns out to be correct, while if "worden ist" (has been) follows, as in (5b), this implies that the correct reading is the accusative one. The head-driven parsing hypothesis predicts that the ambiguous "sie" should not be attached until the first verb ("fragen"). As soon as it is encountered, it is attached to the verb ("fragen"), and so becomes disambiguated as an accusative noun. This analysis turns out to be wrong at the end of the clause in the "hat" condition, (5a), while this is compatible with "worden ist" in (5b). Using this manipulation with two additional control conditions, Bader and Lasser (1994) found that the unambiguous "sie" tends to be analysed as the subject of the forthcoming final verb (i.e., nominative reading). They argued that this finding is incompatible with the head-driven attachment hypothesis.

There is, however, an important concern with German studies of this kind. This stems from the fact that the main manipulations were based on ambiguities of case. It is arguable that certain types of head-driven account could produce effects of the kind that Bader and Lasser (1994) and others interpret as evidence against such models. For example, it is possible to imagine a head-driven system in which case can be assigned to an NP not by the parser itself but by reference to some extraneous strategy—such as automatically assigning nominative case to the first NP in the sentence without any kind of prior higher level structural analysis. For instance, Hopf, Bayer, Bader, and Meng (1998) explicitly acknowledge, in their Footnote 6, that such case effects may be the result of statistical, as opposed to syntactic operations (also, see Hemforth, Konieczny, & Strube, 1993, for evidence of very early signs of case bias in German sentences). Such a possibility is not just a matter of ad hoc speculation: such proposals have a long history in the study of parsing (see also a related statistical proposal by Vosse and Kempen, submitted). For example, Fodor, Bever, and Garrett (1974) proposed that readers and listeners assign preliminary structure to sentences using what they called a "Canonical Order strategy". This involves immediately treating the first NP of a sentence as its subject (and might equally well be interpreted in terms of assigning it nominative case). The crucial feature of any "canonical order" operation is that the decisions are based not on any thorough syntactic analysis of the sentences currently under scrutiny, but on the statistically most common order in which NP category assignments occur in sentences in general (see Hyönä & Hujanen, 1997, for recent evidence that something of this kind might occur in Finnish). Another line of support for these proposals comes from observations concerning assignment of other types of licensing relations during sentence comprehension. Bates, MacWhinney and colleagues have reported numerous studies showing that NPs can be assigned functional roles on the basis of operations that may have little or nothing to do with conventional parsing (see, for example, MacWhinney & Bates, 1989). Such investigations show that these biases are evident even when people are presented with ungrammatical word-strings—indicating that it is implausible to treat them as by-products of any routine forms of syntactic analysis. Because of the close association between case and functional roles, it seems highly likely that there is also a (non-syntactic) predisposition to assign case to at least some of the NPs within a sentence. If such NPs can receive case from something other than the results of routine syntactic analysis then the evidence for a nominative or genitive bias in the German studies might not necessarily have any implications for syntactic processing. The preferences might have occurred not because the NP has been structurally linked to a verb that is yet to appear, but because of a broad case assignment in which verb information is not involved. Given these possibilities, there are grounds for being sceptical about the implications of the German findings and, in particular, whether they provide definitive evidence against head-driven models of parsing.

In a more recent study, Koh (1997) has addressed the issue of head-driven parsing in an experiment that is not based on case assignment and is therefore not subject to the reservations raised above. This investigation was organised around a temporary attachment ambiguity in the Korean language, in which a dative-marked NP can potentially be attached either to a subordinate following a word or two later or to a matrix verb scheduled to appear at the end of the sentence. In an eye-tracking study, Koh (1997) compared reading times in sentences of this kind with sentences where there was a forced link between the dative NP and the subordinate verb. According to head-driven accounts, the matrix link should not be an option at any point prior to the appearance of the main verb. Consequently, for most of its length the sentence should be processed exactly as if it were unambiguous, leading to the prediction that there should be no systematic processing differences between the ambiguous sentence and its control. In contrast, a pre-head attachment model would allow the dative NP to be attached to the as-yet-unseen matrix verb where this is permitted (i.e., in the temporarily ambiguous condition). This would lead to processing problems in cases where the final verb rules out the interim matrix attachment. Corresponding difficulties would not, however, be expected in the control condition where matrix attachment was not posited in the first place. In line with the second hypothesis and against the head-driven account, Koh (1997) found that the total reading times were significantly longer in the region of the matrix verb. However, the interpretation of this result was complicated by the fact that different matrix verbs were used in the experimental and control conditions, raising the possibility that there might be a *lexical* rather than a syntactic explanation for the differences obtained. To address this problem, Koh's experiment incorporated two further conditions designed to act as lexical controls. Unfortunately, the difference was not significantly reduced in the lexical control conditions, indicating that the data could not rule out the lexical explanation of the findings. Given this pattern of results, it has to be concluded that Koh's results fail to provide convincing support for the pre-head attachment model of parsing.

The Present Study: Japanese Argument Attachment Ambiguity

As seen, previous empirical studies (Bader & Lasser, 1994; Koh, 1997; Scheepers et al., 1994) have not succeeded in providing solid support for the hypothesis that structural attachment analyses of pre-verbal constituents are accomplished prior to the host verb. To overcome the problems of both the German and Korean studies, it is necessary to conduct experiments that avoid the theoretical and methodological objections outlined above. In the present paper, we report a series of off-line/on-line experiments in Japanese that look at whether the parser initiates structural analyses of pre-verbal constituents before the host verb. Using a Japanese ambiguity enables us to avoid the potential problem of the previous German experiments (Bader & Lasser, 1994; Scheepers et al., 1994) discussed above, namely, the possibility that the head-driven parser might pre-verbally assign cases independent of (and prior to) structural analyses. The following ambiguity will be examined (the ambiguity is based on Koh, 1997):

(6) Kyooju-ga gakusee-ni toshokansisho-ga kasita mezurasii komonjo-o miseta.
Professor-Nom student-Dat librarian-Nom lent unusual ancient manuscript-Acc showed.
"The professor showed [HA: the student] the unusual ancient manuscript which the librarian had lent [LA: the student]."

The ambiguity in (6) is that the dative NP "gakusee-ni" (student-Dat) can be attached either to the VP headed by the subordinate verb "kasita" (lent) or that headed by the matrix verb "miseta" (showed) (we shall hereafter refer to the first option as "low attachment" and the second option as "high attachment", as well as "subordinate attachment" and "matrix attachment", respectively). The ambiguity is "global" in the sense that the grammar does not force either attachment to be confirmed at any point in the sentence. The Japanese global ambiguity is possible since a dative Goal argument is *always* optional for Japanese ditransitive verbs. Both attachment decision form a grammatical construction. In the high attachment analysis, "mezurasii komonjo" (unusual ancient manuscript) was *shown* to "gakusee" (student), while the Goal argument of "kasita" (lent) is assigned to a "pro" (or left empty), representing perhaps someone who is not mentioned in the sentence. In contrast, the low attachment decision leads to the interpretation that "mezurasii komonjo" was *lent* to "gakusee" whereas it was shown to someone else, filling the Goal of the alternative verb with a "pro". The earliest indication of the ambiguity is the appearance of the second nominative NP "toshokansisho-ga" (librarian-Nom), since there has been only one dative NP for two clauses. However, note that it is impossible at this stage to establish whether the host verb of each clause can legitimately take a dative verb.

The two different types of parser under investigation, namely the head-driven and pre-head attachment systems, would process the Japanese sentence (especially the dative NP) in a different manner.

We start by giving detailed consideration of the step-by-step operations of a head-driven parser. By hypothesis, this would not start structural analysis of the pre-verb arguments until the verbs are encountered. When the first verb ("kasita") appears, the dative NP would presumably be analysed as the indirect object of the verb. In Pritchett's framework this follows from the tendency to define licensing relations as soon as possible (Generalized Theta Attachment; (3)). Within the Vosse/Kempen U-Space model the same would occur for the mere reason that the NP and "kasita"-frames co-exist for a time in U-space without any competition for their mutual connections. In either framework, the low-attached link would be retained at least until the alternative verb appears. When the matrix verb "miseta" is encountered, the parser faces the problem that both verbs can take a dative argument. At this point there are two ways in which a head-driven parser might resolve the dilemma. On the one hand it might retain the initially established low-attachment decision and avoid possible reanalysis costs (leading to a durable low-attachment preference at the end of the sentence). On the other hand, it might try to achieve a balance between the two alternatives, being guided by the competing constraints associated with the two heads. Assuming (a) that there is no additional cost associated with unravelling existing decisions (reanalysis) and (b) that there is no imbalance between the acceptabilities of the two dative roles in the two respective analyses, then this state of affairs might eventually lead to 50% low and 50% high attachment preferences. In short, head-driven accounts would predict at one extreme a 50/50 attachment bias and this would tilt in the direction of a low-attachment preference on the plausible assumption that there is some "inertia" in the system (favouring existing links over restructuring or reanalysed relations).

In contrast with this, an incremental pre-head attachment parser would be capable of making its high-level attachment decisions without having to wait for either of the verbs to appear, for example, as soon as the NP-arguments are encountered. Thus, making use of the early availability of top-down information (e.g., a "generic sentence frame" discussed earlier) the parser would link the first two NPs to the generic verb slot within the top-down frame well before a verb arrives. The later arrival of the subordinate verb ("kasita") would provide a competing set of links for the dative NP. Potentially this could lead to a steady reduction in the strengths of the links to the matrix verb depending on the exact details of the conflict-resolution process. In some variants of the account, the procedural details might favour the links to the explicitly-realised bottom-up verb slots rather than to the postulated generic verb frames. This might lead to ultimate (though not necessarily immediate) predictions that are indistinguishable from those for the head-driven models outlined above. In other variants, initially robust links may be preserved at the expense of later-arriving competitors. Such models would predict a completely different (high-attached) preference at the end of the sentence. However, although the former type of pre-head attachment hypothesis is theoretically possible, we shall hereafter deal with only the latter account in our discussion on incremental pre-head attachment parsing for simplicity.

The study presented in the present paper consists of one questionnaire study (Experiment 1) and one self-paced reading task (Experiment 2). Experiment 1 aims to demonstrate an off-line preference for the ambiguity. Note that the two opposite accounts predict different eventual preferences as discussed above.[2] On the other hand, Experiment 2 looks at on-line processing of the ambiguity under investigation. Additionally, before Experiment 1, a preliminary test is conducted to rate how strongly an optionally ditransitive verb requires a dative Goal argument. The rating results are to be used to counterbalance the strength of the dative requirement in the two attachment host verbs in the globally ambiguous sentences (e.g., (6)) used in the subsequent experiments. Although corpora would provide argument structure information based on data from a wider range of materials/readers, it has to be noted that no reliable corpora are available for Japanese verbs at present.

[2] Note that the constraint-satisfaction approach (MacDonald et al., 1994; Trueswell & Tanenhaus, 1994) argues that both attachment hosts are equally preferred off-line given that the dative requirement strength is counterbalanced between the two verbs. Thus, the approach predicts no off-line attachment preference for the ambiguity given the lexical counterbalance.

EXPERIMENT 1

The present experiment examines the off-line preference for the attachment ambiguity under consideration. The eventual preference for the ambiguity has important implications for the question of whether Japanese parsing is head-final or incremental, since the two opposite accounts make different predictions about the preferences that will prevail. As already noted, head-driven accounts predict either (a) that low attachment should be eventually preferred as a consequence of immediate satisfaction of an argument structure requirement (without reanalysis), or (b) that both attachments should be equally preferred because both attachment decisions equally satisfy argument structure requirements (with reanalysis) (see the Introduction above, and also Table 2 below). In contrast, the incremental pre-head attachment hypothesis predicts that high attachment should be preferred since it is the first attachment option that the parser commits itself to.

Preliminary Test

Before Experiment 1, a preliminary questionnaire study was carried out. The purpose of this was to obtain norms in order to establish how strongly various Japanese ditransitive verbs require a Goal (dative) argument. The results of this analysis will be used to provide a basis for selecting materials for use in Experiment 1 and later also in Experiment 2. To counter against biases originating from the properties of individual verbs, we require two groups of Japanese ditransitive verbs that require a Goal argument with the same strength. Such counterbalancing should ensure that any possible attachment preference can be attributed to structural biases as opposed to lexical biases.

Eighty-eight native speakers of Japanese participated in the Preliminary Test. All of them were students (undergraduates and postgraduates) or academic staff at the Kumamoto University, Japan.

Initially, 24 globally ambiguous complex sentences such as (6) above were constructed, using 48 Japanese ditransitive verbs from Mizutani (1985).[3] Then, the 24 complex sentences were divided into two unambiguous simplex sentences (e.g., (7a) and (7b) were made out of (6)):

(7a) Kyooju-ga gakusee-ni mezurasii komonjo-o miseta.
"The professor showed the student the unusual ancient manuscript."

[3] The material set of 24 ambiguous sentences is given in Appendix 2: the sentences were used as the experimental sentences in Experiments 1 and 2, as we shall discuss below.

(7b) Toshokansisho-ga gukasee-ni mezurasii komonjo-o kasita.
"The librarian lent the student the unusual ancient manuscript."

Furthermore, versions of the sentences in which the dative arguments were omitted were constructed (e.g., (8a) and (8b) for (7a) and (7b), respectively):[4]

(8a) Kyooju-ga mezurasii komonjo-o miseta.
"The professor showed the unusual ancient manuscript."

(8b) Toshokansisho-ga mezurasii komonjo-o kasita.
"The librarian lent the unusual ancient manuscript."

In the Preliminary Test, subjects were asked to use a numerical scale to rate how well they understood the "dative missing" sentences like (8), given the benchmark that they were called on to use the score of 100 to rate their understanding of the "full" sentences like (7). All materials were presented as pairs (e.g., (7a) and (8a) or (7b) and (8b)) in Japanese script on one-sided A4 sheets. In total, there were 48 unambiguous pairs. There was no explicit instruction as to whether or not numerical ratings could exceed 100.

The rating score for each Japanese ditransitive verb is given in Appendix 1. The score varied from 66.4 to 76.14, and the mean score was 72.21. It was revealed that the ditransitive verbs which served as a subordinate verb and those those which served as a matrix verb in the initially-constructed material set (24 sentences like (6)) contained statistically equal strengths of dative requirements on average (mean scores: Subordinate Verbs: 71.40; Matrix Verbs: 71.01; $F2(1,47) = 0.266$, $P = .609$, MSe = 3.956). Therefore, the results suggested that the original material set would provide counterbalanced dative requirement biases in the further experiments (Experiments 1 and 2).

Method

Subjects. Eighty-eight native speakers of Japanese participated in Experiment 1. All of them had previously participated in the preliminary test.

Materials and procedure. All materials were presented in Japanese script on one-sided A4 sheets. The task was to read sentences like (6) (repeated as (9a)), and to answer two subsequent questions like (9b) and

[4] This somewhat reversed order of constructing materials was chosen in order to examine the same combinations of objects and verbs in both the preliminary test and further experiments.

(9c) (the (9a) versions of all sentences examined in Experiment 1 are given in Appendix 2 as the globally ambiguous (GA) condition sentences for Experiment 2):

(9a) Kyooju-ga gakusee-ni toshokansisho-ga kasita mezurasii komonjo-o miseta.
Professor-Nom student-Dat librarian-Nom lent unusual ancient manuscript-Acc showed.
"The professor showed [HA: the student] the unusual ancient manuscript which the librarian had lent [LA: the student]."

(9b) Dare-ni-kyooju-ga kononjo-o misemasitaka.
"To whom did the professor show the ancient manuscript?"

(9c) Dare-ni toshokansisho-ga komonjo-o kasimasitaka.
"To whom did the librarian lend the ancient manuscript?"

Twenty-four dative ambiguous sentences (e.g., (9a)) were tested. The subsequent questions were about Goal roles for the ditransitive verbs in the sentence. Dative NPs stood for a person or a group of people in all sentences. Subjects were explicitly instructed that they could use the same persons for both Goal roles in a sentence, and also that they could use "sonata" (someone else) when they did not find any overt Goal in the sentence. The order of the matrix question (e.g., (9b)) and a subordinate question (e.g., (9c)) was counterbalanced. Also, there were two different versions in the order of all 24 experimental sentences. Altogether, each of the four versions was presented to 22 subjects. As mentioned earlier, the ditransitive verbs used for the subordinate verb and those used for the matrix verb had statistically the same strength of dative requirements on average, based on the results from the preliminary test.

Results and Discussion

Six patterns of attachment were found in the questionnaire study. Table 1 gives those attachment patterns and percentages.

The first column indicates the name of each attachment pattern found in Experiment 1. The result (as percentage) for each pattern is shown in the second column. The alternative attachment patterns depend on which participants (constituents) were selected for the answers of the questions (9b) and (9c) above. The third column represents which constituent is the Goal role of the matrix verb in each pattern. For instance, in the MS attachment pattern (first row), the dative NP ("gakusee" (the student) for (9a)) is the answer for the question like (9b) above. On the other hand, the constituent in the fourth column indicates which constituent is the Goal role of the subordinate verb in each attachment pattern. For example,

TABLE 1
Percentage of each Attachment Pattern in Experiment 1

Pattern	*Percentage*	*Constituent for Goal of Matrix Verb (answer to (9b))*	*Constituent for Goal of Subordinate Verb (answer to (9c))*
Matrix Subject (MS)	60.32	Dative NP	Matrix Subject
High Attachment (HA)	19.03	Dative NP	"someone else"
Both	15.43	Dative NP	Dative NP
Subordinate Subject (SS)	2.84	Subordinate Subject	Dative NP
Low Attachment (LA)	2.04	"someone else"	Dative NP
Null	0.43	"someone else"	"someone else"

"kyooju" (the professor) is the answer for the question like (9c) above in the MS attachment pattern. Among all the six patterns, there was a robustly significant difference across attachment pattern ($F1(5,435)$ = 269.67, $P < .001$, MSe = 9.76; $F2(5,115) = 48.81$, $P < .001$, MSe = 196.66). The preference for the MS analysis was significantly greater than that for any of the alternatives (e.g., MS *vs* HA: $F1(1,87) = 127.42$, $P < .001$, MSe = 34.45; $F2(1,87) = 28.90$, $P < .001$, MSe = 547.81). In all attachment patterns, it is possible to categorise the MS and HA analyses as the high attachment group, and the SS and LA analyses as the low attachment groups, according to the attachment of the dative NP under investigation. Thus, Experiment 1 showed that readers opt for variations of high attachment significantly more frequently than those of law attachment (HA and MS *vs* LA and SS: 79.88% *vs* 4.88%; $F1(1,87) = 1687.99$, $P < .001$, MSe = 8.25; $F2(1,23) = 192.25$, $P < .001$, MSe = 263.13). This is inconsistent with any of the head-driven predictions for the ambiguity (which ranged from a low-attachment preference to a 50/50 attachment preference). The results are also incompatible with versions of the pre-head driven model based on the premise that the initial high-attached preference is substantially *reversed* before the end of the sentence (as might occur, for example, if links to explicitly-realised verbs were favoured over those to *postulated* verbs). The overwhelming bias in favour of high-attachment is not consistent with competing effects of this kind. In contrast, the results are fully in line with the predictions of the pre-head driven models in which an initial attachment to a verb-slot within a hypothesised top-down structure is lodged so strongly by virtue of its early arrival that it cannot be displaced by its competitors.

EXPERIMENT 2

Finally, a self-paced reading task on the ambiguity was conducted. The purpose of the experiment is to demonstrate on-line preferences for the ambiguity. There were the following three experimental conditions in Experiment 2 (the slashes show the segmentation pattern used in the self-paced experiment; the dative NP is italicised; the verb(s) in bold is the legitimate attachment host; (11) gives the name of each segmented region):

(10a) Globally Ambiguous (GA) condition:
Kyooju-ga / *gakusee-ni* / toshokansisho-ga / **kasita** / mezurasii komonjo-o / **miseta**.
Professor-Nom student-Dat librarian-Nom lent unusual ancient manuscript-Acc showed
"The professor showed [HA: the student] the unusual ancient manuscript which the librarian had lent [LA: the student]."

(10b) High Attachment (HA) condition:
Kyooju-ga / *gakusee-ni* / toshokansisho-ga / yabutta / mezurasii komonjo-o / **miseta**.
Professor-Nom student-Dat librarian-Nom tore unusual ancient manuscript-Acc showed
"The professor showed the student the unusual ancient manuscript which the librarian had torn."

(10c) Low Attachment (LA) condition:
Kyooju-ga / *gakusee-ni* / toshokansisho-ga / **kasita** / mezurasii komonjo-o / yabutta.
Professor-Nom student-Dat librarian-Nom lent unusual ancient manuscript-Acc tore
"The professor tore the unusual ancient manuscript which the librarian had lent the student."

(11) Matrix Subject / Dative NP / Subordinate Subject / Subordinate Verb / Accusative NP / Matrix Verb.

(10a) contains a ditransitive verb (i.e., a potential attachment host for the dative NP) for both the subordinate and matrix verbs, while (10b) and (10c) contain one ditransitive verb for only the matrix and subordinate verbs, respectively. The other verbs (the subordinate verb in (10b) and the matrix verb in (10c)) are monotransitives that cannot take a dative indirect object. The legitimate reading: both attachments for (10a), high attachment only for (10b), and low attachment only for (10c). Therefore, each condition ((10a), (10b), and (10c)) is referred to as the "Globally Ambiguous (GA)" condition, the "High Attachment (HA)" condition, and the "Low Attachment (LA)" condition, respectively.

Examining the three conditions enables us to have a close look at attachment procedures at each part of the sentences. Table 2 shows

TABLE 2
Predictions of Attachment Patterns at Key Regions in Each Condition

Hypothesis	*Attachment before Subordinate Verb*	*Attachment at Subordinate Verb*	*Attachment at matrix Verb*
Head-driven Parsing Hypothesis	GA: NO HA: NO LA: NO	GA: LOW HA: NO LA: LOW	GA: LOW or 50/50* HA: HIGH LA: LOW
Pre-head Attachment Hypothesis	GA: HIGH HA: HIGH LA: HIGH	GA: HIGH HA: HIGH LA: HIGH	GA: HIGH HA: HIGH LA: LOW*

Note: GA, Globally Ambiguous condition; HA, High Attachment condition; LA, Low Attachment condition; *, reanalysis required.

attachment decisions that each account predicts at three position in each condition.[5]

According to head-driven accounts, the parser delays all argument-attachment decisions until it comes across a verb. Such accounts therefore predict that no attachment is established prior to the first verb in any of the three conditions. However, when the first verb is encountered, head-derived information becomes available, and the parser tries to fill the associated requirements as soon as possible. Thus the prediction of head-driven accounts is that, for the GA and LA conditions, low attachment takes place at the subordinate verb—because in these two cases the verb enables a dative NP to receive a thematic role. In the LA condition, this structural analysis should be retained, without further problem or reanalysis, until the end of the sentence. Note that the LA sentence is comparable to the following sentence in which Pritchett (1992) predicts no processing breakdown occurs:

(12) Frank-ni Tom-ga Guy-o syookai suru to John-wa omotteiru.
Frank-dat Tom-Nom Guy-Acc introduce Comp John-Top thinking.
"John thinks that Tom will introduce Guy to Frank."

[5] In Table 2, we include only predictions made by the head-driven and pre-head attachment parsing hypotheses. However, there are a number of other theoretically possible attachment patterns. The following shows such patterns excluded in Table 2:
(i) no attachment → low attachment at NP-Nom2 in all conditions
(ii) high attachment → low attachment at NP-Nom2 in all conditions
(iii) low attachment → high attachment at the subordinate verb in the GA LA conditions
(iv) no attachment → high attachment at the subordinate verb in the GA and LA conditions
(v) high attachment → low attachment at the matrix verb in the GA condition
(vi) high attachment → 50/50 at the matrix verb in the GA condition
(vii) low attachment → low attachment at the matrix verb in the ga condition.

There are two differences between the sentence structures in (10c) (the LA condition) and (12). Firstly, the subordinate clause is a sentential complement clause in (12) whereas it is a relative clause in (10c). Secondly, the matrix subject ("John-wa") is placed just before the matrix verb in (12) whereas it ("toshokansisho-ga") is placed three constituents before the matrix verb in (10c). Despite these differences, Sentence (12) provides a good pointer to the prediction Pritchett (1992) would make for (10c), since, in both sentences, attachment of the dative NP is in principle ambiguous until the matrix verb appears and the matrix verbs cannot take dative arguments. Pritchett (1992) argues that his head-driven parser would attach the dative NP ("Frank-ni" in (12)) to the first verb ("shookai suru" in (12)) as soon as the verb is encountered. The clause is first analysed as simplex (i.e., the matrix clause), but the subsequent appearance of the second subject "John-wa" indicates that the clause is subordinate. According to Pritchett (1992), the initial attachment of the dative NP, which would be referred to as low attachment in (10c), is retained throughout the sentence, and no reanalysis is required, as described in the following:

(13) Such sentences (N.B. the original simplex sentence analysis prior to the complementiser and the final complex sentence analysis at the matrix verb) are both fully grammatical and acceptable and yield no conscious processing difficulty whatsoever (Pritchett, 1992; p.153).

Thus, it seems safe to argue that Pritchett (1991, 1992) unambiguously predicts no reanalysis at the matrix verb in the LA condition.

In the GA condition, it is revealed that the matrix verb also holds a thematic requirement. As previously discussed, the parser might resolve this conflict in either of two different ways. The parser might retain the previously established low attachment avoiding reanalysis (low attachment). Alternatively, it could opt equally for both attachments, with competition being resolved in favour of the low attachment decision in half of the cases, while reanalysis occurs in the other half (50/50 attachment). Turning next to the HA condition, the basic prediction is that the dative NP initially remains unattached (because the head properties of the subordinate verb prevent it from taking dative arguments). At the matrix verb, matrix verb attachment is established—as this is the first, and only linkage, which licenses the dative thematic role. This process should be relatively low-cost, since there is no competition or reanalysis involved in this case.

The corresponding predictions for pre-head attachment accounts are markedly different. Such models posit that the parser attaches the dative NP to an attachment host (e.g., the matrix IP, the matrix VP, or a verb-slot

TABLE 3
Predictions of Reading Time Patterns at the Verb Regions

Hypothesis	*Reading Time Pattern at Subordinate Verb*	*Reading Time Pattern at Matrix Verb*
Head-driven Parsing Hypothesis	GA = HA = LA	GA = HA = LA or GA > HA = LA
Pre-head Attachment Hypothesis	GA = HA = LA	LA > GA = HA

Note: GA, Globally Ambiguous condition; HA, High Attachment condition; LA, Low Attachment condition.

postulated as part of a top-down generic sentence frame), and that this commitment is made well before the subordinate verb is first encountered.[6] At the matrix verb, the parser has to reconcile this initial commitment with the argument structure of the final two-place matrix verb. In the GA and HA conditions the initial commitment and the final argument structures are entirely compatible with one another and so the prediction is that the analysis will run through quickly and easily in these two conditions. In the LA condition, on the other hand, the initial commitment and the matrix argument structure are in conflict with one another. Here, it is predicted that the conflict should lead to a revision, and consequently an increment in reading time for the final verb.

The predictions in Table 2 will result in particular reading time patterns in the self-paced reading task. Table 3 summarises the various reading time predictions that can be made on the basis of the two classes of parsing model.

Head-driven parsing accounts predict different attachment operations at the subordinate verb across the conditions: low attachment occurs in the GA and LA conditions, while no attachment decision is made in the HA condition. It seems reasonable to consider that the accounts (as well as other types of parsing models) predict making no attachment and making an attachment requires statistically indistinguishable reading times when no reanalysis is involved. Thus, no reading time difference is predicted across the conditions at the subordinate verb within the head-driven framework (GA = HA = LA). At the matrix verb, the accounts predict no reading time difference across the conditions given the low attachment

[6] Given the outcome of Experiment 1, we assume that there is little or no reanalysis of the generic verb (high-attached) link when the subordinate verb is encountered. (Such reanalysis would have yielded end-of-sentence results different from those already reported and so there is little point in entertaining this possibility any further.)

prediction (GA = HA = LA). On the other head, reanalysis is involved in half of cases in the GA condition given the 50/50 prediction. It is predicted that the GA condition takes more time to red than the other conditions (GA > HA = LA).[7] On the contrary, incremental parsing accounts predict no reading time difference across the conditions at the subordinate verb, since they predict that the previously established high attachment is retained in all conditions (GA = HA = LA). At the matrix verb, the accounts predict that the LA condition takes more time to read due to a reanalysis from high to low attachment (LA > GA = HA).[8]

Method

Subjects. Twenty-four native speakers of Japanese participated in Experiment 2. All of them were students (undergraduates and post-graduates) at the University of Exeter. All of them had corrected or uncorrected normal vision. None of them had participated in a similar psycholinguistic experiment before, or was aware of the purpose of the experiment. Subjects were paid £2 for their participation. The average total duration of their stay in English-speaking countries was 10.42 months (minimum: one month; maximum: eight years).

Apparatus. A NEC laptop computer (98 NOTE SX/T) was used for controlling the experiment procedure and recording date. The experiment was set up and run with an experimental package for NEC computers written in N88-BASIC. Two keys on the computer keyboard were used for Yes and No keys.

Materials and conditions. As discussed above, three experimental conditions were examined as shown in (10) (the experimental sentences of Experiment 2 are given in Appendix 2). There were 24 sets of three

---

[7] Alternatively, head-driven accounts can predict that the reanalysis processes do not result in producing statistically longer reading times in the GA condition at the matrix verb, since analysis takes place only in 50% of all cases given this prediction (i.e., GA = HA = LA).

[8] On the other hand, it is possible to assume that assigning a "pro" causes some measurable costs. The operation could occur at the subordinate verb in the GA and LA condition or at the matrix verb in the GA condition: the pre-head attachment parser might decide to leave the Goal role of the low attachment verb unfilled as soon as the verb is encountered (i.e., at the subordinate verb), or after all items have appeared in the sentence (i.e., during wrap-up processes at the matrix verb). Given the former, the GA andLA conditions take equally longer than the HA condition at the subordinate verb (i.e., GA = LA > HA). Given the latter, the GA condition takes longer than the HA condition at the matrix verb, while the relation between the LA and GA conditions is arbitrary (i.e., LA > HA; GA > HA).

experimental conditions. The sentences in the GA condition had been tested in Experiment 1. As fillers, 48 other sentences with irrelevant structures were included. The 24 sets of experimental sentences were divided into three material files. Each material set was read by one of three subject groups (eight subjects for each group). As shown in (10), one of three conditions contained a different lexical item from the others in the Subordinate Verb region and Matrix Verb region. Table 4 shows the mean number of characters for the Subordinate Verb and Matrix Verb region for each material file:

As indicted in (10), there were three groups of verbs in the subordinate and matrix verb positions (e.g., "kasita" (lent), "miseta" (showed) and "yabutta" (torn)). We conducted a 5-scale familiarity rating questionnaire on 46 Japanese native speakers using the 72 experimental verbs and 72 filler verbs. The mean familiarity ratings of the verbs were found to be statistically indistinguishable across the verb groups (mean rating scores (1—very unfamiliar; 5—very familiar)): "kasita" verbs: 4.55 (SD = 0.39); "miseta" verbs: 4.55 (SD = 0.40); "yabutta" verbs: 4.52 (SD = 0.38); $F1(2,90) = 0.97$, $P = .424$, MSe = 0.01; $F2(2,46) = 0.04$, $P = .961$, MSe = 0.11). In particular, there was no significant familiarity difference between the "kasita" verbs and the "yabutta" verbs (see the reading time predictions for the matrix verbs in Table 3) ($F1(1,45) = 1.49$, $P = .228$, MSe = 0.01; $F2(1,23) = 0.06$, $P = .804$, MSe = 0.11).

Out of 24, four sentences were followed by a yes/no question. The number of correct yes/no answers was counterbalanced (two for each).

Procedure. A self-paced reading technique was used in the experiment. The stimuli were presented in a non-cumulative segment-by-segment fashion with a moving-window technique. Also, they were randomised by the computer without any constraint. In 16.7% of all trails (12 in total: 4 experimental sentences, 8 fillers), a yes/no question about

TABLE 4
Mean Number of Characters for the Subordinate Verb and Matrix Verb Regions in each Condition in each Material File in Experiment 2

	Subordinate Verbs				*Matrix Verbs*			
	GA	*HA*	*LA*	*Mean*	*GA*	*HA*	*LA*	*Mean*
File 1	3.25	3.25	3.5	3.33	3.125	3.5	3.125	3.25
File 2	3.5	3.5	4.125	3.708	3.5	3.625	3.375	3.5
File 3	3.5	3.5	3.75	3.58	3.75	3.75	3.75	3.75
Mean	3.417	3.417	3.792	3.539	3.458	3.625	3.458	3.5

the content followed the material sentence. Two keys on the computer keyboard were used for the Yes and No keys for questions. First, the first display showing "Sentence Comprehension Experiment" (in English) appeared in the centre of the screen. Then, instructions for the experimental procedure were presented on an A4 sheet. Subjects were asked to read them silently. The instructions included that the task was to read stimuli on the screen as naturally and correctly as possible while pressing the space bar. Also, other operative instructions were included, as shown below. After subjects read the instructions, the experimenter indicated all keys to be used in the experiment. Then the Practice Trial block (consisting of four trials) and the Experimental Trial block (consisting of 72 trials) followed. Subjects were allowed to ask any question about experimental procedure before/during/after the Practice Trial block. If they were certain that they understood the experimental procedure, the Experimental Trial block was started, and the experimenter withdrew from the test-room. Each trial was presented by the instruction "Press space bar" (in English). When the subject did this, the first display appeared. In both the Practice and Experimental Trial blocks, the beginning of each trial was indicated by a display consisting of only this instruction. When subjects did this, dots (●) appeared in the centre of the screen, indicating the length of the subsequent material sentence. Further space bar pressing triggered the first segment of the sentence, replacing dots with the first fragment. When subjects read the first segment, they were asked to press the space bar, so that the first segment was replaced with dots again, and the second segment was opened. Subjects continued this operation until the end of the sentence was reached, which was indicated by no further dots on the right hand site. The dots and final segment of the sentence disappeared when the space bar was pressed again. Next, a yes/no question followed in some trials. Answering the question by pressing the allocated Yes/No keys triggered the very first display of the next trial (i.e., "Press space bar"). When there was no question, the instruction appeared just after the final space bar pressing of the previous trial. The end of the Experimental Trial block was marked by a display saying "Thank you very much!!". Then, subjects were asked to fill in a form asking about their name, affiliation, age, sex, languages they spoke (other than English and Japanese), the duration of having lived in an English-speaking country. After answering the personal information questions, the subjects were asked to call the experimenter who had been waiting outside. Then, they were paid £2 for their participation and dismissed. All sessions were carried out in a dim silent test room in the Washington Singer Laboratories, University of Exeter. The average session took approximately 30 minutes.

Results

Table 5 gives reading times per character for all regions in each condition.

Among the six regions, only the subordinate verb and matrix verb comprise different lexical items across the conditions. ANOVAs confirmed that the same materials were read with the same difficulty in the other regions: there were no statistical differences in reading times across the conditions in other regions (Matrix Subject, Dative NP, Subordinate Subject, and Accusative NP). Thus we shall discuss reading times for only the two critical verb regions. At the subordinate verb, the effect of condition was not significant ($F1(2,46) = 0.03$, $P = .973$, MSe = 3800.98; $F2(2,46) = 0.01$, $P = .991$, MSe = 445.25). There was no significant difference between any pair of the three conditions. On the other hand, at Matrix Verb, the main effect of condition was significant ($F1(2,46) = 5.33$, $P = .008$, MSe = 7216.96; $F2(2,46) = 3.38$, $P = .043$, MSe = 10005.82). Furthermore, it was shown that reading times were increased at the matrix verb in the LA condition compared to the mean reading times of the other two conditions (LA *vs* the mean of GA and HA: $F1(1,23) = 6.00$, $P = .022$, MSe = 9379.73; $F2(1,23) = 4.23$, $P = .051$, MSe = 11625.32). In contrast, the GA and HA conditions produced statistically indistinguishable reading times for Matrix Verb ($F1(1,23) = 0.99$, $P = .33$, MSe = 1927.58; $F2(1,23) = 0.43$, $P = .519$, MSe = 4511.31). The results, therefore, suggest that readers had a problem when it turned out that the matrix verb could not take a dative argument (i.e., in the LA condition). This suggests that the parser must have been unravelling a commitment already made prior to this point—namely a link between the dative NP and the as-yet-unread matrix verb. Hence, the prolonged reading times in the LA condition are consistent with the incremental pre-head attachment hypothesis, but not with the head-driven parsing hypothesis. Also, the lack of any difference between the GA and HA conditions throughout the whole sentence

TABLE 5
Mean Reading Times per Character (msec) for all Regions in Experiment 2

Condition	*Matrix Subject*	*Dat NP*	*Subordinate Subject*	*Subordinate Verb*	*Acc NP*	*Matrix Verb*
GA	235.79	238.65	243.65	240.92 (126.45)	141.83	225.44 (108.86)
HA	255.97	237.28	252.03	237.22 (141.93)	133.25	212.83 (96.23)
LA	251.30	251.01	253.48	237.37 (108.22)	139.56	287.61 (198.91)

Note: The values inside the parentheses show the standard deviations.

suggests that the global ambiguity did not yield significant extra processing costs.

Discussion

Overall, the whole pattern of data was compatible with the pre-head attachment hypothesis, but inconsistent with head-driven accounts: the increased reading times for the matrix verb region were found in the condition where the matrix attachment analysis turned out to be ungrammatical (i.e., the LA condition). This is an indication of early commitment to high attachment, which can be predicted only by pre-head attachment accounts. More specifically, the head-driven model failed to predict the increased processing load at the ends of sentences resolved in favour of low-attachment. Prior to the arrival of the final verb, such models have no basis for postulating anything other than low attachment, and so when the final verb eventually turns out to be fully compatible with this analysis, the model cannot fail to predict a quick and easy completion of the syntactic analysis. Equally, there was no sign at all of the positive predictions of such models—namely that there might be a cost associated with a high-attached resolution compared with the globally ambiguous control (the numerical difference was in the opposite direction—albeit non-significant).

In contrast, the results were exactly as predicted by the variant of the pre-head driven model in which the dative NP is initially attached to a postulated head-free structure and remains attached in this way up until the arrival of the final word in the sentence.

Although the reading times results may look straightforward, however, there are some possible criticisms to the present study. One of the more obvious criticisms would be that there was no manipulation before the first verb across the conditions (see (10)). The lack of manipulation made it impossible to identify the exact point at which the preferred high attachment is established. In fact, there are three possible decision-making points that are compatible with the pattern of data from Experiment 2: at the dative NP ("gakusee-ni"), at the second nominative NP ("toshokan-sisho-ga"), and before the subordinate verb ("kasita"). Although we have pointed out that effects in any of these three regions would be compatible with the present paper's definition of he pre-head attachment parsing hypothesis (see the Introduction), further empirical specification of the attachment point would certainly play a helpful role in clarifying the details of pre-head attachment mechanisms. Moreover, the uncertainty could make some variants of a head-driven parser consistent with the findings on certain assumptions. Specifically, one could posit a head-driven parser (a) that makes no attachment decision for the dative NP prior to he subordinate verb, and (b) that, when the verb is encountered, decides *not* to attach the NP to the verb and to leave it unattached instead (see the Introduction). This variant of a head-driven parser can be reconciled with the data if we make the additional assumption that attaching a constituent to an already-closed clause (e.g., the subordinate clause in the structure under investigation) is significantly more costly than attaching it to a currently-open clause (e.g., the matrix clause) (this account was suggested to us by Altmann, pers. comm.). The second variant of head-driven parsing that could account for the data is that the parser makes a low attachment decision at the subordinate verb but reanalyses it to the alternative (high) attachment option when the matrix verb appears—perhaps because the order of "NP-Nom + NP-Dat", as in high attachment, is canonical in Japanese whereas the order of "NP-Dat + NP-Nom" as in low attachment is non-canonical (this account was suggested to us by Kempen, pers. comm.). The observed processing cost at the matrix verb in the LA condition can be explained on the assumption that cost of making an attachment to a previously-closed clause is higher than the cost of standard reanalysis in the GA condition. Moreover, this variant of head-driven parser ought to assume that there analysis in the GA condition costs as little as in the HA condition where there should be no reanalysis at the matrix verb. Such variation in attachment costs is completely acceptable within the framework of the U-Space model (Vosse & Kempen, submitted) since, within this framework, certain attachment decisions can be reversed at a cost depending on the strength of information in support of the link (Kempen, pers. comm.). Although these two variants of the head-driven hypothesis are consistent with our results, there does not seem to be any motivation (other than that of explaining our data) for a head-driven parser to behave in this way.

A second possible criticism to the present study may be that the experimental manipulation may involve a potential problem caused by the fact that the data points come at the end of a clause. In Experiment 2, there were two critical data points: the subordinate verb and the matrix verb. A possible criticism is that an end-of-clause critical region might not reflect only structural/lexical effects but also some others such as wrap-up effects. However, it should be noted that it is almost impossible to avoid having a critical region at the end of a clause in Japanese experiments of this kind. Moreover, even if the present results reflect wrap-up effects, it must still be explained why these wrap-up effects cause the differences we found.

GENERAL DISCUSSION

The experiments used in the present study were based on the Japanese ambiguity in which a dative NP can be attached to either one of two verbs:

a verb within a subordinate clause or a matrix verb. Using the only globally ambiguous version of this sentence structure (as in (6)), Experiment 1 revealed that subjects showed a very strong tendency to interpret the dative NP as being attached to the matrix verb (and not, therefore, to its subordinate competitor) (this interpretation also dominated over various other potential readings of the material, such as interpretations in which the NP was somehow "shared" by the two verbs). Experiment 2 confirmed this bias in a self-paced reading study. Where the thematic properties of the matrix verb forced the dative NP to be tied in to the alternative host, the reading time for the verb was raised relative to that in the globally ambiguous control condition (which presumably forced neither matrix nor subordinate verb attachment). In contrast there was no corresponding processing load when the combined thematic properties of the two verbs together forced the dative attachment to the matrix host. This is taken to indicate that what was being forced here was precisely the commitment that had already been made prior to this point, and as a matter of preference during earlier phases in the processing of the sentence. Nor can any of these biases plausibly be attributed to systematic differences in the dative NP attracting properties of the individual verbs themselves or to differences in their overall familiarities. Prior measurements of such tendencies (from the Preliminary Test and the familiarity-rating questionnaire in the Method Section of Experiment 2) had been used to equate these properties of the matrix and subordinate verbs in the main study.

In short, the data provided persuasive evidence that, in this Japanese ambiguity, the dative NP is preferentially attached to the matrix verb (high attachment) rather than the subordinate verb (low attachment).

As spelt out in the Introduction, this bias is in line with the predictions of pre-head attachment models and contrary to the predictions of head-driven accounts. In pre-head attachment accounts, a dative NP is attached to the only verb-structure that can confidently be projected even when the verb itself has not yet been processed—namely the structure associated with the matrix verb that *has to* turn at some subsequent point in the sentence. Such a link-up is compatible with the data in the sense that subsequent processing is rapid and unproblematic in all conditions where the thematic properties of the matrix verb are compatible with this arguably premature decision. Where there is conflict, however, there is also an increase in processing time—as would be expected if the preliminary analysis were being reviewed and altered, shifting the dative NP from (say) its initial slot within matrix argument structure to its final place in the subordinate verb structure.

In contrast with this, the results run contrary to the predictions of head-driven accounts. The increased processing costs associated with forcing subordinate verb attachment are not readily explained in accounts in which this interpretation is the initial commitment. According to Pritchett's model (Pritchett, 1991, 1992), the parser should attach the dative NP to the first verb when it is encountered (i.e., the subordinate verb). This follows from the Generalized Theta Attachment principle (Pritchett, 1992) in that this particular link-up satisfies the Theta Criterion for the dative NP by locating a verb that offers it an acceptable thematic role, thereby ending the brief interval during which it is left unattached. If this is indeed what happened in the course of processing, it is not at all obvious why the subsequent reading latencies should show that it is apparently costly to retain this linkage (in the condition forcing subordinate verb attachment), while breaking and reversing the link is cost-free (i.e., at this point there are two ways where matrix attachment is forced).

In short, the results systematically and consistently support pre-head attachment models and run against the prediction of head attachment accounts.

These conclusions are consistent with those reached on the basis of German data (Bader & Lasser, 1994; Scheepers et al., 1994). However, unlike the German studies the present results could not have been distorted by the potential influence of a non-syntactic mechanism for assigning case to otherwise ambiguous NPs. To this extent the current findings go beyond the earlier data and strengthen the findings against head-driven models.

Overall, then, the present findings seem to provide clear evidence against head-driven accounts of parsing—at least as applied to the syntactic analysis of the Japanese language. While this clearly implies that such models cannot provide a universal account of human parsing, what it does not do, of course, is establish that pre-head driven parsing is necessarily any more general than head-driven parsing. It could be that the parsing machinery is differentially parameterised in different languages in such a way that the system is configured (say) as a head-driven system when it is called upon to handle head-initial languages, whereas it takes the alternative pre-head driven form when dealing with head-final languages like Japanese. The question of whether pre-head driven accounts apply universally or whether they are restricted to a subset of languages, cannot be resolved without further research designed to examine the status of the two competing accounts in a range of different languages.

In the meantime, the present study not only raises questions about strictly head-driven accounts. It also highlights imperfections in approaches which, while not purely head-driven, place very strong emphasis on those aspects of syntactic analysis that are contingent upon the prior use of such head information (e.g., the model proposed by MacDonald et al., 1994). One consequence of this heavy emphasis on head-based processing is that such models have neglected to provide well fleshed-out accounts of the various kinds of syntactic processing that must occur in the absence of prior lexical head information. Detailed accounts of processes that occur once the verb has been read are not typically matched by clear statements about the kinds of operations that might occur prior to the appearance of a verb in languages like German, Korean and Japanese. Arguably, viable constraint-based models could be developed for this purpose—perhaps by appealing to the "emergent" biases derived from past contact with individual verbs (e.g., by following the kinds of theoretical moves set out by Tabor, Juliano, & Tanenhaus, 1997). On such accounts it may well be feasible to tap into the emergent biases of generic verb representations well in advance in specific sentences of the kind examined here. The averaged thematic properties of such schematic representations might conceivably offer mechanisms for explaining the data—namely, in this particular case, the evidence for early matrix verb attachment. However, as far as we are aware, such extensions to the constraint-based account have not yet been explicitly developed by proponents of these theories. In the absence of such explicit refinements, it is difficult to assess the prospects constraint-based models may have in accounting for argument attachment biases in head-final languages.

REFERENCES

Abney, S.P. (1989) A computational model of human parsing. *Journal of Psycholinguistic Research, 18*, 129–144.

Altmann, G.T.M., & Steedman, M. (1988). Interaction with context during human sentence processing. *Cognition, 30*, 191–238.

Bader, M., & Lasser, I. (1994). German verb-final clauses and sentence processing: Evidence for immediate attachment. In C. Clifton, Jr., Frazier, & K. Rayner (Eds), *Perspectives on sentence processing*, pp.225–242. Hillsdale, NJ: Lawrence Erlbaum Associates Inc.

Chomsky, N. (1981). *Lectures on government and binding*. Dordrecht: Foris.

Chomsky, N. (1986). *Knowledge of Language*. New York: Praeger Publishers.

Cuetos, F., Mitchell, D.C., & Dorley, M.M.B. (1996). Parsing in different languages. In M. Carreiras, J. Garcia-Albea, & N. Sabastian-Galles (Eds), *Language processing in Spanish*, pp.145–187. Hillsdale, NJ: Lawrence Erlbaum Associates Inc.

Fillmore, C.J. (1968). Lexical entries for verbs. *Foundations of Language, 4*, 373–393.

Fodor, J.A., Bever, T.G., & Garrett, M.F. (1974). *The psychology of language*. New York: McGraw-Hill.

Fodor, J.D. (1998). Learning to parse. *Journal of Psycholinguistic Research, 27*, 285–319.

Ford, M., Bresnan, J., & Kaplan, R. (1982). A competence-based theory of syntactic closure. In J. Bresnan (Ed.), *The mental representation of grammatical relations*, pp.727–796. Cambridge, MA: MIT Press.

Frazier, L. (1987). Sentence processing: A tutorial review. In M. Coltheart (Ed.), *Attention and performance*, XII, pp.559–585. Hove, UK: Lawrence Erlbaum Associates Ltd.

Gorrell, P. (1995). *Syntax and parsing*. Cambridge: Cambridge University Press.

Grimshaw, J. (1990). *Argument structure*. Cambridge, MA: MIT Press.

Hemforth, B. (1993). *Kognitives parsing: Repräsentation and verarbeitung sprachlichen wissens*. Sankt Augustin: Infix.

Hemforth, B., Konieczny, L., & Strube, G. (1993). Incremental syntax processing and parsing strategies: *Proceedings of the XVth Annual Conference of the Cognitive Science Society*, pp.539–554. Hillsdale, NJ: Lawrence Erlbaum Associates Inc.

Hopf, J-M., Bayer, J., Bader, M., & Meng, M. (1998). Event-related brain potentials and case information in syntactic ambiguities. *Journal of Cognitive Neuroscience, 10*, 264–280.

Hyönä, J., & Hujanen, H. (1997). Effects of case marking and word order on sentence parsing in Finnish: An eye fixation analysis. *Quarterly Journal of Experimental Psychology, 50(A)*, 841–858.

Inoue, A., & Foder, J.D. (1995). Information-paced parsing of Japanese. In R. Mazuka & N. Nagai (Eds), *Japanese sentence processing*, pp.9–63. Hillsdale, NJ: Lawrence Erlbaum Associates Inc.

Jackendoff, R.S. (1972). *Semantic interpretation in generative grammar*. Cambridge, MA: MIT Press.

Koh, S. (1997). The resolution of the dative NP ambiguity in Korean. *Journal of Psycholinguistic Research, 26*, 265–273.

Konieczny, L. (1996). *Human sentence processing: A semantics-oriented parsing approach*. IIG-Berichte 3/96.

Konieczny, L., Hemforth, B., Scheepers, S., & Strube, G. (1997). The role of lexical heads in parsing: Evidence from German. *Language and Cognitive Processes, 12*, 307–328.

MacDonald, M.C., Pearlmutter, N.J., & Seidenberg, M.S. (1994). The lexical nature of syntactic ambiguity resolution, *Psychological Review, 101*, 676–703.

MacWhinney, B., & Bates, E. (1989). *The crosslinguistic study of sentence processing*. Cambridge: Cambridge Univesity Press.

Mazuka, R., & Itoh, K. (1995). Can Japanese speakers be led down the garden path? In R. Mazuka & N. Nagai (Eds), *Japanese sentence processing*, pp.295–329. Hillsdale, NJ: Lawrence Erlbaum Associates Inc.

Mazuka, R., & Nagai, N. (Eds) (1995). *Japanese sentence processing*. Hillsdale, NJ: Lawrence Erlbaum Associates Inc.

Mizutani, S. (1985). *Bunpoo to imi*. Asakura nihongo kooza, Vol. 3. Tokyo: Asakura Shoten.

Pollard, C., & Sag, I.A. (1987). Information-based syntax and semantics. CSLS lecture notes (No. 13), Stanford: Centre for the study of language and information, 1.

Pollard, C., & Sag, I.A. (1994). *Head-driven phrase structure grammar*. Chicago, London: Univesity of Chicago Press and CSLI Publications.

Pritchett, B.L. (1987). Garden path phenomena and the grammatical basis of language processing. Unpublished PhD thesis. Harvard University.

Pritchett, B.L. (1988). Garden path phenomena and the grammatical basis of language processing. *Language, 64*, 539–576.

Pritchett, B.L. (1991). Head position and parsing ambiguity. *Journal of Psycholinguistic Research, 20*, 251–270.

Pritchett, B.L. (1992). *Grammatical competence and parsing performance*. Chicago: Univesity of Chicago Press.

Scheepers, C., Hemforth, B., & Konieczny, L. (1994). Resolving NP-attachment ambuguities in German verb-final constructions. In B. Hemforth, L. Konieczny, C. Scheepers, & G. Strube (Eds), *First Analysis, reanalysis, and repair*, pp.51–76. Freiburg, Germany: IIG-Berichte 8/94.

Tabor, W., Juliano, C., & Tanenhaus, M.K. (1997). Parsing in a dynamical system: An attractor-based account of the interaction of lexical and structural constraints in sentence processing. *Language and Cognitive Processes, 12*, 211–271.

Trueswell, J.C., & Tanenhaus, M.K. (1994). Toward a lexicalist framework of constraint-based ambiguity resolution. In C. Clifton, Jr., L. Frazier, & K. Rayner (Eds), *Perspectives on sentence processing*, pp.155–179. Hillsdale, NJ: Lawrence Erlbaum Associates Inc.

Vosse, T., & Kempen, G. (submitted). Syntactic structure assembly in human parsing: A computational model based on competitive inhibition and a lexicalist grammar.

Weinberg, A. (1995). Licensing constraints and the theory of language processing. In R. Mazuka & N. Nagai (Eds), *Japanese sentence processing*, pp.339–364. Hillsdale, NJ: Lawrence Erlbaum Associates Inc.

APPENDIX 1: RATING RESULTS OF PRELIMINARY TEST

The following table shows the results of the preliminary test. Low rating scores indicate that the verbs require a dative Goal argument strongly. The English translation of the results can be obtained from the first author.

	VERB	RATE	POSITION		VERB	RATE	POSITION
1	望む	66.40	S	25	表現する	71.71	S
2	勧める	68.10	S	26	説く	71.73	M
3	残す	68.15	S	27	知らせる	71.79	M
4	贈る	68.35	M	28	見せる	71.84	M
5	譲る	68.48	S	29	紹介する	71.88	S
6	質問する	68.49	S	30	伝える	71.99	M
7	説明する	68.78	M	31	語る	72.04	M
8	向ける	69.00	M	32	送る	72.07	S
9	ご馳走する	69.04	M	33	約束する	72.08	S
10	返す	69.10	M	34	保証する	72.10	M
11	貸す	69.25	S	35	報告する	72.17	M
12	手渡す	69.27	M	36	支給する	72.53	S
13	尋ねる	69.74	S	37	もたらす	72.54	S
14	言う	69.84	M	38	通知する	72.84	M
15	あげる	70.11	S	39	任せる	72.85	M
16	預ける	70.40	S	39	払う	72.85	M
17	渡す	70.42	M	41	請う	73.01	S
18	許可する	70.64	M	42	提案する	73.02	S
19	売る	71.01	M	43	申請する	73.52	S
20	与える	71.12	M	44	配る	73.62	S
21	述べる	71.33	S	45	投げる	73.70	M
22	処方する	71.42	M	46	誓う	74.43	S
23	話す	71.44	M	47	支持する	74.87	S
24	書く	71.56	S	48	求める	76.17	S

Note: S, used as a Subordinate Verb; M, used as a Matrix Verb.

APPENDIX 2: EXPERIMENTAL MATERIALS FOR EXPERIMENT 2

The following shows experimental sentences for each condition in Experiment 2. The GA condition was also tested in Experiment 1. "/" indicates the segmentation pattern. All sentences were presented in one line. The English translation of the materials can be obtained from the first author.

1:GA 教授が/学生に/図書館司書が/貸した/珍しい古文書を/見せた
1:HA 教授が/学生に/図書館司書が/破った/珍しい古文書を/見せた
1:LA 教授が/学生に/図書館司書が/貸した/珍しい古文書を/破った

2:GA 研究助手が/学部長に/学長が/請った/実験結果を/報告した
2:HA 研究助手が/学部長に/学長が/まとめた/実験結果を/報告した
2:LA 研究助手が/学部長に/学長が/請った/実験結果を/まとめた

3:GA 中国政府が/日本の大蔵省に/アメリカの外務省が/約束した/貿易協定を/説明した
3:HA 中国政府が/日本の大蔵省に/アメリカの外務省が/違反した/貿易協定を/説明した
3:LA 中国政府が/日本の大蔵省に/アメリカの外務省が/約束した/貿易協定を/違反した

4:GA 哲二が/順一に/美香が/預けた/新しいスーツケースを/返した
4:HA 哲二が/順一に/美香が/壊した/新しいスーツケースを/返した
4:LA 哲二が/順一に/美香が/預けた/新しいスーツケースを/壊した

5:GA ある中年女性が/ある２０代女性に/ある老婦人が/あげた/中古のピアノを/売った
5:HA ある中年女性が/ある２０代女性に/ある老婦人が/懐かしがった/中古のピアノを/売った
5:LA ある中年女性が/ある２０代女性に/ある老婦人が/あげた/中古のピアノを/懐かしがった

6:GA 貴子が/恋人に/美容院店員が/勧めた/ビートルズのＣＤを/贈った
6:HA 貴子が/恋人に/美容院店員が/愛した/ビートルズのＣＤを/贈った
6:LA 貴子が/恋人に/美容院店員が/勧めた/ビートルズのＣＤを/愛した

7:GA 真弓が/章子に/キャンペーンガールが/配った/化粧品のサンプルを/投げた
7:HA 真弓が/章子に/キャンペーンガールが/落とした/化粧品のサンプルを/投げた
7:LA 真弓が/章子に/キャンペーンガールが/配った/化粧品のサンプルを/落とした

8:GA 医者が/喘息患者に/医療雑誌が/紹介した/漢方薬を/処方した
8:HA 医者が/喘息患者に/医療雑誌が/疑った/漢方薬を/処方した
8:LA 医者が/喘息患者に/医療雑誌が/紹介した/漢方薬を/疑った

9:GA 厚生部が/社員食堂係員に/新入社員が/提案した/新しいポットの購入を/保証した
9:HA 厚生部が/社員食堂係員に/新入社員が/話し合った/新しいポットの購入を/保証した
9:LA 厚生部が/社員食堂係員に/新入社員が/提案した/新しいポットの購入を/話し合った

10:GA 田中が/鈴木に/佐藤が/譲った/他社とのプロジェクトを/任せた
10:HA 田中が/鈴木に/佐藤が/企画した/他社とのプロジェクトを/任せた
10:LA 田中が/鈴木に/佐藤が/譲った/他社とのプロジェクトを/企画した

11:GA 男Ａが/男Ｂに/男Ｃが/書いた/重要な文書を/手渡した
11:HA 男Ａが/男Ｂに/男Ｃが/盗んだ/重要な文書を/手渡した
11:LA 男Ａが/男Ｂに/男Ｃが/書いた/重要な文書を/盗んだ

12:GA 浩平が/妻に/弟が/誓った/半年間の禁煙を/話した
12:HA 浩平が/妻に/弟が/始めた/半年間の禁煙を/話した
12:LA 浩平が/妻に/弟が/誓った/半年間の禁煙を/始めた

13:GA 智恵が/従姉妹に/両親が/尋ねた/新居での暮らしを/知らせた
13:HA 智恵が/従姉妹に/両親が/想像した/新居での暮らしを/知らせた
13:LA 智恵が/従姉妹に/両親が/尋ねた/新居での暮らしを/想像した

14:GA 大旦那が/番頭に/若旦那が/述べた/斬新なアイデアを/伝えた
14:HA 大旦那が/番頭に/若旦那が/実現した/斬新なアイデアを/伝えた
14:LA 大旦那が/番頭に/若旦那が/述べた/斬新なアイデアを/実現した

15:GA 兄が/元恋人に/叔父が/送った/とりたてのカニを/ご馳走した
15:HA 兄が/元恋人に/叔父が/嫌った/とりたてのカニを/ご馳走した
15:LA 兄が/元恋人に/叔父が/送った/とりたてのカニを/嫌った

16:GA 義姉が/子供に/来客が/残した/チョコレートケーキを/与えた
16:HA 義姉が/子供に/来客が/賞賛した/チョコレートケーキを/与えた
16:LA 義姉が/子供に/来客が/残した/チョコレートケーキを/賞賛した

17:GA 部長が/係長に/事務員が/申請した/１０日間の休暇を/許可した
17:HA 部長が/係長に/事務員が/忘れていた/１０日間の休暇を/許可した
17:LA 部長が/係長に/事務員が/申請した/１０日間の休暇を/忘れていた

18:GA 未亡人が/子供に/死んだ夫が/もたらした/耐え難い不幸を/語った
18:HA 未亡人が/子供に/死んだ夫が/克服した/耐え難い不幸を/語った
18:LA 未亡人が/子供に/死んだ夫が/もたらした/耐え難い不幸を/克服した

19:GA 大学病院が/受付に/患者が/求めた/人間ドックの結果を/通知した
19:HA 大学病院が/受付に/患者が/憂いだ/人間ドックの結果を/通知した
19:LA 大学病院が/受付に/患者が/求めた/人間ドックの結果を/憂いだ

20:GA 物理学者が/理科教師に/生徒の一人が/質問した/ビックバンの原因を/説いた
20:HA 物理学者が/理科教師に/生徒の一人が/知っていた/ビックバンの原因を/説いた
20:LA 物理学者が/理科教師に/生徒の一人が/質問した/ビックバンの原因を/知っていた

21:GA 直子が/美樹に/涼子が/表現した/本当の気持ちを/言った
21:HA 直子が/美樹に/涼子が/尊重した/本当の気持ちを/言った
21:LA 直子が/美樹に/涼子が/表現した/本当の気持ちを/尊重した

22:GA 洗濯業者が/新人工員に/工場が/支給した/地味な作業服を/渡した
22:HA 洗濯業者が/新人工員に/工場が/汚した/地味な作業服を/渡した
22:LA 洗濯業者が/新人工員に/工場が/支給した/地味な作業服を/汚した

23:GA 祐也が/成美に/正樹が/望んだ/熱いまなざしを/向けた
23:HA 祐也が/成美に/正樹が/笑った/熱いまなざしを/向けた
23:LA 祐也が/成美に/正樹が/望んだ/熱いまなざしを/笑った

24:GA 主婦が/郵便局に/郵政省が/指示した/新規定の手数料を/払った
24:HA 主婦が/郵便局に/郵政省が/心配した/新規定の手数料を/払った
24:LA 主婦が/郵便局に/郵政省が/指示した/新規定の手数料を/心配した

LANGUAGE AND COGNITIVE PROCESSES, 1999, *14* (5/6), 663–686

A U-shaped Relative Clause Attachment Preference in Japanese

Edson T. Miyamoto
University of Tokyo

Edward Gibson
Massachusetts Institute of Technology

Neal J. Pearlmutter
Northeastern University

Takako Aikawa
Microsoft

Shigeru Miyagawa
Massachusetts Institute of Technology

This paper presents results from a self-paced reading experiment in Japanese investigating attachment preferences for relative clauses to three ensuing potential nominal heads. Similar to previous results from the processing of English, Spanish and German, we observed the following non-monotonic preference ordering among the three attachment sites: most local, least local, intermediate. We discuss the result in light of two types of parsing models: models that only consider attaching a modifier to candidate sites whose lexical heads have already been encountered, and models in which predicted categories are also considered as possible modification sites. We contend that the preference to attach to the least local site over the intermediate site

---

Requests for reprints should be addressed to Edson Miyamoto, Tsujii Lab., Department of Information Science, Faculty of Science, University of Tokyo, 7-3-1 Hongo Bunkyo-ku Tokyo, 113-0033 Japan. Email: etm@is.s.u-tokyo.ac.jp

We would like to thank the participants in the sentence processing laboratory at MIT and the audience at the 11th CUNY Conference on Human Sentence Processing for helpful discussions on earlier presentations of this work. All remaining errors are our own. Partial funding for the project was provided by the JST/MIT joint international research project "Mind/Articulation". The first author was supported by a fellowship from CNPq (Brasília, Brazil).

argues against the first type of model, and supports the second type of model with a factor such as predicate proximity or anaphor resolution driving the preference to attach the RC to the least local candidate site.

INTRODUCTION

In the sentence processing literature, principles such as *right association*, *late closure*, and *locality* have often been assumed to apply universally across languages, favouring the interpretation in which a modifying phrase is attached to the closest possible site in linear terms (Frazier, & Fodor, 1978; Gibson, 1991, 1998; Kimball, 1973; Phillips, 1995). Recent proposals by Gibson, Pearlmutter, Canseco-Gonzalez, and Hickok (1996) and Hemforth, Konieczny, Scheepers, and Strube (1998) have refined this view by suggesting factors that modulate locality, so as to account for cross-linguistic results in the attachment of relative clauses (RCs) (see Mitchell & Brysbaert, 1998, for a recent overview). The purpose of the present paper is to investigate the attachment preferences of head-final RCs in Japanese.

In an experiment measuring reading time and grammaticality judgement accuracy Gibson et al. (1996) showed that, in sentence fragments such as (1a) and (1b) with three potential host nouns, native speakers preferred to attach the RC to the low noun (i.e., N_3, the lowest candidate noun in the tree structure) both in Spanish and English. Furthermore, attachment to the high noun (N_1) was preferred over the middle noun (N_2). Note that RC attachment in (1) was disambiguated by manipulating number on the head nouns so that only one of them is compatible with the verbs in the RC (namely, fue dañada in (1a) and was in (1b)).

Example (1) *head-initial RCs*

	N_1		N_2		N_3	RC
a.	la(s) *lámpara(s)*	cerca de	la(s) *pintura(s)*	de	la(s) *casa(s)*	[que fue dañada en la inundación]
b.	the *lamp(s)*	near	the *painting(s)*	of	the *house(s)*	[that was damaged in the flood]

Cuetos, Mitchell, and Corley (1996) raised some potential methodological problems with the grammaticality judgement task used by Gibson et al. (1996). However, the original pattern of results was replicated using reading time measures in Spanish (Gibson, Pearlmutter, & Torrens, in press) and German (Walter, & Hemforth, 1998).

The overall preference for low attachment found by Gibson et al. (1996) is compatible with locality. However, the advantage of the high over the middle noun is not. In order to explain this U-shaped preference curve (i.e., with the middle noun as the least preferred site), Gibson et al. (1996)

proposed a second factor, *predicate proximity*, which prefers the attachment of the modifying phrase to the high site (N_1) and therefore competes with locality. The attachment preference then results from the interaction of these two factors. According to predicate proximity, modifiers are preferentially attached to the phrase closest in structural terms to the predicate of the sentence. In the construction in (1), predicate proximity is not strong enough to override locality, resulting in the preference for N_3. But it is strong enough to yield the preference for N_1 over N_2.

Hemforth and colleagues (Hemforth et al., 1998; Walter, & Hemforth, 1998) suggested an alternative proposal in which the factor favouring the attachment of a RC to the higher site is related to the process of finding the antecedent for the relative pronoun in the RC (e.g., who in English) as this process may be biased towards discourse salient entities such as the head of a complex NP (e.g., N_1 in (1)).

The purpose of this paper is to explore some aspects of RC attachment when three potential host nouns are available. In particular, we will consider the case in which the RC precedes the head nouns and is not initiated by a complementiser or a relative pronoun, as in (2).

Example (2) *head-final RCs*
RC N_3 postposition N_2 postposition N_1

In (2), we have the head-final RC construction in languages such as Japanese, Korean and Tamil, which have postpositions rather than prepositions and therefore present the nouns in the opposite order to that of head-initial languages (cf. (1)). In linear terms (i.e., in terms of the number of intervening words), N_3 is still the closest site to the RC and consequently should be favoured by locality more than the other two sites. Moreover, structurally, N_3 is the lowest noun available for attachment, and the farthest one (N_1) is the highest.

Assuming an incremental parser, which processes each incoming word immediately and tries to integrate it without delay to the phrase marker built so far (e.g., Marslen-Wilson, & Tyler, 1980, 1981), the positioning of the head nouns after the RC in the head-final RC construction makes it particularly interesting to compare to its head-initial counterpart. In head-initial RC constructions, the attachment decision is made after the three nouns have been encountered. In head-final RCs, however, the RC is processed first and only then are the nouns detected. Hence, under an incremental model, the parser should attempt to attach the RC to each incoming noun in turn until a successful attachment is made.[1] Because the

[1] Here, *attachment* refers to the process of determining the head noun that the RC modifies independent of whether the actual constituent being processed and incorporated into the mental representation at that point is the RC (as in head-initial constructions) or the head noun (as in head-final constructions).

first noun (N_3) is the only available candidate initially, it is natural to expect it to be the most preferred site for attachment. If attachment to the first noun is not successful, incrementality predicts that the middle noun is favoured over the high noun as the parser attempts to resolve the attachment as soon as possible.

However, this overlooks an important factor in the processing of head-final constructions in that the parser's decisions may be influenced by a category that is predicted to be upcoming in the input string. Evidence that predicted categories influence the parser's behaviour is provided by Yamashita (1994) who showed that native Japanese speakers do not wait for the detection of a verb in order to start interpreting a sequence of NPs. Instead these NPs are interpreted as the arguments of a predicted verb whose properties (e.g., ditransitivity) are only partially determinable from the case markers on those NPs.

Thus, when discussing the processing of head-final RC constructions with multiple potential heads, it is necessary to consider whether there is partial information predicting a category, and, if so, how such information could affect the attachment of the RC. First, partial information may be available in this construction in the form of a particle (e.g., a postposition) marking a noun being processed, which indicates that a higher noun is to come. For example, when processing N_3 in (2) above, the parser may be already predicting another noun because of the postposition that immediately follows N_3, assuming that the postposition can be seen parafoveally while the noun is read (see Rayner, Sereno, Morris, Schmauder, & Clifton, 1989, for evidence in English). Second, if a particle does predict a higher noun, then there are two alternative ways for the parser to treat such partial information with respect to attachment decisions. It is conceivable that whenever a lexicalised candidate (i.e., a category whose head has already been read in the input) is available, the parser ignores any predicted category as a potential site for attachment. In other words, the parser may only use predicted categories as a last resort when no lexicalised options are available. We will refer to this strategy as parsing with lexically-realised candidates, or *lexicalised-parsing* (cf. the *head attachment principle*; Konieczny, Hemforth, Scheepers, & Strube, 1997). Alternatively, the parser may consider associating the RC to a predicted site whose head is still to be processed, even if a lexically-realised candidate is also available. We will refer to this type of model as a *predictive-parsing* model.

The following are the predictions that lexicalised- and predictive-parsing make in the head-final RC construction with three candidate sites. In lexicalised-parsing, whenever there is one lexicalised candidate noun available, the parser will not consider a predicted category as a possible candidate, preferring instead to use a lexicalised noun as the head of the

RC. This is exactly the situation when the low noun is read together with the following postposition in the sense that there is a lexicalised noun (the low noun) and a predicted noun (the middle noun), thus the low noun should be preferred over the middle noun. Similarly when the middle noun and the ensuing postposition are read, the high noun is being predicted but it is not yet lexicalised. Consequently, if the low noun was not previously interpreted as the head of the RC, then the middle noun should now be preferred over the high noun. Thus, according to lexicalised-parsing, the parser favours attachment to the nouns in the order that they become available—low, middle, high—a monotonic decreasing preference ordering of the sites. In more general terms, lexicalised-parsing is incompatible with any preference for a higher site (N_H) in detriment of a lower one (N_L) because, at some point during parsing, N_L will be lexicalised and available for attachment whereas N_H will not have been lexicalised yet and therefore is not available as a head for the RC. Note that the strength with which factors such as predicate proximity (Gibson et al., 1996) and anaphor resolution (Hemforth et al., 1998) favour higher sites is irrelevant in lexicalised-parsing because the lower sites are lexicalised sooner, hence preempting any preference to attach to a higher (upcoming) site.

In contrast, under predictive-parsing, it is possible that an upcoming noun may be preferred as the attachment site for the RC over a noun already available. In fact, most preference patterns in the Japanese RC construction would be compatible with predictive-parsing. The predictions in this case will crucially depend on the weights of the factors favouring the low site (locality) and the high site (predicate proximity or anaphor resolution) at each point during the processing of the RC heads. With the exception of the middle site being preferred overall, varying such an assignment of weights within predictive-parsing could account for most outcomes in the present experiment, but if the weights of the factors in the Japanese construction should mirror the ones proposed for Spanish and English (Gibson et al., 1996), then a U-shaped preference ordering of the sites would be the expected result.

Kamide and colleagues provide some suggestive evidence for predictive-parsing in two self-paced reading experiments testing the attachment of head-final RCs with two potential hosts in Japanese. In the first experiment, Kamide and Mitchell (1997) reported an initial advantage for low attachment, supporting locality. In a follow-up experiment (Kamide, Mitchell, Fodor, & Inoue, 1998), the segmentation for their self-paced presentation was modified so that, contrary to the presentation in the original experiment, the first head noun and the following particle (the genitive market no) were presented in the same region. Although the low condition was still faster than the high condition, this difference was no longer significant. This suggests that locality was weakened by the visibility of the genitive marker, which signalled that another site was upcoming. However, based on the lack of statistical significance in this second study alone, it is not possible to determine the extent to which the predicted category is in fact exerting an influence in the process. More convincing evidence in support of predictive-parsing would be a statistically significant preference to associate an RC to a predicted candidate over a lexicalised one.

In summary, there are two distinct predictions being made in relation to attachment preferences in head-final RC constructions with three head nouns. First, there is the prediction for a monotonic curve with the middle (N_2) being preferred over the high (N_1). And second, there is the prediction for a U-shaped curve, in which the middle site (N_2) is the least preferred. In both cases, the most local site (N_3) is predicted to be the most preferred. We investigated these predictions in the head-final RC construction with three potential attachment sites in Japanese.

METHOD

Participants

Thirty-nine native speakers of Japanese participated for $20 each. They had all come to the U.S. as adults and were residents of the Boston area. One participant was eliminated for answering the comprehensive questions at chance level, and two were eliminated because of extremely long or short baseline reading times (see the Analysis section for details).

TABLE 1
Regions for Self-paced Reading Presentation

	Region					
Condition	1	2	3	4	5	6
Low	RC_A	N_A $postp_1$	N_B $postp_2$	N_C topic	$pred_1$	$pred_2$
Mid	RC_B	N_A $postp_1$	N_B $postp_2$	N_C topic	$pred_1$	$pred_2$
High	RC_C	N_A $postp_1$	N_B $postp_2$	N_C topic	$pred_1$	$pred_2$
Mid	RC_A	N_C $postp_1$	N_A $postp_2$	N_B topic	$pred_1$	$pred_2$
High	RC_B	N_C $postp_1$	N_A $postp_2$	N_B topic	$pred_1$	$pred_2$
Low	RC_C	N_C $postp_1$	N_A $postp_2$	N_B topic	$pred_1$	$pred_2$
High	RC_A	N_B $postp_1$	N_C $postp_2$	N_A topic	$pred_1$	$pred_2$
Low	RC_B	N_B $postp_1$	N_C $postp_2$	N_A topic	$pred_1$	$pred_2$
Mid	RC_C	N_B $postp_1$	N_C $postp_2$	N_A topic	$pred_1$	$pred_2$

Note: letter subscripts indicate attachment, so that RC_A plausibility attaches only to N_A, for example. Postp = postposition; topic = topic marker; pred = predicate.

Materials

Sentences like those in (3) were presented using Japanese characters, with the attachment of the RC disambiguated by plausibility. The potential attachment sites are in italics in (3); the slashes indicate the divisions between regions for the self-paced reading presentation. In (3a), the RC is biased towards the low site (N_3); in (3b), towards the middle site (N_2); and in (3c), towards the high site (N_1). Appendix B contains a complete list of the stimuli.

Example (3) *head-final RCs*

a.

RC / N_3 $postp_1$ / N_2 $postp_2$ /

[$_{RC}$ Eda-ga oreteiru]/ *shigemi*-no yoko-no/ *hito*-no ushiro-no/
branch-$_{Nom}$ broken / bush beside / person behind /

N_1-topic / $pred_1$ / $pred_2$
jitensha-wa/ kireide/ ooki-katta
bicycle-$_{Top}$ / pretty / big-was

b.
[$_{RC}$ Paati-de atta]/ …
party-$_{Loc}$ met

c.
[$_{RC}$ Gakkou-made notta]/ …
school-to rode

'The bicycle behind the person beside the bush that *has a broken branch*
I met at the party
I rode to school

was pretty and big.'

In order to control for potential lexical and plausibility differences, the three head nouns were rotated through the three attachment sites for each of the three plausibility-biased RCs, yielding a total of nine subconditions, as schematically represented in Table 1.

Because of the plausibility biases, each RC in Table 1 has to attach to the same noun (as the subscripts A, B, C indicate), but the position of the noun itself varies from condition to condition. For example, in (3b), the RC that I met at the party always attaches to person, but the position of this head noun (high, middle or low) depends on the subcondition.

In order to make all of the head noun rotations plausible within an item, only locative postpositions were used in the items. Eight different complex postpositions were used (**beside, near, on the left (side) of, on the right (side) of, in front of, next to, behind, on the other side of**) in the sense that they all included a noun as part of their complex (e.g., the noun **front** in **in front of** or the noun **left** in **on the left of** in English). As in English, this head noun is not a grammatical candidate attachment site for any modifier, so there are exactly three potential attachment sites for the RC in all of the target items.

In the segmentation of the sentences for the self-paced reading presentation, regions 2 and 3 included a head noun and a postposition together. Words are not usually separated by spaces in written Japanese, hence there is no a priori natural way to segment the regions. However, two factors led us to display each PP (i.e., a postpositional phrase comprised of a postposition with its preceding noun) as a single region. First, particles such as **no** (which initiated the locatives used as postpositions) mark the previous noun and are not used on their own. Second, the comparison between lexicalised-parsing and predictive-parsing is only possible if the partial information (i.e., the postposition predicting a higher noun) is available at the earliest possible point. For lexicalised-parsing any such delay would not have any impact (as the parser is not taking partial information into account), but for predictive-parsing a slight delay may disrupt the use of information and could create a confound.

Nine lists were created by distributing the 36 stimuli in a Latin Square design. Each participant saw exactly one of the lists intermixed with 65 unrelated items in pseudo-random order. After each sentence, participants answered a yes/no comprehension question presented on a new screen.

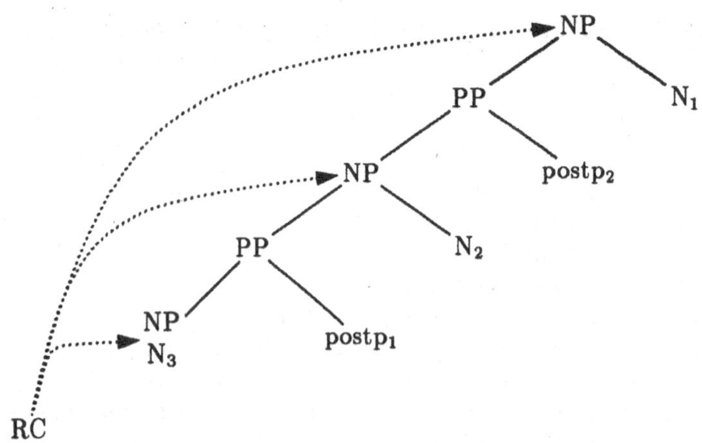

FIG. 1. N_3 modifying N_2—RC can attach to any of the 3 nouns.

Stimulus norming

A crucial assumption in this experiment is that attachment to each of the three sites is grammatical. In particular, in the present case, it is necessary to guarantee that attachment of the RC to N_2 is grammatical by making sure that the first PP (N_3 postp$_1$) modifies N_2 (see Figure 1) and not N_1 (see Figure 2). In the latter structure, it would not be possible to attach the RC to N_2, assuming that attachments leading to crossed branches are ungrammatical.

To ensure that the PP containing N_3 modified N_2 and not N_1 in our stimuli, we presented a separate group of 46 native Japanese speakers with fragments like (4a) and questions about which of N_1 or N_2 was modified by N_3, as in (4b).

Example (4)

	N_3	postp$_1$	N_2	postp$_2$	N_1
a.	shigemi-no	yoko-no	hito-no	ushiro-no	jitensha
	bush	beside	person	behind	bicycle

"the bicycle behind the person beside the bush"

b.	shigemi-no	yoko-ni-wa	hito-ga	imasuka	soretomo
	bush	beside$_{\text{-Loc -Top}}$	person$_{\text{-Nom}}$	is	or
	jitensha-ga	arimasuka?			
	bicycle$_{\text{-Nom}}$	is			

"Is the person or the bicycle beside the bush?"

As in Table 1, each triple of head nouns was rotated through three different orderings, yielding a total of nine different orderings for each item in the main experiment. Each participant saw exactly one of the nine orderings of each of the 36 items mixed pseudo-randomly with 44 filler items. Some of the fillers were biased for low or high attachment and were

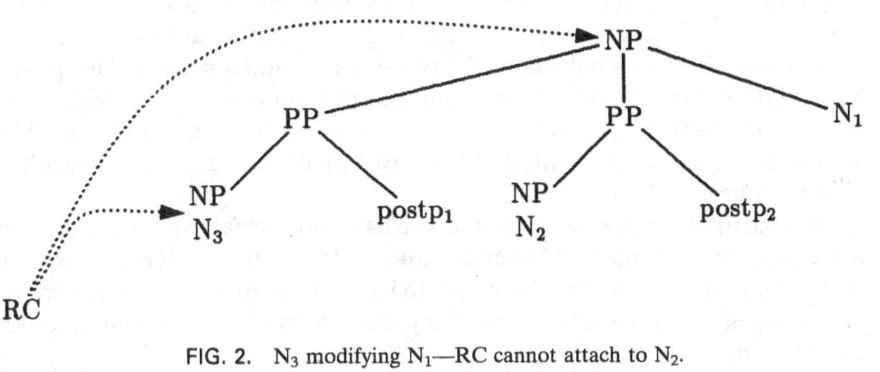

FIG. 2. N_3 modifying N_1—RC cannot attach to N_2.

used to ensure that participants were not using any particular strategy in the survey. Nine participants' data were eliminated for not answering these foil items appropriately.

As expected, participants had a strong preference for the low attachment, choosing to attach N_3 to the lower noun (N_2) more than 85% of the time. In each of the 36 triples, low attachment was preferred at least 75% of the time.

Procedure

The experiment was conducted on a Power Macintosh 7500/100 running PsyScope (Cohen, MacWhinney, Flatt, & Provost, 1993) with a button-box. Participants were timed in a phrase-by-phrase self-paced non-cumulative moving-window reading task (Just, Carpenter, & Woolley, 1982). The characters initially appeared as dots, and participants pressed the leftmost button of the button-box to reveal each subsequent region of the sentence and cause all other regions to revert to dots. At the end of each sentence, the yes/no question appeared on a new screen, which participants answered by pressing one of two buttons. No feedback was given.

The experimental trials were preceded by one screen of instructions and eight practice trials. All sentences were presented on a single line. The experiment took participants approximately 20 minutes.

Analysis

We analysed comprehension question response accuracy and reading times. For the purposes of analysis and presentation of the data, the nine subconditions in Table 1 were collapsed into the three conditions of interest (low, mid, high attachment).

Analyses were conducted on residual reading times per region (Ferreira & Clifton, 1986), derived by subtracting from raw reading times each participant's predicted time to read regions of the same length (measured in number of characters), which in turn was calculated from a linear regression equation across all of a participant's sentences in the experiment. The residual reading times were trimmed so that data points beyond four standard deviations from the relevant condition × region cell mean were discarded, corresponding to less than 1% of the total data. The means and analyses presented below are based on the trimmed residual reading times.

Two participants were eliminated for having unusual intercepts in their regression equations (1949 msec and −1505 msec). The other 36 participants had intercepts between 155 and 1008 msec ($M = 524$ msec; $SD = 232$ msec). Inclusion of the two participants eliminated did not alter the patterns in the data.

RESULTS

Comprehension question response accuracy

Performance in the low attachment condition (91% correct) was better than in the middle (85%) ($F_1(1,35) = 8.51$, $P < .01$; $F_2(1,35) = 12.3$, $P < .01$) or the high (86%) conditions ($F_1(1,35) = 9.33$, $P < .01$; $F_2(1,35) = 8.23$, $P < .01$), but the high and middle conditions did not differ (*F*s < 1).

Reading times

Figure 3 shows the residual reading times by region. No differences were present (*F*s < 1) in the first region (the RC). In region 2 (the first PP), the low attachment condition was significantly faster than the middle condition ($F_1(1,35) = 5.37$, $P < .05$; $F_2(1,35) = 5.67$, $P < .05$) and the high condition ($F_1(1,35) = 10.5$, $P < .01$; $F_2(1,35) = 7.87$, $P < .01$). The high and middle conditions did not differ (*F*s < 1).

In region 3 (the second PP), the high condition was faster than the low condition ($F_1(1,35) = 13.2$, $P < .01$; $F_2(1,35) = 11.9$, $P < .01$) and the middle condition ($F_1(1,35) = 8.76$, $P < .01$; $F_2(1,35) = 10.2$, $P < .01$); but the low and middle conditions did not differ ($F_1(1,35) = 1.17$, $P = .287$; $F_2(1,35) = 1.21$, $P = .278$).

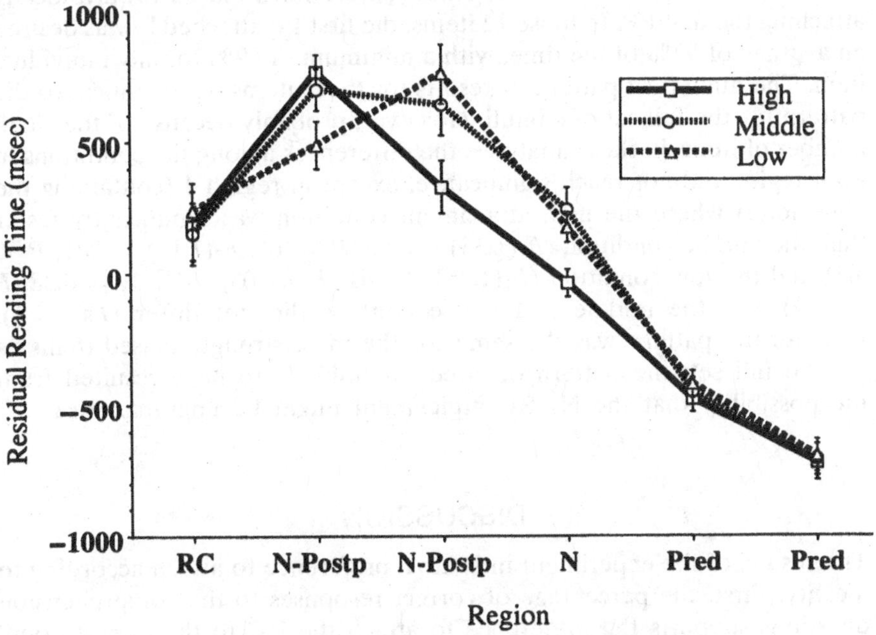

FIG. 3. Residual reading times for each region.

Region 4 (the third noun and the topic marker) presented the same pattern as region 3: the high condition was faster than the low condition ($F_1(1,35) = 9.76$, $P < .01$; $F_2(1,35) = 10.4$, $P < .01$) and the middle condition ($F_1(1,35) = 15.4$, $P < .01$; $F_2(1,35) = 19.2$, $P < .01$); and the low and middle conditions did not differ ($F\text{s} < 1$).

In region 5 (the initial segment of the main predicate), the high condition was still faster than the low condition ($F_1(1,35) = 4.18$, $P < .05$; $F_2(1,35) = 4.34$, $P < .05$); but the middle condition did not differ from either the high condition ($F_1(1,35) < 1$; $F_2(1,35) = 1.06$) or the low condition ($F_1(1,35) = 1.55$, $P = .222$; $F_2(1,35) < 1$).

There were no differences in region 6 (the second part of the main predicate; $F\text{s} < 1$).

The statistical analyses with the raw reading times yielded a pattern identical to that for residual reading times, except that the high and low conditions did not differ reliably in region 5 for the raw reading times. See Appendix A for presentation of the raw reading times in each condition.

Because the results of the norming study did not yield a 100% preference to attach the first PP low, it is possible that difficulty attaching the RC to the middle site could arise from the ungrammatical instances in which the first PP attached high. To ensure that our results were not due to these instances, separate analyses were conducted on the 12 items that, according to the off-line norming study, were most biased toward locally attaching the first PP. In those 12 items, the first PP attached low as desired an average of 92% of the time, with a minimum of 89% for any individual item. The numerical pattern of results for these items was identical to the pattern for the full set of stimuli. However, probably because of the small number of items in these analyses, the differences among the conditions in each region did not reach significance, except in region 4 (containing the high noun) where the high attachment condition was significantly faster than the middle condition ($F_1(1,35) = 8.83$, $P < .01$; $F_2(1,11) = 7.81$, $P < .05$) and the low condition ($F_1(1,35) = 4.41$, $P < .05$; $F_2(1,11) = 6.38$, $P < .05$), but the middle and low conditions did not differ ($F\text{s} < 1$). Because the pattern was the same for the most strongly biased items as for the full set, the pattern of effects is unlikely to have resulted from the possibility that the N_2 RC attachment might be ungrammatical.

DISCUSSION

The results of the experiment indicate a preference to attach according to locality. First, the percentage of correct responses to the comprehension questions supports the preference to attach the RC to the closest noun. Second, a preference for the closest site was detected in region 2 of the self-paced reading presentation (i.e., the first PP). This result indicates that even when a head noun and its ensuing postposition are presented in the same region in a self-paced reading experiment, there is a preference for the low attachment condition, thus suggesting that the lack of statistical significance in the advantage for the low attachment condition in Kamide et al. (1998) was probably accidental. (Analysing our data using raw reading time per character, which is the method used by Kamide and colleagues, yielded the same overall pattern of results as in the reported analyses.)

The results also support a U-shaped preference ordering over a monotonic preference ordering of the candidate sites, which argues against lexicalised-parsing models in general. The evidence for the U-shared preference curve comes from region 3, where the reading time of the high condition was faster than in the middle condition.

The reading times of the high condition in regions 2 (containing the low noun) and 3 (containing the middle noun) are particularly informative because in both cases the RC in this condition is incompatible with the head noun being read, but it is only in region 2 that the high condition is slow. This suggests that the relatively slow reading time in region 2 in the high condition is not caused by the incompatibility between the head noun and the RC alone, otherwise a similar slow reading time should have occurred in region 3 as well. It is conceivable then that participants are attempting to attach the RC to each of the three incoming heads, and that they are only slow when the attachment fails with a favoured site (N_3) but not when the attachment fails at a less preferred site (N_2), as long as another potential site is to come.

The U-shaped preference curve supports a predictive-parsing model in which the preference to attach to the high site over the middle site is explained by an independent factor. The anaphor resolution process could be such a factor as it is not bound to either lexicalised- or predictive-parsing. Another possibility for the factor preferring the high site is predicate proximity, as it favours the site structurally closest to a predicate and remains neutral to the use of partial information during parsing. Consider how a high site factor may interact with locality within a predictive-parsing model to generate the U-shaped preference pattern observed in our experiment. When processing the low site, the parser considers attaching the RC to the current noun (N_3 in (2), repeated below as (5)) as well as to the noun predicted by the first postposition. However, because of the strength of locality at this point, the closest site (N_3) is preferred; hence, the low attachment is fast. In the middle and high attachment conditions, however, plausibility disfavours the low site in region 2, contradicting locality and leading to the slow-down in these two conditions.

Example (5) *head-final RCs*
RC N_3 postposition N_2 postposition N_1

In cases when the low attachment fails, the parser proceeds to region 3 and considers the middle noun (N_2) and the newly predicted noun as possible candidates for attachment. At this point, the high site factor is stronger than locality, making the parser prefer to attach the RC to the upcoming noun (N_1), therefore making the high attachment unproblematic. However, in the middle condition, the middle noun (N_2) is favoured by plausibility, which in this case contradicts the parser's preference to attach to the high noun, thus leading to the slowdown observed in region 3.

The following discusses three other types of factors that may be involved in the results obtained in the experiment. The first is related to priming, the second to discourse complexity and the third to RC length.

An anonymous reviewer suggested that the faster reading times for the low attachment condition in region 2 may be caused by semantic priming, as the RC in region 1 (and possibly some words contained therein) may have primed the low candidate noun in the low condition, leading to faster lexical access in region 2 when compared to the other two conditions. However, priming effects in English sentences are on the order of 30–40 msec (Foss, 1982), whereas the effect in region 2 is around 200 msec. Furthermore, semantic priming differences are unlikely to account for the comprehension performance advantage for the low attachment condition. An independent preference for locality is required to explain this preference, which can then be used to account for the observed reading time difference.

Another factor that may apply in the RC structures under consideration is related to discourse complexity. Such a factor may explain the relatively slow reading times of the low condition in regions 3 and 4, which were not predicted by any of the models that were considered previously. Note that because the RC attachment was successful in region 2 in the low attachment condition, the processing of the two ensuing regions should have been straightforward. We speculate that such slow reading times could stem from the types of interpretations involved when the RC is attached to the low noun N_3 as compared to the high noun N_1. Consider an English example in which the RC that Mary likes is attached to the high noun bicycle.

Example (6) The *bicycle* beside the *boy* [$_{RC}$ that Mary likes] ...

Because bicycle is already being restricted by the PP beside the boy, it is less likely that the RC further restricts bicycle because, in order to do so, we would have to image several bicycles some of which are beside the boy and, among these bicycles beside the boy, it is the case that Mary likes one of them (as in Altmann & Steedman, 1988; Crain & Steedman, 1985). Thus, restricting an already restricted entity in the discourse may lead to a level of complexity that the parser may not be willing to entertain in a null context (see Thornton, Gil, & MacDonald, 1998, for evidence relevant to attachment decisions modulated by the specificity of the candidate nouns). According to this reasoning, then, when attached high, the RC is more likely to be interpreted as providing some extra (non-restrictive) information about the noun. However, if the RC modifies the low noun boy, then a restrictive interpretation of the RC may obtain. Suppose that this is what is happening in the Japanese head-final RC construction: the RC is sometimes interpreted as restrictive in the low attachment, but always as non-restrictive in the other attachments. In this case, if discourse is more complex for restrictive than non-restrictive information, the low attachment of the RC might have been particularly taxing in regions 3 and 4 as the complexity of the restrictive RC was compounded with the complexity of modifying N_2 with N_3 and then N_1 with N_2 according to the intervening postpositions. Therefore, in the low condition, the initial advantage from locality in region 2 would be replaced by difficulty with discourse complexity in the following two regions. It is unlikely that discourse complexity is the factor favouring the high site overall because, according to the previous reasoning, the middle attachment would also lead to a non-restrictive interpretation of the RC and therefore this hypothesis could not explain the advantage of the high over the middle condition in regions 3 and 4.

Alternatively, reanalysis triggered by long RCs may be another possible explanation for the relatively slow reading times after the attachment is made in the low attachment condition (Fodor, 1998). Kamide and colleagues proposed that the longer the RC, the more likely it will be re-attached to the high noun. Supporting evidence comes from a positive correlation between the length of the RC and the difference between the reading times of the low and the high conditions in their self-paced reading experiment (Kamide et al., 1998). In our experiment, it could be claimed that the relatively slow reading times in regions 3 and 4 in the low condition are due to a late preference that the parser may have to re-attach longer RCs to the high site. If this were the case, longer RCs in the present experiment should lead to greater slow-downs. However, no correlation was found in our data between the number of characters in the RC and the reading times of the low condition in region 2 ($r = -.06$; $P = .53$), region 3 ($r = -.12$; $P = .22$) or region 4 ($r = -.01$; $P = .91$). Similarly, no correlation was found between RC length and the difference in reading times of the low and high conditions in region 2 ($r = -.04$; $P = .67$), region 3 ($r = -.01$; $P = .87$) or region 4 ($r = -.04$; $P = .68$). Each of the two correlation analyses above was conducted with a total of 107 pairs of points (i.e., three subconditions times 36 times, except for one item that had no data available for one subcondition), with the length of the relative clauses varying between 4 and 17 characters (M = 9.6; SD = 2.9). Thus, it is unlikely that the correlations were not significant because too few data points were considered. Moreover, comprehension performance was best in the low condition, which does not support a reanalysis explanation, because more confusion (and hence more comprehension errors) might be expected if such reanalysis had been attempted.

CONCLUSION

There seem to be two factors at work in the Japanese head-final RC construction with multiple candidate hosts. One is locality favouring the closest site, the other (possibly predicate proximity or anaphor resolution) favours the high site, giving rise to a U-shaped preference curve. In addition to these two factors, we tentatively suggest that discourse complexity may also play a role as the type of interpretation for the RC varies.

The U-shaped preference ordering of the candidate sites in the present head-final construction is particularly informative because it supports a parsing framework in which predicted categories are considered as candidates for attachment along with lexically-realised alternatives. We have argued that such use of partial information is crucial to explain the preference to attach to the high site over the middle site, and that any model of modifier attachment must be able to accommodate such a feature in order to account for the preference ordering observed here.

REFERENCES

Altmann, G., & Steedman, M. (1988). Interaction with context during human sentence processing. *Cognition*, *30*, 191–238.

Cohen, J.D., MacWhinney, B., Flatt, M., & Provost, J. (1993). PsyScope: An interactive graphic system for designing and controlling experiments in the psychology laboratory using Macintosh computers. *Behavior Research Methods, Instruments and Computers*, *25*, 257–271.

Crain, S., & Steedman, M. (1985). On not being led up the garden path: The use of context by the psychological syntax processor. In D.R. Dowty, L. Karttunen, & A.M. Zwicky (Eds), *Natural language parsing*, pp.320–358. Cambridge, UK: Cambridge University Press.

Cuetos, F., Mitchell, D.C., & Corley, M.M.B. (1996). Parsing in different languages. In M. Carreiras, J.E. García-Albea, & Sebastián-Gallés (Eds), *Language processing in Spanish*, pp.145–187. Mahwah, NJ: Lawrence Erlbaum Associates Inc.

Ferreira, F., & Clifton, C., Jr. (1986). The independence of syntactic processing. *Journal of Memory and Language*, *25*, 348–368.

Fodor, J.D. (1998). Learning to parse? *Journal of Psycholinguistic Research*, *27*, 285–319.

Foss, D.J. (1982). A discourse on semantic priming. *Cognitive Psychology*, *14*, 590–607.

Frazier, L., & Fodor, J.D. (1978). The sausage machine: A new two-stage parsing model. *Cognition, 6*, 291–325.

Gibson, E. (1991). *A computational theory of human linguistic processing: Memory limitations and processing breakdown.* Unpublished doctorial dissertation, Carnegie Mellon University, Pittsburgh, PA.

Gibson, E. (1998). Linguistic complexity: Locality of syntactic dependencies. *Cognition, 68*, 1–76.

Gibson, E., Pearlmutter, N.J., Canseco-Gonzalez, E., & Hickok, G. (1996). Recency preference in the human sentence processing mechanism. *Cognition, 59*, 23–59.

Gibson, E., Pearlmutter, N.J., & Torrens, V. (in press). Recency and lexical preferences in Spanish. *Memory and Cognition.*

Hemforth, B., Konieczny, L., Scheepers, C., & Strube, G. (1998). Syntactic ambiguity resolution in German. In D. Hillert (Ed.), *Sentence processing: A crosslinguistic perspective*, pp.293–312. *Syntax and Semantics, 31*, San Diego, CA: Academic Press.

Just, M.A., Carpenter, P.A., & Woolley, J.D. (1982). Paradigms and processes in reading comprehension. *Journal of Experimental Psychology: General, 3*, 228–238.

Kamide, Y., & Mitchell, D.C. (1997). Relative clause attachment: Non-determinism in Japanese parsing. *Journal of Psycholinguistic Research, 26*, 247–254.

Kamide, Y., Mitchell, D.C., Fodor, J.D., & Inoue, A. (1998). Relative clause attachment ambiguity: Further evidence from Japanese. Poster presented at the eleventh annual CUNY Conference on Human Sentence Processing, Rutgers University, New Brunswick, NJ, March, 1998.

Kimball, J. (1973). Seven principles of surface structure parsing in natural language. *Cognition, 2*, 15–47.

Konieczny, L., Hemforth, B., Scheepers, C., & Strube, G. (1997). The role of lexical heads in parsing: Evidence from German. *Language and Cognitive Processes, 12*, 307–348.

Kuno, S. (1973). *The structure of the Japanese language.* Cambridge, MA: MIT Press.

Marslen-Wilson, W., & Tyler, L.K. (1980). The temporal structure of spoken language understanding. *Cognition, 8*, 1–71.

Marslen-Wilson, W., & Tyler, L.K. (1981). Central processes in speech understanding. *Philosophical Transactions of the Royal Society, Series B, 295*, 317–332.

Mitchell, D.C., & Brysbaert, M. (1998). Challenges to recent theories of crosslinguistic variation in parsing: Evidence from Dutch. In D. Hillert (Ed.), *Sentence processing: A crosslinguistic perspective*, pp.313–335. *Syntax and Semantics, 31*, San Diego, CA: Academic Press.

Phillips. C. (1995). Right association in parsing and grammar. In C.T. Schütze, J.B. Ganger, & K. Broihier (Eds), *Papers on language processing and acquisition*, pp.37–93. *MIT Working Papers in Linguistics, 26*, Cambridge, MA: MIT (MITWPL).

Rayner, K., Sereno, S.C., Morris, R.K., Schmauder, A.R., & Clifton, C. (1989). Eye movements and on-line language comprehension processes. *Language and Cognitive Processes, 4*, 21–49.

Thornton, R., Gil, M., & MacDonald, M.C. (1998). Accounting for crosslinguistic variation: A constraint-based perspective. In D. Hillert (Ed.), *Sentence Processing: A Crosslinguistic Perspective*, pp.211–225. *Syntax and Semantics, 31*, San Diego, CA: Academic Press.

Tsujimura, N. (1996). *An introduction to Japanese linguistics.* Oxford, UK: Blackwell.

Walter, M., & Hemforth, B. (1998). Attachment preferences of extraposed and adjacent relative clauses following three-site NPs in German. Poster presented at the eleventh annual CUNY Conference on Human Sentence Processing. New Brunswick, NJ, March, 1998.

Yamashita, H. (1994). *Processing of Japanese and Korean.* Unpublished doctoral dissertation, Ohio State University, Columbus, OH.

APPENDIX A

The raw reading times (i.e., without normalising according to length), trimmed at 4.0 standard deviations (calculated for each condition), are shown in Figure 4.

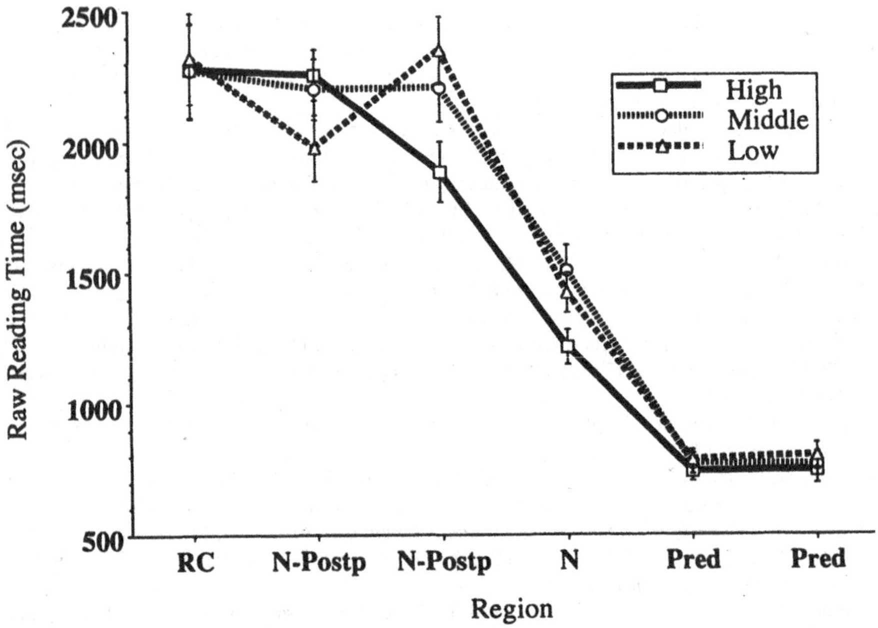

FIG. 4. Raw reading times for each region.

APPENDIX B

The following are the experimental items used in the experiment. All nine subconditions are presented for item 1. For all the other items, only three subconditions are presented as the other six subconditions can be deduced from the pattern presented in Table 1.

The 12 items analysed separately because they showed the strongest local attachment biases of the first PP in the off-line norming study were 10, 11, 13, 14, 16, 21, 22, 24, 32, 33, 34 and 35.

1a. 夕べほえていた / 机の横の / ドアの近くの / 犬は、 / 毛むくじゃらで / 濡れている。

1b. ノブがこわれている / 机の横の / ドアの近くの / 犬は、 / 毛むくじゃらで / 濡れている。

1c. 上の引き出しが壊れている / 机の横の / ドアの近くの / 犬は、 / 毛むくじゃらで / 濡れている。

1d. 夕べほえていた / ドアの横の / 犬の近くの / 机は、 / 英国製の / アンティークだ。

1e. ノブがこわれている / ドアの横の / 犬の近くの / 机は、 / 英国製の / アンティークだ。

1f. 上の引き出しが壊れている / ドアの横の / 犬の近くの / 机は、 / 英国製の / アンティークだ。

1g. 夕べほえていた / 犬の横の / 机の近くの / ドアは、 / いい鍵がついていて / 盗難を防ぐ。

1h. ノブがこわれている / 犬の横の / 机の近くの / ドアは、 / いい鍵がついていて / 盗難を防ぐ。

1i. 上の引き出しが壊れている / 犬の横の / 机の近くの / ドアは、 / いい鍵がついていて / 盗難を防ぐ。

2a. その中にほうきがしまってあった / 皿洗機の右側の / こんろの反対側の / 戸棚は、 / 引き出しが三段ついていて / かなり幅がある。

2e. 野菜を調理していた / こんろの右側の / 戸棚の反対側の / 皿洗機は、 / 昨日デパートで / 買った。

2i. 今、皿を洗っている / 戸棚の右側の / 皿洗機の反対側の / こんろは、 / 昨日デパートで / 買った。

3a. 私が夕べ読んだ / 鉛筆の近くの / ディスケットの右側の / 本は、 / 長くて / 退屈だった。

3e. 私が夕べ消した / ディスケットの近くの / 本の右側の / 鉛筆は、 / 教室に / あった。

3i. 私がしんを折ってしまった / 本の近くの / 鉛筆の右側の / ディスケットは、 / 便利で / 仕事が捗った。

4a. きのうの消印が押された / 缶の左側の / ホッチキスの前の / 絵葉書は、 / 小さくて / 奇麗だった。

4e. 針が入っていなかった / ホッチキスの左側の / 絵葉書の前の / 缶は、 / ひょろ長くて / 滑り易い。

4i. コカコーラが一杯入っていた / 絵葉書の左側の / 缶の前の / ホッチキスは、 / 重くて / 黒い。

5a. 山田さんが群集に砲火した / 鍵の隣の / ズボンの後ろの / 銃は、 / 本物の弾が / 入っていた。

5e. 椅子でひっかけてやぶってしまった / ズボンの隣の / 銃の後ろの / 鍵は、 / 鋭くて / ギザギザだった。

5i. 山田さんがきのう金物屋で買った / 銃の隣の / 鍵の後ろの / ズボンは、 / 茶色で / 短すぎた。

6a. きのう巣を作っていた / 水たまりの横の / 小枝の隣の / クモは、 / 小さいが / 恐い。

6e. 木から折れて落ちてしまった / 小枝の横の / クモの隣の / 水たまりは、 / 深くて / 大きかった。

6i. 子供がピチャピチャ水を飛び散らした / クモの横の / 水たまりの隣の / 小枝は、 / 曲がっていて / 脆かった。

7a. とてもうるさく鳴っていた / ペンの近くの / コップの左の / 電話は、 / 軽くて / 使い易い。

7e. 水がこぼれ落ちそうに入っている / コップの近くの / 電話の左の / ペンは、 / 古いが / とてもよく書ける。

7i. インクがきれている / 電話の近くの / ペンの左の / コップは、 / 罅が入っていて / 壊れている。

8a. 羽毛が一杯つまった / ベルトの右側の / ナイフの反対側の / 枕は、 / ふかふかしていて / 心地よい。

8e. 鋭く尖れた / ナイフの右側の / 枕の反対側の / ベルトは、 / 擦り切れていて / 小さい。

8i. いつも川野さんがズボンにしている / 枕の右側の / ベルトの反対側の / ナイフは、 / 切れ味が / 悪い。

9a. すごいスピードで走っていた / 道路の横の / 標識の前の / バスは、 / 明るい黄色で / とても長かった。

9e. 読みにくかった / 標識の横の / バスの前の / 道路は、 / 狭くて / カーブが多い。

9i. 車が止めてあった / バスの横の / 道路の前の / 標識は、 / 古くて / 雨や風で傷んでいる。

10a. ページが破れている / ラジオの近くの / コンピューターの隣の / 雑誌は、 / 三十年前のものだが / まだそのまま保存されている。

10e. 画面が緑の / コンピューターの近くの / 雑誌の隣の / ラジオは、 / 楽しませて / リラックスさせてくれる。

10i. 五つの放送局が聞ける / 雑誌の近くの / ラジオの隣の / コンピューターは、 / 便利で / 面白い。

11a. その部屋を照らしていた / ステレオの右側の / ソファの後ろの / ランプは、 / 煌々として / 高い。

11e. 座り心地よいクッションの / ソファの右側の / ランプの後ろの / ステレオは、 / 音が大きくて / 耳障りだ。

11i. うるさい音でなっていた / ランプの右側の / ステレオの後ろの / ソファは、 / 柔らかいが / 丈夫だ。

12a. 夕べ一晩中鳴いていた / 蝶の近くの / 花の前の / カエルは、 / とても機敏で / すばしっこい。

12e. 五月に満開に咲いていた / 花の近くの / カエルの前の / 蝶は、 / そよ風の中を / ひらひらと飛んでいる。

12i. さなぎから出たばかりの / カエルの近くの / 蝶の前の / 花は、 / 鮮やかで / 色彩に富んでいる。

13a. 素晴らしい曲を弾いた / 子猫の横の / 椅子の左の / ギターは、 / 木製で / 美しい音色を出す。

13e. 脚にキャスターが付いている / 椅子の横の / ギターの左の / 子猫は、 / 毛がフサフサしていて / 愛らしい。

13i. 毛糸玉とじゃれている / ギターの横の / 子猫の左の / 椅子は、 / 柔らかくて / 座り心地がよい。

14a. ハスの葉が浮いていた / 道の前の / 家の右側の / 池は、 / 風で / 波立っている。

14e. 古れんがでできた煙突がある / 家の前の / 池の右側の / 道は、 / くねくねと曲がっていて / 狭い。

14i. 平野さんが歩き慣れた / 池の前の / 道の右側の / 家は、 / 朽ちて / 倒れかけていた。

15a. 中村さんが木曜日にしていた / ほうきの左の / ティーポットの後ろの / エプロンは、 / 汚れていて / シミが付いている。

15e. ストーブの上で沸き立っていた / ティーポットの左の / エプロンの後ろの / ほうきは、 / ブラシは硬いが / 使い易い。

15i. 中村さんが床を掃いた / エプロンの左の / ほうきの後ろの / ティーポットは、 / 日本製で / 美味しいお茶がいれられる。

16a. 自分の鳴き声で犬を追い立てた / 帽子の近くの / 靴の反対側の / 猫は、 / 年寄りで / 愛想が悪い。

16e. 私が右足にはいていた / 靴の近くの / 猫の反対側の / 帽子は、 / 上に大きな羽が / 付いている。

16i. 私が頭にかぶっていた / 猫の近くの / 帽子の反対側の / 靴は、 / キメの細かい革で / できている。

17a. 自分の父親に微笑みかけた / ベッドの隣の / ボールの前の / 男の子は、 / 優しくて / 朗らかだ。

17e. その子供が池に投げすてようとした / ボールの隣の / 男の子の前の / ベッドは、 / 寝心地がよくて / 小さい。

17i. 犬が寝ていた / 男の子の隣の / ベッドの前の / ボールは、 / ゴム製で / よく弾む。

18a. マリーがパイのために切った / 手紙の近くの / スプンの後ろの / りんごは、 / つるつる光っていて / 赤い。

18e. マリーがヨーグルトをすくった / スプンの近くの / りんごの後ろの / 手紙は、 / 長くて / 詳しく書かれている。

18i. マリーがけさ叔父宛に書いた / りんごの近くの / 手紙の後ろの / スプンは、 / 罅が入っていて / 欠けている。

19a. 観光客に噛みついた / プールの隣の / 檻の左側の / ライオンは、 / 大きくて / 美しい。

19e. 鎖で出来ている / 檻の隣の / ライオンの左側の / プールは、 / 大きくて / 美しい。

19i. 観光客が泳いだ / ライオンの隣の / プールの左側の / 檻は、 / 大きくて / 美しい。

20a. 学校まで乗った / 茂みの横の / 人の後ろの / 自転車は、 / きれいで / 大きかった。

20e. パーティーで会った / 人の横の / 自転車の後ろの / 茂みは、 / きれいで / 大きかった。

20i. 枝がおれている / 自転車の横の / 茂みの後ろの / 人は、 / きれいで / 大きかった。

21a. 妹が描いた / テーブルの隣の / テレビの右側の / 絵は、 / 高くて / 小さかった。

21e. うるさい音がしている / テレビの隣の / 絵の右側の / テーブルは、 / 高くて / 小さかった。

21i. 私が夕べ食事をした / 絵の隣の / テーブルの右側の / テレビは、 / 高くて / 小さかった。

22a. お茶がいっぱい入っている / 写真の横の / 新聞の反対側の / 茶碗は、 / 古くて / 黄ばんでいた。

22e. うその話が書いてある / 新聞の横の / 茶碗の反対側の / 写真は、 / 古くて / 黄ばんでいた。

22i. 昨日焼き増しした / 茶碗の横の / 写真の反対側の / 新聞は、 / 古くて / 黄ばんでいた。

23a. ワインを急冷凍した / 缶切りの隣の / 流しの左側の / 冷蔵庫は、 / 古くて / 使いにくかった。

23e. 我々が食器洗いをした / 流しの隣の / 冷蔵庫の左側の / 缶切りは、 / 古くて / 使いにくかった。

23i. 研ぐ必要のある / 冷蔵庫の隣の / 缶切りの左側の / 流しは、 / 古くて / 使いにくかった。

24a. 木に登った / 街灯の隣の / 郵便受けの反対側の / りすは、 / 小さくて / 可愛かった。

24e. 郵便やさんがあけた / 郵便受けの隣の / りすの反対側の / 街灯は、 / 小さくて / 可愛かった。

24i. 道を明るく照らしている / りすの隣の / 街灯の反対側の / 郵便受けは、 / 小さくて / 可愛かった。

25a. 女の子にささやいた / コピー機の近くの / 壁の横の / 図書館員は、 / 大きくて / 醜かった。

25e. コンクリートで出来ている / 壁の近くの / 図書館員の横の / コピー機は、 / 大きくて / 醜かった。

25i. 私が以前論文を複写した / 図書館員の近くの / コピー機の横の / 壁は、 / 大きくて / 醜かった。

26a. 清掃婦がほうきではいた / アライグマの後ろの / バケツの反対側の / 砂は、 / 茶色で / きれいだった。

26e. 水がいっぱい入っている / バケツの後ろの / 砂の反対側の / アライグマは、 / 茶色で / きれいだった。

26i. 追いかけた / 砂の後ろの / アライグマの反対側の / バケツは、 / 茶色で / きれいだった。

27a. 警笛を吹いた / 車の横の / 木の右側の / 警察官は、 / 美しくて / 有名だった。

27e. 葉っぱが落ちてしまった / 木の横の / 警察官の右側の / 車は、 / 美しくて / 有名だった。

27i. バックミラーがとれている / 警察官の横の / 車の右側の / 木は、 / 美しくて / 有名だった。

28a. 弦が切れた / スツールの左側の / トランペットの前の / ハープは、 / 古くて / 小さかった。

28e. 吹き口がなくなった / トランペットの左側の / ハープの前の / スツールは、 / 古くて / 小さかった。

28i. 花子がすわった / ハープの左側の / スツールの前の / トランペットは、 / 古くて / 小さかった。

29a. 田中さんに書いた / 鏡の横の / 練り歯磨きの反対側の / メモは、 / 新しくて / 白かった。

29e. 虫歯を防ぐ / 練り歯磨きの横の / メモの反対側の / 鏡は、 / 新しくて / 白かった。

29i. 光っている / メモの横の / 鏡の反対側の / 練り歯磨きは、 / 新しくて / 白かった。

30a. まだ飲んでいない / スプーンの後ろの / ステーキの近くの / お茶は、 / 高くて / 有名だ。

30e. こんがりと焼いてある / ステーキの後ろの / お茶の近くの / スプーンは、 / 高くて / 有名だ。

30i. 銀で出来ている / お茶の後ろの / スプーンの近くの / ステーキは、 / 高くて / 有名だ。

31a. ヒールが高い / 上着の隣の / 傘の右側の / ブーツは、 / 古くて / 破れていた。

31e. 柄が奇麗な / 傘の隣の / ブーツの右側の / 上着は、 / 古くて / 破れていた。

31i. いい生地で出来ている / ブーツの隣の / 上着の右側の / 傘は、 / 古くて / 破れていた。

32a. 消えてしまった / バラの前の / 彫像の左側の / ローソクは、 / 大きくて / きれいだった。

32e. 腕が一本おれている / 彫像の前の / ローソクの左側の / バラは、 / 大きくて / きれいだった。

32i. きれいに咲いている / ローソクの前の / バラの左側の / 彫像は、 / 大きくて / きれいだった。

33a. はさみが一つしかない / タオルの近くの / ピンの前の / カニは、 / 小さくて / 赤かった。

33e. コーラが入っている / ピンの近くの / カニの前の / タオルは、 / 小さくて / 赤かった。

33i. 洗濯した / カニの近くの / タオルの前の / ピンは、 / 小さくて / 赤かった。

34a. くぎを打った / 鋸の横の / ドライバーの後ろの / カナズチは、 / 新しくて / 使いやすかった。

34e. ネジをしめた / ドライバーの横の / カナズチの後ろの / 鋸は、 / 新しくて / 使いやすかった。

34i. 板を切った / カナズチの横の / 鋸の後ろの / ドライバーは、 / 新しくて / 使いやすかった。

35a. ガットのはりかえが必要な / ロッカーの前の / トレーナーの右側の / ラケットは、 / 新しくて / 高かった。

35e. 袖が長い / トレーナーの前の / ラケットの右側の / ロッカーは、 / 新しくて / 高かった。

35i. 鍵がかかっている / ラケットの前の / ロッカーの右側の / トレーナーは、 / 新しくて / 高かった。

36a. 10 分おくれている / マグカップの隣の / カタログの反対側の / 時計は、 / 高くて / 重かった。

36e. ２００ページもある / カタログの隣の / 時計の反対側の / マグカップは、 / 高くて / 重かった。

36i. コーヒーが入っている / 時計の隣の / マグカップの反対側の / カタログは、 / 高くて / 重かった。

LANGUAGE AND COGNITIVE PROCESSES, 1999, *14* (5/6), 687–714

The Effects of Case Marking Information on Korean Sentence Processing

Youngjin Kim

Ajou University, Suwon, South Korea

Two experiments were conducted to determine whether a parser's on-line processes are affected by manipulation of case markings in Korean sentence processing, and to evaluate the usefulness of a Ranked Flagged Serial Parser (RFSP) model in predicting Korean ambiguity resolution processes. By using a self-paced word-by-word reading task, in Experiment 1, relative and coordinate sentences of the form NP-*ka* (nominative), NP-*lul* (accusative), and Verb were compared to those sentences of the form NP-*nun* (topic marker), NP-*lul*, and Verb. In Experiment 2, relative sentences that have NP-*ka*, NP-*ka*, and Verb sequence were compared to those sentences of NP-*nun*, NP-*ka*, and Verb sequence. In addition, reversed relative clause sentences were compared after changing case markings of the last NP. The topic marker -*nun* changed overall patterns of word-by-word reading times of the sentences in both experiments. The results clearly showed that local grammatical cues, such as case markings, are used in generating syntactic hypotheses. We also found that the RFSP model successfully predicted local processing loads and reparsing difficulties in Korean sentence comprehension. Suggestions for further studies were made.

INTRODUCTION

The universality of processing in human language has been an important issue in psycholinguistics. To address the issue, it is necessary to examine various languages both theoretically and experimentally. A lot of cross-linguistic studies have been reported (Cuetos, Mitchell, & Corley, 1996;

Requests for reprints should be addressed to Youngjin Kim, Department of Psychology, Ajou University, San-5, Wonchun-Dong, Paldal-Ku, Suwon, 442-749, South Korea. Email: yjkim@madang.ajou.ac.kr

I thank Jin-Deok Jang for running subjects, and thank Byeong-Taek Lee who read and commented on earlier drafts. I have benefited from the comments that an anonymous reviewer and the editor, Hsuan-Chih Chen, provided. In particular, I would like to express my gratitude to another anonymous reviewer who provided invaluable suggestions. The suggestions greatly improved the paper.

Inoue & Fodor, 1995; Koh, 1997). Especially East Asian languages, like Korean and Japanese, constitute a particularly valuable contrast with languages like English, because the languages differ structurally in ways that profoundly affect the flow of information available as a sentence is heard or read. The data from psycholinguistic experiments of the East Asian languages are ideal types of sources to consider the issue of universality.

In linguistic terms, Korean is head final and left branching, has subject-object-verb word order, permits scrambling, and allows phonological null arguments. What this means is that in Korean crucial information (e.g., information included in verbs) comes late in the sentence; verbs are clause final, and so are the complementisers and adverbs that mark subordinate clauses. Therefore, the positions of clause boundaries tend to be highly uncertain during the processing of most of the words of a sentence. That is, in Korean, there can be multiple ambiguity with respect to basic facts, such as which noun phrases belong together as the subject and object of the same proposition. Another interesting characteristic of Korean that drastically distinguishes it from English is the phenomenon of Korean particles, the counterpart of which is largely lacking in many languages.

There are about 47 different particles that can be categorised into two types in Korean; one is case markers that are suffixed to nouns, the other is delimiters that delimit the semantic scope of the attached words (clauses). Unlike English, these morphemes are not free, but are always bound to nouns, adverbs, or conjunctions. As many psycholinguists suggest, in languages such as Korean, Japanese, and German, the information of particles attached to NPs might be an important source for generating a hypothesis of a syntactic structure before predicates (Carlson & Tanenhaus, 1988; MacDonald, Pearlmutter, & Seidenberg, 1994).

The current study focused on a Korean nominative case marker *-ka* (which becomes *-i* after a consonant) and a Korean delimiter (or topic maker) *-nun* (which becomes *-un* after a consonant). In ordinary conversations and texts, these two particles are used inter-changeably. So it is very difficult to say when use *-ka/i* and when to use the alternative *-nun/un* instead. Many grammatical and functional studies have been attempted to explain the differences between them. Kuno (1972) argued that the Japanese *-wa* (almost the same as the Korean *-nun/un*) marks either the theme or the contrasted element of a sentence. The theme must be either anaphoric (i.e., previously mentioned) or generic, while there is no restriction for the contrasted element. However, Yang (1973) argued that the Korean delimiter *-nun/un* has the following semantic functions: presupposition, assertion, and implication. That is, these linguists argued that the subjective case marker *-ka/i* and the delimiter (or topic marker) *-nun/un* have different semantic/pragmatic functions.

Hong (1985) examined the distribution of the use of the subject marker in written and spoken data, and he found that *-nun/un* is used more in written language and *-ka/i* is used more in spoken style. He also found that new information favours *-ka/i* while old and inferable information favours *-nun/un*. The subject of the main clause favours *-nun/un* and the subject of subordinate and relative clause favours *-ka/i*. Thus his results showed that two markers have different preference for different syntactic structures.

There are some experimental results that showed the effects of these particles on sentence comprehension. For example, Uehara (1997) reported an effect of more than two consecutive noun phrases with the same nominative case markers, *-ga* (almost the same as the Korean *-ka*), on ratings of processability for Japanese multiply centre-embedded sentences. In particular, she compared a sentence which contained three consecutive NP-*ga* to a sentence which contained one topic marker and two *-ga*, and found the latter rated significantly more processable than the former. Yamashita (1997) also showed that the Japanese parser was sensitive to the variety of case-marked arguments. We will discuss Yamashita's results in more detail below. However, it is not yet known whether the Korean *-nun/un* and *-ka/i* have different effects on on-line sentence comprehension processes. To date we have no evidence that the changes of a particle produce different patterns of reading times in sentence comprehension processes. So, the first purpose of this study was to investigate whether the grammatical and semantic/pragmatic information associated with those particles is utilised in Korean sentence processing.

As has previously been stated, in Korean, there can be multiple ambiguity with respect to basic facts, such as which noun phrases belong together as subjects and objects of the same proposition. That is, the predicate-argument structure within clauses is the major source of local and mild garden-path effects in Korean. For example:

[1] Bob-ka Mary-lul manna-n. .
-Nom[1] -Acc meet-rel
(Bob met Mary . .)

[2] a. Bob-ka Mary-lul manna-n Jack-lul ttaraessta.
-Nom -Acc meet-rel -Acc hit
(Bob hit Jack who met Mary.)
b. Bob-ka Mary-lul manna-n sagun-i allaegussta.
-Nom -Acc meet-rel event-Nom was known
(The event that Bob met Mary was known.)

[1] Nom, nominative; Acc, accusative; rel, relativisation suffix.

Two NPs in [1] are ambiguous, e.g., they can be grouped as the two arguments of a clause and constitute a complement clause like [2b], or the second NP as an argument of new relative clause like [2a]. So, a lot of interesting questions can be raised. Are there any processing load differences between the two sentences [2a and 2b], especially at the ambiguous third word position and at the disambiguating fourth word? Is syntactic processing delayed until the disambiguating location (i.e., the fourth word)? Is there any evidence for parallel syntactic analysis? Evidence that Korean parsing is serial and committal comes from an eye-tracking experiment of Koh (1997). He argued that, in Korean, the attachment of each phrase is not delayed until a head, such as a verb, is available, and Korean parsing can be explained by the garden-path theory (Frazier, 1978; Frazier & Rayner, 1982). However, we do not have enough information to picture word-by-word procedures of Korean parsing. As Inoue and Fodor (1995) said for Japanese, there are so many questions unanswered linguistically and experimentally in Korean. Therefore, it is very difficult to generate a plausible hypothesis for experimentation. What we need is a theoretical model that could embrace the grammatical characteristics of Korean. The most promising candidate might be the Ranked Flagged Serial Parser (RFSP) (Inoue & Fodor, 1995), because of its general applicability. We will use the RFSP model to generate predictions of word-by-word parsing or reparsing loads (or reading time increases) of Korean sentences.

Ranked Flagged Serial Parser

Everyone agrees that the human sentence processing mechanism must be universal to a certain degree, although the grammars of languages may vary systematically from one to another. The question is how to account for differences across languages within the framework of a universal theory of language processing. The RFSP of Inoue and Fodor (1995; Fodor & Inoue, 1994) provides a strong form of the universal hypothesis. It is an attempt to embrace the massive ambiguities found in Japanese sentences. The main characteristics of the RFSP model can be summarised as follows:

(i) At a choice point, a flag is posted to note the existence of each alternative, though only the first one to arrive is developed in subsequent processing (i.e., serial processing).

(ii) The RFSP records at each point not just what alternative parses there are, but also how highly each is valued (i.e., confidence rankings or ratings).

(iii) In RFSP, the various analyses are logged and clocked. Their arrival times will mirror their relative difficulty for the parser. These times can serve as ratings.

(iv) The parsing strategies such as minimal attachment (Frazier, 1978) and minimal everything (Inoue & Fodor, 1995) are just reflections of what the parser finds easiest (i.e., fast clock time).
(v) In case of first-pass breakdown, the parser re-starts at one ambiguity point, selecting the second choice on the list of alternative stored there, and simply proceeds from left to right as usual, applying the usual strategies and preference rankings.
(vi) Revision difficulty is a function of the relative values of alternative analyses as established by the first-pass parsing routine.

The RFSP model is well specified enough to generate specific predictions of local processing loads and reparsing difficulties of Korean sentence processing. However, there are several things needed to complement the model experimentally and theoretically. As has previously been stated, in the RFSP model, all candidate analyses are logged in, though only the first one to arrive is continued. There is a very slightly greater element of parallel processing in the model than in a standard serial processor, though considerably less than in a standard parallel processor. So, does this sort of parallelism produce any measurable processing loads? For example, if more than two flaggings are possible at a position of a sentence, does it create greater processing load (or reading time) than one flagging? Inoue and Fodor (1995) seemed to assume flaggings are resource free. The number of flags at a word location may be not important for parsing. However, there is no evidence to support this assumption. We need experimental evidence.

Secondly, a key concept of the RFSP model is the confidence rankings or ratings of each alternative analysis, but Inoue and Fodor (1995) do not provide any concrete schemes that can assign the ratings in each word position of a sentence. What we need is a simple, but reasonable system that assigns a number (i.e., rating values) to each location. As a first approximation, we will use a simple scheme that assigns 1 to 5 points in each word position of the sentence. We will assume that the strongly preferable syntactic analysis that follows the minimal attachment principle has a strong rating (i.e., 5 points) and alternative analyses have values between 1 and 4 points. All rating values will depend on the parsing principles and the available syntactic (or semantic) information such as word order and case markings. We will discuss how this simple scheme will be applied to Korean sentences in the introductory part of Experiment 1.

In summary, the first aim of this study was to examine whether the parser's on-line decisions are affected by manipulations of the case markings in Korean sentences. Secondly, we also tried to verify the predictions of the RFSP model on the local processing loads and reparsing difficulties (or word-by-word reading times) of Korean sentences.

EXPERIMENT 1

In Experiment 1 we used Korean centre-embedded relative clause sentences and coordinate sentences. Examples [3] and [4] are the relative clause structure. The only difference between [3] and [4] is the case marking of the first NP, i.e., subjective marking (*-ka/i*) in [3] and topic marking (*-nun/un*) in [4]. If we changed the first verb ending (or suffix) of rhe relative clause sentences (i.e., *sealduk-han* → *sealduk-hago*), structures in [3] and [4] become coordinate structures like [5] and [6]. The ending *-han* is a relativisation marker of a verb and the ending *-hago* is a coordinate marker of a verb.

[3] Wunchensoo-ka chunksoboo-lul sealduk-han gunchukka-lul bipanhanda.
Driver-Nom janitor-Acc persuade-rel architect-Acc criticised.
(The driver criticised the architect who persuaded the janitor.)

[4] Wunchensoo-nun chunksoboo-lul sealduk-han gunchukka-lul bipanhanda.
Driver-Topic janitor-Acc persuade-rel architect-Acc criticised.
(The driver criticised the architect who persuaded the janitor.)

[5] Wunchensoo-ka chunksoboo-lul sealduk-hago gunchukka-lul bipanhanda.
Driver-Nom janitor-Acc persuade-coor architect-Acc criticised.
(The driver persuaded the janitor and criticised the architect.)

[6] Wunchensoo-nun chunksoboo-lul sealduk-hago gunchukka-lul bipanhanda.
Driver-Topic janitor-Acc persuade-coor architect-Acc criticised.
(The driver persuaded the janitor and criticised the architect.)

Based on the RFSP model, the assumption that a human parser follows the principle of minimal attachment (Frazier, 1978), and the simple ranking scheme we will discuss, we can generate predictions of word-by-word Korean syntactic analysis procedures and confidence rankings (or ratings) for each analysis. The two NPs in [3] and [5], in which the *-ka* and *-lul* case markers are included, are ambiguous. They can be grouped as co-arguments of a single clause or the second noun can be analysed as a start of the new clause. So, two flags must be posted at the second noun position according to the RFSP model. The first syntactic analysis is the strongly preferred co-argument analysis, because it agrees with the minimal attachment principle (Frazier, 1978) or minimal everything principle (Inoue & Fodor, 1995), and it also corresponds to the canonical word order in Korean. We will call this analysis "flag 1 (the co-argument analysis)". However, the second analysis, in which the two NPs appear in different clauses, is less preferred, because it does not agree with the minimal attachment principle. We will call this analysis as "flag 2 (the separate clause analysis)". Therefore, the flag 1 (the co-argument analysis) should have a higher rating (or ranking) than the flag 2 (the separate clause analysis). We will simply assume the ranking of the flag 1 has 5 points and the flag 2 has 1 point (flag 1 = 5, flag 2 = 1). The RFSP model will assume that only the first syntactic analysis (flag 1) is continued in subsequent processing.

The two NPs in [4] and [6] seem to have the same ambiguity (i.e., flags) as the NPs in [3] and [5]. However, there may be a subtle difference between them. Hong (1985) examined the distribution of the use of the subject marker in written and spoken data. He found that the subject of a main clause favours *-nun* and the subject of a subordinate and relative clause favours *-ka*. Kuno (1973) argued that the Japanese topic maker *-wa* could not be used in the relative clause. Functions of the Japanese topic maker may be almost the same as the Korean topic maker *-nun*. So, we can infer that there may be a syntactic constraint in Korean that the topic maker cannot be used in the relative clause. However, there is an exception to this syntactic constraint. That is, if the *-nun* marker is used as a contrastive particle instead of a topic or thematic particle, the NP *-nun* can be used in the relative clause (Lee, 1979). The Korean *-nun* may induce some expectation about what sequence of words will be next in the input. However, the exception means that it may not be a strong enough cue to disambiguate the two NPs in [4] and [6].

So, is this the kind of frequency information and syntactic expectation that the topic maker has used in syntactic parsing? Right now we do not have enough theoretical basis and empirical evidence to answer the question. We can only guess that the flag 1 (the co-argument analysis) in [4] and [6] might have low ratings compared to the flag 1 in [3] and [5]. This is presumabaly because the topic maker could reduce the confidence rating of flag 1 (the co-argument analysis). That is, in [4] and [6], the first (topic marked) NP is most likely to appear in the main clause, so if the second (accusative marked) NP turns out to appear in a subordinate clause, it is unlikely that the two NPs will be co-arguments. In contrast, the first (nominative marked) NP in [3] and [5] could easily appear in a subordinate clause, so if the second (accusative marked) NP appears in a subordinate clause, these two NPs are more likely to be co-arguments. Therefore, in [4] and [6], we could simply assume the flag 1 (the co-argument analysis) has 4 points and the flag 2 (the separate clause analysis) has 1 point (flag 1 = 4, flag 2 = 1). The RFSP model will assume that only the flag 1 (co-argument analysis) is continued in subsequent processing.

The third word in [3] and [4] produces another ambiguity. The three words can be constructed as a complement clause like an example in [2b], or the second noun and the third verb can be grouped as an embedded relative clause and the first word can be raised as the subject of the main clause. The former is a continuation of the flag 1 (the co-argument analysis) and the latter is the continuation of flag 2 (the separate clause analysis). However, there may be some additional information in the third word. As Suh (1994) discussed, when the third verb word *sealduk-han* is received, it becomes clear that there is (at least) one degree of embedding, since it contains suffix (i.e., *-han*), which functions either as a relative clause or as a complementiser heading a complex NP clause. When the noun following the verbal suffix can be an argument of the verb, the verbal suffix functions as relative clause marker and the following noun becomes the head noun of the relative clause. When it cannot be an argument of the verb, the verbal suffix functions as a complementiser heading a complex NP clause. These two analyses seem to compete, because the head noun is not received yet.

Therefore, we could guess that the third word *sealduk-han* may function as a cue which signals that the flag 2 (the separate clause analysis) may be more possible, compared to the flag 2 analysis addressed only based on the initial two NPs. The third word also may reduce the difference in the confidence ratings between the flag 1 and the flag 2. That is, it may weaken the flag 1 analysis and strengthen the flag 2 analysis. So, we can predict that the confidence ratings of each analysis in [3] will be 4 and 2 respectively (flag 1 = 4, flag 2 = 2), and those in [4] will be 3 and 2 respectively (flag 1 = 3, flag 2 = 2).

The third word in [5] and [6] also produces another ambiguity. The three words can be constructed as a single clause, or the second noun and the third verb can be grouped as a more deeply embedded relative or complement clause.[2] The former is a continuation of the flag 1 (the co-argument analysis) and the latter is the continuation of flag 2 (the separate clause analysis). However, the third word in [5] and [6] is a verb which signals the end of the sentence, and it has a coordinate suffix (i.e., *-hago*) which functions like English 'and'. So, the verb and suffix may strongly signal the end of the clause that has constructed so far. That is, the flag 1 analysis must be more preferred than the flag 2 analysis. We can predict that the confidence ratings of each analysis in [5] will be 5 and 1 respectively (flag 1 = 5, flag 2 = 1) and the confidence ratings of each analysis in [6] will be 4 and 1 respectively (flag 1 = 4, flag 2 = 1). Like the second word position, only the flag 1 analysis will be continued in subsequent processing in [5] and [6].

The fourth word in [3] and [4] is in a position of disambiguation. The analysis performed until the third word, i.e., the flag 1 (co-argument analysis), must be reparsed, because the fourth word must function as one of the arguments of the relative clause, and so one of the previous NPs

[2] An anonymous reviewer pointed out this possibility.

must be raised to the main clause. In other words, the second and third words must be reanalysed as an embedded relative clause with the fourth word, and the first word must be a subject of the main clause, i.e, flag 2 (the separate clause analysis). As mentioned before, we predicted that the confidence ratings of two alternative analyses in [3] are 4 and 2 respectively (flag 1 = 4, flag 2 = 2), and those in [4] and 3 and 2 respectively (flag 1 = 3, flag 2 = 2). We also predicted that only the flag 1 analysis was adopted in both sentences. However, it must be changed to the flag 2 analysis when the fourth word occurred. The RFSP model can make an interesting prediction about local processing loads or reparsing difficulties of the fourth word. As Inoue and Fodor (1995) argued, "revision difficulty is a function of the relative values of alternative analyses as established by the first-pass parsing routines" (p. 36). Therefore, if we follow this argument, the reanalysis may be easy in [4], compared to [3], because the flag 1 analysis has a low rating value in [4]. That is, we can predict that reading times of the fourth word position be shorter in [4] than those in [3]. The ambiguity in [5] and [6] continues at the fourth word. The final word is a verb that closes the sentences, and there is no ambiguity in it.

In summary, the RFSP model predicted that reading times of the fourth word position should be shorter in [4] than those in [3] because of the ease of the revision in the former condition.

Methods

Subjects. Sixty undergraduate students of Ajou University participated in the experiment, all of whom were native speakers of Korean and were naive about the purpose of the experiment.

Materials. Twenty-eight test sentences and forty-two fillers were constructed for the experiment. There were four versions of each test sentence. One version of the test sentences had centre-embedded relative clauses and contained the nominative case marker *-ka* in the initial noun phrase; one version of the test sentences had centre-embedded relative clauses and contained the topic marker *-nun* in the initial noun phrase; one version of the test sentences had coordinate clause sentences and contained the nominative case marker *-ka* in the initial noun phrase; and finally, one version of the test sentences had coordinate clause sentences and contained the topic case marker *-nun* in the initial noun phrase. The following is an example of one complete set of test sentences[3]:

[3] Nom, nominative; Acc, accusative; rel, relativisation suffix; Topic, topic marker; coor, coordinate suffix.

Relative -ka sentence
Wunchensoo-ka chunksoboo-lul sealduk-han gunchukka-lul bipanhanda.
Driver-Nom janitor-Acc persuade-rel architect-Acc criticised.
(The driver criticised the architect who persuaded the janitor.)

Relative -nun sentence
Wunchensoo-nun chunksoboo-lul sealduk-han gunchukka-lul bipanhanda.
Driver-Topic janitor-Acc persuade-rel architect-Acc criticised.
(The driver criticised the architect who persuaded the janitor.)

Coordinate -ka sentence
Wunchensoo-ka chunksoboo-lul sealduk-hago gunchukka-lul bipanhanda.
Driver-Nom janitor-Acc persuade-coor architect-Acc criticised.
(The driver persuaded the janitor and criticised the architect.)

Coordinate -nun sentence
Wunchensoo-nun chunksoboo-lul sealduk-hago gunchukka-lul bipanhanda.
Driver-Topic janitor-Acc persuade-coor architect-Acc criticised.
(The driver persuaded the janitor and criticised the architect.)

All nouns in the test sentences were Korean occupation names (e.g., driver and lawyer) and all verbs in the test sentences were transitive. All words were randomly assigned to each sentence to remove any semantic relatedness. A counterbalanced design yielded four lists of stimuli, such that no more than a single version of any particular test sentence was presented in each list. Each of the four lists contained 28 test sentences (with 7 tokens of each of the 4 versions). These sentences were interspersed among 42 filler sentences. The fillers included a variety of structures. Fifteen subjects were randomly assigned to one of the four lists. The presentation orders of 70 sentences were randomised to each subject.

Procedure. Each set of sentences was presented word-by-word, using a subject-paced moving window paradigm (Just, Carpenter, & Woolley, 1982) on an IBM compatible computer. When the subject first pressed the space bar on the keyboard, the first word appeared. Then at the next button press, letters of the first word were replaced by the same number of underlines, and the next word appeared at the right of the first word position. The computer recorded the time elapsed, in milliseconds, between the onset of each new word and the next key press. Subjects were instructed to read the sentences as quickly as possible, without sacrificing their comprehension of each sentence, and to read carefully to figure out "Who did what to whom". After the last word of each sentence, a question sentence appeared below the test sentence position. The subjects were instructed to press a key marked <YES> whenever a question sentence was true based on the sentence just read, and to press <NO> whenever a question was false.

Results and Discussion

All subjects showed more than 87% accuracy to the 70 question sentences, indicating they were reading carefully. Two-way ANOVA on the accuracy data revealed no significant differences across the four conditions. So, we analysed the data focusing on the reading times. The reading times of each word were divided by the number of syllables included in each word. Figure 1 depicts the mean syllable reading times at each word position.

Based on the suggestions of Pollatsek & Well (1995), three-way ANOVAs (*-ka/-nun*, relative/coordinate, and four counterbalancing groups) were performed separately at each word position. The ANOVAs examined the two types of structures (relative/coordinate) and the two types of grammatical markers (*-kal/-nun*) as two main factors. Planned comparisons in each type of structure (e.g., relative *-ka* vs. relative *-nun*) were also performed to verify the predictions we made. The ANOVAs revealed no significant differences across the four conditions at the first and the second word positions.

However, at the third word position, there was a significant difference between the two tapes of structures [$F_1(1,56) = 48.760$, $MSe = 6786.155$, $P < .002$, $F_2(1,24) = 46.017$, $MSe = 3355.677$, $P < .001$]. The relative structures showed longer reading times than the coordinate structures (respectively, 426 ms vs. 352 ms). As we mentioned before, Inoue and Fodor (1995) assumed that flaggings themselves are resource free and the confidence ratings of each alternative analysis themselves do not matter in parsing. That is, as the parser follows only one analysis (i.e., flag 1, the co-argument analysis) in both structures, the only difference between the two structures was the confidence rating values of each alternative analysis. So, the RFSP predicted no difference in reading times between the two conditions. The experimental result did not confirm their assumption. We assumed the third word in [5] and [6] produces the almost same ambiguity as the third word in [3] and [4]. Then, it is not clear why the reading time difference between the two structures was found at the third word. Our assumption might be wrong. The significant reading time difference might reflect the relative strength of the confidence rating of the flag 1 (the co-argument analysis). The rating values of the flag 1 were higher in the

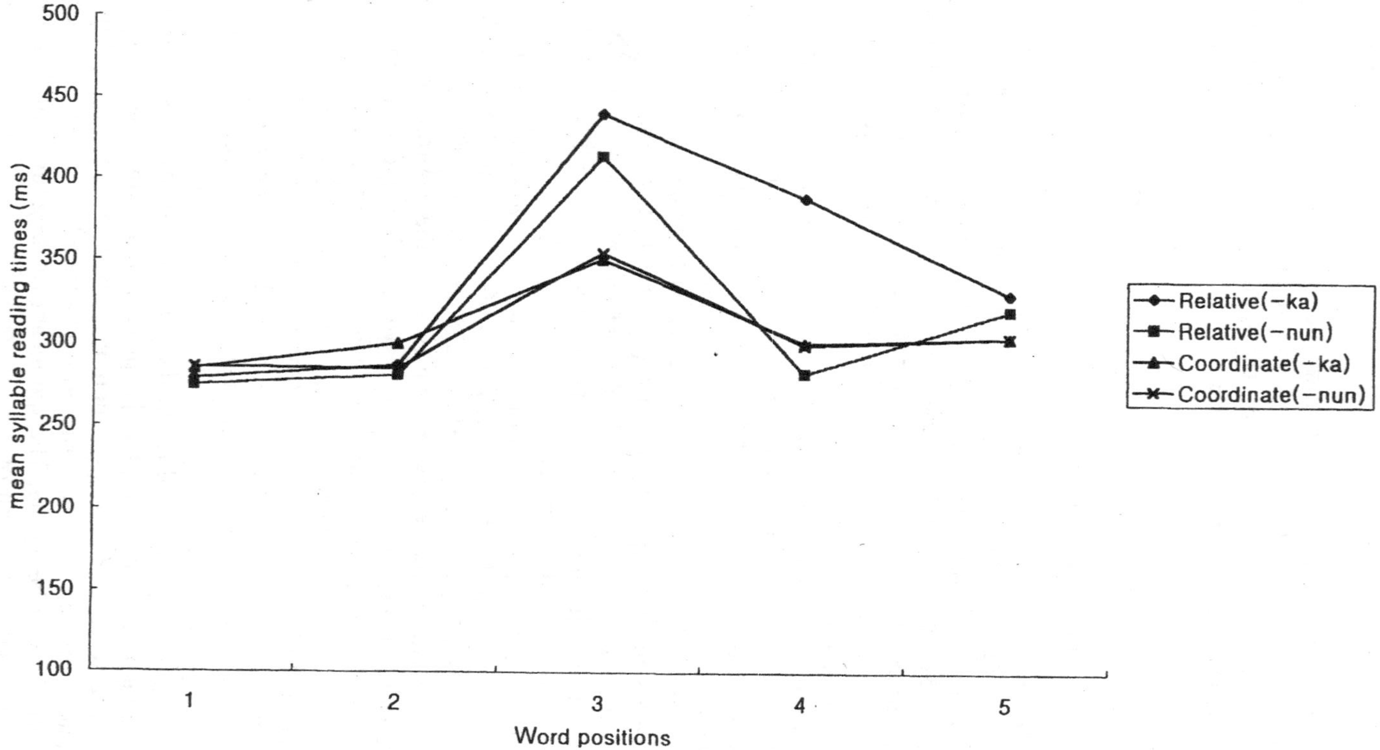

FIG. 1. Mean syllable reading times of Experiment 1.

coordinate structures (flag 1 = 5 in [5] and flag 1 = 4 in [6]) than those in the relative structures (flag 1 = 4 in [3] and flag 1 = 3 in [4]).

We predicted that the confidence ratings of each analysis (flagging) at the third word position were different in the two types of the relative structure. As we discussed in our Introduction, we predicted that the confidence ratings of two syntactic analyses in the relative *-ka* sentences will be 4 and 2 respectively (flag 1 = 4, flag 2 = 2). However, those ratings in the relative *-nun* sentences will be 3 and 2 respectively (flag 1 = 3, flag 2 = 2). So, do these different confidence ratings of each analysis produce any difference in processing loads? The third word in the relative *-ka* condition showed longer reading times than the word in the relative *-nun* condition (respectively, 439 ms vs. 413 ms). However, planned comparison between the two conditions was marginally significant only in F_1 [$F_1(1,56) = 3.570$, $MSe = 5654.198$, $P = .061$, $F_2(1,24) = 3.038$, $MSe = 3100.536$, $P = .091$].

At the fourth word position, there was a significant difference between the two types of structures [$F_1(1,56) = 25.315$, $MSe = 200941.703$, $P < .001$, $F_2(1,24) = 52.645$, $MSe = 45092.625$, $P < .001$]. The relative structures showed longer reading times than the coordinate structures (respectively, 334 ms vs. 299 ms). There was a marginally significant difference between the two types of grammatical markers [$F_1(1,56) = 3.533$, $MSe = 72205.492$, $P = .062$, $F_2(1,24) = 4.098$, $MSe = 29048.635$, $P = .052$]. The *-ka* condition showed longer reading times than the *-nun* condition (respectively, 343 ms vs. 290 ms). However, an interaction effect was not significant [$F_1(1,56) = 3.229$, MSe = 67404.297, $P = .074$, $F_2(1,24) = 2.790$, MSe = 36412.316, $P = .104$].

The fourth word in the relative structures is in a position of disambiguation. The analysis performed until the third word, i.e., the analysis that grouped three words as a single clause (flag 1, the co-argument analysis), must be reparsed. So, we can analyse the reparsing difficulties by examining the reading times of the fourth word. At the fourth word position, the relative *-ka* condition showed the longest reading times compared to the other three conditions. A planned comparison between the relative *-ka* and the relative *-nun* (respectively, 387 ms *vs.* 281 ms) was significant [$F_1(1,56) = 5.203$, $MSe = 90715.438$, $P = .025$, $F_2(1,24) = 6.406$, $MSe = 34387.473$, $P = .017$]. The results were consistent with the predictions of the RFSP model. That is, it showed that reanalysis was easy in the topic marker *-nun* condition compared to the nominative marker *-ka* condition, because the first pass analysis (flag 1, the co-argument analysis) has a low rating value in the relative *-nun* condition. At the fifth word position, only the main effect of the structures was significant [$F_1(1,56) = 5.203$, $MSe = 90715.438$, $P = .025$, $F_2(1,24) = 6.406$, $MSe = 34387.473$, $P = .017$]. The relative structure showed longer reading times than the coordinate structure (respectively, 323 ms vs. 302 ms).

The findings in the present experiment clearly showed important points about Korean sentence processing. First, they confirmed that Korean particles attached to NPs are an important source for generating a hypothesis of a syntactic structure before predicates. The simple change of a particle (*-ka* into *-nun*) in a relative clause sentence produced different patterns of reading times or local processing loads. Secondly, the findings showed that the RFSP model could explain most of the results of the experiment nicely. That is, the results showed that the RFSP model and the simple ranking scheme we used are enough to predict word-by-word parsing loads. Especially, the results nicely showed that the RFSP model could explain reparsing difficulties at the disambiguating position in Korean relative clause sentences. The results of Experiment 1 also showed that the confidence ratings of each alternative analysis might be an important factor that should be considered in predicting local parsing and reparsing difficulties. Based on these considerations, Experiment 2 extended the first experiment by using different types of relative structure.

EXPERIMENT 2

In Korean, eight different types of relative clause structure are possible. Thus these are good stimuli to examine local processing strategies (Clancy, Lee, & Zoh, 1986) or processing loads (Kim, 1995) in sentence comprehension processes. Therefore, in order to get further evidence for the effects of the case marking information in Korean sentences, and to verify the predictions of the RFSP model, in Experiment 2, we used two different types of relative structure as follows:

[9] Wunchensoo-ka chunksoboo-ka sealduk-han gunchukka-lul bipanhanda.
Driver-Nom janitor-Nom persuade-rel architect-Acc criticised.
(The driver criticised the architect whom the janitor persuaded.)

[10] Wunchensoo-nun chunksoboo-ka sealduk-han gunchukka-lul bipanhanda.
Driver-Topic janitor-Nom persuade-rel architect-Acc criticised.
(The driver criticised the architect whom the janitor persuaded.)

[11] Wunchensoo-lul chunksoboo-ka sealduk-han gunchukka-ka bipanhanda.
Driver-Acc janitor-Nom persuade-rel architect-Nom criticised.
(The architect whom the janitor persuaded criticised the driver.)

[12] Wunchensoo-lul chunksoboo-ka sealduk-han gunchukka-nun bipanhanda.
Driver-Acc janitor-Nom persuade-rel architect-Topic criticised.
(The architect whom the janitor persuaded criticised the driver.)

These four examples are all centre-embedded relative clause structures. The word order of the main clause in [9] and [10] is subject-object-verb (SOV) which is dominant in Korean, but the word order of the main clause in [11] and [12] is object-subject-verb (OSV). The only difference between [9] and [10] is, as in Experiment 1, the case marking of the first NP, i.e., subjective marking *-ka* in [9] and topic marking *-nun* in [10]. The only difference between [11] and [12] is also the case marking of the third NP, i.e., subjective marking in [11] and topic marking in [12]. The structures of [9] and [10] are exactly the same as the structures of [3] and [4] that were used in Experiment 1, except for the case marking on the second NP. That is, we changed the objective case marking (*-lul*) into the nominative case marking (*-ka*) in the second NPs. Although they have the same surface form, their syntactic analyses will not be the same.

Considering the RFSP model, we can generate predictions about word-by-word parsing procedures as we did in the Introduction section of Experiment 1. The two NPs in [9], at which the first *-ka* and the second *-ka* case markers are attached, are ambiguous. They can be grouped as co-arguments of a clause, i.e., flag 1 (the co-argument analysis) or the second noun can be analysed as the start of a new clause, i.e., flag 2 (the separate clause analysis). The first analysis agrees with the minimal attachment principle (Frazier, 1978). This kind of double subject case marking sentence is not an infrequently used expression style in Korean. But it is grammatical only if it is followed by adjective predicates (e.g., '*chota* (like)' or '*mipta* (hate)') or psych-verbs (e.g., '*kekcensulepta* (is worried about)') (Suh, 1994). So, the subjective case marker *-ka* that was attached at the second NP can act as a cue that the second NP would be the start of a new clause. Therefore, the confidence rating difference between the two syntactic analyses will be relatively small (flag 1 = 4, flag 2 = 2) compared to the corresponding structure (3) used in Experiment 1. The two NPs in (10), at which the first *-nun* and the second *-ka* case markers are attached, are ambiguous too. Like the two NPs in (9), they can be grouped as co-arguments of a clause (flag 1) or the second noun can be analysed as a start of a new clause (flag 2). So, these two analyses may have the same confidence rating values as the example sentence in [9]. However, there is another cue in [10]. As we mentioned in the Introduction section of Experiment 1, the topic marker *-nun* has a syntactic constraint or frequency information that a noun that has topic marker *-nun* may be the subject of the main clause. Therefore, the confidence rating of the second analysis, i.e., flag 2 (the separate clause analysis) in [10] will be stronger and the difference between the two syntactic analyses will be smaller (flag 1 = 4, flag 2 = 3) compared to the sentence in [9].[4]

Another thing we must consider is an ambiguity of grammatical (or thematic) role assignments in [9] and [10]. If two NPs are grouped as co-arguments of a clause (flag 1), two ways of role assignments are possible. The first possibility is that the subject (agent) role can be assigned to the first NP *-ka* (or *-nun*) and the object (patient) role can be assigned to the second NP *-ka* (flag 1-1). Another possibility is that the object (patient) role can be assigned to the first NP *-ka* (or *-nun*) and the subject (agent) role can be assigned to the second NP *-ka* reversibly (flag 1-2). So, which one will have a higher confidence rating? We do not have any clear answer to this question. The only plausible guess is that the first possibility of the role assignment (flag 1-1), which is consistent with canonical word order (i.e., SOV), might have a high confidence rating (i.e., flag 1-1 = 4, flag 1-2 = 3).

In summary, the two NPs in [9] and [10] are triply ambiguous; that is, three possible syntactic analyses (flag 1-1, flag 1-2, and flag 2) are possible. We can observe consequences of the ambiguity by examining the third word.

The two NPs in [11] and [12] are ambiguous too, and are the same as the two NPs of the sentences in [3] and [5] used in Experiment 1, except that they have non-canonical OSV word order. They can be grouped as co-arguments of a clause (flag 1, the co-argument analysis) or the second noun can be analysed as the start of a new clause (flag 2, the separate clause analysis). The confidence ratings of each analysis will be same as the corresponding structures of Experiment 1 (flag 1 = 5, flag 2 = 1). In all conditions, only the flag 1 (more specifically, flag 1-1) analysis will be continued in subsequent processing. Although different confidence rating values for each analysis are assigned to four conditions, the RFSP model predicts that there will be no difference among four conditions.

The third word in [9] is in a disambiguating position. The three words can not be grouped as a clause; that is, double subjective case markers and

---

[4] We assumed that when two consecutive nominative NPs are encountered they are preferentially analysed as co-arguments of one clause. However, as an anonymous reviewer pointed out, readers may prefer the analysis that two nominative NPs will trigger two different clauses. In addition, when one topicalised NP and a following nominative NP are provided, readers may also prefer the analysis that two NPs will trigger two different clauses. The clause initiated by the first NP will be the main clause and the clause by the second NP will turn out to be a relative or complement clause. If two clauses are postulated before a relative verb, it can be predicted that the reading times in the topicalised NP condition [9] will not be different from those in the nominative NP condition [10] at the relative head. As we mentioned in the result section, there was a significant difference between the two conditions only in F1. We need further experimentation to verify this possibility.

a given transitive verb (e.g., *sealduk-han*) can not be constructed into a single clause (i.e., flag 1-1 and flag 1-2 analyses are excluded). As we mentioned before, the sequence is grammatical only if adjective verb or psych-verb follows it. So, those word strings must be reanalysed, i.e., flag 2 (the separate clause analysis) must be adopted. The reparsing may be relatively easy, because revision difficulty is a function of the relative values of alternative analyses and the confidence rating of the alternative syntactic analysis is high relative to the first choice (i.e., flag 1-1 = 4, flag 2 = 2).

However, the third word in [10] is not in a disambiguating position. In spite of the appearance of the third word (i.e., transitive verbs), the three words still can be analysed as a single clause (i.e., continuation of flag 1-2). That is, the topic marked NP can be analysed as an argument (i.e., object or patient) of the verb, and the second nominative marked NP can be analysed as another argument (i.e., subject or agent) of the verb. So, the sequence of 'NP-topic NP-nom Verb-rel' can be constructed as a single clause, perhaps as part of a relative or complement clause. Alternatively, the second and the third words can be grouped as an embedded clause (i.e., continuation of flag 2, the separate clause analysis). The ratings of each flag will be the same as those at the second word (i.e., flag 1-2 = 3, flag 2 = 2). Therefore, based on the RFSP model and the results that we get from the Experiment 1, we can predict longer reading times in [9] than those in [10], because reparsing must be performed in [9] (i.e., 9 > 10). Ambiguities at the third word in [11] and [12] still continue; thus the RFSP model predicts no difference between them.

The fourth word in [10] is in a position of disambiguation. That is, the analysis performed until the third word, i.e., the analysis that grouped three words as a single clause (flag 1-2, co-argument analysis) must be reparsed. The second and third words must be constructed as an embedded relative clause with the fourth word, and the first word must be a subject of the fourth word. According to the RFSP model, we can expect a difference between the two SOV relative clause sentences. That is, if we compare the reading times of the fourth word between the [9] and the [10], the former will be shorter than the latter because reparsing has been already performed in the former condition (i.e., 10 > 9). The fourth word in [11] and [12] is in a position of disambiguation and the same reanalysis must be performed both conditions. So, the RFSP model does not make any expectation of reading time differences between the fourth word in [11] and in [12].

In summary, the RFSP model predicts different patterns of local processing loads among four types of the sentences, especially from the third word position to the fourth position. Experiment 2 was designed to test these predictions, using a word-by-word reading paradigm.

Methods

Subjects. Thirty-six undergraduate students of Ajou University participated in the experiment, all of whom were native speakers of Korean and were naive about the purpose of the experiment.

Materials. Twenty-eight test sentences and forty-two fillers were constructed for the experiment. There were four versions of each test sentence. Two of them were centre-embedded relative clause structures whose word order of the main clause was subject-object-verb (SOV). Two of the test sentences were also centre-embedded relative clause structures, in which the word order of the main clause, however, was OSV. One version of the test sentences contained the subjective case marker *-ka* in the initial noun phrase and one version of the test sentences contained the topic marker *-nun* in the third noun phrase. The following is an example of one complete set of test sentences:

SOV -ka sentence

Wunchensoo-ka	chunksoboo-ka	sealduk-han	gunchukka-lul	bipanhanda.
Driver-Nom	janitor-Nom	persuade-rel	architect-Acc	criticised.

(The driver criticised the architect whom the janitor persuaded.)

SOV -nun sentence

Wunchensoo-nun	chunksoboo-ka	sealduk-han	gunchukka-lul	bipanhanda.
Driver-Topic	janitor-Nom	persuade-rel	achitect-Acc	criticised.

(The driver criticised the architect whom the janitor persuaded.)

OSV -ka sentence

Wunchensoo-lul	chunksoboo-ka	sealduk-han	gunchukka-ka	bipanhanda.
Driver-Acc	janitor-Nom	persuade-rel	architect-Nom	criticised.

(The architect whom the janitor persuaded criticised the driver.)

OSV -nun sentence

Wunchensoo-lul	chunksoboo-ka	sealduk-han	gunchukka-nun	bipanhanda.
Driver-Acc	janitor-Nom	persuade-rel	architect-Topic	criticised.

(The architect whom the janitor persuaded criticised the driver.)

All nouns in the test sentences were occupation names (e.g., driver and lawyer) and all verbs in the test sentences are transitive. All words were randomly assigned to each sentence to remove any semantic relatedness. A counterbalanced design yielded four lists of stimuli, such that no more than a single version of any particular test sentence was presented in each list. Each of the four lists contained 28 test sentences (with 7 tokens of each of the 4 versions). These sentences were interspersed among 42 filler sentences. The fillers included a variety of structures. Six subjects were randomly assigned to one of the four lists. The presentation orders of 70 sentences were randomised to each subject.

Procedure. The procedure was the same as Experiment 1.

Results and Discussion

All subjects showed 76% accuracy to the question sentences, which is lower than the accuracy in Experiment 1. However, two-way ANOVAs on the accuracy data revealed no significant differences across the four conditions. Figure 2 depicts the mean syllable reading times at each word position. An interesting result of Experiment 2 was the overall increase in reading times. As we know from Figures 1 and 2, the mean syllable reading times at each word position of Experiment 2 showed a rise of 30 to 100% over those of Experiment 1.[5]

Based on the suggestions of Pollatsek & Well (1995), three-way ANOVAs (*-ka/-nun*, SOV/OSV, and four counterbalancing conditions) were performed separately at each word position like Experiment 1. These ANOVAs examined the two types of structures (SOV/OSV) and the two types of grammatical markers (*-ka/-nun*) as two major factors. Planned comparisons in each type of structure (e.g., SOV *-ka vs.* SOV *-nun*) were also performed to verify the predictions we made. The ANOVAs revealed no significant differences across the four conditions at the first word positions. However, at the second word position, there was a significant difference between the SOV structure and the OSV structure [$F_1(1,32) = 8.797$, $MSe = 214591.453$, $P = .005$, $F_2(1,24) = 12.424$, $MSe = 120621.648$, $P = .002$]. The SOV structures, which are canonical in Korean, showed shorter reading times than the OSV structures (487 ms *vs.* 545 ms). This result could be easily explained by the well-known word order effects (Clark & Clark, 1977). The results also showed that the mean syllable reading times of the *-nun* condition were smaller than the *-ka* condition (respectively, 475 ms and 498 ms). However, the difference (23 ms) was not statistically significant.

[5]The subjects in Experiment 1 might be more skilled readers relative to those in Experiment 2 in terms of both reading speed and accuracy on the comprehension questions. However, the subjects in both experiments were recruited from the same subject pool, and two experiments were performed consecutively. So, we believe that there was no difference in subject characteristics between the two experiments. The overall increase in reading times might be caused by difficulties of the test sentences. In Experiment 2, all of the test sentences were centre-embedded relative clause structures, and half of them were scrambled structures. The difficulties of the test sentences might make the subjects in Experiment 2 read more carefully.

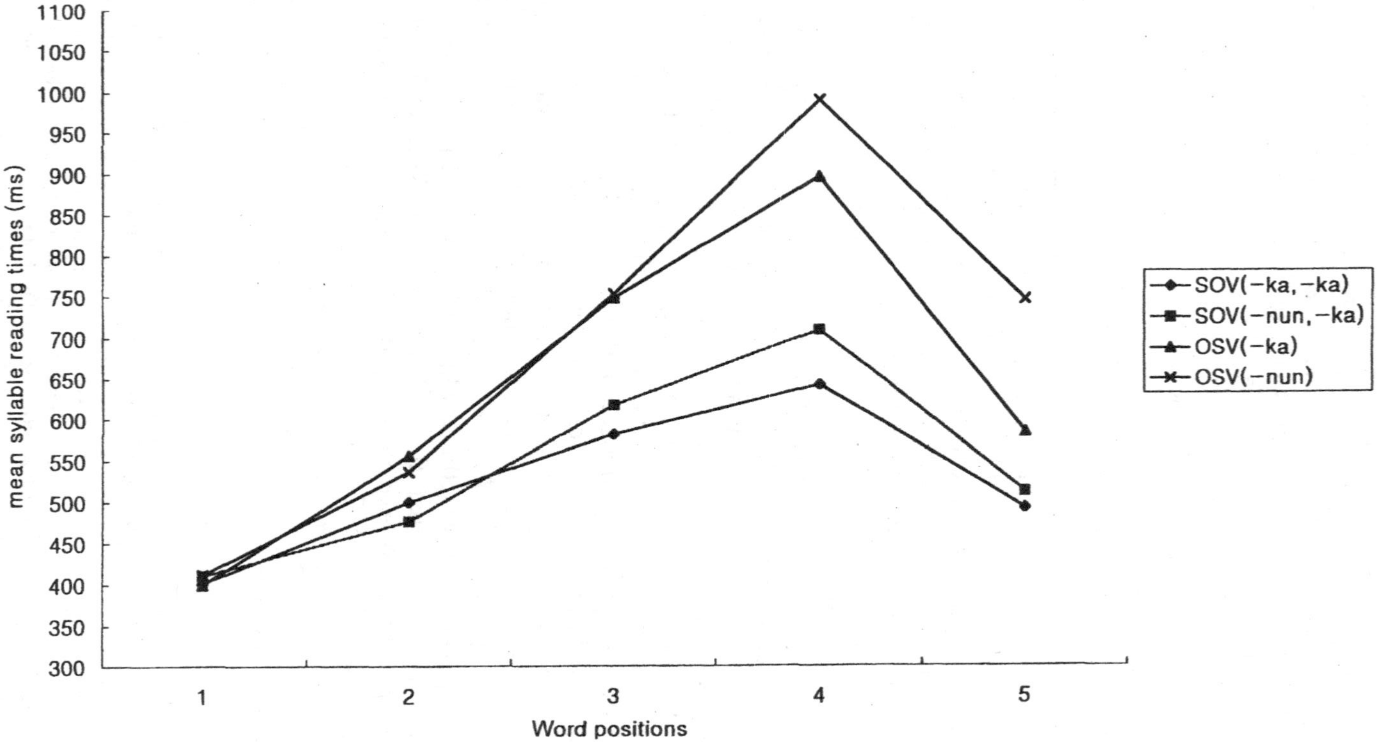

FIG. 2. Mean syllable reading times of Experiment 2.

At the third word position, there was also a significant difference between the two types of structures [$F_1(1,32) = 24.556$, $MSe = 298703.906$, $P < .001$, $F_2(1,24) = 32.240$, $MSe = 176950.328$, $P < .001$]. The SOV structures showed shorter reading times than the OSV structures (597 ms *vs.* 746 ms). The third word, especially in SOV structures, is the position in which we can verify the predictions of the RFSP model. As we mentioned, the RFSP model predicted that the third word reading times in [9] (i.e., SOV *-ka* sentences) would be longer than those in [10] (i.e., the SOV *-nun* sentences), because the third word in the former is in the position of disambiguation and reparsing must be done at that position. The results did not correspond to the prediction of the RFSP model. That is, contrary to the prediction, the third word reading times of the SOV *-ka* sentences were shorter than those of the SOV *-nun* sentences (respectively, 579 ms vs. 615 ms). However, planned comparison between two conditions was not significant [$F_1(1,32) = 1.608$, $MSe = 133811.375$, $P = .212$, $F_2(1,24) = 1.160$, $MSe = 144254.797$, $P = .292$].

At the fourth word position, the OSV *-nun* condition showed the longest reading times compared to the other three conditions. The RFSP model predicted that the SOV *-ka* condition was easier than the SOV *-nun* condition. The results seemed to confirm the RFSP model. However, a planned comparison test between the SOV *-ka* and SOV *-nun* (respectively, 638 ms vs. 705 ms) was significant only in F_1 [$F_1(1,32) = 6.002$, $MSe = 215009.672$, $P = .019$, $F_2(1,24) = 2.776$, $MSe = 361528.844$, $P = .105$].

The RFSP model predicted no difference between the OSV *-nun* condition and OSV *-ka* condition at the fourth word. A planned comparison test between these conditions (OSV *-ka*: 891 ms and OSV *-nun*: 985 ms) was marginally significant only in F_1 [$F_1(1,32) = 3.315$, $MSe = 765064.875$, $P = .075$, $F_2(1,24) = 2.564$, $MSe = 769355.063$, $P = .119$]. At the final verb, the interaction effect was significant [$F_1(1,32) = 7.060$, $\text{MSe} = 409143.531$, $P = .012$, $F_2(1,24) = 9.768$, $MSe = 229997.453$, $P = .005$]. That is, the difference between the OSV *-ka* and the OSV *-nun* (respectively, 580 ms *vs.* 741 ms) was significant [$F_1(1,32) = 6.959$, $MSe = 1081462.375$, $P = .012$, $F_2(1,24) = 13.235$, $MSe = 442264.781$, $P = .002$], but the difference between the two SOV conditions was not significant. The RFSP model did not expect the significant difference at the final verb between the two OSV conditions.

We do not have any clear explanations for the significant difference between the OSV *-ka* condition and the OSV *-nun* condition right now. It presumably reflected that the topic marker *-nun* at the fourth NP made the final wrap-up processing difficult. Sheldon (1974) proposed that an important factor in determining the psycholinguistic complexity of sentences with relative clause is "parallel function". According to the parallel function hypothesis, readers find it easier to understand complex sentences in which the relativised NP has the same grammatical function in both main and embedded clause. The fourth word ('*gunchukka*') in [9] and [10] has the parallel function, but the fourth word in [11] and [12] does not have the same grammatical function. It must be an object in the embedded relative clause, but it must be a subject in the main clause. So, we can explain the significant difference between the SOV and the OSV at the fourth NP and at the final verb by the parallel function hypothesis. However, how to explain the longer reading times at the fourth word (and at the final verb) in the OSV *-nun* condition compared the OSV *-ka* condition? It might be caused by the grammatical category ambiguity of the topic marker *-nun*. The fourth word in [11] has the subject marker *-ka* that signals grammatical function of the NP in the main clause. However, the fourth word in [12] has the topic marker that can be used as both a subject and an object. So, it presumably made the main clause processing difficult.

GENERAL DISCUSSION

The purpose of the current study was, first, to examine whether the parser's on-line processes are affected by manipulations of the case markings in Korean. That is, we tried to answer the question that the mere change of a particle in a sentence, without changing the other elements of a sentence, could produce different parsing or reparsing procedures, which are reflected in different patterns of reading times. This question is important theoretically and experimentally, because there must be a way to reduce the massive local ambiguity that is the characteristic of the Korean language. As many psycholinguists presume, the particle information attached to NPs should be an important information source for reducing syntactic ambiguity and for generating possible hypotheses of a syntactic structure before predicates.

The results from the two experiments confirmed our expectation. The mere change of the particle (i.e., *-ka* into *-nun*) in the relative clause sentences drastically modified the patterns of the word-by-word reading times in Experiments 1 and 2. Although the change of the particle in the coordinate structure did not alter the reading time patterns in Experiment 1, and some differences at the local reading times among conditions in Experiment 2 failed to reach statistical significance, overall reading time patterns were consistent with our expectation. Our findings were consistent with the results of Yamashita (1997) that showed the Japanese parser was sensitive to the variety of case-marked arguments.

Generally, these results showed that local grammatical cues, such as particles that attached to NPs and inflections of verbs, are rich sources of information for syntactic analysis in Korean (Suh, 1994). The results are not compatible with lexically based theories (Pritchett, 1992) that argue, in head-final languages such as Korean, that the attachment of each phrase is delayed until a head such as a verb is available. On the other hand, the results seem to be more compatible with the garden-path theory (Frazier, 1978; Frazier & Rayner, 1982) that assumes incoming material is immediately attached to a phrase in the current phrase marker regardless of whether the head of that phrase has been received.

One interesting finding that we should mention was the direction of the particle effects. That is, the particle *-nun* reduced the word-by-word reading times in the relative clause sentences used in Experiment 1, especially at the fourth word position. However, it increased the reading times in the relative clause sentences used in Experiment 2, especially at the fourth word position. It means that grammatical or semantic information included in the local cues would interact with structural characteristics of the whole sentence. Sometimes they can facilitate the syntactic parsing processes, but sometimes they can make parsing and reparsing processes difficult. Therefore, it carries a moral. As we mentioned, there are 47 different types of particles in Korean. We should not only examine grammatical or thematic/semantic functions of these particles themselves, but also consider their parsing functions in the context of a given sentence structure.

The second purpose of this study was to evaluate the usefulness of the RFSP model in predicting Korean ambiguity resolution processes. Broadly speaking, most of the results of Experiment 1 and 2 coincided with the predictions of the model. The RFSP model and the simple ranking schemes that we used were enough to predict many of the local parsing and reparsing difficulties in the Korean sentences used in Experiment 1, but were not wholly successful in predicting the results of Experiment 2. Before accepting the RFSP model as a guide in predicting word-by-word reading times in Korean sentence comprehension, we have to hold an assumption that Inoue and Fodor (1995) suggested in suspension.

One assumption that was not consistent with our experimental results is that the confidence ratings of each alternative analysis themselves do not matter in parsing. In the RFSP model, all candidate syntactic analyses are logged in (i.e., flagged), though only the first one to arrive is continued. In order to maintain the characteristics of a serial parser, Inoue and Fodor (1995) argued that the confidence ratings themselves do not matter in most situations. However, we found the reading time increases at the third word position, at which two flags must be posted, of the relative clause sentences compared to the same location, at which the same number of two flags must be needed, of the coordinate sentences in Experiment 1. If Korean parser follows the same analysis in both conditions, there must be no reading time difference between the two conditions. So, what made the difference? We do not have any clear explanation for the difference. We could guess that the relative strength (i.e., the confidence rating) of the first pass parsing might be a factor in producing local processing loads.

The significant difference of reading times between the *-nun* condition and the *-ka* condition at the fourth word position (Experiment 1) means that reanalysis was easy in the former condition compared to the latter condition. Although we tried to explain the result based on the RFSP model and the ranking schemes, it might also be explained by the various theories of revision that have been suggested recently (Ferreira & Henderson, 1998; Fodor & Inoue, 1998; Frazier & Clifton, 1998; Hirose & Inoue, 1998; Sturt & Crocker, 1996).

Especially, the work of Hirose and Inoue (1998) may be relevant for our data. Hirose and Inoue (1998) examined reanalysis processes of Japanese relative clause ambiguities that are very similar to the Korean sentences we used. They compared the 'subject reanalysis structure' to the 'subject and object reanalysis structure' by using a word-by-word reading task. They found that thematic ambiguity of the head noun increased reading times, and argued that cost of the reanalysis was determined by the ambiguity of the head noun. However, their explanation may not be applied to the results of Experiment 1, because the head nouns of the *-ka* and *-nun* conditions have same thematic ambiguities, and both conditions require only the subject reanalysis. The notions of the 'thematic processing domains (TPDs)' (Ferreira & Henderson, 1998) and 'lowering operations' (Sturt & Crocker, 1996) may not be applied to the reanalysis ease of the *-nun* condition too, because the two conditions seem to have identical thematic domains, and to require same reanalysis operations.

Fodor and Inoue (1998) summarised claims of recent reanalysis theories that, "revision is easy only if it does not alter the meaning assigned the sentence; if it does not require erasure of domination statements; if it involves only local restructuring" (p. 138). Based on these hypotheses, we may explain why the coordinate structures that we used in Experiment 1 showed fast reading times, i.e., ease of reanalysis. The Diagnosis model (Fodor & Inoue, 1994; 1998) can provide a possible explanation for the reanalysis ease of the *-nun* condition. That is, it is easy to diagnosis that topic marked NP is not part of a relative clause, because it does not normally occur in relative clauses. Suh (1994) discussed two possible structuring processes in the following relative structure that is the same type of structure as we used in Experiment 1.

[13]	John-i	[Bill-ul	ttayli-n]	salam-ul	mannassta.
	-Nom	-Acc	hit-Rel	man-Acc	met.

(John met the man who hit Bill.)

Regarding the parser's structural commitment at the point of receiving the relativised verb ('*ttayli-n*') in [13], Suh (1994) suggested two hypotheses. One is a momentary delay hypothesis. Since the relativised verb contains suffix *-n* that signals (at least) one degree of embedding, and the grammatical role of the clause containing the relativised verb is determined by the following input item, the parser delays structure building among three words until the next word is seen. In other words, the parser may construct a clause node dominating the first nominative marked NP ('John') and another node for the relative clause. The other hypothesis is an immediate structuring hypothesis. It predicts that the parser computes a clause structure from the three words ('John-i Bill-ul ttayli-n') as soon as suffix *-n* is encountered. Suh (1994) argued, "Given that minimal structure building is the basic strategy to deal with structural ambiguity, why does not the parser computer the minimal structure upon receiving the relativised verb" (p. 160). That is, he argued that the latter hypothesis must be true in [13].

From this discussion, we could guess a reason for the ease of analysis in *-nun* condition. Although the nominative case marker *-ka* favours the latter hypothesis, the topic marker *-nun* favours the former hypothesis. That is, we can consider the possibility that the topic maker *-nun* may momentarily delay immediate structuring of a string. As previously stated, the first topic marked NP is most likely to appear as a subject in the main clause. The topic marker *-nun* can be used instead of a subject case marker or an object case marker. It is also used as a delimiter that does not specify the grammatical role of the NPs it is attached to. So, given that Korean topic maker *-nun* has such information, why does not the Korean parser use the information? Does the Korean parser neglect such information? Does it just follow the minimal attachment principle in first-pass parsing without considering the information that the topic marker has? We do not have any answer to these questions. However, a possible guess may be that the Korean parser would consider such information seriously. If the parser uses the information immediately, the former, i.e., the momentary delay hypothesis may be a reasonable candidate although it will conflict with the principle of minimal attachment. The local delay of structuring would not produce any serious problems, and would not increase short-term storage loads, because it is usually disambiguated by the next words. So, by assuming the former as structuring process of the topic marked NP (and by assuming the latter as structuring process of the nominative case marked NP), we could explain the short reading times at the fourth word position in [4]. However, we need to do further experiments to verify this possibility.

Frazier and Clifton (1998) argued that revision cost can not be calculated in purely structural terms, and suggested non-structural factors, such as the length of an ambiguous phrase, semantic effects, and the frequency of a verb's sub-categorisation frames might be important for predicting reparsing difficulties. In line with this argument, we may explain the reanalysis ease of the *-nun* condition by phonological coding associated with the topic maker, rather than the structural characteristics. Our intuition is that the topic marked NPs are usually stressed, and there is some pause after the topic marked NPs in normal conversation. That is, the topic marked NPs and the subject case marked NPs may have different prosodic structures that have been computed via phonological coding. As Bader (1998) suggested, the prosodic structure of the topic marker might be used in reanalysis procedures.

We applied the RFSP model to Korean sentence processing. However, some results, such as the word order effect and the long reading times at the final verb of the OSV *-nun* condition in Experiment 2, showed that the RFSP model is not enough to predict local word-by-word reading times. We should consider those effects in the framework of the RFSP model to make more accurate predictions on local processing loads in further studies. One finding that we should mention is the word order effect found in Experiment 2. Our result is not consistent with the result of Yamashita (Experiment 1, 1997). She found no processing cost for scrambled word order in comparison with canonical word order in Japanese and suggested that this supports a non-configurational approach to Japanese syntax. The Korean results in Experiment 2 seem to contradict this finding. However, there is some difference between our Experiment 2 and her Experiment 1. A major difference is the type of sentence structure. She used the simple sentence structure, but, in Experiment 2, we used the centre-embedded relative clause sentences that are well known to take longer reading times (Ford, 1983; Holmes & O'Regan, 1981). The word order effect might not be detected in the simple sentence structure, because all parsing procedures in the simple structure might be performed too fast to be detected by the self-paced reading task.

In fact, there is an experimental result that failed to show the word order effect in Korean. Kim and Zoh (1981) compared the SOV simple sentence structure to the OSV simple sentence structure by measuring click-monitoring times at the end of the manipulated clause (i.e., at the end of verb stem of the SOV or OSV clause). They did not find any difference between the two conditions. That is, they failed to confirm the word order effect in Korean. However, several experiments that used the more complex relative clause sentences reliably showed the word order effect in Korean (Kim 1995). It may be very difficult to make a valid conclusion about the word order effect in free word order languages such as Korean and Japanese right now, because the word order effect can be affected by various factors such as sentence length, experimental tasks and measures, and types of sentence structure. Sometimes it shows up and sometimes it fails to show up. In order to pinpoint the conditions that the word order effect is observed, we need more sensitive on-line measures and more experiments on various types of sentence structures. It might be an interesting research topic for further studies.

REFERENCES

Bader, M. (1998). Prosodic influences on reading syntactically ambiguous sentences. In J.D. Fodor & F. Ferreira (Eds), *Reanalysis in sentence processing*, pp.1–46. Boston, MA: Kluwer Academic Publishers.

Carlson, G.N., & Tanenhaus, M.K. (1988). Thematic roles and language comprehension. In W. Wilkins (Ed.), *Syntax and semantics: Vol. 21. Thematic relations*, pp.263–300. San Diego, CA: Academic Press.

Clancy, P.M., Lee, H., & Zoh, M.-H. (1986). Processing strategies in the acquisition of relative clauses: Universal principles and language-specific realisations. *Cognition*, *24*, 225–262.

Clark, H.H., & Clark, E.V. (1977). *Psychology and language: An Introduction to psycholinguistics.* New York: Harcourt Brace Jovanovich.

Cuetos, F., Mitchell, D.C., & Corley, M.M.B. (1996). Parsing in different language. In M. Carreiras, J. Garcia-Albea, & N. Sabastian-Galles (Eds), *Language processing in Spanish*, pp.145–187. Hillsdale, NJ: Lawrence Erlbaum Associates Inc.

Ferreira, F. & Henderson, J.M. (1998). Syntactic reanalysis, thematic processing, and sentence comprehension. In J.D. Fodor & Ferreira (Eds), *Reanalysis in sentence processing*, pp.73–100. Boston, MA: Kluwer Academic Publishers.

Fodor, J.D., & Inoue, A. (1994). The diagnosis and cure of garden paths. *Journal of Psycholinguistic Research*, *23*, 407–434.

Fodor, J.D., & Inoue, A. (1998). Attach anyway. In J.D. Fodor & Ferreira (Eds), *Reanalysis in sentence processing*, pp.101–141. Boston, MA: Kluwer Academic Publishes.

Ford, M. (1983). A method for obtaining measures of local parsing complexity throughout sentences. *Journal of Verbal Learning and Verbal Behavior*, *13*, 203–218.

Frazier, L. (1978). *On comprehending sentences: Syntactic parsing strategies.* Unpublished doctoral dissertation, University of Connecticut.

Frazier, L., & Rayner, K. (1982). Making and correcting errors during sentence comprehension: Eye movements in the analysis of structurally ambiguous sentences. *Cognitve Psychology*, *43*, 178–210.

Frazier, L., & Clifton, C. (1998). Sentence reanalysis, and visibility. In J.D. Fodor & F. Ferreira (Eds), *Reanalysis in sentence processing*, pp.143–176. Boston, MA: Kluwer Academic Publishers.

Hirose, Y., & Inoue, A. (1998). Ambiguity of reanalysis in parsing complex sentences in Japanese. In D. Hillert (Ed.), *Syntax and semantics: Vol. 21. Sentence processing: A Crosslinguistic perspective*. New York: Academic Press.

Holmes, V.M., & O'Regan, J.K. (1981). Eye fixation patterns during the reading of relative clause sentences. *Journal of Verbal Learning and Verbal Behavior*, *20*, 417–430.

Hong, Y. (1985) A Quantitative analysis of KA/I and (N)UN as subject markers in spoken and written Korean. *Proceedings of the 1985 Harvard Workshop on Korean Linguistics*, 145–153.

Inoue, A., & Fodor, J. (1995). Information-paced parsing of Japanese. In R. Mazuka & N. Nagai (Eds), *Japanese sentence processing*, pp.9–63. Hillsdale, NJ: Lawrence Erlbaum Associates Inc.

Just, M.A., Carpenter, P.A., & Woolley, J.D. (1982). Paradigms and processes in reading comprehension. *Journal of Experimental Psychology: General, 111*, 228–238.

Kim, Y. (1995). Comprehension processes and structures of Korean relative clause sentences. *Korean Journal of Cognitive Science, 6*, 5–22 (in Korean).

Kim, Y., & Zoh, M.-H. (1981). Syntactic and semantic factors in the sentence processing for comprehension. *Language Research, 17*, 1–21 (in Korean).

Koh, S. (1997). The resolution of the dative NP ambiguity in Korean. *Journal of Psycholinguistic Research, 26*, 265–273.

Kuno, S. (1972). Functional sentence perspective. *Linguistic Inquiry, 3*, 269–320.

Kuno, S. (1973). *The structure of the Japanese language*. Cambridge, MA: MIT Press.

Lee, H.-B. (1979). Generative grammar of Korean (III). *Grammar Studies, 4*, 3–36 (in Korean).

MacDonald, M.C., Perlmutter, N.J., & Seidenberg, M.S. (1994). Lexical nature of syntactic ambiguity resolution. *Psychological Review, 101*, 676–703.

Pritchett, B.L. (1992). *Grammatical competence and parsing performance*. Chicago, IL: University of Chicago Press.

Pollatsek, A., & Well, A.D. (1995). On the use of counterbalanced designs in cognitive research: A suggestion for a better and more powerful analysis. *Journal of Experimental Psychology: Learning, Memory, and Cognition, 21*, 785–794.

Sheldon, A. (1974). The role of parallel function in the acquisition of relative clauses in English. *Journal of Verbal Learning and Verbal Behavior, 13*, 272–281.

Sturt, P., & Crocker, M. (1996). Monotonic syntactic processing: A cross-linguistic study of attachment and reanalysis. *Language and Cognitive Processes, 11*, 449–494.

Suh, S. (1994). *The syntax of Korean and its implications for parsing theory*. Unpublished doctoral dissertation, University of Maryland.

Uehara, K. (1997). Judgements of processing loads in Japanese: The effects of NP-ga sequences. *Journal of Psycholinguistic Research, 26*, 255–263.

Yamashita, H. (1997). The effects of word-order and case marking information on the processing of Japanese. *Journal of Psycholinguistic Research, 26*, 163–188.

Yang, I.-S. (1973). Semantics of delimiters. *Language Research, 9*, 84–121.

LANGUAGE AND COGNITIVE PROCESSES, 1999, *14* (5/6), 715–743

Comprehension of Referring Expressions in Chinese

Chin Lung Yang, Peter C. Gordon and Randall Hendrick
University of North Carolina at Chapel Hill

Jei Tun Wu
National Taiwan University

Studies of English have shown that reduced referential expressions (e.g. pronouns) contribute more to discourse coherence than do unreduced expressions (e.g. proper names). To test the generality of these findings, a series of reading-time studies was conducted to examine the processing of co-reference in Chinese discourse. The results obtained for Chinese were similar to those obtained previously for English. Furthermore, comparisons of the comprehension of overt pronouns and zero pronouns (a phologically-null form not present in English) showed that the two types of reduced referring expressions contribute equally to discourse coherence for the kinds of passages studied in the experiments. A formal model of the structure and processing of reference in discourse, developed to handle co-reference phenomena in English, is shown to provide an account of these experimental results on the reading of Chinese.

INTRODUCTION

It is generally believed that the use of referring expressions plays a fundamental role in well-formed discourse by providing critical links that integrate successive utterances to form a coherent discourse representation (Grosz, Joshi, & Weinstein, 1995; Halliday & Hassan, 1976; Kintsch & van Dijk, 1978) and that different forms of referring expressions have distinct functions in promoting discourse comprehension (Gordon, Grosz, & Gilliom, 1993). However, most of the research that supports these conclusions has been conducted in English, and there is no certainty that they can be generalised to other languages. The present research extends

Requests for reprints should be addressed to Peter C. Gordon, Department of Psychology, The University of North Carolina at Chapel Hill, CB# 3270, Davie Hall, Chapel Hill, N.C. 27599-3270.

The research reported here was supported by a grant from the National Science Foundation (SBR-98-07028). We would like to thank Tai Li Chou for advice on experiment design and helping to conduct the experiments.

this psycholinguistic investigation of referential expressions to the study of Chinese.

Reduced expressions (e.g. pronominal expressions such as *he* or *she*) appear to contribute more to discourse coherence than do full lexical expressions (e.g. proper names like *John* or definitive descriptions like *the table*). This is illustrated in the following passage.

(1) a. John went to the grocery store this morning.
    b. *John/He* lost his wallet along the way.

The second sentence (1.b) seems more natural when a pronoun (he) is used to refer to a prominent discourse entity (JOHN) than when a repeated name (John) is used for the same purpose.

The phenomenon illustrated intuitively in (1) above has been the object of substantial study in psycholinguistics. Demonstrations that discourse coherence is promoted more by co-reference with pronouns than by co-reference with repeated names has been found using a variety of experimental paradigms including: response times to related and unrelated probe words (Cloitre & Bever, 1988), production of coherent speech (Brennan, 1995), judgements of coherence or grammaticality (Gordon & Hendrick, 1997; Hudson, Tanenhaus & Dell, 1986), self-paced reading time (Gordon et al., 1993) and eye-tracking during reading (Kennison & Gordon, 1997). Under specific circumstances, sentences with repeated names are read more slowly than sentences with pronouns, an effect that has been called the repeated-name penalty (Gordon et al., 1993). Other research looking at recognition memory for probe words has been interpreted as indicating that co-reference is achieved more easily with repeated names (or repeated descriptions) than with pronouns (Gernsbacher, 1989; Greene, McKoon, & Ratcliff, 1992), but the methodology used has been criticised because it may tell more about the relation between the repeated name and the probe word than about the repeated name and its referent in the discourse (Gordon et al., 1993; Garrod, Freudenthal, & Boyle, 1994).

The effect of a pronoun on discourse comprehension has been explained in several ways that are broadly similar. Garrod and Sanford (1982, 1988) suggested that the use of a pronoun in a discourse indicated that its referent is in discourse focus whereas the use of a repeated name reintroduced its referent back into the discourse focus. Cloitre and Bever (1988) argued that different forms of referring expressions trigger different levels of representation, with pronouns directly activating semantic information while repeated nouns activate phonological information first. Gordon and Hendrick (1998), drawing on work in model-theoretic semantics (Kamp & Reyle, 1993) and computational linguistics (Grosz et al., 1983, 1995) have presented a model in which reduced expressions (such as pronouns) are interpreted as referring to entities already represented in a discourse universe while expressions (such as proper names) are interpreted as invoking more general knowledge.

However, since most of the evidence showing differences in the ease of interpreting co-reference with pronouns and names comes from studies of English, the generality across languages of the explanations discussed above is unclear. The current paper addresses this issue by examining the comprehension of co-reference in Chinese, a very different language system from English.

Chinese Anaphora

Chinese has three kinds of anaphoric expressions: zero pronouns, overt pronouns, and referring expressions. The zero pronoun is a non-overt, reduced expression that co-refers with an expression that appears earlier in a discourse (Chen, 1984; Huang, 1984; Li, 1985; Li & Thompson, 1981, 1984; Tai, 1978; Xu, 1986). It is a characteristic of anaphoric reference that distinguishes Chinese and many other East Asian languages from some European languages such as English or French. A sample zero pronoun discourse, taken from Li and Thompson (1981, p.669), is shown below.

(2) a. Speaker A:

他	看見	你	沒有？
ta	kanjian	ni	meiyou?
3sg	see	you	not

"(Did) he see you?"

b. Speaker B:

	看見		了。
____	kanjian	______	le
(ta)	see	(wo)	ASPECT

"he saw me."

A Chinese addressee has no difficulty in using discourse context to determine the intended referents in utterance 2.b, even though the expressions that indicate those referents ("*ta*" and "*wo*") have been omitted. However, if context is removed by eliminating utterance 3.a, then the intended referents in 3.b cannot be determined. Accordingly, it is commonly assumed that Chinese-speakers and listeners have to rely upon contextual and pragmatic knowledge in order to interpret zero pronouns rather than upon syntactic and semantic factors (Chen, 1984; Li & Thompson, 1981, 1984). Some European languages, like Italian or Spanish, contain zero pronouns. But these languages have morphosyntactic systems that redundantly encode pronominal information in the verbal agreement system. Chinese has an impoverished morphosyntactic system that lacks verb agreement. Elliptical expressions in English might be considered zero pronouns but these are under far greater syntactic control than are zero pronouns in Chinese.[1] The phenomenon of zero pronouns in Chinese raises two theoretical issues that merit examination.

First, do the two kinds of reduced expressions in Chinese (overt and zero pronouns) have different effects on discourse coherence? Generally speaking, linguists studying Chinese believe that zero pronouns in pro-drop languages perform specific roles with respect to meaning that are different from the roles of overt pronouns (Chen, 1984; Givon, 1983, 1992; Huang, 1991; Li, 1985; Li & Thompson, 1981, 1984; Tao, 1996). A traditional view attributes the choice of the form of a referring expression to the degree of familiarity or accessibility of its referent; the more accessible a referent, the more likely speakers are to choose a reduced expression. Building on this view, it has been argued that zero pronouns require referents with a higher degree of accessibility than do overt pronouns (Ariel, 1990, 1991; Halmari, 1996; Givon, 1983). Ariel (1990, 1991) proposed that a zero pronoun is a referential expression that signals the retrieval of the antecedent with highest accessibility from a mental representation of a discourse. Further, Givon (1981, 1983) proposed a cross-linguistic ranking of the impact of topic continuity on the form of referring expressions. According to this ranking, speakers use zero pronouns when the referent is the most accessible topic in discourse context, whereas they tend to use overt pronouns when the referent becomes less accessible.

The second theoretical issue posed by zero pronouns is whether their interpretation depends exclusively on pragmatic factors or whether syntactic factors also help to determine the referent of a zero pronoun. It has been generally believed that the interpretation of omitted referential expressions in a Chinese zero-pronoun discourse heavily depends upon the integrated semantics of a discourse (Chen, 1984; Li, 1985; Li & Thompson, 1981, 1984). However, views differ with regard to the role that syntactic factors play in deciphering omitted referential expressions in a zero-pronoun discourse. Li and Thompson (1981, 1984) contended that the interpretation of omitted referential expressions relies upon context and

[1] The null subjects in English infinitives such as "John wanted to go to school" appear to have different empirical properties than Chinese zero pronouns. For example, they typically have an antecedent within their sentence or when one is not present they are given a generic interpretation (cf. Chomsky, 1986). Gerundives show similar restrictions. The Chinese zero pronoun do not show these characteristics.

pragmatic information only. In contrast, Chen (1984) and Li (1985) both asserted that syntactic structure partially determines the choice between overt pronoun and zero pronoun, but primarily for the special syntactic constructions that involve "coverb" and "pivotal" sentences. Because relatively little psycholinguistic research has been done on anaphoric reference in Chinese discourse, there is no immediate answer to this question with regard to language comprehension. However, the context-and-pragmatics-only approach advocated by Li and Thompson (1984) is not consistent with characterisations of anaphoric reference in other languages, where referential processing is found to be influenced by syntactic factors (Gordon et al., 1993; Gordon & Chan, 1995; Gordon & Scearse, 1995; Kennison & Gordon, 1997; McKoon, Ratcliff, & Ward, 1993; McKoon, Ward, & Ratcliff, 1993).

The experiments reported in this paper use self-paced reading time methodology to address the questions raised above. The first two experiments were conducted using designs that are very similar to those developed by Gordon et al. (1993) to study the comprehension of co-reference in English. Accordingly, comparison of the findings from those experiments with the findings reported by Gordon et al. (1993) provides a basis for cross-linguistic comparison in the comprehension of co-reference. The second two experiments focus specifically on similarities and differences in the comprehension of zero and overt pronouns in Chinese.

EXPERIMENT 1

This experiment examined how the timecourse of reading Chinese sentences was influenced by three types of referring expressions: repeated names, pronouns, and zero pronouns. A self-paced reading task was employed to examine the reading of passages such as the one shown in Table 1. Each passage consisted of three sentences in a semantically coherent discourse. The first sentence introduced two named individuals of different genders using a subject-verb-object word order. Subject-verb-object order was used because it is the most common order in Chinese and does not use the special markings ("把 '*Ba*'" and "被 '*Bei*'") required by other orders (Chu, 1979; Sun & Givon, 1985). One discourse entity was introduced as a grammatical subject, and the other was introduced as the postverbal object. This assignment of syntactic roles for these two discourse entities was maintained in the second sentence. In the second, critical sentence the form of referring expressions was manipulated. There were six versions constructed by the combinations of assigning different forms of anaphoric expression (repeated name, overt pronoun, and zero pronoun) to different syntactic positions (subject or object). However, zero pronouns were only used for the expression in the position of grammatical

TABLE 1
Sample Stimuli for Experiment 1

Initial Sentence:

小明	告訴	小玲	這一帶	住宅區	不	安全。
Xiaoming	gaoshu	*Xiaolin*	zheyidai	zhuzaiqu	bu	anquan.
3rd sing.	tell(told)	3rd sing.	here	community	not	safe.

"*Xiaoming* told *Xiaolin* that the community here is not safe".

Second Sentence:

小明/他/	警告	小玲/她	平常	隨時	提高	警覺。
Xiaoming / Ta/∅	jinggao	*Xiaolin /Ta*	pinchang	suishi	tigao	jingjie.
Xiaoming /Ta/∅	warn(ed)	*Xiaolin /Ta*	usually	always	keep	alert.

"*Xiaoming /He/∅* warned *Xiaolin /her* to keep alert aways".

Passage-final Sentence:

提高	警覺	是	預防	意外	的	不二	法門。
Tigao	jingjie	shi	yufang	yiwai	de	buer	famen.
Keep	alert	is	prevent	accident	prep.	best	way.

"To keep alert is the best way to prevent an accident".

Note: For all the Chinese Sample Stimuli in this paper, we adopted the system of "Hanyupinyin" (Wentzu Kaiko Chupanshe, 1958) for the Pinyin Spellings

subject because the appearance of zero pronouns in object position must meet strict discourse and syntactic constraints such as the absence of any complement or modifier after the object (Huang, 1984; 1991). With the exception of the inclusion of the zero-pronoun condition, the experiment matches the design of reading-time studies that have been done in English by Gordon et al. (1993) and by Kennison and Gordon (1997). This allows a comparison of the current results in Chinese to those previously obtained in English.

The first goal of the experiment was to examine the effect of the form of the referring expression on reading time. As discussed earlier, Gordon et al. (1993) demonstrated a repeated-name penalty in English where sentences with repeated names are read more slowly than matched sentences with pronouns. The various explanations of such differences between names and pronouns all incorporate in some way or another the notion that there are fundamental differences in the way that unreduced expressions (such as names) and reduced expression (such as pronouns) achieve reference (Cloitre & Bever, 1988; Garrod & Sanford, 1982; Gordon et al., 1993; Gordon & Hendrick, 1998). If these accounts are generalised to comprehension in Chinese as well as in English, they predict that a repeated-name penalty should occur in Chinese so that the sentence in Table 1 with the repeated name (*Xiaoming*) would be read more slowly than the matched sentence with the overt pronoun (*Ta*) or the zero pronoun (∅). However, these theoretical explanations make no distinction in how different types of pronouns, as reduced referring expressions, are interpreted. Accordingly, they do not predict a difference in reading time between the reading time of sentences with overt pronouns (*Ta*) and those with zero pronouns (∅). This prediction contrasts with the traditional view that the zero pronoun makes the strongest contribution to discourse coherence in Chinese (Chen, 1984; Givon, 1983, 1992; Li, 1985; Li & Thompson, 1981, 1984; Tao, 1996). If the zero pronoun plays a unique role in forging coherence in a Chinese discourse then one might expect that it would also render a discourse easier to understand than would an overt pronoun. It is that expectation that our first experiment evaluates.

The second goal of this experiment was to examine whether the interpretation of referential expressions in Chinese depends on the syntactic role of the expression as it does in other languages. Gordon et al. (1993; Kennison & Gordon, 1997) found that the repeated-name penalty for a referring expression appeared when the expression occupies a syntactically prominent position, such as the position of grammatical subject, but disappeared when it was in a less prominent position, such as the position of grammatical object. If the role of syntactic factors in the interpretation of reference in Chinese is similar to that in English, then we would predict that the repeated-name penalty would only be observed for expressions in subject position. In contrast, the context-and-pragmatics-only approach that has been advanced for the interpretation of reference in Chinese (Li & Thompson, 1981; 1984) would not lead normally to an explanation for why the repeated-name penalty would only be observed in subject position.

Method

Participants. Sixty undergraduate students attending introductory psychology courses at National Taiwan University (NTU) participated in a single session lasting about 40 minutes. They were all native Chinese speakers and received course credit for their participation.

Stimuli. A set of 42 three-sentence passages like the one shown in Table 1 was constructed. There were six alternative versions of the second sentence constructed by varying the forms of the anaphoric expressions in different syntactic positions. The third sentence did not mention either of the two discourse entities. It was included so that the critical sentence did not appear at the end of the passage. Each passage was followed by a true-or-false comprehension question. The names of the two characters in a passage were conventionally of different genders so that there was no gender ambiguity in interpreting overt pronouns. All named characters were two-character Chinese word with as simple strikes and visual forms as possible, such as "小明", "大興", "小美", and "文英". For example, in Table 1, the name "*Xiaoming*" and "*Xiaolin*" conventionally refer to male and female characters, respectively. Also, in Chinese, there is no phonological differentiation for overt pronouns with different genders. Overt pronouns with different genders have exactly the same pronunciation: "Ta". However, in written Chinese, gender influences the visual form of overt pronouns. Thus, male pronominal "Ta" in our experimental passages was indicated as "他" and female pronominal "Ta" as "她". The gender sequence for the two characters in the first sentence of each passage was counterbalanced across passages so that half of the passages were *male-female* and half were *female-male.*

A set of 102 filler passages was constructed. The fillers, like the experimental passages, consisted of three-sentence passages which included named referents. Approximately half of them (48 out of 102) had similar syntactic structures to those of the experimental passages and had roughly equal numbers of the six types of NP sequences in the second sentences. The rest of the filler passages were also semantically coherent discourses, with various syntactic structures that are not relevant to our experimental manipulations. Each filler passage was followed by a comprehension question like those for the experimental passages.

Design. Six sets of materials were constructed by assigning one of the six versions of each experimental passage to each material set. In this design, each experimental passage occurred in all its six versions across six material sets, but within each material set each experimental passage appeared in only one version. Participants read one of the six material sets as well as the 102 filler passages. The stimulus material for each set along with fillers was divided into six blocks of 24 passages each. In each block, there were seven experimental passages as well as 17 filler passages. The order of trials was randomised. An initial practice block consisting of 10 filler passages was used to familiarise participants with the reading task.

Procedure. The experiment was conducted on a personal computer. Participants read the instructions on the computer screen and performed the practice block to become familiar with the self-paced reading task. At the start of each trial, the sentence "請按任意鍵開始" (*Please press any key to begin trial*) was presented in the centre of the screen. Participants initiated a trial by pressing a key and the passage was presented one sentence at a time in the centre of the screen. They pressed the space bar to move on to the next sentence. They were instructed to read each sentence at a natural pace, neither slowly nor rushed. The reading time for each sentence was calculated from the onset of a sentence to the time the participants pressed the space bar. At the end of each passage, the screen went blank for one second and a true-or-false comprehension question was presented in the centre of the screen. This question assessed knowledge of the event described in the passage but did not require knowledge of the characters names. Participants responded by pressing "T" (true) or "F" (false) keys. Feedback on the accuracy of the response to the true-false question was presented only for incorrect responses. Also, participants received feedback about the percentage of correct responses and incorrect responses after they had finished each block.

Results

Table 2 shows the mean reading time of the critical (second) sentence and the mean accuracy for the comprehension questions for all combinations of the two variables: form and syntactic role of the referring expressions. Outliers were excluded from the data analysis according to the criterion of Gordon et al. (1993, p.326): reading times below 500 ms per sentence or greater than 6000 ms were considered as premature or careless responses and therefore excluded. Excluded observations comprised 2.9% of the data. The same criterion was adopted for the remaining experiments reported in this article.

The reading times of the critical sentences containing repeated-names as grammatical subjects were 156 ms slower than those with overt pronouns as grammatical subjects, an instance of the repeated-name penalty. In contrast, this difference was only 54 ms for referring expressions in the position of grammatical object. Further, the difference in reading times of sentences with overt pronouns compared to those with zero pronouns was just 52 ms. Analysis of variance was conducted both by participants (F_1)

TABLE 2
Mean Reading Times (in ms) with 95% Confidence Interval for the Second Sentence and Mean Accuracy (% in parenthesis) for the Comprehension Questions in each of the Experimental Conditions

Syntactic status		*Object*		
		Repeated name	*Overt pronoun*	
	Repeated name	1965 ± 83 (94.4)	1923 ± 89 (94.5)	1944 ± 61 (94.4)
Subject	*Overt pronoun*	1784 ± 79 (95.3)	1791 ± 82 (94.8)	1788 ± 57 (95.1)
	Zero-pronoun	1798 ± 76 (95.1)	1673 ± 81 (93.7)	1736 ± 56 (94.4)
Average		1849 ± 46 (94.9)	1795 ± 49 (94.3)	

and by items (F_2) to test the generality of these effects. The results indicated that when an anaphoric expression was in the grammatical subject position, the effect of form of expression was significant both by participants; ($F_1(2,118) = 16.39$, $P < .001$) and by items ($F_2(2,82) = 13.37$, $P < .001$). In contrast, when the anaphoric expression was in the grammatical object position, the effect of form of expression failed to reach significance by participants; ($F_1(1,59) = 2.93$, $P = .092$) or by items ($F_2(1,41) = 2.31$, $P = .136$). The interaction of the effect of form of anaphoric expression and the syntactic status of such anaphoric expression was not significant by participants; ($F_1(2,118) = 1.49$, $P = .229$) or by items ($F_2(2,82) = 1.69$, $P = .190$).

Post hoc contrasts for different forms of expression in subject position, adjusted by the Bonferroni method, showed that the reading times for repeated-names were slower than those for overt pronouns by participants ($t_1(59) = 4.11$, $P < .005$) as well as by items ($t_2(41) = 3.69$, $P < .005$); however, the difference between the reading times for overt pronouns and those for zero pronouns was not significant by participants ($t_1(59) = 1.396$, $P > .1$) or by items ($t_2(41) = 1.256$, $P > .20$). Further analysis illustrated that the reading time of sentences with repeated-name subjects was significantly slower than the pooled reading times for sentences with overt pronoun subjects and zero pronoun subjects both by participants ($t_1(59) = 5.55$, $P < .005$) and by items ($t_2(41) = 4.99$, $P < .005$).

Table 3 also shows the mean reading times for the first and third sentences of the passages as a function of the experimental manipulations. The manipulations had no significant effects on these measures of performance. The finding that manipulation of the form of a referring expression has effects confined to the sentence in which it occurs is consistent with previous self-paced reading experiments of this sort (Gordon et al., 1993; Gordon & Chan, 1995; Gordon & Scearce, 1995). The mean accuracy for comprehension questions was 94.6% overall with a

TABLE 3
Mean Reading Times for the Initial and Final Sentence of Experimental Passages in Experiment 1 in each of the Experimental Conditions

		Mean reading times for the initial sentence		*Mean reading times for the final sentence*	
		Object		*Object*	
Syntactic status		*Repeated name*	*Overt pronoun*	*Repeated name*	*Overt pronoun*
Subject	*Repeated name*	3440 (± 192)	3490 (± 182)	1571 (±115)	1537 (± 93)
	Overt pronoun	3352 (± 175)	3330 (± 187)	1517 (± 88)	1457 (± 79)
	Zero pronoun	3375 (± 171)	3316 (± 189)	1565 (± 97)	1509 (± 89)

Note: The numbers in parenthesis indicates the 95% confidence interval of the mean

range from 93.7% in the zero pronoun-pronoun condition to 95.3% in the pronoun-name condition. Statistical analysis showed that no significant effects on accuracy were observed for the experimental conditions.

Discussion

The results of the experiment show that the form of a referring expression in Chinese contributes to discourse comprehension in a manner that is similar to that which has previously been observed for English. Sentences containing reduced referential expressions (overt or zero pronouns) in subject position were read more quickly than matched sentences containing repeated names. This repeated name penalty has previously been observed in self-paced reading time experiments in English (Gordon et al., 1993). It suggests that pronouns can facilitate discourse comprehension in Chinese just as they can in English. Further, the experiments showed no significant differences between the reading times of sentences containing overt pronouns and those containing zero pronouns. The absence of a significant difference between these conditions suggests that accounts of referential processing that incorporate a basic distinction between reduced and unreduced forms (Cloitre & Bever, 1988; Garrod & Sanford, 1982; Gordon et al., 1993; Gordon & Hendrick, 1998) are sufficient and that at least for the kinds of passages examined in this experiment there is no need to assign special status to the zero pronoun in Chinese (Chen, 1984; Givon, 1983, 1992; Li, 1985; Li & Thompson, 1981, 1984).

Furthermore, the facilitating effect of pronominal reference on discourse comprehension occurred only for expressions in subject position and not for expressions in object position, again showing a parallel between the effects of form of reference in Chinese and what has previously been shown for English (Gordon et al., 1993). This result suggests that in Chinese syntactic information plays an important role in the processing of co-reference at a local discourse level, a conclusion that is not consistent with the context-and-pragmatics-only approach proposed by Li and Thompson (1981, 1984).

In this experiment, as well as in the subsequent ones, the lengths of the critical sentences varied slightly as a function of the form of the critical referring expression. Sentences with repeated names were one character longer than matched sentences with overt pronouns which were one character longer than matched sentences with zero pronouns. These length differences do not provide a general explanation of the pattern of reading times observed here because the repeated-name penalty was only found for expressions in subject position but not for expressions in object position even though manipulating the form of the expressions in the two positions causes the same differences in length. In a similar way length differences cannot explain results obtained in English where the magnitude of the repeated-name penalty is determined by syntactic and discourse factors rather than by the greater number of letters in names as compared to pronouns (Gordon et al., 1993; Gordon & Chan, 1995; Gordon & Scearce, 1995). An explanation in terms of length differences is also inconsistent with eye-tracking results that show that repeated names cause elevated durations for fixations after the repeated name and also cause an increase in regressive saccades (Kennison & Gordon, 1997). Subsequent experiments in this paper will further show that the effect of form of referring expression on reading time does not reduce to an effect of length.

EXPERIMENT 2

Experiment 1 demonstrated that the repeated-name penalty in Chinese depends on the syntactic role of the referring expression. As in English, it occurs for expressions in subject position but not for expressions in object position. An additional finding in English is that the repeated-name penalty depends not only on the syntactic role of an expression in an utterance but on the syntactic role of the expression that mentioned the referent in the immediately preceding sentence. Building on centering theory (Grosz et al., 1983; 1995), Gordon et al. (1993) examined how the effect of form of reference on reading time was influenced by whether a sentence *continued* or *shifted* a critical referent from the preceding sentence. The continue and shift conditions are illustrated in Table 4. In the continue condition, the subject of the critical (second) sentence is also the subject of the preceding sentence. In the shift condition, the subject of the critical sentence was an object in the preceding sentence and the subject of the preceding sentence is not mentioned. Gordon et al. (1993) found that the repeated-name penalty occurred in the continue condition but not in the shift condition, thus showing that the facilitating effect of a pronoun on discourse comprehension depends on the structural relation between successive sentences. Centering theory (Grosz et al., 1983, 1995) explains such effects through the theoretical construct of a set of forward-looking centres that are ordered in prominence, and where subsequent pronominal reference to prominent entities is easier than to nonprominent entities. Gordon and Hendrick (1998) have incorporated the notion of forward-looking centres into a model of discourse processing in which syntactic prominence (defined in terms of depth of embeddedness) is a central determinant of prominence in the discourse model. This model provides an account of why the repeated-name penalty is present in the continue condition and absent in the shift condition.

The current experiment examines whether the syntactic relation between successive sentences has the same impact on the ease of

TABLE 4
Sample passage for Experiment 2

Initial Sentence

大明 喜歡 告訴 文瑩 每晚 作 的 夢。
Daming xihuan gaoshu *Wenying* meiwan zuo de meng.
"*Daming* likes to tell *Wenying* the dream he has every night."

Second Sentence

Continue Condition

大明/他 描述 夢境 時 興致 盎然。
Daming /Ta miaoshu mengjing shi xingzhi angran
"*Daming/He* describes his dreams with great excitement."

Shift Condition

文瑩/她 聽了 都 覺得 索然 無味。
Wenying /Ta tingle dou juede suoran wuwei
"*Wenying /She* feels insipid every time she hears those dreams."

Passage-final Sentence.

夢 的 趣味 只有 作夢 的 人 才 能 了解。
meng de quwei ziyou zuomeng de ran cai neng liaojie.
"Only those who dream can enjoy the fun from their dreams."

comprehending different forms of referring expressions in Chinese as it does in English. It has been argued that the processing of discourse comprehension in Chinese is different from that in English in that the interpretation of referring expressions in Chinese relies primarily upon context and pragmatics and does not involve syntactic structure as in English (Li & Thompson, 1981, 1984). Examining the effect of structure on the repeated-name penalty provides one way of addressing this position. The experiment employs passages like those shown in Table 4.

In these passages, two named individuals of different genders were introduced in the first sentence. One was introduced as the grammatical subject, a syntactically prominent position, while the other was introduced as the postverbal object, a less prominent position. The second sentence was the critical sentence in which two factors were manipulated. One was the continue-shift factor; in the continue condition, the subject of the second sentence (*Daming*) was identical to that of the first sentence, whereas in shift condition the subject of the second sentence (*Wenying*) differed from that of the first sentence. The second factor was the form (name vs. overt pronoun) of the referring expression in subject position of the second sentence. These Chinese passages closely match those studied in English by Gordon et al. (1993, also Kennison & Gordon, 1997) and therefore provide a test of whether discourse structure has a similar influence on the comprehension of referring expressions in the two languages.

Method

Participants. Sixty new undergraduate students from the same population of Experiment 1 participated in this experiment.

Stimuli, design, and procedure. Forty three-sentence experimental passages were constructed as shown in Table 3. A preliminary questionnaire study was conducted to ensure that the predicate of the second sentence for each experimental passage led naturally to the intended interpretation of reduced expressions for sentences in both the Continue and Shift conditions. Passages were tested, revised, and re-tested until approximately 92% of the participants identified the grammatical subject of the second sentence in the expected way. Two groups of eight participants participated in this preliminary study. Other than the structure of the passages, the experiment was run in the same manner as Experiment 1 except for minor design changes to accommodate the differing number of conditions. In particular, the experimental passages along with fillers were divided into five blocks of 28 passages each. Each block consisted of eight experimental passages as well as 20 filler passages. Participants performed one initial practice block of 16 filler passages at the beginning of the session.

Results

Figure 1 shows the mean reading time for the critical sentence for all combinations of the two factors: form of referring expression (name vs. overt pronoun) and discourse structure (continue vs. shift).

In the Continue condition, the reading times of sentences with repeated-names were 147 ms slower than those of sentences containing overt pronouns, an instance of the repeated-name penalty. In contrast, in the Shift condition, sentences with repeated names were read as fast as those with pronouns. Analysis of variance showed that the main effect of Continue/Shift did not reach significance by participants ($F_1(1,59) = 0.59$, $P = .45$) nor items ($F_2(1,39) = 0.12$, $P = .73$). The main effect of form of

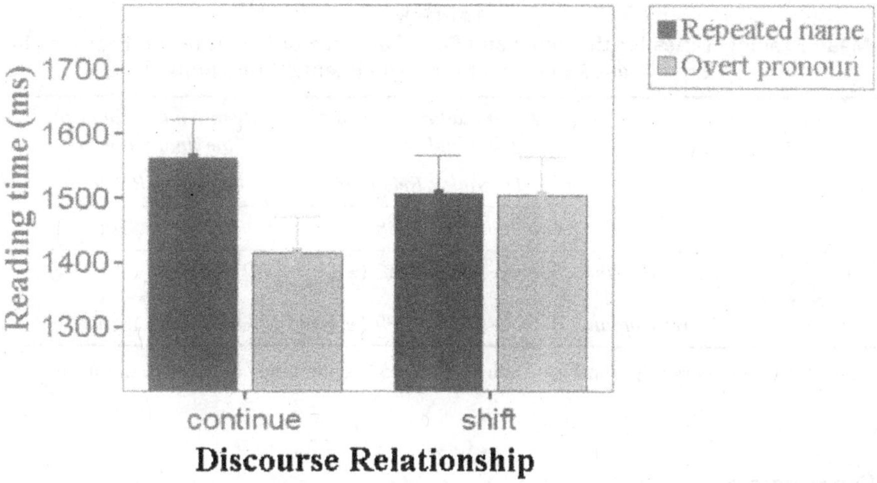

FIG. 1. Mean reading times (ms) of the critical sentences that include the experimental manipulations. Error bars show 95% confidence interval of mean. The mean accuracy rates for comprehension questions in each condition are: Continue-Name: 95%, Continue-Pronoun: 94%, Shift-Name: 95%, and Shift-Pronoun: 92%.

referring expression was significant both by participants ($F_1(1,59) = 6.52$, $P < .05$) and by items ($F_2(1,39) = 7.75$, $P < .01$). A significant interaction was observed between forms of referring expression and Continue/Shift by participants ($F_1(1,59) = 6.12$, $P < .05$), as well as by items ($F_2(1,39) = 4.65$, $P < .05$). A planned contrast showed that the repeated-name penalty was significant in the continue condition ($t_1(59) = 3.58$, $P < .01$; $t_2(39) = 3.09$, $P < .01$) but not in the shift condition ($t_1(59) = 0.024$, $P > .25$; $t_2(39) = 0.021$, $P > .25$). A further contrast showed that reading times for sentences containing pronouns were faster in the continue condition than in the shift condition when tested by subjects ($t_1(59) = 2.19$, $P < .05$) but not when tested by items ($t_2(39) = 1.89$, $P > .05$). In addition, no significant difference was found for reading times of sentences containing repeated names in different discourse relationship ($t_1(59) = 1.34$, $P > .10$; $t_2(39) = 1.16$, $P > .20$).

Table 5 shows the mean reading times for the initial and final sentences of the passages as a function of the experimental manipulations. The manipulations did not significantly influence the reading times of those sentences. The mean accuracy for comprehension questions was 94.6% overall with a range of 92.0% in the *shift-pronoun* condition to 95.9% in the *shift-name* condition. Accuracy was not influenced significantly by experimental condition.

TABLE 5
Mean Reading Times for the Initial and Final Sentence of Experimental Passages in Experiment 2 in each of the Experimental Conditions

		Mean reading times for the initial sentence		*Mean reading times for the final sentence*	
		Discourse Relations		*Discourse Relations*	
		Continue	*Shift*	*Continue*	*Shift*
Referring expressions	*Repeated name*	3255 (± 159)	3112 (± 140)	1422 (± 67)	1353 (± 60)
	Overt pronoun	3156 (± 145)	3139 (± 140)	1389 (± 62)	1350 (± 60)

Note: The numbers in parenthesis indicates the 95% confidence interval of the mean

Discussion

The results of this experiment show that for the most part local discourse structure has a similar effect in Chinese to that which it has in English. In both English and Chinese, a repeated-name penalty is observed in the continue condition, where the subject of the critical sentence co-referred with the subject of the preceding sentence, while no repeated-name penalty occurred in the shift condition, where the subject of the critical sentence co-referred with object of the preceding sentence. This similarity suggests that discourse structure in the types of passages studied here may be processed in similar ways in Chinese and English despite the many differences between the two languages.

The results of this experiment also provide additional evidence that in Chinese, as in English, differences in the length of different types of referring expressions cannot account for the repeated-name penalty. Length differences been the repeated-name and pronoun versions of the sentences were the same in the continue and shift conditions but a repeated-name penalty was only observed in the continue condition, indicating that the effect depends on the relation between successive sentences.

One difference between the results of this experiment on Chinese and those previously done on English is that there was a marginally significant trend for sentences with pronouns to be read more quickly in the continue condition than in the shift position. Such a difference was originally predicted based on centering theory (Grosz et al., 1983) but was not observed in our reading time studies of English. Experiment 4 of Gordon et al. (1993) found a difference of 53 ms in this direction but the difference was not significant. Experiment 2 of Gordon and Chan (1995) and Experiment 2 of Kennison and Gordon (1997) also failed to find significant effects. Given that the difference between the continue and shift conditions in the present experiment was only marginally significant it is unclear whether or not the present result points to a real difference between English and Chinese.

EXPERIMENTS 3 AND 4

Experiment 1 indicated that the two types of reduced expressions in Chinese, overt pronouns and zero pronouns, make similar contributions to discourse coherence. This finding does not support the view that a zero pronoun in Chinese has a special role in promoting discourse coherence (Chen, 1984; Givon, 1981, 1983; Li, 1985; Li & Thompson, 1981, 1984). Experiments 3 and 4 provide additional tests of whether zero pronouns promote discourse coherence more than overt pronouns and also examine whether there are situations where overt pronouns are preferred (Chen, 1984; Li, 1985; Li & Thompson, 1981). In the model of discourse processing proposed by Gordon and Hendrick (1998), the occurrence of a pronoun triggers a construction rule by which the entities in the discourse model are searched in order of prominence for a "suitable antecedent". As discussed earlier, the syntactic role of the expression that introduced an entity is a major determinant of prominence. A suitable antecedent is defined as one that matches the pronoun on grammatically encoded semantic features such as gender, number or animacy. This model leads to the prediction that the ease of understanding the two types of pronouns should not differ in cases where they refer to the most prominent entity in the discourse nor in cases where the semantic features encoded in the overt pronoun do not specifically identify a suitable antecedent. However, in cases where the referent of the pronoun is not the most accessible entity and where semantic features do specifically identify an antecedent, the Gordon and Hendrick (1998) model predicts an advantage of overt pronouns, which grammatically encode semantic features, over zero pronouns, which as null expressions convey no semantic information about their referents.

Experiments 3 and 4 examine these predictions measuring the reading time for passages such as those shown in Table 6. The two named characters in the first sentence are the same gender in Experiment 3 and different genders in Experiment 4. Thus, in Experiment 3 the gender of a pronoun in the second sentence cannot unambiguously pick out its referent while in Experiment 4 it can (as was the case in Experiment 2). For both experiments, the second sentence varies two factors: the continue/shift manipulation and whether the referring expression is subject position is an overt pronoun or a zero pronoun.

TABLE 6
Sample passage for Experiment 3 and Experiment 4

Initial Sentence

小美[3] / 大興[4] 告訴 小蓉 花園 裏 應 種 蔬菜 而 不 種 花。
Xiaomei(3)/Daxing(4) gaoshu *Xiaorong* huayuan li ying zhong sucai er bu zhong hua.
"*Xiaomei(3)/Daxing(4)* told *Xiaorong* that vegetables, instead of flowers, should be planted in the garden."

Second (Critical) Sentence

Continue Condition

她[3] / 他[4] / 認爲 蔬菜 比 花 還要 實用。
Ta(3)/Ta(4)/∅ renwei sucai bi hua haiyao shiyong.
"*She(3)/He(4)/∅* thought vegetables are of more utility than flowers."

Shift Condition

她[3] / 她[4] / 卻 認爲 蔬菜 和 花 都 要 種。
Ta(3)/Ta(4)/∅ que renwei sucai han hua dou yao zhong.
"*She(3)/She(4)/∅* thought, however, that both vegetables and flowers should be planted."

Passage-final Sentence

花園 的 使用 及 規劃 是 很大 的 學問。
Huayuan de shiyong ji guihua shi henda de xuewen.
"The usage and planning of a garden are worth studying."

Note: The numbers in parentheses in the passage indicates the version of different experiments. For instance, in the initial sentence, the grammatical subject in Experiment 3 is *Xiaomei* (a Female name) whereas it is *Daxing* (a Male name) in Experiment 4. Also, both Experiment 3 and 4 use the same postverbal object *Xiaorong* (Female name). This changes in the pronominalisation of the grammatical subjects in different conditions of the second sentence across Experiment 3 and 4. For Experiment 3, the grammatical subject for all conditions are all female pronominal expressions ("她 ", *She*); for Experiment 4, the grammatical subjects are pronominal expressions with different genders for different conditions, "他 " (*He*) in the continue condition and "她 " (*She*) in the shift condition

Method

Participants. Experiment 3 tested 64 new participants while Experiment 4 tested 48 new participants. They were all from the same population as the previous experiments.

Stimuli, design, and procedure. Both Experiment 3 and 4 used 36 experimental passages that were constructed as shown in the sample stimuli above. Most of the passages were adopted from the experimental passages of Experiment 2. Thirty-three of the 36 passages were taken directly from those used in Experiment 2; only the referring expressions in those passages were changed so that they contained the kinds of referential relationships to be investigated in the study. For the remaining three passages, changes in content were necessary so that the passage made sense when the characters were the same gender (Experiment 3) or were of different gender (Experiment 4). The changes in these three passages were validated with a preliminary study (using five native Chinese speakers who were naïve to the purposes of the study) of plausibility like that conducted for Experiment 2. Within each experiment, appropriate changes were made for the second sentence of each passage in terms of the type of referring expressions used. Across Experiments 3 and 4, appropriate changes were made for the first sentence of each passage in terms of the gender of the two characters. Both experiments were conducted in a similar manner to Experiment 2 in terms of the assignment of experimental passages to conditions, participants, and trial blocks. For Experiment 3, each stimulus material set along with additional 89 fillers were divided into five blocks of 25 passage each, and for Experiment 4, each stimulus material set along with additional 94 fillers were divided into five blocks of 26 passage each. Participants performed one initial practice block of 16 filler passages at the beginning of each experiment.

Results

Experiment 3. Figure 2 shows the mean reading time in Experiment 3 for the critical sentence as a function of the experimental conditions. Analysis of variance indicated that only the main effect of Continue/Shift reached statistical significance both by participants ($F_1(1,63) = 33.24$, $P <$

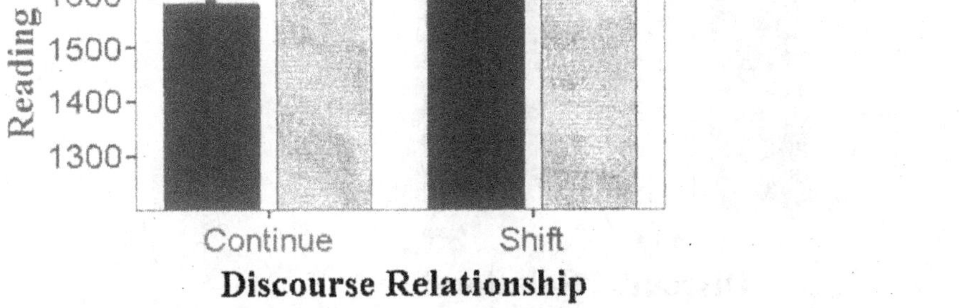

FIG. 2. Mean reading times (ms) of the critical sentences that include the experimental manipulations. Error bars show 95% confidence interval of mean. The accuracy rates for comprehension questions in each condition are: Continue-Zero: 93%, Continue-Pronoun: 93%, Shift-Zero: 91%, and Shift-Pronoun: 87%.

TABLE 7
Mean Reading Times for the Initial and Final Sentence of Experimental Passages in Experiment 3 in each of the Experimental Conditions

		Mean reading times for the initial sentence *Discourse Relations*		*Mean reading times for the final sentence* *Discourse Relations*	
		Continue	*Shift*	*Continue*	*Shift*
Referring expressions	*Overt pronoun*	3619 (± 165)	3491 (± 151)	1382 (± 65)	1395 (± 66)
	Zero pronoun	3620 (± 169)	3613 (± 171)	1379 (± 64)	1427 (± 68)

Note: The numbers in parenthesis indicates the 95% confidence interval of the mean

.001), and by items ($F_2(1,35) = 12.81$, $P < .001$). Neither the main effect of type of reduced expressions was significant ($F_1(1,63) = 2.34$, $P = .131$; $F_1(1,35) = 1.59$, $P = .22$) nor was the interaction between type of reduced expression and continue/shift ($F_1(1,63) = .19$, $P = .66$; $F_2(1,35) = .10$, $P = .75$). Table 7 shows the mean reading times for the initial and final sentences of the passages. The experimental manipulations had no significant effects on the reading times of these sentences.

Experiment 4. Figure 3 shows the mean reading time in Experiment 4 for the critical sentence as a function of the experimental conditions.

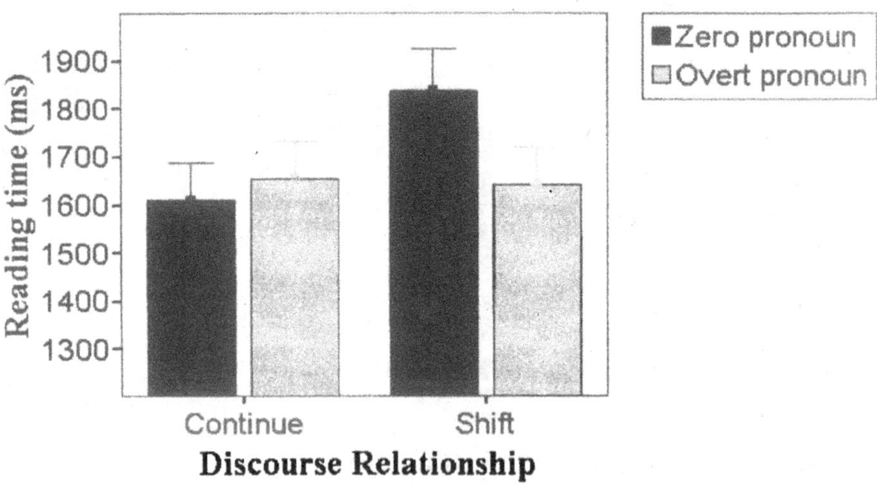

FIG. 3. Mean reading times (ms) of the critical sentences that contain the experimental manipulations. Error bars show 95% confidence interval of mean. The accuracy rates for comprehension questions in each condition are: Continue-Zero: 95%, Continue-Pronoun: 96%, Shift-Zero: 93%, and Shift-Pronoun: 93%.

Analysis of variance showed that the reading times of sentences with zero pronouns were significantly slower than those with overt pronouns ($F_1(1,47) = 4.60$, $P < .05$; $F_2(1,35) = 4.88$, $P < .05$). Also, significantly slower reading times were observed in the Shift condition than in the Continue condition by participants ($F_1(1,47) = 14.14$, $P < .001$), but not by items ($F_2(1,35) = 4.06$, $P = .052$). The interaction of type of reduced expressions and Continue/Shift was significant by participant ($F_1(1,47) = 11.48$, $P < .01$) and by items ($F_2(1,35) = 9.95$, $P < .01$). Table 8 shows the mean reading times for the initial and final sentences of the passages. The experimental manipulations had no significant effects on the reading times of these sentences. Accuracy on the comprehension questions was marginally higher in the continue condition (95.4%) than in the shift condition (92.9%); $F(1,47) = 3.96$, $P < .1$).

A planned contrast on the difference between reading times of critical sentences with pronouns in the continue and shift conditions revealed no significant differences ($t_1(47) = 0.24$, $P > .25$; $t_2(35) = 0.22$, $P > .25$).

Discussion

The results of the continue conditions of Experiments 3 and 4 show no significant difference in reading times between sentences with overt pronouns and those with zero pronouns. This finding, consistent with the results of Experiment 1, does not support the notion that the zero pronoun makes a unique contribution to the coherence of Chinese discourse in cases where it refers to a highly accessible entity (Ariel, 1990, 1991; Givon, 1983, 1992). The finding supports models (Cloitre & Beaver, 1988; Garrod & Sanford, 1982; Gordon et al., 1993; Gordon & Hendrick, 1998) in which the same mechanisms underlie the interpretation of different types of reduced referring expressions.

TABLE 8
Mean Reading Times for the Initial and Final Sentence of Experimental Passages in Experiment 4 in each of the Experimental Conditions

		Mean reading times for the initial sentence		*Mean reading times for the final sentence*	
		Discourse Relations		*Discourse Relations*	
		Continue	*Shift*	*Continue*	*Shift*
Referring expressions	*Overt pronoun*	3714 (± 196)	3764 (± 203)	1461 (± 77)	1394 (± 65)
	Zero pronoun	3573 (± 190)	3729 (± 190)	1489 (± 76)	1457 (± 76)

Note: The numbers in parenthesis indicates the 95% confidence interval of the mean

In Experiment 4 the continue/shift factor was manipulated for sentences with overt pronouns, as it was in Experiment 2. While Experiment 2 found a marginally significant effect of this factor, Experiment 4 did not find such an effect. This supports the idea that the continue/shift manipulation does not have a substantial impact on the processing of sentences with overt pronouns where the pronoun can unambiguously indicate its referent because of a gender cue. Thus, the marginal effect observed in Experiment 2 contrasts with the absent effect or small hints of effects that were observed in this experiment and in several experiments on English (Gordon et al., 1993; Gordon & Chan, 1995; Gordon & Scearce, 1995). For both Chinese and English it appears that effects of the form of referring expressions are much more robust than the main effect of continue-shift with unambiguous pronouns.

Again, the results of these experiments show that differences in the length of the different types of referring expressions do not account for differences in reading time. Length differences between the overt-pronoun and zero-pronoun versions of the sentences were the same in the continue and shift conditions and when gender was ambiguous or unambiguous. However, differences in reading time as a function of the type of referring expression depended on these factors rather than reflecting a constant influence of length.

The overall pattern of the continue/shift effects in the two experiments is consistent with the predictions from the Gordon and Hendrick (1998) model. As discussed above, that model predicts that the form of the reduced referring expression should not interact with the continue/shift manipulation in Experiment 3 because the gender of the overt pronoun provides no information about its referent beyond what is conveyed by the zero pronoun (since the two possible referents are the same gender). In contrast, in Experiment 4 the continue/shift manipulation should have a greater impact for sentences with zero pronouns than with overt pronouns because the gender of the overt pronoun can unambiguously pick out its referent. The results of the two experiments show this pattern exactly.

GENERAL DISCUSSION

The goal of the current experimental research was to examine how referring expressions in brief locally coherent discourses contribute to the comprehension of Chinese. The results of a series of experiments showed that the form of referring expressions affects reading time for Chinese text in a manner that is very similar to what has been observed in English (Gordon et al., 1993) despite the different linguistic properties of the two languages. In particular, reduced expressions (both overt and zero pronouns) contribute more to discourse coherence than do full expressions (repeated names) for the types of passages studied here; this facilitating effect of reduced expressions only occurs when the antecedent expression is syntactically prominent. These results suggest that overt and zero pronouns are for the most part interpreted by the same structure-dependent processes when they refer to an entity introduced into the discourse by a syntactically prominent expression. When these expressions refer to an entity that was introduced by an expression that is not syntactically prominent, the relative ease of understanding the two types of pronouns depends on whether the inherent semantic features of the overt pronoun allow it to unambiguously indicate its referent. When the overt pronoun is ambiguous then no difference is observed in the comprehension of sentences with overt and zero pronouns. When the overt pronoun unambiguously indicates its referent, then sentences with overt pronouns are understood more easily than matched sentences with zero pronouns. This pattern shows a specific situation where overt pronouns are more easily understood than zero pronouns; this advantage is readily understood in terms of the relative ability of the two types of pronouns to convey information about the identity of their referents.

The basic similarity that we have observed in the processing of overt and zero pronouns contributes to the assessment of different approaches to the comprehension of referring expressions. Several approaches that have been developed for the study of English (Cloitre & Bever, 1988; Garrod & Sanford, 1982; Gordon et al., 1993; Gordon & Hendrick, 1998) make a basic distinction between how unreduced and reduced referring expressions contribute to discourse coherence. These approaches do not distinguish among different types of reduced expressions. In contrast, several approaches to the study of Chinese and other languages (Ariel, 1990, 1991; Chen, 1984; Givon, 1983; Li, 1985; Li & Thompson, 1981, 1984) advance the position that under some circumstances zero pronouns contribute more to discourse coherence than do overt pronouns. Our results show that at least for the types of discourses that we examined, there is no need to posit special mechanisms for how zero pronouns contribute to discourse coherence, thereby supporting approaches that do not distinguish among different types of reduced referring expressions.

Our results also show that the ease of interpreting reduced expressions in Chinese depends on the accessibility of the intended referent as determined by the syntactic prominence of the antecedent expression that introduced the referent. This finding is in accordance with what has been observed in English (Gordon et al., 1993; Gordon & Hendrick, 1997) and it is consistent with a number of theories (Ariel, 1991; Gordon & Hendrick, 1998; Halmari, 1996) in which the ease of interpreting reduced expressions depends on the accessibility of their referents. The model developed by

Gordon and Hendrick (1998) provides an explicit account of how differing degrees of accessibility influences referential interpretation and also places substantial emphasis on the contributions of syntax to this process. We review that model here in order to show how it can provide an account of the findings observed in the present work.

The Gordon and Hendrick (1998) model addresses the distribution and comprehension of different forms of referring expressions both within and between sentences. It is developed using the formalism of *Discourse Representation Theory* (Kamp & Reyle, 1993), a framework that applies model-theoretic semantics to natural language. Kamp and Reyle (1993) characterise a discourse model as a semantic representation mediating between linguistic expressions and objects in the world. A set of *Construction Rules* determines the way in which syntactic expressions are mapped onto a *Discourse Representation Structure.* Each construction rule consists of a linguistic triggering condition and a set of instructions for modifying the current model of discourse. In this view, syntactic expressions trigger the building of a discourse representation structure through dynamic interaction with the discourse model. Gordon and Hendrick (1998) modify the construction rules of Kamp and Reyle (1993) so that they can account for how the form of referring expressions influences the ease of establishing co-reference.

Gordon and Hendrick (1998) propose three major construction rules. The construction rule for pronouns is triggered by the occurrence of a pronoun and then searches the current discourse entities in order of their (syntactically-derived) prominence in order to find a "suitable antecedent"—one that matches in terms of gender, number, animacy and reflexivity. Thus, the construction rule for pronouns establishes co-reference directly. The construction rule for names is triggered by the occurrence of a name (or a description) and then posits a new entity into the discourse model with the name predicated on that entity. Thus, the construction rule for names introduces new entities and does not establish co-reference directly. This is done through the construction rule for equivalence which is triggered by the occurrence in the discourse model of the same name predicated on different entities. The construction rule for equivalence operates in the opposite fashion in that it has greater difficulty establishing co-reference when the antecedent is prominent. The differing operations of the construction rules for pronouns and for equivalence account for the patterns of co-reference and disjoint reference that have been observed in reading-time studies and in judgments of co-reference (Gordon et al., 1993; Gordon & Hendrick, 1997).

The results of the current experiments show that the Gordon and Hendrick (1998) model can account for phenomena in the comprehension of co-reference in Chinese as well as in English. Experiments 1 and 2 both show that the repeated-name penalty (slower reading of sentences with repeated names as compared to matched sentences with pronouns) occurs in Chinese. In the Gordon and Hendrick (1998) model, this effect occurs because co-reference with pronouns is established in one step via the construction rule for pronouns whereas co-reference with repeated names is established in two steps via the construction rules for names and for equivalence. Experiments 1 and 2 also show that the repeated-name penalty occurs for expressions that refer to the entity that was the grammatical subject in the preceding sentence but not the grammatical object. This pattern (which also occurs in English) is explained by the fact that syntactic prominence facilitates operation of the construction rule for pronouns and inhibits operation of the construction rule for names. Experiment 1 shows that the repeated-name penalty occurs for pronouns as a class, but that there is no difference between reading times for overt and zero pronouns. This pattern is explained in the Gordon and Hendrick (1998) model by the fact that pronouns are interpreted directly in relation to the discourse universe while names are interpreted in relation to the world; the model makes no distinction between types of pronouns. Experiments 3 and 4 show that both overt and zero pronouns are processed more easily when they refer to a prominent entity than when they refer to a nonprominent entity in cases where the pronoun could match either of two entities in terms of gender. When the gender of an overt pronoun allows it to refer unambiguously to a nonprominent entity it is processed more easily than a matched zero pronoun which cannot convey gender information. This pattern is easily explained by the construction rule for pronouns which preferentially interprets pronouns as referring to the most prominent entity in the discourse model unless features of the pronoun (gender, number, etc.) mean that the prominent entity is not a suitable antecedent. The operation of the rule causes substantial processing difficulty when subsequent semantic information forces a pronoun to be reinterpreted and this reinterpretation leads to the finding that reading times are elevated (as found in Experiment 3 with ambiguous overt pronouns and Experiment 4 with zero pronouns) when ambiguous pronouns refer to nonprominent entities as compared to when they refer to prominent entities.

The construction rule for pronouns also suggests that an unambiguous pronoun that refers to a nonprominent entity should be less easy to understand than a pronoun that refers to the most prominent entity because the most prominent entity is always evaluated first as a suitable antecedent. However, with a clear gender cue mismatch the most prominent entity is easily rejected as a suitable antecedent and measurable differences in reading time are not consistently found in comparing unambiguous pronouns in the continue and shift conditions (as seen in Experiments 2, 4 and comparable experiments in English). Similarly, the construction rule for equivalence suggests that repeated-name co-reference should be easier when the repeated name refers to a less prominent entity than when it refers to a prominent entity because the construction rule for equivalence evaluates the entities as suitable antecedents from the least prominent to the most prominent. Once again, however, name mismatches are a clear cue for rejecting an entity as a suitable antecedent and measurable differences in reading time are not found in comparing repeated names in the continue and shift conditions (Experiment 2 and comparable experiments in English). Combined, the greater ease of establishing co-reference with pronouns in continue as compared to shift conditions and with repeated names in shift as compared to continue conditions leads to a significant interaction between continue-shift and pronoun vs. name (as seen in Experiment 2 and comparable experiments in English).

In beginning our research on the comprehension of referring expressions in Chinese we believed that it was important to study passages of a type that were similar to those that we have previously studied in English. Some researchers (e.g., Li & Thompson, 1981) prefer to analyse an unmarked, sentence-initial NP in Chinese as a topic rather than as a grammatical subject. A topic is defined in relation to a discourse rather than in relation to a sentence; it extends through a sequence of sentences in a "topic chain". A topic does not necessarily have any direct semantic relation to the subsequent verb (Li & Thompson, 1981). In contrast, a subject does have a direct semantic relation to the subsequent verb (Li & Thompson, 1981; Tsao, 1977). In more formal terms, the subject is an argument of a semantic function expressed by a predicate. To illustrate, sentence (3) has both a topic (zhe ke shu) and a subject (yezi) with the sentence-initial NP as a topic whose semantic scope dominates the following predicate. Example (4) shows a "topic chain" because two sentences show the continued prominence of a single topic (zhe ke shu). Sentence (5) shows a sentence-initial NP preferentially defined as a subject because of its direct relationship with the following VP.

(3)

這	棵	樹	葉子	很	大。
zhe	ke	shu	yezi	hen	da.
This	CL	tree	leaf	very	big

"This tree, (its) leaves are very big."

(Li & Thompson, 1981, p.15)

(4) 這棵樹 葉子很大 花很小。

zhe ke shu yezi hen da hwa hen xiao.

This CL tree leaf very big flower very small

"This tree, (its) leaves are very big (its) flowers are very small."

(5) 我 喜歡 吃 蘋果。

wo xihuan chi pinguo.

I like eat apple.

"I like to eat apple."

The passages in our experiments were designed so that the initial NP of both the first and second sentences had direct semantic relations to the subsequent verb. Using this type of passage minimised possible influences of a topic chain and provides support for our characterisation that the syntactic role of the NPs was the level of language that influenced comprehension processes. According to the Gordon and Hendrick (1998) model, the initial steps in comprehension are driven by syntactic and sequential factors that influence how linguistic expressions are mapped onto discourse expressions. These initial steps in processing can be observed through online measures such as reading time. In the Gordon and Hendrick (1998) model, semantic and pragmatic processing occur subsequently within the discourse model. The distinction between subject and topic in Chinese is based exclusively on linguistic analyses that used off-line data such as classical written Chinese text, or recorded discourse. Those data may reflect later integrative processes that occur after the initial discourse model is created.

As just described, the Gordon and Hendrick (1998) model provides a clear account of the findings reported in this paper. However, this conclusion raises questions about why the zero pronoun is used so extensively in Chinese given that our experiments found no evidence that the zero pronoun plays a special role in making Chinese discourse coherent at least for the types of discourses that we studied. One obvious line of explanation is that zero pronouns involve less articulatory effort than overt pronouns and that some principle of least effort is involved. A second avenue is that the zero pronoun has some specific stylistic value. For example, it might relate to social stratification or be expressive of social attitudes; one might expect that the choice of a zero pronoun is influenced by the same kinds of factors that influence the use of contracted negatives in English. Finally, many interesting questions remain concerning how the immediate processing of syntactic structure of Chinese interacts with more functionally oriented aspects of the language, such as topic-chain structure, to achieve coreference and discourse coherence in the comprehension of Chinese.

REFERENCES

Ariel, M. (1990) *Accessing NP antecedents*. London: Routledge.

Ariel, M. (1991). The function of accessibility in a theory of grammar. *Journal of Pragmatics, 16*, 443–463.

Brennan, S. (1995). Centering attention in discourse. *Language and Cognitive Processes, 10*, 137–167.

Chen, P. (1984). *Discourse analysis of third person zero anaphora in Chinese*. Bloomington, Indiana: Indiana University Linguistics Club.

Chomsky, N. (1986). *Knowledge of language: Its nature, origin, and use*. New York. Praeger.

Chu, C. (1979). The word order change in Chinese and its problems. In C.C. Chu (Ed.), *Yuyanxue Lunji* [*On Linguistics*], pp.87–121, Taipei, Taiwan: Crane Books.

Cloitre, M. & Bever, T.G. (1988). Linguistic anaphors, levels of representation, and discourse, *Language and Cognitive Processes, 3(4)*, 293–322.

Garrof, S., & Sanford, A. (1982). The mental representation of discourse in a focussed memory system. Implications for the interpretation of anaphoric noun phrases. *Journal of Semantics, 35*, 21–41.

Garrod, S., & Sanford, A. (1988). Thematic subjecthood and cognitive constrains on discourse structure. *Journal of Pragmatics, 12*, 519–534.

Garrod, S., Freudenthal, D., & Boyle, E.A. (1994). The role of different types of anaphors in the on-line resolution of sentences in a discourse. *Journal of Memory and Language, 33(1)*, 39–68.

Gernsbacher, M.A. (1989). Mechanism that improve referential access. *Cognition, 32*, 99–156.

Givon, T. (1981). Topic continuity in discourse: the functional domain of switch-reference. In J. Haiman, & P. Munro. (Eds), *Switch-reference and universal grammar: Proceedings of a symposium on switch reference and Universal Grammar*. Amsterdam, Philadelphia: J. Benjamins Pub. Co.

Givon, T. (1983). Introduction. In T. Givon (Ed.), *Topic continuity in discourse: A quantitative cross-language study*. Amsterdam, Philadelphia: J. Benjamins Pub. Co.

Givon, T. (1992). The grammar of referential coherence as mental processing instructions. *Linguistics, 30*, 5–55.

Gordon, P.C., Grosz, B.J., & Gilliom, L.A. (1993). Pronouns, names, and the centering of attention in discourse. *Cognitive Science, 17*, 311–347.

Gordon, P.C., & Chan, D. (1995). Pronouns, passives, and discourse coherence. *Journal of Memory and Language, 34*, 216–231.

Gordon, P.C., & Scearce, K.A. (1995). Pronominalization and discourse coherence, discourse structure, and pronoun interpretation. *Memory and Cognition, 23*, 313–323.

Gordon, P.C., & Hendrick, R. (1997). Intuitive knowledge of linguistic coreference. *Cognition, 62*, 325–370.

Gordon, P.C., & Hendrick, R. (1998). The representation and processing of co-reference in discourse. *Cognitive Science, 22*, 389–424.

Greene, S.B., McKoon, G., & Ratcliff, R. (1992). Pronoun resolution and discourse models. *Journal of Experimental Psychology: Learning, Memory, and Cognition, 18*, 266–283.

Grosz, B.J., Joshi, A.K., & Weinstein, S. (1983). Providing a unified account of definite noun phrases in discourse. *Proceedings of the 21st Annual Meeting of the Association for Computational Linguistics*, Cambridge, MA.

Grosz, B.J., Joshi, A.K., & Weinstein, S. (1995). Centering: A framework for modelling the local coherence of discourse, *Computational Linguistics*, *21*, 203–226.

Halliday, M.A., & Hassan, R. (1976). *Cohesion in English*, London: Longman.

Halmari, H. (1996). On accessibility and coreference. In T. Fretheim, & J.K. Gundel (Eds), *Reference and referent accessibility*. Philadelphia, PA: John Benjamins Publishing Co.

Huang, C.-T.J. (1984). On the distribution and reference of empty pronouns. *Linguistic Inquiry*, *15*, 531–574.

Huang, C.-T.J. (1991). Remarks on the status of the null object. In R. Freidin (Ed.), *Principle and parameters in comparative grammar*. Cambridge, MA: The MIT Press.

Hudson, S.B., Tanenhaus, M.K., Dell, G.S. (1986). The effect of the discourse centre on the local coherence of a discourse. In *Proceedings, the 8th Annual Conference of the Cognitive Science Society*, 96–101. Hillsdale, NJ: Lawrence Erlbaum Associates Inc.

Kamp, H., & Reyle, U. (1993). *From Discourse to logic. Introduction to model-theoretic semantics of natural language, formal logic and discourse representation theory*. Dordrecht: Kluwer Academic Publishers.

Kennison, S.M., & Gordon, P.C. (1997). Comprehending referential expressions during reading: Evidence from eye tracking. *Discourse Processes*, *24*, 229–252.

Kintsch, W., & van Dijk, T.A. (1978). Toward a model of text comprehension and production. *Psychological Review*, *85*, 363–394.

Li, C.I. (1985). *Participant anaphora in Mandarin Chinese*. Unpublished PhD Dissertation. University of Florida, Linguistics Department.

Li, C.N., & Thompson, S.A. (1984). Third person pronouns in zero-anaphora in Chinese discourse. In T. Givon (Ed.), *Discourse and Syntax*, pp.311–335. New York: Academic Press.

Li, C.N., & Thompson, S.A. (1981). *Mandarin Chinese: A functional reference grammar*. University of California Press.

McKoon, G., Ratcliff, R., & Ward, G. (1993). Syntactic prominence effects on discourse processes. *Journal of Memory and Language*, *32*, 593–607.

McKoon, G., Ward, G., & Ratcliff, R. (1993). Morphosyntactic and pragmatic factors affecting the accessibility of discourse entities. *Journal of Memory and Language*, *32*, 56–75.

Sun, C., & Givon, T. (1985). On the so-called SOV word order in Mandarin Chinese: A quantified text study and its implications. *Language*, *61*, 329–351.

Tai, J.H.Y. (1978). Anaphoric constraints in Mandarin Chinese narrative discourse. In J. Hinds (Ed.), *Anaphora in discourse*. Edmonton, Alberta, Canada: Linguistic Research Inc.

Tao, L. (1996). Topic discontinuity and zero anaphora in Chinese discourse: Cognitive strategies in discourse processing. In B. Fox (Ed.), *Studies in anaphora*. Philadelphia, PA: John Benjamins Publishing Co.

Wentzuk Kaiko Chupanshe (1958). *Hanyu pinyin fanan*. Peiching: Wentzu Kaiko Chupanshe.

Xu, L. (1986). Free empty category. *Linguistic Inquiry*, *17*, 75–93.

Subject Index